Colégio Bandeirantes

B2

PERSPECTIVES
Combo
Special Edition
for Colégio Bandeirantes

Hugh **DELLAR**

Andrew **WALKLEY**

Lewis **LANSFORD**

Daniel **BARBER**

Amanda **JEFFRIES**

 NATIONAL GEOGRAPHIC LEARNING

Australia · Brazil · Mexico · Singapore · United Kingdom · United States

Perspectives Combo Special Edition for Colégio Bandeirantes
Hugh Dellar, Andrew Walkley, Lewis Lansford, Daniel Barber, Amanda Jeffries

Publisher: Sherrise Roehr
Executive Editor: Sarah Kenney
Publishing Consultant: Karen Spiller
Senior Development Editor: Lewis Thompson
Senior Development Editor: Brenden Layte
Editorial Assistant: Gabe Feldstein
Director of Global Marketing: Ian Martin
Product Marketing Manager: Anders Bylund
Director of Content and Media Production: Michael Burggren
Production Manager: Daisy Sosa
Media Researcher: Leila Hishmeh
Manufacturing Customer Account Manager: Mary Beth Hennebury
Art Director: Brenda Carmichael
Production Management, and Composition: 3CD
Cover Design: Raquel Braik Pedreira
Cover Image: © Leonardo Da/Shutterstock.

© 2018 National Geographic Learning, a Cengage Learning Company

ALL RIGHTS RESERVED. No part of this work covered by the copyright herein may be reproduced or distributed in any form or by any means, except as permitted by U.S. copyright law, without the prior written permission of the copyright owner.

"National Geographic", "National Geographic Society" and the Yellow Border Design are registered trademarks of the National Geographic Society ® Marcas Registradas

> For product information and technology assistance, contact us at
> **Cengage Learning Customer & Sales Support, cengage.com/contact**
> For permission to use material from this text or product, submit all requests online at **cengage.com/permissions**
> Further permissions questions can be emailed to
> **permissionrequest@cengage.com**

Student Edition
ISBN: 978-0-357-46253-9

National Geographic Learning
20 Channel Center Street
Boston, MA 02210
USA

National Geographic Learning, a Cengage Learning Company, has a mission to bring the world to the classroom and the classroom to life. With our English language programs, students learn about their world by experiencing it. Through our partnerships with National Geographic and TED Talks, they develop the language and skills they need to be successful global citizens and leaders.

Locate your local office at **international.cengage.com/region**

Visit National Geographic Learning online at **NGL.Cengage.com/ELT**
Visit our corporate website at **www.cengage.com**

4 (tl1) Lutz Jaekel/laif/Redux, (tl2) epa european pressphoto agency b.v./Alamy Stock Photo, (cl) Michael Christopher Brown/Magnum Photos, (bl1) Tasso Marcelo Leal/AFP/Getty Images, (bl2) © Bryce Duffy, **5** (tl1) © Marla Aufmuth/TED, (tl2)(cl)(bl1)(bl2) © James Duncan Davidson/TED, **6** (tl1) Christian Ziegler/National Geographic Creative, (tl2) © Hassan Hajjaj/A-WA, (cl) Yva Momatiuk and John Eastcott/National Geographic Creative, (bl1) VCG/Getty Images, (bl2) © Intuitive Surgical, **7** (tl1)(tl2)(cl) © Ryan Lash/TED, (bl1) © James Duncan Davidson/TED, (bl2) © TED, **8-9** Lutz Jaekel/laif/Redux, **10-11** Digital Vision./Getty Images, **13** Paul Darrows/Reuters, **14** Michael Christopher Brown/Magnum Photos, **15** Paul Chesley/Stone/Getty Images, **16-17** © Marla Aufmuth/TED, **18-19** Ed Norton/Lonely Planet Images/Getty Images, **20-21** epa european pressphoto agency b.v./Alamy Stock Photo, **22-23** © Rainforest Connection, www.rfcx.org, **26** (tl) Morten Falch Sortland/Moment Open/Getty Images, (cl) Ellisha Lee/EyeEm/Getty Images, (bl) wundervisuals/E+/Getty Images, **28-29** © James Duncan Davidson/TED, **30-31** © www.fairafric.com, **32-33** Michael Christopher Brown/Magnum Photos, **34-35** Mirco Lazzari gp/Getty Images Sport/Getty Images, **36** Michael Regan/Getty Images Sport/Getty Images, **38** Harry How/Getty Images Sport/Getty Images, **39** Adrian Dennis/AFP/Getty Images, **40-41** © James Duncan Davidson/TED, **42-43** Giovani Cordioli/Moment/Getty Images, **44-45** Tasso Marcelo Leal/AFP/Getty Images, **46-47** © Jeroen Koolhaas, **48** Juan Barreto/AFP/Getty Images, **50** Scott R Larsen/Moment/Getty Images, **51** David Pereiras/Shutterstock.com, **52-53** © James Duncan Davidson/TED, **54-55** James Bagshaw/Alamy Stock Photo, **56-57** © Bryce Duffy, **58-59** (spread) © National Geographic Learning, **58** (br) Maxx-Studio/Shutterstock.com, **61** Robert Clark/National Geographic Creative, **62** Puwadol Jaturawutthichai/Alamy Stock Photo, **63** © Hero Images/Getty Images, **64-65** © James Duncan Davidson/TED, **66** Sakura Photography/Moment/Getty Images, **67** © National Geographic Learning, **68-69** Christian Ziegler/National Geographic Creative, **70-71** Dietmar Temps, Cologne/Moment/Getty Images, **73** (bgd) Bryan Mullennix/Stockbyte/Getty Images, (inset) Color4260/Shutterstock.com, (t) Thaiview/Shutterstock.com, **74** Wf Sihardian/EyeEm/Getty Images, **75** Jonathan Blair/National Geographic Creative, **76-77** © Ryan Lash/TED, **78-79** Phil Moore/AFP/Getty Images, **80-81** © Hassan Hajjaj/A-WA, **82-83** © Dave Devries, **85** (bdg) tomograf/E+/Getty Images, © National Geographic Learning, **86** Troy Aossey/The Image Bank/Getty Images, **87** XiXinXing/Shutterstock.com, **88-89** © Ryan Lash/TED, **90-91** Thomas Barwick/Taxi/Getty Images, **92-93** Yva Momatiuk and John Eastcott/National Geographic Creative, **94-95** Jiro Ose/Redux, **97** AP Images/Dario Lopez-Mills, **98** Bettmann/Getty Images, **99** © Leila Dougan, **100-101** © Ryan Lash/TED, **102-103** CKN/Getty Images News/Getty Images, **104-105** VCG/Visual China Group/Getty Images, **106-107** © Patrick Meier, **108** Polina Yamshchikov/Redux, **110** Julian Broad/Contour/Getty Images, **111** © Laurie Moy, **112** © James Duncan Davidson/TED, **114** Carrie Vonderhaar/Ocean Futures Society/National Geographic Creative, **116-117** © Intuitive Surgical, **118-119** Reuters/Alamy Stock Photo, **121** Pasieka/Science Source, **122** ZUMA Press, Inc./Alamy Stock Photo, **123** Noor Khamis/Reuters, **124-125** © TED, **126-127** Media Drum World/Alamy Stock Photo.

Printed in Brazil
Print Number: 01   Print Year: 2019

ACKNOWLEDGMENTS

Paulo Rogerio Rodrigues
Escola Móbile, São Paulo, Brazil

Claudia Colla de Amorim
Escola Móbile, São Paulo, Brazil

Antonio Oliveira
Escola Móbile, São Paulo, Brazil

Rory Ruddock
Atlantic International Language Center, Hanoi, Vietnam

Carmen Virginia Pérez Cervantes
La Salle, Mexico City, Mexico

Rossana Patricia Zuleta
CIPRODE, Guatemala City, Guatemala

Gloria Stella Quintero Riveros
Universidad Católica de Colombia, Bogotá, Colombia

Mónica Rodriguez Salvo
MAR English Services, Buenos Aires, Argentina

Itana de Almeida Lins
Grupo Educacional Anchieta, Salvador, Brazil

Alma Loya
Colegio de Chihuahua, Chihuahua, Mexico

María Trapero Dávila
Colegio Teresiano, Ciudad Obregon, Mexico

Silvia Kosaruk
Modern School, Lanús, Argentina

Florencia Adami
Dámaso Centeno, Caba, Argentina

Natan Galed Gomez Cartagena
Global English Teaching, Rionegro, Colombia

James Ubriaco
Colégio Santo Agostinho, Belo Horizonte, Brazil

Ryan Manley
The Chinese University of Hong Kong, Shenzhen, China

Silvia Teles
Colégio Cândido Portinari, Salvador, Brazil

María Camila Azuero Gutiérrez
Fundación Centro Electrónico de Idiomas, Bogotá, Colombia

Martha Ramirez
Colegio San Mateo Apostol, Bogotá, Colombia

Beata Polit
XXIII LO Warszawa, Poland

Beata Tomaszewska
V LO Toruń, Poland

Michał Szkudlarek
I LO Brzeg, Poland

Anna Buchowska
I LO Białystok, Poland

Natalia Maćkowiak
one2one, Kosakowo, Poland

Agnieszka Dończyk
one2one, Kosakowo, Poland

WELCOME TO *PERSPECTIVES*!

Perspectives teaches learners to think critically and to develop the language skills they need to find their own voice in English. The carefully-guided language lessons, real-world stories, and TED Talks motivate learners to think creatively and communicate effectively.

In *Perspectives*, learners develop:

● AN OPEN MIND

Every unit explores one idea from different perspectives, giving learners opportunities for practicing language as they look at the world in new ways.

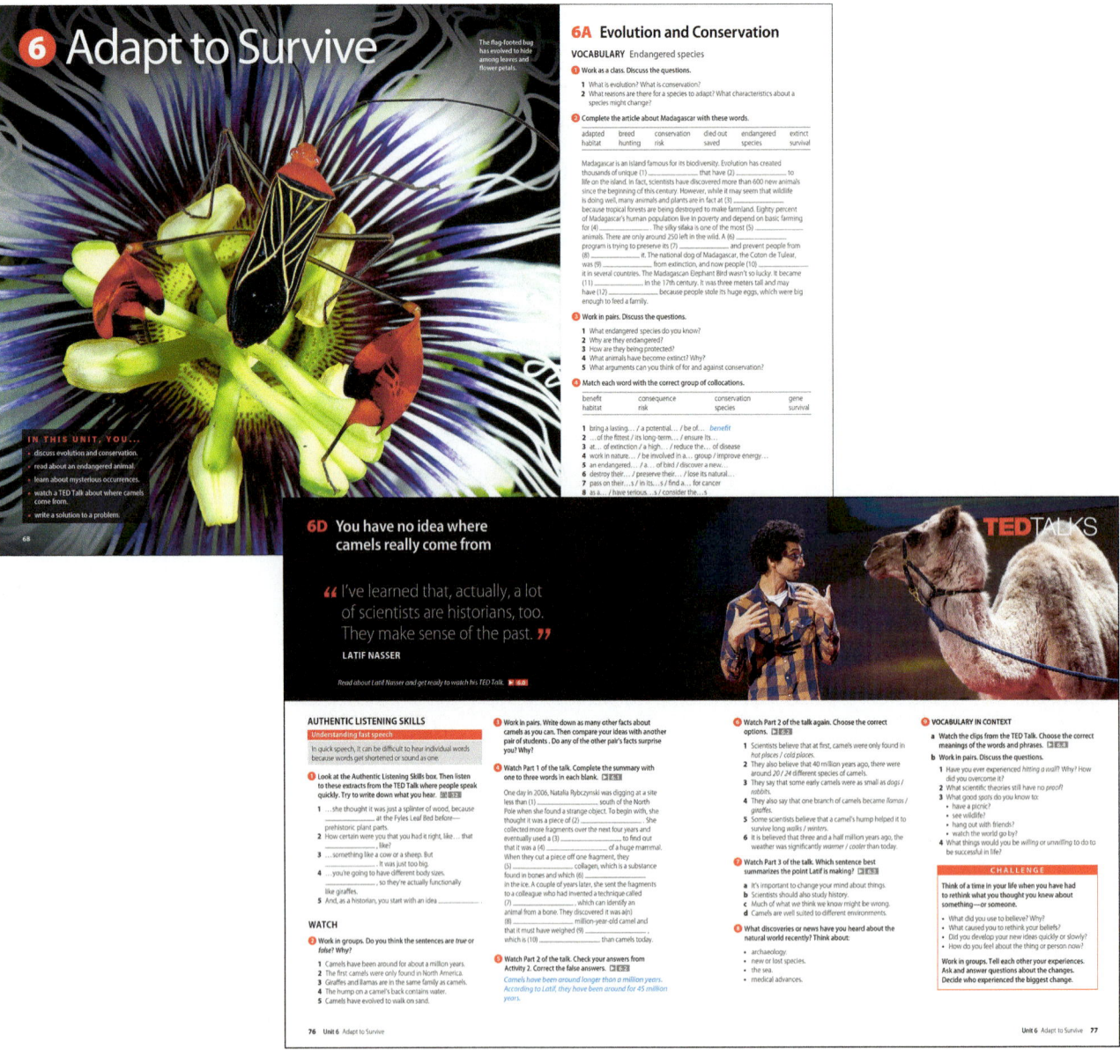

● A CRITICAL EYE

Students learn the critical thinking skills and strategies they need to evaluate new information and develop their own opinions and ideas to share.

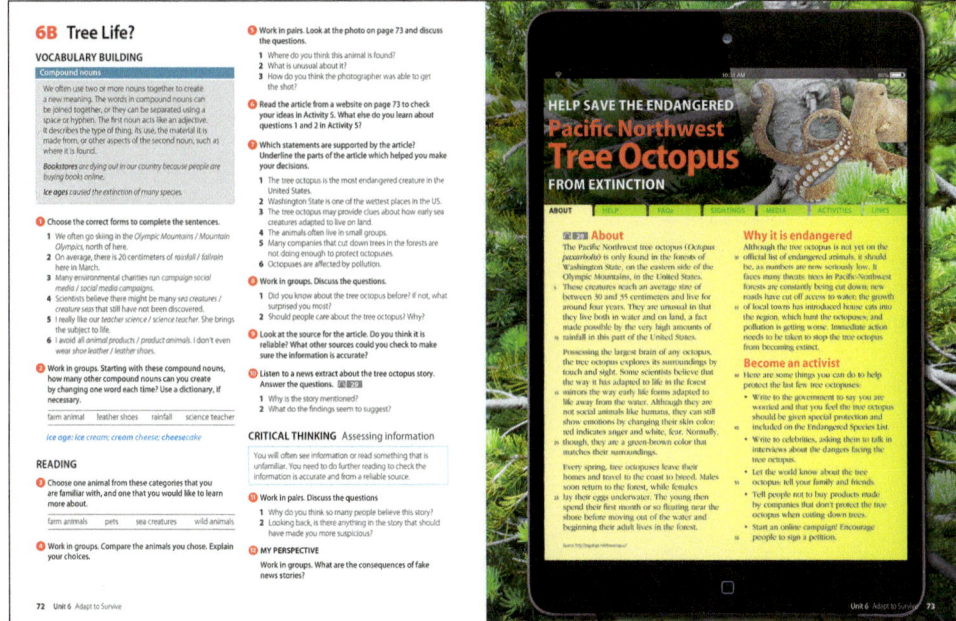

● A CLEAR VOICE

Students respond to the unit theme and express their own ideas confidently in English.

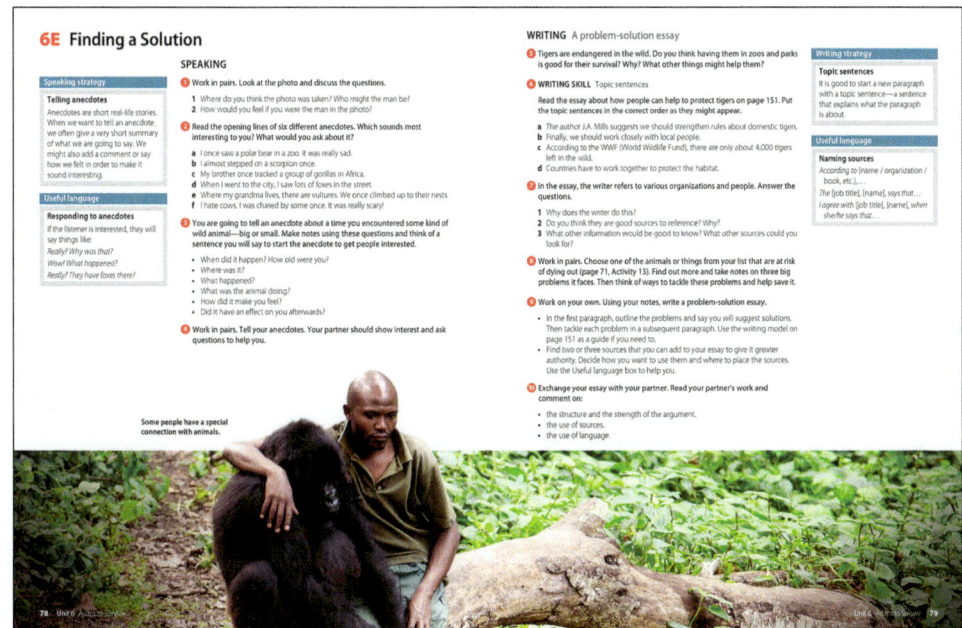

3

CONTENTS

UNIT	VOCABULARY	LISTENING	GRAMMAR	READING
1 Travel, Trust, and Tourism Pages 8–19	Experiences abroad **Vocabulary Building** Phrasal verbs	A podcast about study-abroad programs	Present and past forms	Hitchhiking **Critical Thinking** Evaluating ideas
2 The Business of Technology Pages 20–31	Setting up a new business **Vocabulary Building** Adjective and noun collocations 1	A lecture about young entrepreneurs	Present perfect forms and the simple past	Online Crime **Critical Thinking** Interpreting data
3 Faster, Higher, Stronger Pages 32–43	Describing athletes **Vocabulary Building** Synonyms in texts	Four people talking about athletes they admire	Determiners	Olympic Gold **Critical Thinking** Supporting arguments
4 Cultural Transformation Pages 44–55	Cultural events **Vocabulary Building** Adjective and noun collocations 2	A podcast about art projects	Future forms 1	A System That's Leading the Way **Critical Thinking** Understanding and evaluating ideas
5 It's Not Rocket Science Pages 56–67	Science in action **Vocabulary Building** Adjective endings	A radio program about life hacks	Passives 1 **Pronunciation** Stress in passives	Back to the Future? **Critical Thinking** Asking critical questions

4

GRAMMAR	TEDTALKS		SPEAKING	WRITING
Used to and *would* **Pronunciation** *To* in natural speech	How Airbnb designs for trust	**JOE GEBBIA** Joe Gebbia's idea worth spreading is that we can design products, services, and experiences that feel more local, authentic, and that strengthen human connections. **Authentic Listening Skills** Reporting	Advice / Making recommendations	A review **Writing Skill** Adding comments
Verb patterns (*-ing* or infinitive with *to*)	This is what happens when you reply to spam email	**JAMES VEITCH** James Veitch's idea worth spreading is that spam email can lead us to some surprising, bizarre, and often hilarious exchanges with others. **Authentic Listening Skills** Intonation and pitch	Persuading	A persuasive article **Writing Skill** Getting people's attention **Pronunciation** Intonation for persuasion
Comparatives and superlatives **Pronunciation** Linking words together in fast speech	Are athletes really getting faster, better, stronger?	**DAVID EPSTEIN** David Epstein's idea worth spreading is that the amazing achievements of many modern-day athletes are thanks to a complex set of factors, not just natural ability. **Authentic Listening Skills** Slowing down and stressing words	Reporting findings	A survey **Writing Skill** Describing statistics
Future forms 2 **Pronunciation** Contrastive stress	Building a Park in the Sky	**ROBERT HAMMOND** Robert Hammond's idea worth spreading is that we can work together to turn abandoned and neglected parts of our cities into vibrant community spaces. **Authentic Listening Skills** Recognizing words you know	Making suggestions	A *for* and *against* essay **Writing Skill** Introducing arguments
Passives 2	Science is for everyone, kids included	**BEAU LOTTO AND AMY O'TOOLE** Beau Lotto and Amy O'Toole's idea worth spreading is that all of us can be scientists if we approach the world with the curiosity, interest, innocence, and zeal of children. **Authentic Listening Skills** Fillers	Staging and hypothesizing	A scientific method **Writing Skill** Describing a process

CONTENTS

UNIT	VOCABULARY	LISTENING	GRAMMAR	READING
6 Adapt to Survive Pages 68–79	Endangered species **Vocabulary Building** Compound nouns	An interview with a conservationist about extinction	Modals and meaning	Help Save the Endangered Pacific Northwest Tree Octopus **Critical Thinking** Assessing information
7 Outside the Box Pages 80–91	Breaking the mold **Vocabulary Building** Noun forms	A podcast about the importance of creativity	First, second, third, and mixed conditionals	Testing Creative Thinking **Critical Thinking** Fact and opinion
8 Common Ground Pages 92–103	Identity and communication **Vocabulary Building** Compound adjectives	An interview with a girl about intercultural communication	Reported speech **Pronunciation** Stress for clarification	A Place to Be **Critical Thinking** Understanding other perspectives
9 Lend a Helping Hand Pages 104–115	Dealing with disaster **Vocabulary Building** *the* + adjective	A radio program about crisis mapping	Relative clauses	Shouting Out for the Young **Critical Thinking** Detecting bias
10 Life-changing Pages 116–127	Illness and injury **Vocabulary Building** Dependent prepositions	A radio program about inspiring movies	Expressing past ability **Pronunciation** Stress on auxiliaries	Avoiding the Antibiotic Apocalypse **Critical Thinking** Thinking through the consequences

GRAMMAR	TEDTALKS		SPEAKING	WRITING
Modals and infinitive forms **Pronunciation** Weak form of *have*	*You have no idea where camels really come from*	**LATIF NASSER** Latif Nasser's idea worth spreading is that in science, and in life, we are making surprising discoveries that force us to reexamine our assumptions. **Authentic Listening Skills** Understanding fast speech	Telling anecdotes	A problem-solution essay **Writing Skill** Topic sentences
Wish, if only, would rather **Pronunciation** Elision of final consonants *t* and *d*	*Go ahead, make up new words!*	**ERIN MCKEAN** Erin McKean's idea worth spreading is that making up new words will help us use language to express what we mean and will create new ways for us to understand one another. **Authentic Listening Skills** Speeding up and slowing down speech	Offering solutions	A report **Writing Skill** Cohesion
Patterns after reporting verbs	*Why I keep speaking up, even when people mock my accent*	**SAFWAT SALEEM** Safwat Saleem's idea worth spreading is that we all benefit when we use our work and our voices to question and enlarge our understanding of what is "normal." **Authentic Listening Skills** *Just*	Challenging ideas and assumptions	A complaint **Writing Skill** Using appropriate tone
Participle clauses **Pronunciation** *ing* forms	*(Re)Touching Lives through Photos*	**BECCI MANSON** Becci Manson's idea worth spreading is that photographs hold our memories and our histories, connecting us to each other and to the past. **Authentic Listening Skills** Intonation and completing a point	Countering opposition	A letter of application **Writing Skill** Structuring an application
Emphatic structures **Pronunciation** Adding emphasis	*A Broken Body Isn't a Broken Person*	**JANINE SHEPHERD** Janine Shepherd's idea worth spreading is that we have inner strength and spirit that is much more powerful than the physical capabilities of even the greatest athletes. **Authentic Listening Skills** Collaborative listening	Developing conversations	A success story **Writing Skill** Using descriptive verbs

Grammar Reference 128   Irregular Verbs 148   Writing Bank 149   Word Lists 154

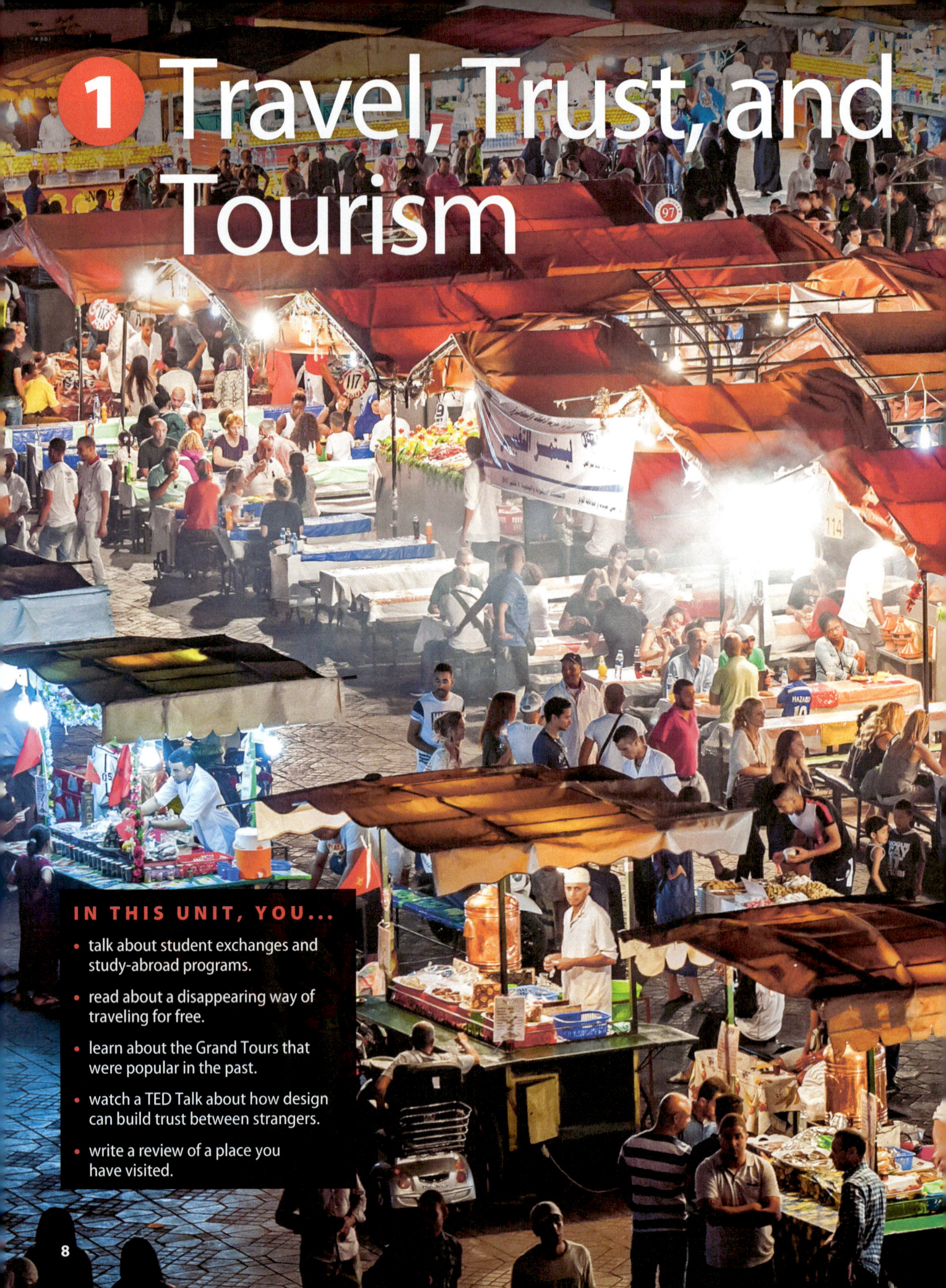

1 Travel, Trust, and Tourism

IN THIS UNIT, YOU...

- talk about student exchanges and study-abroad programs.
- read about a disappearing way of traveling for free.
- learn about the Grand Tours that were popular in the past.
- watch a TED Talk about how design can build trust between strangers.
- write a review of a place you have visited.

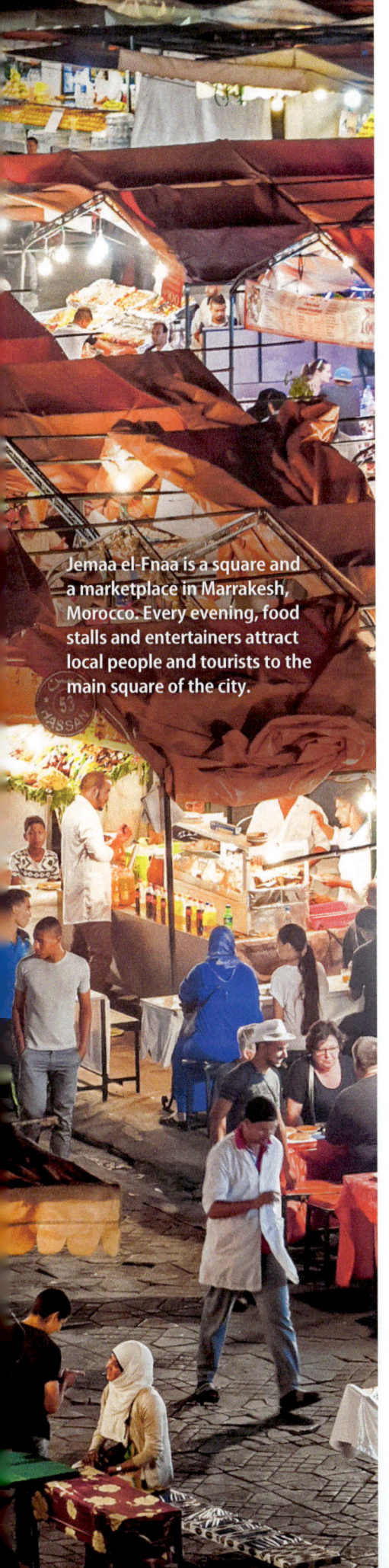

Jemaa el-Fnaa is a square and a marketplace in Marrakesh, Morocco. Every evening, food stalls and entertainers attract local people and tourists to the main square of the city.

1A Cultural Exchange

VOCABULARY Experiences abroad

1 Work in pairs. Discuss the questions.

1 What do you normally do on vacation?
2 Have you been abroad? If yes, where? If no, would you like to? Why?
3 What do you know about student exchanges and study-abroad programs?

2 Check that you understand the words and phrases in bold. Use a dictionary, if necessary. Then tell your partner which experiences you think are good and which are bad. Give your reasons.

1 be **left to your own devices**
2 experience **culture shock**
3 find people very **welcoming**
4 **get a real feel for** the place
5 get **food poisoning**
6 get **robbed**
7 go **hiking** in the mountains
8 **hang out** with local people
9 **lie around** a house all day
10 see all **the sights**
11 stay in a **B&B**
12 stay with **a host family**
13 take a while to **get used to the food**
14 travel **off the beaten path**

3 Work in groups. Look at the words and phrases in Activity 2. Discuss the questions.

1 Which are the most connected to visitors to your country? The least?
2 Which have you done, or which have happened to you? When?
3 Which three do you most want to remember and use? Why?

4 Work in pairs. Look at the photo and discuss the questions.

1 How is the market different from markets near where you live? How would visiting this place make you feel? Why?
2 Which words and phrases from Activity 2 can you use to describe what is happening? Make a list. Then explain your choices to a partner.

5 Complete the description with words or phrases from Activity 2.

In the past, it was very common for teenagers to do student exchanges, where they would go abroad and stay in each other's homes. The idea was not only to learn a new language, but also to (1) _____ with the local teenagers, go to their school, and get a (2) _____ the place and culture. Sometimes the (3) _____ was very welcoming and students got along well with the people in the home; other times the (4) _____ was too much. The students couldn't (5) _____ the food and ended up being left to their (6) _____ . Maybe that's why these days it is more common for teenagers to go on a group trip abroad, where everyone stays in a (7) _____ or hostel together. During the trip, students go and see (8) _____ and only briefly meet up with a group from a local school. This way teenagers don't (9) _____ a foreign house all day, and there is no awkwardness. The worst that could happen might be a case of (10) _____ from a bad clam and some sore feet from walking around the town.

6 Work in pairs. Do you think that the old or new way of doing student exchanges is better? Why?

Unit 1 Travel, Trust, and Tourism 9

LISTENING

7 Listen to the first part of a podcast about study-abroad programs. Find out: 🎧 1

1. who can do these programs.
2. how long people can go abroad and study for.
3. when the system started.
4. what the possible benefits are.

8 Listen to Kenji and Catalina. Answer the questions. 🎧 2

1. Where did they do their study-abroad programs?
2. How long did they stay for?
3. Did the trip increase their understanding of other cultures and develop their language skills? If yes, how do you know?

9 Work in pairs. Are the sentences *true* or *false*? Listen again to check your answers. 🎧 2

1. Kenji had visited several countries before studying abroad in Munich.
2. He was really excited about studying abroad.
3. His host family helped him develop a better understanding of the German language.
4. He's still in touch with his host family.
5. Catalina has family roots* in Italy.
6. She felt at home as soon as she arrived.
7. After a few weeks, she spoke enough Italian to do what she needed to do.
8. She's glad she went to Italy, but has no plans to go back.

family roots *original place where a family is from*

10 MY PERSPECTIVE

Work in pairs. Think of two more benefits and three possible issues students might face when doing a study-abroad program. Then discuss the questions.

1. What do you think the biggest benefit is? Why?
2. What do you think the biggest issue is? Why?

GRAMMAR Present and past forms

11 Look at the sentences in the Grammar box. Then answer the questions.

1. Which two are about the present?
2. Which four are about the past?
3. Which two describe actions that happened before something else in the past?
4. Which three use simple forms?
5. Which three use continuous forms?

Present and past forms

a *I was actually thinking about canceling my trip.*
b *I'd been wanting to go there for ages.*
c *We're talking about study-abroad programs.*
d *I'd never left Argentina!*
e *I spent six months in Germany last year.*
f *I miss my host family.*

Check the Grammar Reference for more information and practice.

Some study-abroad programs allow students to visit countries like China, where they can go to places like the Great Wall.

10 Unit 1 Travel, Trust, and Tourism

12 Match the rules (1–6) with the examples (a–f) in the Grammar box.

1 We use **the simple present** to talk about habits, permanent states, and things that are generally true.
2 We use **the present continuous** to talk about actions we see as temporary, in progress, and unfinished.
3 We use **the simple past** to describe finished actions in the past, especially when there is one finished action after another.
4 We use **the past continuous** to emphasize an action in progress around a time in the past.
5 We use **the simple past perfect** to emphasize that one thing happened before a particular point in the past.
6 We use **the past perfect continuous** to talk about an action that was in progress over a period of time *up to* or *before* a particular point in the past.

13 Complete the text with the correct form of each verb.

I really (1) _____ (love) traveling. It's probably the most important thing in my life. I'm 17, and I (2) _____ (plan) to spend the summer on a National Geographic Student Expedition! I actually (3) _____ (go) on my first adventure trip a few years ago when I (4) _____ (spend) two months in China. It was the first time I (5) _____ (ever / go) abroad, and I (6) _____ (love) every minute of it! While we (7) _____ (stay) in Beijing, we (8) _____ (visit) the Great Wall of China, which was something I (9) _____ (dream) of doing ever since I was a child. It was amazing! I (10) _____ (hope) to do an expedition to Iceland next year and stay somewhere really off the beaten path.

14 Complete the pairs of sentences with the correct simple form of one of the verbs and the correct continuous form of the other.

1a We usually _____ (spend) the summers with my grandparents at their house on the coast.
1b This summer, though, my brother is in Costa Rica. He _____ (stay) with a host family there.
2a This weekend I _____ (go) hiking in the mountains with some friends.
2b The bus _____ (leave) at six every morning, so we should be at the station 15 minutes before.
3a I _____ (get) really bad food poisoning while I was in Scotland. I have no idea why!
3b Things got worse when somebody stole my suitcase while I _____ (wait) in line to buy train tickets to Glasgow.
4a I spoke good French by the time I left Quebec because I _____ (hang out) with the locals for the last few months of the ski season.
4b It was a great trip, but it was scary, because I _____ never _____ (try) skiing before.

15 Choose one of the situations below. Then plan what you want to say about where you were, when you went, and what happened. Think about how to use all four past forms at least once.

a Something that happened while you were on vacation
b A time you stayed with other people
c A place you have visited

16 Work in pairs. Tell each other your stories.

1B Ask for a Ride

VOCABULARY BUILDING

Phrasal verbs

Phrasal verbs are often used in conversation instead of more formal words. They are very common in English. The meaning of a verb often changes when it is used in a phrasal verb.

1 Rewrite the words in italics using the correct forms of these phrasal verbs.

| break down | come down to | line up |
| pick up | pull over | turn out |

1 They offered to give me a ride to the airport and *got me* from the hotel at eight o'clock.
2 The bus *stopped working* on the way there, so we were five hours late.
3 It was New Year's Day, so I had to *wait in line* for hours to get a train ticket.
4 I think the changes *are basically because of* two things: wealth and technology.
5 A car *stopped by the side of the road* and the driver asked us for directions.
6 I was worried because I'd never been abroad before, but everything *was* great in the end.

2 Write sentences using these phrasal verbs.

| hang out | lie around | look after | step out |

3 Work in pairs. Look at the photo on page 13 and discuss the questions.

1 What is happening?
2 Which of the phrasal verbs from Activity 1 can you connect to the photo? Explain your choices.

READING

4 Read the article about hitchhiking. Match these headings with the numbered paragraphs.

a Fear
b More wealth
c New needs and opportunities
d Legal restrictions
e Low-cost flights
f Greater access to cars

5 Work in pairs. Which of these ideas does the author present? What evidence is given?

1 There used to be far more hitchhikers.
2 There was a high number of robberies involving hitchhikers.
3 It's difficult to find a place to hitchhike these days.
4 More people drive now than in the past.
5 Air travel is safer than driving or hitchhiking.
6 We are wasting a lot of energy by driving alone.
7 People only hitchhike now if they are poor.
8 Hitchhiking brings benefits to communities and individuals.

6 Work in pairs. Imagine you are standing at the side of a road, trying to hitchhike. Tell your story. Before you do, talk and make notes about:

- where you are going.
- why you are hitchhiking.
- how you are feeling.
- what happens next.
- how the story ends.

7 Tell your stories to other people in your class. Vote on the best one. Explain why it is the best story.

CRITICAL THINKING Evaluating ideas

Evaluating ideas and judging them against other perspectives helps to form a basis for developing your own point of view.

8 Work in groups. Discuss the questions.

1 Which is the most important reason the author gives for the decline in hitchhiking? Do you agree? How important are the other reasons?
2 What comparison does the author provide from the website Wand'rly? Is it a fair comparison? Why?
3 How is the example of hitchhiking in Virginia different from other kinds? Does this make it safer? Why?
4 Why do you think the author says he gained a different perspective from other tourists? Do you think that is true? Do you think his perspective was better? Why?

9 MY PERSPECTIVE

Work in pairs. Discuss the questions.

1 Do you think hitchhiking is a good idea? What other reasons could there be for doing it?
2 How could you make hitchhiking safer?

Hitchbot, a hitchhiking robot, waits for a ride at the side of a road. Read more about Hitchbot on page 129.

Hitchhiking

Where did all the hitchhikers go?

3 I was driving along the other day, and I passed a man sticking his thumb out. He was asking for a ride. When we had gone past, my daughter, who is 15, asked me, "What was that man doing?" The question surprised me, because hitchhiking used to be so common. I used to do it all the time when I was a student going home to visit friends, and I also spent one summer hitchhiking around South America. Often when you went to some hitching spots, you'd have to line up behind several others already waiting for a ride—it was so popular. So what happened? Why is it so rare now? The authors of *Freakonomics*, Stephen Dubner and Steve Levitt, have also asked this question in one of their regular podcasts. They suggest that it probably comes down to five main reasons.

(1) _____
Several horror movies have shown psychotic drivers who kidnap and murder the hitchhiker they pick up (or vice versa). This has been reinforced by certain stories in the media of people getting robbed and being left in the middle of nowhere. Unsurprisingly, this has caused trust to break down. Some people believe that the chances of these things happening are small. The website Wand'rly, for example, suggests that people are far more likely to die by tripping and falling than by hitchhiking.

(2) _____
There are more major roads now than there used to be, and hitching is either banned or drivers are not allowed to pull over on these roads.

(3) _____
Alan Piskarsi, a transportation expert, points to the fact that cars last longer, so there are more of them available at a cheaper price. What's more, many more people have driver's licenses than they used to.

(4) _____
In the past, young people simply couldn't afford to fly long distances, and traveling by train wasn't necessarily much quicker than traveling by car. Now, however, we have budget airlines, making air travel more accessible.

(5) _____
Along the same lines, people's standard of living has increased. Perhaps people opt for higher levels of comfort, privacy, or reliability when they travel.

(6) _____
The trouble is that privacy comes at a cost. Levitt and Dubner state that in the United States, 80 percent of passenger space in cars is unused, which makes them more costly to operate and creates unnecessary traffic and pollution. The solution could be more hitchhiking! They give the example of a city in Virginia, where commuters have organized a spot where they meet to hitch a ride so drivers with no passengers can use carpool lanes on the highway that are reserved for cars that contain more than one person.

Fresh Fears

But what about general travel? I often argued with my parents about the dangers of hitchhiking, and I would tell them about all the amazing experiences I'd had and the generous, interesting people I'd met. I think it genuinely gave me a different perspective on other travelers and tourists. But now, I look at my daughter and think about her going on a trip. Would I want her to go hitchhiking?

Andrew Skurka's longest "Grand Tour" was 7,775 miles.

1C The Grand Tour

GRAMMAR Used to and would

1 Look at the Grammar box. Match the structures with the uses, based on the examples in bold.

1 simple past
2 used to, would, simple past
3 used to or simple past

a to describe a past state over a period of time
b to describe individual past events and situations
c to describe a habit or regular action in the past

> **Used to and would**
>
> Hitchhiking **used to be** so common. I **used to do it** all the time when I **was** a student going home to visit friends, and I also **spent** one summer hitching around South America. Often when you went to some hitching spots, **you'd have to line up** behind several others already waiting for a ride—it was so popular. **I often argued** with my parents about the dangers of hitching, and **I would tell them about** all the amazing experiences I'd had.

Check the Grammar Reference for more information and practice.

2 Read about Grand Tours. Find out what they were and why people did them.

Humans have always been travelers, moving out of Africa to all parts of the world in search of space, food, and resources. But the idea of guided tourism for leisure and education (1) **didn't really start** until the 17th century, when the Grand Tour (2) **began** to be established. Young aristocrats* from different parts of the world (3) **spent** several months traveling around important sights in Europe after they had finished their schooling. The Tour often (4) **started** in the Netherlands, where the tourists (5) **hired** a horse and carriage, servants, and a tutor to show them the sights and teach them about what they saw.

From the Netherlands, they went to Paris, where they (6) **did** a French language course, before moving on to Switzerland and then crossing the Alps to Italy. After an extensive tour of Italy, they (7) **went** home directly, (8) **traveled** back to the Netherlands via Austria and Germany, or (9) **continued** south to Greece.

The Grand Tour (10) **played** an important part in education and in spreading culture. The tourists would often bring back paintings and books, which influenced artists in their own country. The Venezuelan Francisco de Miranda even (11) **saw** the beginnings of the French Revolution on his Grand Tour, which (12) **led** him to fight for independence for his country.

aristocrat *person belonging to a high class*

3 Change the words in bold in Activity 2 from the simple past to *used to* or *would* + verb, where possible.

4 MY PERSPECTIVE

Work in pairs. Discuss the questions.

1 Do you think anyone does Grand Tours today? Why?
2 Where would you go on a Grand Tour? Why? Think about:
   • the sights you would visit.
   • the food you would eat.
   • the people you would meet.

14 Unit 1 Travel, Trust, and Tourism

5 PRONUNCIATION *To* in natural speech

> When unstressed, the word *to* is usually pronounced "tuh."
> *I was a student going home to visit friends.*
>
> It can also be reduced and joined with the previous word.
> *Hitchhiking used to be so common.*
> *You'd have to line up behind several others.*

a Listen to the sentences from the Pronunciation box. Notice the differences between unstressed *to* and the sentences with reductions. 🎧 4

b Listen and repeat. 🎧 4

6
Read about Andrew Skurka. Decide if *used to*, *would*, and the simple past are used correctly or incorrectly. Change the ones which are incorrect.

Andrew Skurka is an ultra-hiker. Every year, he (1) *used to go* on hikes that are thousands of miles long, walking between 25 and 40 miles a day. One of his most amazing tours was circling the Arctic in 176 days. His boots (2) *got very wet* for 156 of those days and they (3) *used to froze* overnight. He (4) *would then have to* force his feet into the icy boots each morning. Unsurprisingly, he (5) *didn't use to see* many people during his tours and once, he (6) *would spend* 24 days completely on his own. He'd sometimes (7) *get depressed* and (8) *cried*, but one day he came across a herd of caribou and it (9) *used to change* his perspective. He (10) *realized* he was very similar to them—just one more creature on Earth, like them.

7 CHOOSE

Choose one of the following activities.

- What did your parents or grandparents do on vacation when they were growing up? Write any similarities and differences to what you do.
- Work in groups. Share what you know about tourism in your country in the past compared to now. Talk about:
  – resorts.
  – the kinds of people who visit or visited.
  – the kinds of vacations.
  – the number and length of vacations.
  – destinations people from your country visit or visited.
- Work in pairs. Tell your partner about two of the following.
  – Something you used to believe and why you changed your mind.
  – Something you used to like doing and why you don't like it or do it now.
  – Something you do now that you never used to do and why.
  – Someone you used to spend a lot of time with and what you would do.

In the past, only young aristocrats were able to visit classical sites such as the Pantheon in Rome, Italy.

Unit 1 Travel, Trust, and Tourism

1D How Airbnb Designs for Trust

> **"** We were aiming to build Olympic trust between people who had never met. **"**
>
> **JOE GEBBIA**

Read about Joe Gebbia and get ready to watch his TED Talk. ▶ 1.0

AUTHENTIC LISTENING SKILLS

Reporting

When people tell stories, they often use present tenses to make events sound more immediate. They also often report what people said or what was going through their mind at the time, as if they were speaking.

1 Look at the Authentic Listening Skills box. Listen and complete the extracts. 🎧 5

1 I make the mistake of asking him,
   "_____?"
2 And I'm thinking,
   "_____?"
3 And the voice in my head goes,
   "_____?"
4 I'm staring at the ceiling, I'm thinking,
   "_____?"

2 Look at your completed extracts in Activity 1. What do you think happened before? What do you think will happen next?

3 Work in pairs. Read the sentences below. Discuss what may have happened before somebody said each one.

1 So I'm thinking to myself, "What do I do now?"
2 She looks at me and goes, "I've met you somewhere before."
3 The voice in my head says, "Don't do it!"

WATCH

4 Work in groups. Discuss the questions.

1 Have you or your family ever asked for help from a stranger while on vacation? What happened?
2 Have you or someone in your family ever helped a stranger while on vacation? What happened?
3 Why might you trust or not trust a stranger? How do you decide who to trust for help or advice?

5 Watch Part 1 of the talk. Choose the correct options. ▶ 1.1

1 From his meeting with the "Peace Corps guy," Joe learns
   a he should always have an airbed.
   b he should start a hosting business.
   c we should be less fearful of strangers.
2 He decided to start his business because
   a there weren't many hotels in the city.
   b he really needed somewhere to stay.
   c it offered him an opportunity as a designer.
3 The business wasn't immediately successful because
   a people didn't trust Joe and his co-founder.
   b the website wasn't very well designed.
   c it didn't get any additional investment.

6 MY PERSPECTIVE

How can you make people feel that they can trust each other more? Think of three ideas. Then share them with the class. Does anyone have the same ideas as you?

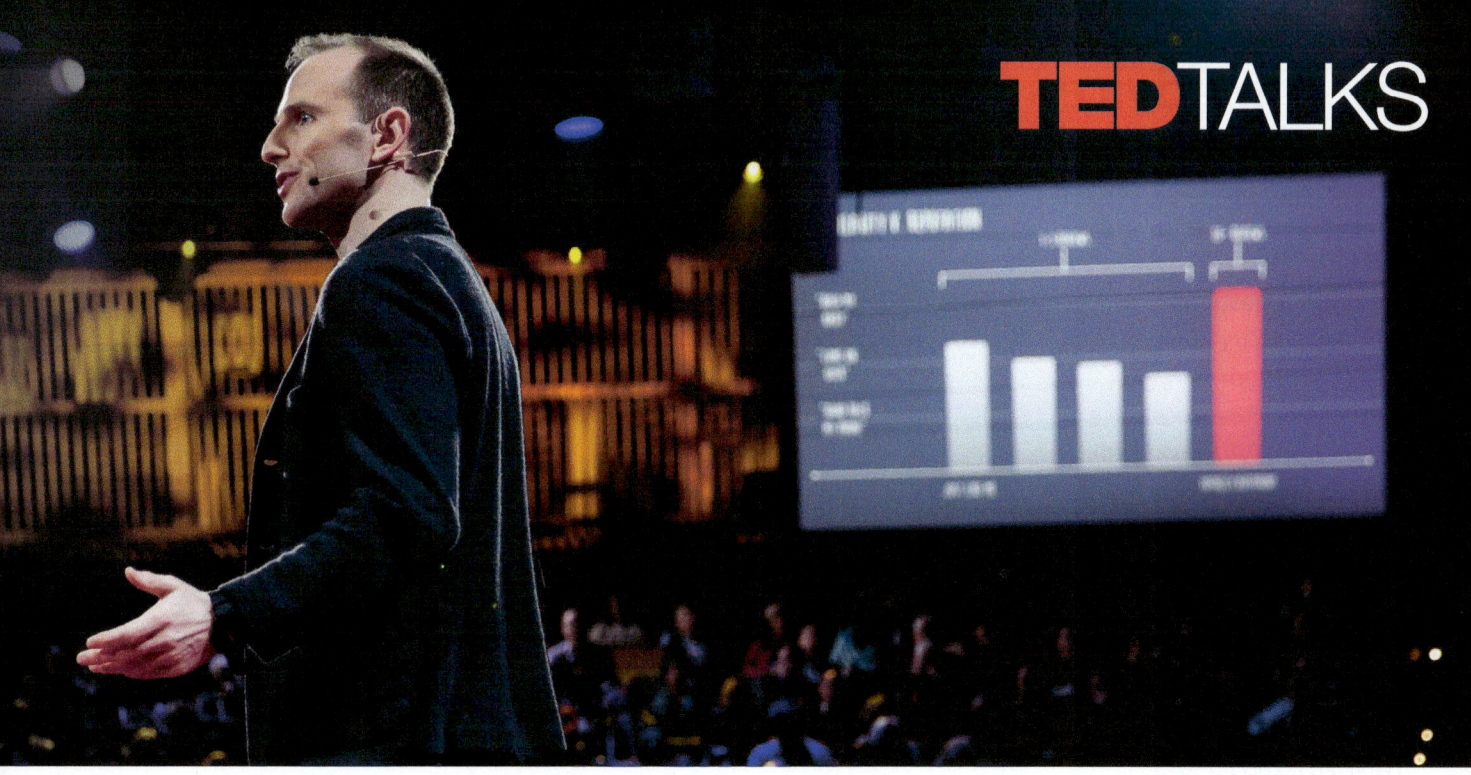

TEDTALKS

7 Watch Part 2 of the talk. Complete these notes. ▶ 1.2

- Experiment—shows how host can feel _____ but guest can feel _____ = how business works. Well-designed reputation (review) system—key to _____ .
- _____ must leave reviews before they are revealed.
- _____ = people stop worrying about differences (reputation beats similarity).
- _____ and prompts = right amount of honesty and sharing (disclosure).

8 Watch Part 3 of the talk. Then work in groups and summarize what Joe said using these ideas. What did you like about these ideas? ▶ 1.3

- when trust works
- a man having a heart attack
- the sharing economy
- human connection
- Seoul, South Korea
- students and empty-nesters*

empty-nesters *parents whose children have left home*

9 Look back at your ideas in Activity 6. Did Joe mention any of your ideas? Have any of them changed?

10 VOCABULARY IN CONTEXT

a Watch the clips from the TED Talk. Choose the correct meanings of the words and phrases. ▶ 1.4

b Work in groups. Discuss these questions.

1 What things can increase or reduce *anxiety* when traveling?
2 Have you ever met someone on vacation you got along with? Have you *kept in touch*? Why?
3 Would you be *up for* doing any of these things on vacation? Why?
   - rafting or bungee jumping
   - going to a nightclub
   - doing a guided tour of a museum
   - going camping
4 When did you last *rush* somewhere? Why?
5 Have you ever experienced anything that *tripped you up*? What?

CHALLENGE

Work in groups. Make a list of things you have which you could share with others in your area or with people visiting you on vacation. Think about:

- skills and abilities.
- knowledge.
- possessions that you do not use all the time.

How could you share the things in your list in a way that people could trust and avoid danger?

Unit 1 Travel, Trust, and Tourism

1E Trip Advice

Useful language

Making suggestions

If sightseeing is their thing, then the best place to go is…

If they want to experience a genuine local night out, I'd suggest trying…

If they're only staying here for a little while, they should probably…

If you ask me, the one place they really have to go to is…

Reacting to suggestions

If they'd rather try something different, …might be worth a shot.

I wouldn't bother going to…, personally.

They'd be better (off) going to…

SPEAKING

1. Work in pairs. Make a list of three places close to where you live that you would recommend to each of these groups of people. Think about places to stay, eat, shop, and visit.

   | a couple in their 50s or 60s | a father with a young teenage son |
   | a group of teenage friends | a young married couple with a child |

2. Compare your list with another pair. Make suggestions for the best places for each group of people. Use the Useful language box to help you.

3. Put the sentences in the correct order to make a conversation between a local person and a guest. Then listen and check your answers. 🎧 6

   a Well, there's a great steak place down by the river.
   b I'm thinking of seeing some sights today. Can you recommend anywhere?
   c In that case, you'd be best off going to Madragora—a nice little vegetarian place near the park.
   d OK. Well, I'll check that out this morning, then. And do you know anywhere good to have lunch?
   e Great. Thanks for the tip.
   f Oh, right. Well, actually, I don't eat meat, so…
   g Well, the Old Town is well worth a visit. There are some amazing buildings there.

4. Roleplay two conversations similar to the one in Activity 3, using places you know. Underline phrases from Activity 3 that you want to use. Then have the conversations. Take turns being the local person and the guest.

Tourists walk across the Perito Moreno Glacier in Santa Cruz Province, Argentina.

WRITING A review

5 Look at page 149 and read the four short online reviews. What kind of place is each review about?

6 Work in pairs. Which reviewer:

1 does not feel that he or she got a good value?
2 managed to negotiate a deal?
3 strongly recommends a place?
4 had to entertain himself or herself quite a lot?
5 complained?
6 had to wait far longer than he or she had been expecting to?
7 felt very comfortable where he or she was?
8 mentions local sights?

7 Look at page 149 again. Underline the sentences in the reviews that helped you answer the questions in Activity 6.

8 WRITING SKILL Adding comments

Match the first half of each excerpt (1-4) with the second half (a-d).

1 Our room had a great view of the ocean, but the hotel restaurant closed at nine,
2 We had an amazing time, but terrible weather on the day we left,
3 We complained about the room, so they offered us two full days at the spa,
4 The beach was a five-minute walk from the hotel, but so was the snake market,

a which meant we were delayed for several hours.
b which was rather disappointing.
c which was a bit of a culture shock, to say the least.
d which was kind of them.

9 Choose one of these places and write a review. Use the Useful language box to help you.

- vacation destination
- local cafe or restaurant
- local tourist attraction
- place you have stayed

Writing strategy

Writing reviews

In reviews, it's quite common to use a relative clause starting with *which* to add a comment about a whole sentence.

*I was far from my school, **which wasn't ideal**.*

*It serves great breakfasts, lunches, and snacks, **which is perfect if you're feeling hungry**.*

Useful language

Introducing follow-up comments

On top of that,…
What's more,…
One other thing was the fact that…

Recommending and not recommending

I can't recommend it enough.
It's well worth a visit.
It's just not worth it.
I'd skip it (if I were you).

2 The Business of Technology

IN THIS UNIT, YOU...

- discuss young entrepreneurs.
- read about online scams.
- learn how to be a responsible user of social media.
- watch a TED Talk about responding to email scams.
- persuade people to invest in a product.

A man stands inside a virtual cave at the Gdansk University of Technology in Poland. Virtual caves can be used by architects, doctors, and firefighters to simulate real-world scenarios.

2A Young Business

VOCABULARY Setting up a new business

1 Look at the photo and read the caption. How do you think the virtual cave works? How can it help people? In what other jobs might the virtual cave be useful?

2 Work as a class. Discuss the questions.
1 What is the difference between an **entrepreneur** and a **businessperson**?
2 What qualities and skills do you think you need to be an entrepreneur?
3 How easy is it for young people to become businesspeople or entrepreneurs?
4 Can you think of any young entrepreneurs? Who was the youngest? What was his or her business?

3 Work in pairs. Discuss the questions.
1 How do people **raise money** for a business or a charity?
2 Who might businesspeople **negotiate with**? What about?
3 In what ways do businesses **market products**?
4 What might a business or a person **recover from**?
5 What are good and bad ways of **handling pressure**?

4 What skills do you need to start a new business? Choose the correct option to complete each skill.

1 _____ something new
   a negotiate   b invent   c redesign
2 _____ money from investors
   a raise   b lend   c ask
3 _____ with suppliers to get the best deal
   a handle   b manage   c negotiate
4 find partners to _____ the product in different countries
   a send   b distribute   c deal
5 have the confidence to _____ from failure
   a recover   b repair   c accept
6 be good at _____ your product to increase sales
   a meeting   b networking   c marketing
7 be capable of _____ stress and pressure
   a preparing   b holding   c handling
8 be able to _____ a diverse range of people
   a deal with   b talk   c get on
9 _____ a team of people
   a apply for   b figure   c put together
10 _____ in an impressive office
   a live   b be based   c show

5 MY PERSPECTIVE

Work in pairs. What are the three most important skills from Activity 4 that make a new business a success? Can you think of any other skills?

6 Explain your choices from Activity 5 to another pair. Do they agree? Why?

Unit 2 The Business of Technology   21

LISTENING

7 Listen to a woman talking about entrepreneurs. Think about the questions and take notes. 🎧 7

1 How is being an entrepreneur changing?
2 According to the speaker, what is the most important aspect of being an entrepreneur?

8 Work in pairs. Discuss the sentences. Are they *true* or *false*? Listen again to check. 🎧 7

1 Nick D'Aloisio became a millionaire when he was eighteen.
2 Amanda Hocking didn't go through a traditional publisher to market her books.
3 The speaker suggests that most investments from banks in the past went to older, wealthy businessmen.
4 D'Aloisio's first investor chose him because he was young and had potential.
5 Kickstarter investors buy a share of the company.
6 Projects advertised on Kickstarter aim to make a profit.
7 The majority of Kickstarter projects get no investments.
8 Hocking is an example of recovering from failure.

9 Work in pairs. Discuss the questions.

1 How has the internet changed entrepreneurship?
2 Do you think Kickstarter is a good idea? What are the benefits and risks of raising money this way?
3 What do you think might be good or bad about being an entrepreneur?

GRAMMAR Present perfect forms and the simple past

10 Look at the Grammar box. Read the sentences. Then answer the questions.

1 Which tense is each of the verb forms in bold?
2 Why do you think the different forms are used?

> **Present perfect forms and the simple past**
>
> a *D'Aloisio's first investor **contacted** him by email from Hong Kong.*
> b *Kickstarter **has been running** for several years now.*
> c *Most successful entrepreneurs **have failed** at least once.*

Check the Grammar Reference for more information and practice.

11 Based on your ideas from Activity 10, complete the summary. Use each form once.

The number of entrepreneurs (1) _____ (grow) ever since the arrival of new technology and online services. This new technology (2) _____ (reduce) the barriers that previously (3) _____ (discourage) people from setting up a business.

12 Do the underlined verbs use the correct forms? Change the ones you think are incorrect.

Topher White is a young entrepreneur. In college, he (1) <u>trained</u> as a physicist, but since 2012 he (2) <u>ran</u> a non-profit company, Rainforest Connection, to help prevent the illegal practice of logging.* He (3) <u>has invented</u> a system using old cell phones and solar power to hear the sound of saws and vehicles that illegal loggers use. The phones then send a warning to guards so they can stop the activity before it does too much damage. Topher first (4) <u>has tested</u> the system in Borneo, and in 2014, his Kickstarter campaign (5) <u>has raised</u> almost $170,000 to expand the company. Since then he's (6) <u>been working</u> with groups such as the Tembe tribe in South America, as well as with people in Africa and Indonesia to adapt the system to meet local needs. They successfully (7) <u>detected</u> a lot of illegal activity. The work Topher is doing is important because in some parts of the world they (8) <u>have been losing</u> ten percent of forest cover this century, and deforestation is one of the biggest contributors to climate change.

logging *cutting down trees*

Topher White attaches a Rainforest Connection listening device to a tree in the Amazon Rainforest in Brazil to help stop illegal logging.

13 Complete the sentences so they are true for you.
1. I haven't _____ since _____ .
2. _____ has been doing a lot better since _____ .
3. I _____ over the last five years.
4. I _____ for the first time last year.
5. The number of _____ has grown a lot over the last few years.

14 **MY PERSPECTIVE**

Look again at the three most important skills you listed in Activity 5. Give examples of when you have demonstrated these skills. List any other qualities or ideas you have that show that you would be a good entrepreneur.

15 Work in groups. Try to convince other students that you would make the best entrepreneur. Use the present perfect and simple past forms.

I've been running our school debate team for the last two years, so I believe that I can negotiate well with other people.

I took nine exams last year, so I think I'm capable of handling stress and pressure.

2B Risky Business

READING

1 Complete the sentences with these pairs of words.

confirm + scam	deleted + permission
emails + filter	inbox + attached
infected + backups	profile + edit
social media + posting	store + flash drive

1 Some of my posts were _____ without my _____ . I have no idea why!
2 I can't believe how many _____ manage to get through my spam _____ .
3 He's very active on _____ . He's always _____ new updates and adding photos.
4 I keep my _____ very private, and I often go back and _____ things I've written.
5 This strange email just arrived in my _____ with a file _____ to it, so I deleted it.
6 When they asked me to _____ my bank details, I started to think it must be a _____ .
7 I _____ all my documents in the cloud now, rather than using a _____ .
8 My computer got a virus that _____ a lot of my files and I didn't have any _____ .

2 Work in pairs. How do you think the things in Activity 1 can happen? Why would people do them?

3 Look at the infographic and read the stories. Then answer the questions.
1 What mistake did each person make?
2 What was the result of each mistake?

4 Work in pairs. Answer the questions.
1 Who didn't realize they'd made a mistake for a long time?
2 Who received several emails from the same person?
3 Who thought they had found a bargain?
4 Who was scared into responding too quickly?
5 Who accepted the blame for what happened?
6 Who didn't read a product description carefully enough?

5 Read the stories again to check your ideas in Activity 4. Underline the parts that helped you decide.

6 MY PERSPECTIVE

Make a list of the different ways you could protect yourself from the same kinds of online crimes that Laura, Bruno, and Janella encountered.

VOCABULARY BUILDING

Adjective and noun collocations 1

When you learn adjectives, it is a good idea to remember the nouns that they describe. Sometimes the adjective is next to the noun; however, sometimes it appears later in the sentence.
It's a very user-friendly website with lots of functions and it is also very secure.

7 Match the adjectives with the nouns they are used with in the stories on page 25.

1	the normal	a	hotels
2	a secondhand	b	relative
3	my personal	c	PlayStation
4	luxury	d	documents
5	common	e	fees
6	a distant	f	price
7	official	g	sense
8	legal	h	details

CRITICAL THINKING Interpreting data

You will often see visuals and charts in newspapers, books, and articles online to add information and support the text. You need to check that these statistics are from a reliable source and interpret the data for yourself before you read.

8 Work in groups. Look at the cybercrime graphs on page 25. Discuss the questions.
1 Where does the data come from? Do you think this is a reliable source?
2 What crimes do the graphs focus on? What do you know about them?
3 What's the most common crime? Why do you think that is?
4 Which age groups are the least affected? Which are the most affected? Why do you think that is?
5 Do you think the statistics would be different for your country? Why? Do you know where to find this data?

9 Work in groups. Discuss the questions.
1 Which of the three mistakes do you think is the most serious? Which is the least serious? Why?
2 Why do you think each person acted as they did?
3 What do you think each person did after realizing their mistake?
4 Have you heard any stories about similar mistakes? If so, what happened?

Online Crime

🎧 8 The world becomes more connected every day. It's now easier than ever to keep in touch with friends and family around the world. Online banking allows people to access their accounts from anywhere that has an internet connection. People don't even have to leave the house to go shopping! However, with greater connectivity comes greater risk. Every year, hundreds of thousands of people become victims of online crime. We asked our readers to share some of their terrible tech tales while we examine where the crimes originate.

Laura One day last year, I got a call from what I thought was my bank. They said someone was trying to take money from my account without my permission, and that they needed to confirm my personal details to stop it. I'll be honest—I didn't really understand what was going on and wanted to stop anything bad from happening, so I gave them my name and address and date of birth. I didn't hear back, but a month later I got my credit card statement and found someone had spent over 11,000 pounds on flights and luxury hotels!

Origin of crime: The United States

Bruno I was surfing the web one day when I found a site selling Xboxes and PlayStations. I couldn't believe how cheap they were. They had stuff on there for half the normal price! I clicked on one item and bought what was advertised as a "PlayStation 4 original box and receipt." I assumed it was secondhand and, since it was only 150 euros, I bought it without checking the details. You can imagine how I felt a few days later when the postman brought me just the box and the receipt!

Origin of crime: Romania

Janella Looking back, it was my own fault, but when I got an email saying a distant relative had died and left me millions of dollars, common sense went out of the window! It was from someone claiming to be a lawyer in West Africa. I know my dad's side of the family had connections there, so I thought it must be true. They attached documents that looked official and kept writing, so eventually I sent them 8,000 dollars to pay the legal fees. Of course, it was a scam and I never heard from them again… or got my money back!

Origin of crime: West Africa

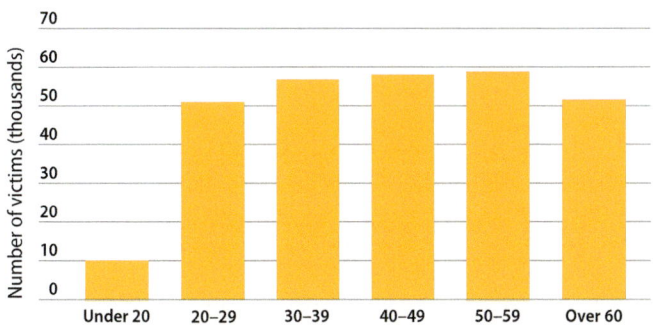

Cybercrime by age (US)

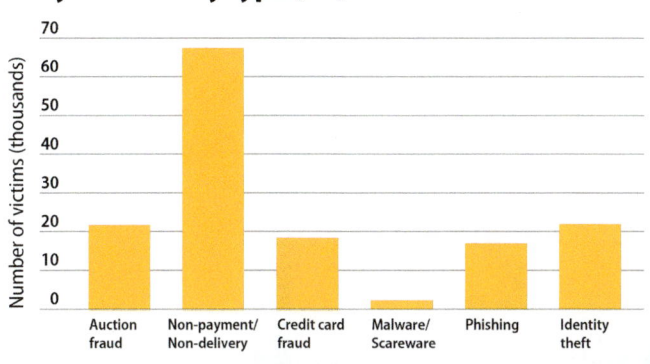

Cybercrime by type (US)

Source: U.S. Department of Justice / Federal Bureau of Investigation Statistics shown are for 2015.

Unit 2 The Business of Technology 25

Do you enjoy posting on social media?

2C What's in a post?

GRAMMAR Verb patterns (*-ing* or infinitive with *to*)

1 Work in pairs. Look at the Grammar box. Which verbs below can be followed by the *-ing* form? Which can be followed by the infinitive with *to*?

admit	agree	arrange	can't stand	consider
decide	delay	enjoy	expect	finish
hope	intend	mind	miss	offer
plan	practice	promise	recommend	refuse

Verb patterns (*-ing* or infinitive with *to*)

When two verbs are used together, the second one often takes the *-ing* form or the infinitive with *to*.
They attached documents that looked official and **kept writing to me**.
Websites such as Kickstarter allow entrepreneurs to **avoid selling** part of their business to an investor.
They **needed to confirm** my personal details.
Over half of the campaigns on Kickstarter don't receive any funding because they **fail to reach** their set target.

Check the Grammar Reference for more information and practice.

2 Choose the correct options to complete the blog post.

If you're anything like most people, you probably enjoy (1) *posting / to post* on social media. Maybe you hope (2) *creating / to create* a particular kind of image of yourself, or intend (3) *showing / to show* others what good taste you have. You're probably not planning (4) *providing / to provide* information that could be used against you in the future, but every time you post online or "like" something, you're agreeing (5) *sharing / to share* that personal information with the world!

Most of us avoid (6) *revealing / to reveal* too much about ourselves face-to-face, but for some reason, we don't mind (7) *doing / to do* this online. Everything you decide (8) *making / to make* public on the internet helps to build a very detailed picture of who you are and what you believe—and we're failing (9) *understanding / to understand* that this helps companies guess your age, gender, education, political views… and much more.

Of course, most social media companies refuse (10) *guaranteeing / to guarantee* privacy for users. After all, we are their product. What they sell is the information we give them! Given this, I recommend (11) *using / to use* science to help us gain control over our data! Sites could warn us of the risks we are taking when we post certain kinds of information, for example. Failing that, of course, we could all just consider (12) *posting / to post* less.

3 Work in pairs. Discuss the questions.

1 How much do you think you reveal about yourself on social media? Why?
2 What kinds of things do you post online? Why?
3 Are you concerned about privacy online? Why?
4 What do you think social media sites do with the personal information they gather? How does this make you feel?

4 Complete the comments with the correct form of these verbs.

be	feel	have	hear
post	protect	quit	spend

Eric Wong — Posted 3 hours ago

I can't stand (1) _____ like everything I do online is being used by someone. Really, we should all promise (2) _____ social media! The only reason we don't is because we're too scared we'd miss (3) _____ from friends!

Luisa Hernandez — Posted 2 weeks ago

If you use social media, you should expect (4) _____ these experiences. Why should companies offer (5) _____ our privacy? They already provide us with free services. That should be enough.

Back to the Future — Posted a month ago

The secret of being happy is to practice (6) _____ more patient! Delay (7) _____ until you're sure you really want the world to have access to what you write—and try (8) _____ as much time offline as you can!

5 Work in groups. Do you agree with the comments in Activity 4? Why?

6 Write your own short response to the blog post in Activity 2. Include two or more verbs from Activity 1. Then share your comments in groups.

Objects before -ing and to

Some verbs always have an object before an -ing form or an infinitive with to.

When they **asked me to confirm** my bank details, I started to think it must be a scam.

Check the Grammar Reference for more information and practice.

7 Look at the Grammar box. Complete the sentences so that they are true for you. Then explain your ideas to a partner.

1 My parents always expected me _____ .
2 In a few years' time, I can see myself _____ .
3 If I could, I'd hire someone _____ .
4 We should do more to prevent _____ .
5 I can still remember begging my parents _____ .

Verbs with two objects

Some verbs can be followed by two objects.

The indirect object is usually a person and the second, direct object is usually a thing.

Can you **email me your essays**, please, instead of **handing them to me** in class?

Check the Grammar Reference for more information and practice.

8 Look at the Grammar box. Complete the sentences with these direct objects. You will also have to add an indirect object. The first one has been done for you.

anything	a loan	a new tablet
a special dinner	permission	the remote control

1 This show is terrible. Let's see what else is on. Pass *me the remote control* .
2 My dad bought _____ for my birthday.
3 If you're under twenty, it's difficult to find a bank that'll give _____ to start a business.
4 By posting on their website, you're basically giving _____ to use your data.
5 If I were you, I wouldn't tell _____ . He can't keep a secret!
6 My sister and I cooked _____ for their wedding anniversary.

9 CHOOSE

Choose one of the following activities.

- Work in pairs. Write a blog post explaining best practices when it comes to using social media. Use as many of the phrases below as you can.

   If I were you, I'd avoid…
   I'd strongly recommend…
   It's best not to agree / try…
   Lots of people fail…
   You may want to prevent people from…
   It's sometimes good to ask friends…
   Don't allow everyone…
   Think carefully before you tell…

- Write a short story about someone who started a new business. Use at least five verbs from pages 21–27.

- Work in groups. Search online for a story about someone who was a victim of cybercrime. Report what happened to another group. Use at least five verbs from pages 21–27.

2D This is what happens when you reply to spam email

> " Crazy stuff happens when you start replying to scam emails. "
>
> **JAMES VEITCH**

Read about James Veitch and get ready to watch his TED Talk. ▶ 2.0

AUTHENTIC LISTENING SKILLS

Intonation and pitch

When we are surprised or shocked by what someone says, we often repeat a key word, phrase, or short sentence with a high pitch and a questioning intonation. We may then add a comment with a falling tone.

1 Look at the Authentic Listening Skills box. Then work in pairs. Practice the exchange.

- **A** We can start with 50 kilograms as a trial shipment.
- **B** Fifty kilograms? There's no point doing this at all unless you're shipping at least a metric ton.

2 Listen to James Veitch. Compare your intonation with his. 🎧 9

3 Work in pairs. Take turns responding to the comments using the same intonation pattern as James.
1. I got an email offering to distribute gold.
2. He's sixteen years old.
3. It cost ten dollars.
4. I've never watched *Star Wars*.
5. Her dad is the mayor of our city.
6. My bank called me and asked for my address.

WATCH

4 Work in groups. Guess what this email means and why it was written.

> The business is on. I am trying to raise the balance for the Gummy Bear so he can submit all the needed Fizzy Cola Bottle Jelly Beans to the Creme Egg for the Peanut M&Ms process to start. Send £1,500.00 via a Giant Gummy Lizard.

5 Watch Part 1 of the talk. Answer the questions. ▶ 2.1
1. How was "Solomon Odonkoh" trying to make money?
2. Do you still have the same answer to Activity 4?

6 Work in pairs. Put the sentences in the correct order.
- **a** I figured I had to knock it on the head.
- **b** On real estate, what about you?
- **c** Dude, you have to use the code!
- **d** I'm a hedge fund executive bank manager.
- **e** I have to go to bed now.
- **f** I could do what I think we've all always wanted to do.
- **g** If we're going to do it, let's go big.
- **h** I didn't hear back. I thought, "I've gone too far."

28 Unit 2 The Business of Technology

7 Watch Part 1 of the talk again to check your ideas in Activity 6. ▶ 2.1

8 Work in groups. Discuss why you think James Veitch replies to spam. Which of these points is he trying to make?

1 He replies to spam email when he is bored.
2 He suggests it is a good way to spend any spare time.
3 He replies to spam email to take up the time of the spammer. He suggests that this stops them from contacting other people.
4 He replies to spam email because he is interested in the financial benefits. He suggests that people can make money by doing business online.

9 Watch Part 2 of the talk. Check your ideas in Activity 8. How effective do you think James's approach is? Why? ▶ 2.2

10 Watch Part 3 of the talk. How are the emails James receives from "Solomon Odonkoh" and the emails he receives this time similar? ▶ 2.3

11 VOCABULARY IN CONTEXT

a Watch the clips from the TED Talk. Choose the correct meanings of the words and phrases. ▶ 2.4

b Work in pairs. Tell your partner about:
- something or someone who *turned up* unexpectedly.
- a situation that *got out of hand* / *went too far*.
- something or someone that / who *intrigues* you.

12 MY PERSPECTIVE

Work in pairs. Come up with five different ways to deal with internet scams. Then discuss which ones are most relevant to these groups of people. Explain your reasons.

- elderly people
- people who enjoy playing video games
- people who do a lot of online shopping

CHALLENGE

Work in groups. Design a questionnaire to find out about people's experiences with internet scams. You should find out how much is already known and what, if anything, people are doing to reduce the risks. You will need at least ten questions.

2E Investment Opportunity

Speaking strategy

Persuading

When we are persuading people, we sometimes turn our own experiences and opinions into a negative question to challenge the other person's ideas.

I think it will lose money.
Don't you think it'll lose money?
I'd find it really useful.
Wouldn't you find it really useful?
I have sometimes had that problem.
Haven't you ever had that problem?

SPEAKING

1 Work in groups. Discuss the questions.

1 Are there any TV shows about business or selling products in your country? Do you watch them? Why?
2 Would you be good at selling a product? Why?
3 Have you ever had to present something in front of people? What did you present? Was the presentation successful? Why?

2 Work in pairs. Read about the Kickstarter project. One person should think of reasons to invest and one person should think of reasons not to invest. Then discuss your reasons and try to persuade each other.

mXers was set up by high school student Bharat Pulgam. He has invented a new kind of earbuds that allow you to easily replace the different parts that can break, so you don't have to buy a whole new set. They also allow you to customize your earbuds for an individual look. mXers needs money to develop the product and start production.

3 Make negative questions from these sentences. Which negative questions could you use to support your reasons from Activity 2? Why?

1 It'd be good to have something like that.
2 I think it's a bad idea to give money to strangers online.
3 There's something similar to that already.
4 Sometimes I've wished that I could do that.
5 I would be happy to pay a little more to help.

4 PRONUNCIATION Intonation for persuasion

a Listen to the negative questions and notice the intonation.
b Practice saying the negative questions.
  1 Wouldn't it be good to have something like that?
  2 Don't you think it's a bad idea to give money to strangers online?
  3 Isn't there something similar to that already?
  4 Haven't you ever wished that you could do that?
  5 Wouldn't you be happy to pay a little more to help?

An woman harvests cocoa in Ghana for Fairafric.

5 Work in pairs. Read about two other Kickstarter projects. Choose one each and try to persuade each other to invest.

> The Possible Project is an after-school program that teaches teenagers, mainly from low-income families, the skills to be entrepreneurs. The project has been running for several years and has trained over 250 students. The team wants to raise money for a laser cutter so that students can make a variety of products quickly.
>
> Hendrik Reimers is a German chocolate maker. He has set up a chocolate-making company, Fairafric, in Ghana. By producing the chocolate bars in their own country, rather than only exporting cocoa beans, people in Ghana can earn over 25 percent more—even compared to fair-trade chocolate. The money raised will help fund production, packaging, shipping, and distribution.

WRITING A persuasive article

6 Read the short article on page 149 and find out:

1 what the aim of the article is.
2 what the nightmare is.
3 what the business is.

7 **WRITING SKILL** Getting people's attention

Work in pairs. Look at the article again and answer the questions.

1 How does the article grab your attention?
2 How does the article try to persuade you to continue reading?
3 Where does the factual information come from?
4 What is the purpose of the final paragraph?

8 Would you invest in the *i-save*? Why? Discuss with a partner.

9 Using the product you chose in Activity 5, a product you have heard about recently, or something you invented yourself, write an article to explain the product and encourage people to invest or find out more about it.

10 Work in groups. Share your article. People in your group should ask you questions or share comments about your article.

Useful language

Getting people's attention
- *Have you ever wanted to…? Well, now you could have the opportunity.*
- *Have you ever wondered…? Well, now scientists have discovered the answer.*
- *Have you ever dreamed of…? Well, that's exactly what happened to…!*
- *Have you ever…? Well, all that could be a thing of the past, thanks to….*
- *Do you think…? Well, think again!*

3 Faster, Higher, Stronger

IN THIS UNIT, YOU...
- describe athletes.
- read about the lengths countries will go to in order to host the Olympics and do well.
- learn about small changes that can make big differences.
- watch a TED Talk about how athletes are improving.
- write and carry out a survey.

Sports fans experience a range of emotions as they watch an event.

3A Incredible Achievements

VOCABULARY Describing athletes

1. Work in groups. Look at the photo and discuss the questions.

   1 Would you like to be in a crowd like this? Why?
   2 Which sport do you think they are watching? Is it popular in your country?
   3 Which are the most popular sports in your country? Do you like them? Why? Do you know any famous people who take part in them?

2. Work in pairs. Choose the option which cannot complete the sentence.

   1 He has… *incredible awareness / very energetic / great technique / a real passion for the game.*
   2 She's… *a very skillful player / a really great attitude / a forward / a positive role model.*
   3 She won… *a great goal / silver at the Olympics / the world championship / a gold medal.*
   4 He scored… *an average of 20 points a game / 300 goals in his career / the most last season / the race.*
   5 *He set a new / He won the / He holds the / He smashed the old*… world record.
   6 *She captained / She was the star of / She competed / She played a key role on*… the team.

3. Complete the sentences with words from Activity 2.

   1 Everyone on the team has a really great _____. They always fight right to the end of the game.
   2 She still _____ the world record she set 30 years ago.
   3 When I was younger, I won a gold _____ in the 400 meters.
   4 He has incredible _____. He can anticipate the other players' moves and create opportunities for scoring.
   5 He was a key player in their success, but he never _____ the team.
   6 I've always had a real passion _____ wrestling.
   7 She's _____ in four Olympics and won two golds, one _____, and one bronze.
   8 He scored the winning _____ in the last World Cup final.

4. Choose five phrases from Activity 2 to describe an athlete, a friend, and a family member. Then tell your partner about the people you thought of.

   My favorite soccer player is Pierre-Emerick Aubameyang. He has incredible awareness and scores some amazing goals.

   I think my big sister is a positive role model for me. She has a great attitude and never gives up.

5. **MY PERSPECTIVE**

   How do you think sports and athletes have changed in your lifetime? With a partner, discuss changes in these categories.

   - fame / celebrity status
   - equipment
   - achievements

LISTENING

6 Listen to four people explain why they admire certain athletes. As you listen: 🎧 11

1 find out where each athlete is or was from.
2 find an example of something each athlete won.

7 Listen to the four people again. What does each person say about the following? 🎧 11

1	275 times	
	over 150	
	eight or nine out of ten	
2	popular	
	Italian	
	celebrations	
3	videos	
	personal problems	
	a great lesson	
4	her future husband	
	introduced	
	fought	

8 Work in groups. Discuss which of the four athletes you think achieved the most. Explain your ideas.

GRAMMAR Determiners

9 Complete the information about the functions of determiners using these words.

articles   demonstratives   possessives   quantifiers

Determiners are words used before nouns. They have two main functions:

- They show which noun we mean, using (1) _____ (*the*, *a[n]*), (2) _____ (*this*, *that*, *these*, *those*), and (3) _____ (*my*, *your*, *his*, *her*, *its*, *our*, *their*).
- They show how much or how many of something there is, using (4) _____ .

10 Look at the Grammar box. Underline the determiners in the sentences.

Determiners

a *That year, Susi won the women's singles.*
b *Ask any Indonesian of his generation.*
c *He won many medals, including one gold.*
d *Without him, fewer people would watch motorcycle road racing.*
e *We'd never won any gold medals.*

Check the Grammar Reference for more information and practice.

Valentino Rossi (left) attempts to overtake Maverick Vinales during a race at the Motorland Aragón Circuit in Alcañiz, Spain.

11 Work in pairs. Complete the sentences with determiners. Then discuss.

1 She used to be _____ forward on _____ US women's soccer team and she's one of the most successful soccer players ever.
2 She played for _____ country 275 times and scored 150 goals. _____ man has ever managed that!
3 Not _____ people can claim to have made a sport popular more or less on _____ own.
4 He has _____ ego problems and _____ great personality.
5 _____ coach has shown me some videos of Joaquín when he was at _____ best.
6 She always fought right to _____ end, even when it seemed there was _____ hope.

12 Work in pairs. Look at the corrected sentences. Discuss why you think the original sentences were wrong.

1 I don't like ~~no~~ *any* sports.
2 Hardly any ~~athlete~~ *athletes* from my country ~~has~~ *have* ever won an Olympic medal.
3 I think I'm pretty healthy. I eat very ~~few~~ *little* junk food.
4 There aren't ~~much~~ *many* places near here where you can exercise outside.
5 A ~~little~~ *few* people I know are crazy about sports.
6 I don't think it's right that some athletes earn so ~~many~~ *much* money.
7 Most ~~of~~ people I know have no interest in soccer.
8 I try to exercise every ~~weekends~~ *weekend* if I can.

13 Decide which sentences you agree with in Activity 12. Change the sentences that you do not agree with. Share your ideas in groups.

Number 1 isn't true for me. I like some sports. I'm really into basketball and baseball.
Number 2 isn't true. Lots of athletes from my country have won medals!

14 Complete the biography with one word in each blank.

Yao Ming is (1) _____ retired professional basketball player. He stopped playing a (2) _____ years ago, but he's still one of (3) _____ most famous athletes in China. I have a (4) _____ of great memories of watching him play. He spent (5) _____ years playing in the NBA in North America, which was amazing because (6) _____ Chinese player had ever done that before—and (7) hardly _____ have done it since. (8) _____, if not all, Chinese people know him and are very proud of what he achieved. He's instantly recognizable because he's 7 feet 6 inches tall. He made (9) _____ other player in the NBA look small in comparison! In the end, though, he had a (10) _____ of injuries that ended his career.

15 Think again about the people you chose in Activity 4. Make notes about their lives, achievements, and why you admire them.

16 Work in groups. Tell each other about the people you wrote about in Activity 15. Ask each other more questions.

Unit 3 Faster, Higher, Stronger

3B Is the cost of coming in first too high?

Fireworks explode at the opening ceremony of the London Olympic Games in 2012.

OLYMPIC GOLD

VOCABULARY BUILDING

Synonyms in texts

Writers often use words or phrases with similar meanings to make their work more interesting and to avoid repetition.

*Countries competing to **host the Olympics** will often spend huge amounts to **hold the 16-day event**.*

1 Complete the sentences with these synonyms. Use a dictionary, if necessary.

establish	funding	hold
selected	sums	top

1 Countries compete to **host** the Olympics.
   Countries spend huge amounts to _____ the 16-day event.
2 Hosts spend huge **amounts**.
   Hosts invest large _____ of money.
3 They have programs for **elite** athletes.
   They support _____ competitors.
4 There is **money** to help develop successful athletes.
   This _____ is directly linked to success.
5 They helped to **set up** a program that promotes excellence in sports.
   They helped to _____ a system that promotes excellence in sports.
6 Children are **chosen** as potential stars.
   Children hope to be _____ as potential stars.

2 Work in pairs. Rewrite the phrases using synonyms.

prove to have talent—*prove to have a natural ability*

1 achieve their targets
2 core principle
3 got its highest ranking
4 linked to success
5 tackle the challenges you face

READING

3 Work in groups. Which of these statements do you agree with?

1 The most important thing is not winning, but taking part.
2 Hosting the Olympics is a waste of money.
3 In sports and in life, you get what you pay for.
4 Increasing participation in sports at low levels could help tackle health and social challenges.

🎧 12 When Baron Pierre de Coubertin set up the first modern Olympics in Athens in 1896, he declared that "The most important thing in the Olympic Games is not winning, but taking part; the essential thing in life is not conquering, but fighting well." These days, it can seem that this core principle has been forgotten, (1) _____ .

The hosting countries spend huge amounts of money to hold the 16-day event. Many of the countries taking part invest huge sums in programs for elite athletes. And that money is not spent to come in fourth; the only thing that matters is having "the best Games" and winning medals—preferably gold.

The figures are enormous! Depending on who you ask, China spent 40 billion dollars on the Beijing Olympics and Russia invested 50 billion in Sochi; the Rio and London Games each cost between 14 and 18 billion dollars. In terms of money for athletes, the UK spent over 400 million dollars supporting 1,300 top competitors. This funding is directly linked to success: those who fail to achieve their targets will have their funding cut and, in some cases, completely removed. (2) _____ !

Similarly, several years ago, China established a system known as *Juguo Tizhi* ("whole country support for the elite sport system") for developing athletes. Children are identified as potential sports stars between the ages of six and nine, and are sent to special sports schools run by the local government, (3) _____ . Those who prove to have talent move on to a semi-professional schedule of four to six hours a day, five or six days a week. Later, the top performers move on to provincial training centers. Students there live and breathe their sport and hope to be selected for their provincial team (4) _____ . There are around 400,000 young people in this system, whose main purpose is to win glory for their nation. In the years before Beijing, it accounted for a very large percentage of all sports funding.

In both sports and life, you tend to get what you pay for; (5) _____ . China came in first in Beijing, and Great Britain got its highest ranking in over 100 years in 2016. The question is whether this search for success at all costs comes at the expense of investing in something which is arguably more valuable: (6) _____ . Seeing your team win can obviously lift your spirits. However, this feeling is only temporary, while taking part in regular exercise and sports has been shown to have long-term physical and psychological benefits. Given this, surely spending more money on increasing sports participation from the lowest levels up would be a better way of tackling some of the health and social challenges that many countries face.

4 Read about what some countries will do to host the Olympics and do well. Complete the text with the phrases (a–f).

a the more money you spend, the better the results
b overtaken by the other motto de Coubertin is known for: "faster, higher, stronger"
c local clubs and competitions; facilities for people to stay healthy and play for fun
d and then to be full-time professional athletes representing their country
e where they train for up to 15 hours a week
f So much for the value of just "taking part"

5 MY PERSPECTIVE

Work in pairs. Discuss the questions.

1 Would you like to participate in a system like *Juguo Tizhi*? Why?
2 Do you know any schools that specialize in sports? Do you think they are a good idea? Why?
3 Do you have to play sports at school? How much importance is given to winning?
4 Have you seen any great sporting events? How did they make you feel? Why?

CRITICAL THINKING Supporting arguments

> Sometimes writers select information to support their point of view.

6 Work in pairs. Read the facts below. Do they support an argument for spending money on the Olympics? Why?

1 Six million dollars of the Beijing Olympics' costs went toward sports. The rest included new subway lines, an airport terminal, a light railway, and roads.
2 The majority of *Juguo Tizhi* athletes retire from their sport without a formal education.
3 According to the Chinese National Audit Office, the Beijing Olympics made a profit of 146 million dollars.
4 Montreal took over 30 years to pay off its debts from holding the Olympics.

7 A city in your country wants to host the Olympics. Divide into two teams—one for and one against. In your teams, discuss the arguments you would give. Then debate the issue as a class. Think about:

- the impact on the local community.
- what would happen after the Olympics.
- alternatives to hosting the Olympics.

3C Getting Better All the Time

GRAMMAR Comparatives and superlatives

1 How much do you agree with this quote? Give examples to show how things are better or worse now than they were in the past.

"This is the best time to be alive—ever."   —TED Speaker Gareth Cliff

> **Comparatives and superlatives**
>
> a Bicycles have improved and become **far** <u>more aerodynamic</u>.
> b There are **many** <u>more people</u> training today.
> c Athletes are training <u>harder and more intelligently</u> than before.
> d The running tracks used in the 1930s were <u>not as fast as</u> the ones today.
> e The soft surface of old running tracks stole **much** <u>more energy</u> from athletes' legs compared to modern tracks.
> f Usain Bolt is <u>the fastest man</u> in history.
> g On average, elite shot-putters now are **two and a half inches** <u>taller</u> and **130 pounds** <u>heavier</u> than they were in the 1920s.
> h The current hour record in cycling is **only slightly** <u>better</u> than it was over 40 years ago.
> i <u>The more money</u> governments spend on athletes, <u>the better</u> the results.

Check the Grammar Reference for more information and practice.

2 Look at the Grammar box. Read the sentences about how sports and athletes have changed. Answer the questions.

1 Which sentences use a comparative form with:
   - an adjective?
   - an adverb?
   - a noun?
2 Which sentence uses a superlative adjective?
3 Which sentence emphasizes that something is "less than"?
4 Which of the words in bold show a small difference and which show a big difference?
5 Why do we say *many more people*, but *much more energy*? What is the opposite of each of them?
6 Which sentence shows how one change causes another change to happen at the same time?

3 PRONUNCIATION Linking words together in fast speech

> When one word ends in a consonant sound and the next begins with a vowel sound, we often link the two words together when speaking.
> *I don't do it as much...* may sound like: *I don't do it as* (tas) *much...*
>
> If one word ends with a consonant sound and the next word starts with the same consonant sound, we often leave out the first consonant sound.
> *...than it did last season* may sound like: *...than it did last season*

a Read about linking words together in fast speech. Then listen to the sentences. Underline where you hear the links. 🎧 13

Swimmers wear caps and body suits to help them move through the water faster than other competitors.

38   Unit 3 Faster, Higher, Stronger

1 I'm better at it than I used to be.
2 It's the best thing I've experienced in my life.
3 I don't do it as much as I used to.
4 It's a lot more popular than it used to be.
5 It's a bit more difficult than it was in the past.
6 It's far easier than it was in the past.
7 I'm not as good at it as I'd like to be.
8 They're doing worse than they did last season.

b Work in groups. Replace *it* in each sentence to make sentences that are true for you.

I'm better at speaking English than I used to be!

4 Read about how small changes made a big difference for the British cycling team. How can small changes make big differences in your life?

Between the Olympics in 1908 and 2004, the British cycling team won just three gold medals. No British cyclist had even come close to winning (1) _____ world's greatest cycle race, the Tour de France. Yet over the next twelve years, the British team won more than 25 gold medals and had two winners of the Tour. How could the team perform so (2) _____ better?

The first thing was that cycling received a (3) _____ more funding (4) _____ it had before and, thanks also to a new Olympic track in Manchester, the team could train (5) _____ intensively. The coaches also began to focus on making small improvements in lots of areas. This was not just about training better and eating (6) _____ healthily, but also included things like teaching the cyclists to wash their hands properly and finding the (7) _____ comfortable pillow for them to use at night! (8) _____ cleaner their hands, the (9) _____ colds and viruses the cyclists pick up, and the more training they can do. If they do not get as much sleep (10) _____ they need, they may ride one percent (11) _____ the next day. The more of these small improvements you can make, the (12) _____ the difference compared (13) _____ your competitors.

With the recent successes in British cycling, there are (14) _____ more people cycling in the country than there used to be. Having a much bigger pool of riders improves the chances of finding talented cyclists to continue that success.

There is a lesson here for all of us. We often set big goals which aren't so easy to achieve when perhaps we should focus on all the things we can do (15) _____ better. Small changes can add up to a big difference.

5 Complete the summary in Activity 4 with one word in each blank. Compare your ideas with a partner.

6 CHOOSE

Choose one of the following activities.

- Write a short essay on the question in Activity 1. Use comparatives in your response.
- What is better now than in the past? What is worse? Make lists of five things that are better and five things that are worse. Use comparatives to explain the differences.
- Work in pairs. How many small changes can you think of which would contribute to these big improvements? Explain how the changes will affect the final result.
  - Improving the performance of a school's sports team
  - Getting better grades at school
  - Increasing people's life expectancy in your country
  - Stopping global warming

On average, elite shot-putters now are two and a half inches taller and 130 pounds heavier than they were in the 1920s.

Unit 3 Faster, Higher, Stronger

3D Are athletes really getting faster, better, stronger?

> "We all have this feeling that we're somehow just getting better as a human race… but it's not like we've evolved into a new species in a century."
>
> **DAVID EPSTEIN**

Read about David Epstein and get ready to watch his talk. ▶ 3.0

AUTHENTIC LISTENING SKILLS

Slowing down and stressing words

Speakers will often slow down and stress words when they are contrasting two ideas. The surrounding language can sound very fast.

1 Look at the Authentic Listening Skills box. Listen to an extract from the TED Talk. Underline where David slows down and stresses words. 🎧 14

The winner of the 2012 Olympic marathon ran two hours and eight minutes. Had he been racing against the winner of the 1904 Olympic marathon, he would have won by nearly an hour and a half.

2 Work in pairs. Underline the contrasts in the extracts. Then practice saying them aloud.

1. Usain Bolt started by propelling himself out of blocks down a specially fabricated carpet designed to allow him to travel as fast as humanly possible. Jesse Owens, on the other hand, ran on cinders.
2. Rather than blocks, Jesse Owens had a gardening trowel that he had to use to dig holes in the cinders to start from.
3. …had he been running on the same surface as Bolt, he wouldn't have been fourteen feet behind—he would have been within one stride.
4. Rather than the last beep, Owens would have been the second beep. Listen to it again.
5. Rather than the average body type, you want highly-specialized bodies that fit into certain athletic niches.

WATCH

3 Work in pairs. Which of these sports do you do or watch? What equipment, skills, and physical attributes do you need for each one?

basketball	cycling	gymnastics	soccer
swimming	tennis	track and field	water polo

4 Watch Part 1 of the talk. Guess what David is going to argue. ▶ 3.1

a. The human body has evolved to be better at sports.
b. New records in sports are largely due to technology and professionalism.
c. Sport is a natural part of human development.

5 Watch Part 2 of the talk. Complete the summary with a number, year, or measurement in each blank. ▶ 3.2

In (1) _____, Jesse Owens held the world record in the (2) _____ meters. If he had run more recently against Usain Bolt, he would've finished (3) _____ feet behind him. However, Owens was competing in very different times, and modern runners are greatly helped by technological advances. Given the same conditions, Owens would have been within (4) _____ stride of Bolt!

Technology also helped to improve the hour record that cyclist Eddy Merckx set in (5) _____ by almost (6) _____ miles, but after the rules were changed in (7) _____, cyclists had to use the same equipment. Subsequently, they were only able to go (8) _____ feet farther than Merckx.

40 Unit 3 Faster, Higher, Stronger

TEDTALKS

6 Watch Part 3 of the talk. Match what David mentions (1–6) with the points he is making (a–f). ▶ 3.3

1 high-jumpers and shot-putters
2 digital technology
3 financial incentives, fame and glory
4 Michael Phelps and Hicham El Guerrouj
5 the Kalenjin tribe
6 a radiator

a The move towards specialized types of bodies for particular sports accelerated.
b Kenyans are the best marathon runners.
c It made elite sports more available to a wider group of people.
d Some people might have long, thin legs because of evolution.
e Swimmers have long torsos, and runners require proportionately longer legs.
f Specific groups of people have advantages for some sports.

7 Watch Part 4 of the talk. Are the statements *true*, *false*, or *not stated*? ▶ 3.4

1 When a person gets an electric shock, it activates their muscles.
2 We only use a small percentage of our brain power at any one time.
3 We can train our brains to accept more pain.
4 Primates are more suited to endurance than humans.
5 Kílian Jornet was the first person to ever run up the Matterhorn.
6 David does not expect Kílian's record to be broken.

8 **VOCABULARY IN CONTEXT**

a Watch the clips from the TED Talk. Choose the correct meanings of the words and phrases. ▶ 3.5

b Work in pairs and think of at least one example of:

1 a recent change or event that has affected people *throughout* the world.
2 someone or something that *changed the face of* your country.
3 two brands which are *essentially* the same.
4 an activity that has *shrunk* in popularity.

9 Work in pairs. Discuss the questions.

1 How much of David's talk was new to you? Was there anything he said you already knew?
2 What were the three most interesting facts for you?
3 What do you think is the most important factor in improving results that David mentions? Why?
4 Do you think all sports are better than they were in the past? Why?

CHALLENGE

Choose a sport you are interested in. Find out:

- if it has changed in the ways David Epstein describes.
- if there have been any other changes.
- how the records today compare to 50 years ago.
- why any changes have occurred.

3E Surveys

Useful language

Introducing main findings

The most surprising / interesting thing we found was that…

You won't be surprised to hear that… but one thing that was interesting was…

The main thing we discovered was…

(By far) the most popular… was…

Introducing other points

Another thing that was interesting was…

Apart from that, we found that…

Some other things worth mentioning are…

SPEAKING

1 Work in groups. The bar graph on this page shows the results of a survey into which sports people had done during the previous month. Discuss:

- whether anything shown surprises you. If so, why?
- why you think certain activities were more or less popular.
- which results you would expect to be similar and different where you live.

2 Work in pairs. Discuss which claims are supported (S) and not supported (NS) by the data in the graph.

1 One fifth of those surveyed used a gym in the month before the survey.
2 Swimming and diving are the most popular sports.
3 One in twenty of those surveyed played golf in the month before the survey.
4 Just under five percent of those surveyed bike to and from work.
5 The popularity of certain sports may change depending on the season.

3 Work in pairs. You are going to conduct a survey. Choose a question from below or think of one that interests you. Your survey should have at least six options.

1 What activities have you done in your free time in the past two weeks?
2 What is your favorite type of movie to watch?
3 What subjects do you want to study in college?

4 Interview as many students as you can and take notes. Discuss your notes with your partner. Then present the findings to the whole class.

WRITING A survey

5 Work in pairs. Read the description on page 150 of the bar graph on this page. Answer the questions.

1 What extra information is included which was not shown in the bar graph?
2 Which part of the description expresses opinion rather than fact?

6 Passive forms are often used in reports. Complete the sentences using the past participles of the verbs in parentheses. You will learn more about passives in Unit 5.

1 The graph shows the result of a survey _____ (conduct) at our school last month.

What sports have you participated in during the last month?

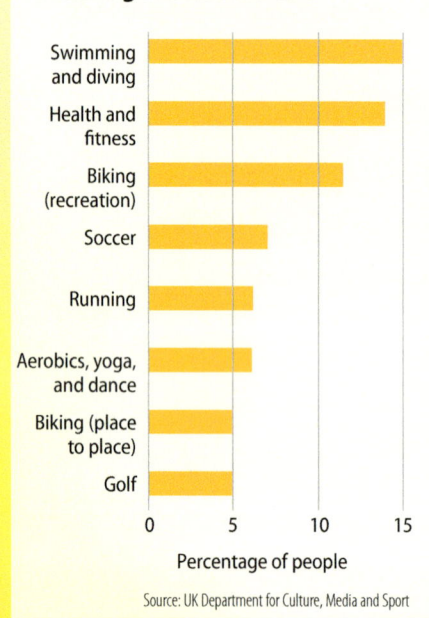

- Swimming and diving
- Health and fitness
- Biking (recreation)
- Soccer
- Running
- Aerobics, yoga, and dance
- Biking (place to place)
- Golf

Percentage of people (0–15)

Source: UK Department for Culture, Media and Sport

Beach soccer is popular on Ipanema Beach in Rio de Janeiro.

42 Unit 3 Faster, Higher, Stronger

2 Fifty students _____ (age) thirteen to fifteen were _____ (interview) about their reading habits.
3 As can be _____ (see), only 20 percent of those _____ (survey) said they had read a novel in the previous six months.
4 The most popular author was J.R.R. Tolkien, _____ (follow) by Anthony Horowitz.
5 We might expect a higher response if the survey were _____ (repeat) with a younger age group.

7 WRITING SKILL Describing statistics

Replace the percentages in italics with these phrases.

| Almost half | A significant majority | A tiny percentage |
| Just under three quarters | Roughly a third | The vast majority |

1 *2%* of those surveyed spend more than an hour a day exercising.
2 *35%* of those who responded play a team sport at least once a month.
3 *48%* of those who responded prefer exercising alone.
4 *65%* of those surveyed would do more sports if they had more free time.
5 *74%* of respondents play fewer sports now than they did five years ago.
6 *96%* of the people I spoke to recognize the importance of exercise.

Writing strategy

Describing statistics
When we describe statistics, we sometimes use phrases or estimates instead of specific percentages. Instead of *10.3 percent cycled*, we might say **one in ten** biked. We do this for variety or to emphasize a point. For example, **over half** may sound bigger than *52 percent*.

8 Work in pairs. Refer to the Writing strategy and use the passive forms in Activity 6 to describe the statistics in this bar graph.

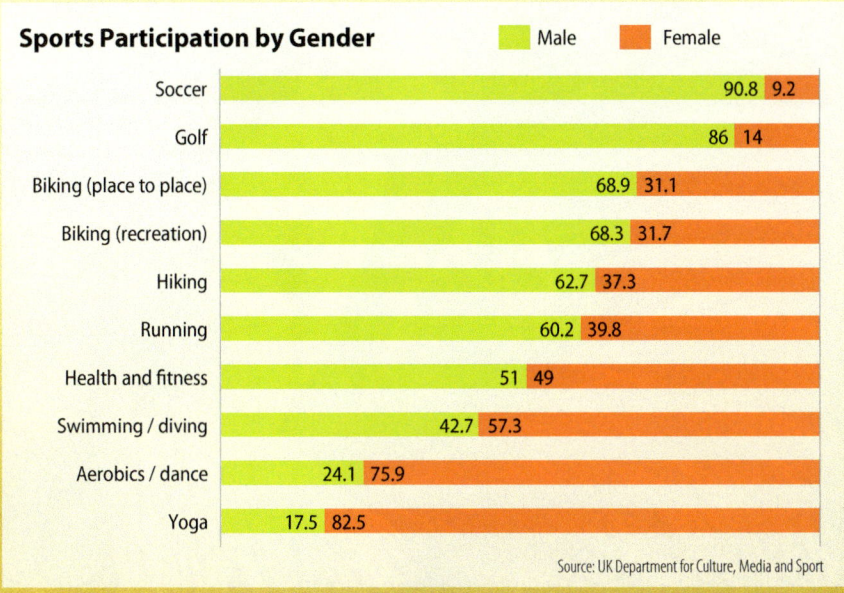

Sports Participation by Gender — Male / Female

Sport	Male	Female
Soccer	90.8	9.2
Golf	86	14
Biking (place to place)	68.9	31.1
Biking (recreation)	68.3	31.7
Hiking	62.7	37.3
Running	60.2	39.8
Health and fitness	51	49
Swimming / diving	42.7	57.3
Aerobics / dance	24.1	75.9
Yoga	17.5	82.5

Source: UK Department for Culture, Media and Sport

4 Cultural Transformation

IN THIS UNIT, YOU...

- discuss how art and cultural events can benefit people and places.
- read about an innovative program for teaching music.
- learn about a Spanish city that was transformed by art and architecture.
- watch a TED Talk about how a park was created on an old railroad line.
- write a *for* and *against* essay.

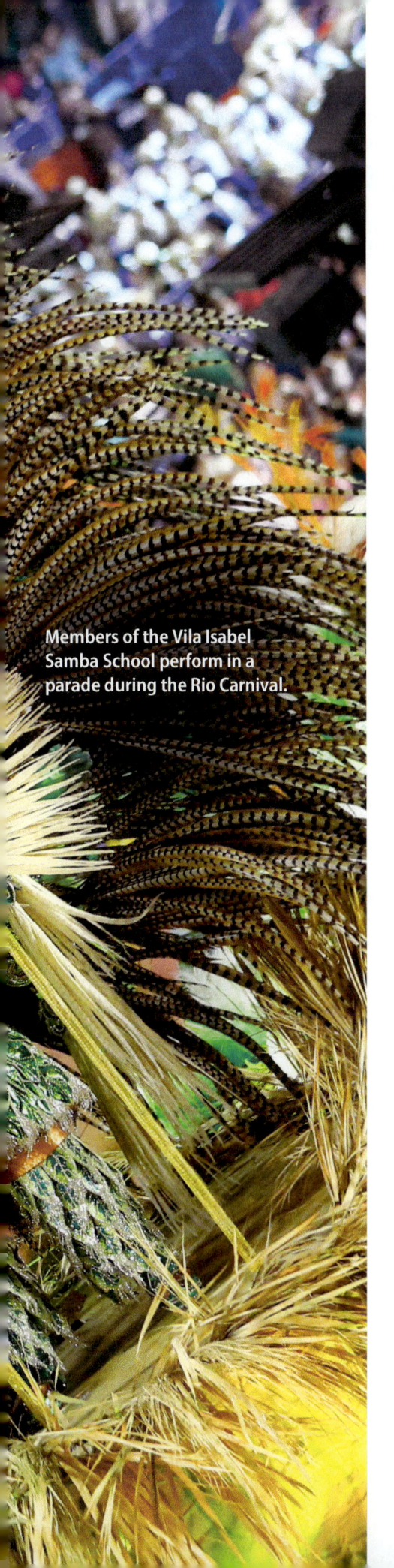

4A Putting the Town on the Map

VOCABULARY Cultural events

1 Work in groups. Look at these cultural attractions and discuss the questions.

art gallery / museum	art / music festival
comedy club	food festival
movie theater	music venue
public art	theater

1 Which of these cultural attractions do you have near where you live?
2 Do you go to any of them? Why?
3 Would you like to have any of them near where you live? Why?

2 Complete the summary by putting the words in bold in the correct order.

The Rio Carnival, one of the world's leading festivals, (1) **every held is February** in Rio de Janeiro, Brazil. During the festival, organizers (2) **huge put on a of parades number** and parties all over the city, which (3) **million tourists almost a attract**. The festival (4) **on impact has a the city big** and on people's cultural lives. The carnival involves around 200 Samba schools which compete to have the best costumes, dance routines, and musical bands. It (5) **million over income $750 in generates** locally in Rio, which comes from tourists who (6) **four-day attend event the** and the Samba schools, which can sometimes spend over 3 million dollars on costumes and preparations. The festival also (7) **Brazil's economy boosts broader**. But it's not just about money. There's (8) **wide for support festival the** because (9) **it together people brings** and helps (10) **create a of pride sense** in the country. Many of the Samba schools are from the poorest neighborhoods in the city, and the festival (11) **opportunities to offers young people part take** in cultural activities and learn new skills. In many ways, the festival has (12) **put map on the Rio** as a world city and cultural hotspot.

3 Listen to the summary. Check your answers in Activity 2. 🎧 15

4 Complete the sentences with six different cultural attractions you know of. Then work in pairs and share your ideas.

1 _____ is held every year.
2 _____ attracts a lot of tourists to our area.
3 _____ has had a big impact on our country.
4 _____ brings people together.
5 _____ has very wide support.
6 I'd like to get involved in _____ .

5 Work as a class. Use the words and phrases in bold from Activity 2 to talk about the places and events you thought of in Activity 1.

We have a music venue near where we live. The promoters put on a lot of small concerts and parties.

6 MY PERSPECTIVE

Work in pairs. Discuss the question.

What other benefits can you think of that are related to cultural attractions and events? Think about the benefits to you, your town, and your country.

Members of the Vila Isabel Samba School perform in a parade during the Rio Carnival.

LISTENING

7 Work in groups. Look at the photo and discuss the questions.

1. Where do you think the photo was taken?
2. What has been done to the building? Why?
3. Do you like it? Why?
4. Have you ever seen anything similar? Where?

8 Listen to a podcast about two big art projects aiming to make a difference. What are the plans for these places? 🎧 16

1. Port-au-Prince, Haiti
2. Birmingham, UK

9 Work in pairs. Do the speakers mention these points in reference to *Port-au-Prince*, *Birmingham*, or *both*. Listen again and check your answers. 🎧 16

1. The project is based on previous work.
2. The project aims to improve the local economy.
3. The project is initially expensive.
4. Local people are involved in creating the work of art.
5. Other things are being built as well.
6. It will bring people together.
7. It may be difficult to keep the art in good condition.
8. There might be an alternative that costs less.

10 MY PERSPECTIVE

Think about your community. What would you choose if you had to decide between the two public art projects and Mark's suggestion of putting on a local festival? Why?

GRAMMAR Future forms 1

11 Look at the Grammar box. Why do you think the forms in bold are used in each sentence?

Future forms

a *And in Haiti, the project **is certainly going to create** jobs, and it'll be employing local artists.*

b *I guess that work **won't last**, but I think the locals are hoping the project **will attract** interest in the area.*

c *The piece should be low maintenance, so they **won't be spending** thousands of pounds every year to keep it in good condition.*

d *What about once it**'s been completed**?*

e *What'll happen when the paint **fades**?*

f *We're **about to put on** a community arts festival.*

g *We're **holding** various shows and events over a week.*

h *You can continue the discussion on the Arts Spot website and get information on Mark's festival, which **starts** soon.*

Check the Grammar Reference for more information and practice.

12 Match each explanation of how to create future forms with an extract in the Grammar box. There are two extracts for one of the explanations.

1. The simple present is used to refer to a scheduled or regular event.
2. The simple present or present perfect is used because it follows a time word.
3. The present continuous is used because they are talking about an arrangement they have made with other people.

With the help of Haas and Hahn, members of a Caribbean community came together to transform a part of their community.

4 *Will* + infinitive is used because they are making predictions about the future they are certain about.

5 The future continuous is used because they are talking about an ongoing or unfinished future action.

6 *Be about to* + verb is used to talk about something which is going to happen in the very near future but has not started yet.

7 *Be going to* + verb is used because they are making a prediction. *Going to* can also be used to talk about arrangements and scheduled events.

13 Choose the correct options.

Our town (1) *holds / is going to hold* a festival next year for the total solar eclipse. There (2) *will be being / are going to be* some small events in the week before the eclipse (3) *takes / is taking* place, like talks and music. On the actual day, the eclipse is expected early in the morning, so we (4) *are about to put on / are putting on* a concert with some local bands as the sun (5) *rises / will rise*. After the concert (6) *has ended / will end*, we're going to have a huge breakfast barbecue to prepare for the big event. It should be great! A lot of people (7) *will be coming to / come to* the area next year to catch the eclipse, so we (8) *will hopefully get / are hopefully getting* a few visitors here, although that's not the main reason for putting on the event. We're really doing it because we want to bring people together, and it's not like we (9) *will be spending / spend* thousands of dollars on it. If (10) *it's going to be / it will be* a success, we'll need lots of volunteers.

14 How many times can you complete the sentences so that they are correct and true? Compare with a partner and see who got the most.

1 I'm _____ next weekend.
2 I'm going to _____ after _____ .
3 There's about to be _____ in our town.
4 I will be _____ , so I can _____ .
5 Next semester, _____ .
6 In five years' time, _____ .

15 Work in pairs. Make a list of at least four ideas for pieces of art, cultural events, or festivals for your community.

16 Work with another pair of students. Compare the ideas you came up with in Activity 15. Discuss which you think would:

- be the most fun.
- be best at bringing the whole community together.
- do most to boost the local economy.
- have the longest lasting impact.
- be the most difficult to organize.

17 Work in the same groups. Choose one of your ideas. Discuss more about the details of the project. Use future forms. Think about:

- the venue.
- how long it will take to set up and how long it will last.
- who will take part.
- who will organize it (professionals / volunteers).
- how much it will cost.
- how you will raise the money.
- any permission you will need.
- how to get people to support the project.
- anything else you think might be important.

18 Present your ideas to the class. Vote for your favorite.

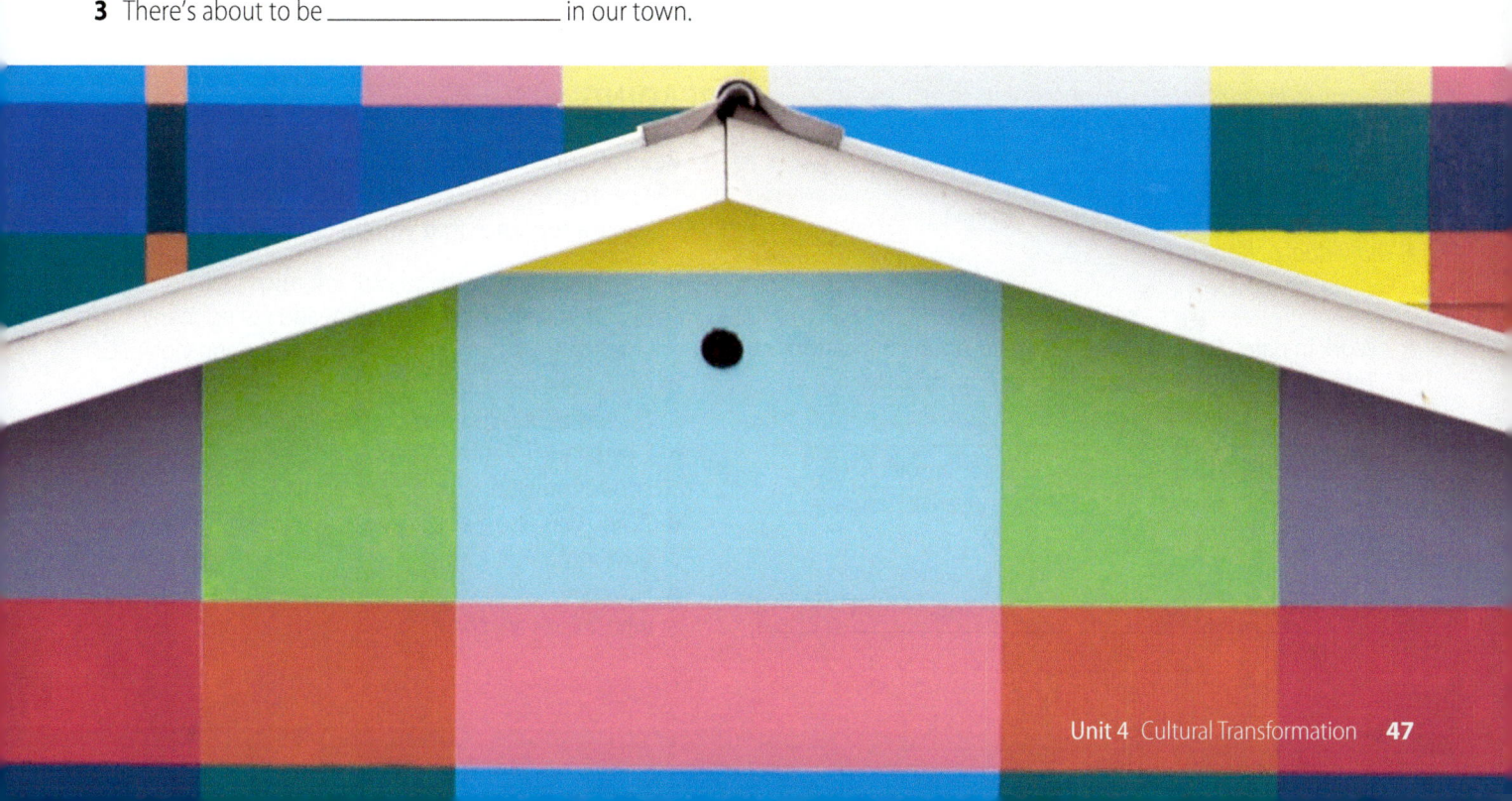

Unit 4 Cultural Transformation

4B Music to Their Ears

A SYSTEM THAT'S LEADING THE WAY

Gustavo Dudamel is the musical director of the Venezuelan Youth Orchestra.

VOCABULARY BUILDING

Adjective and noun collocations 2

It is a good idea to notice and learn adjective-noun collocations. When you learn them, consider how they might be used. Think about:

- what verbs or phrases go with the collocation.

give an **individual performance** */ get a mark for your* **individual performance**

- examples from real life.

We have to work in groups, but we get a mark for our **individual performance**.

1 Work in pairs. Look at these adjective-noun collocations. Take turns explaining what each one means. Use a dictionary, if necessary.

diverse social backgrounds	fierce ambition
hard work	innovative program
leading orchestra	low income
mixed results	private companies
straightforward process	strict set of rules

2 Work in pairs. Put the collocations in Activity 1 in pairs and say how they might be linked together.

fierce ambition / private companies

To get to the top of a private company, you need fierce ambition.

READING

3 Read about *El Sistema*, a program for teaching music. Put the sentences in the correct places in the article. There is one extra sentence that you do not need to use.

  a It has also been credited with improving relations between different communities and saving many children from getting involved in gangs and violence.
  b Obviously, the resources that the Venezuelan government puts into *El Sistema* are important.
  c Central to *El Sistema* is a focus on discipline and commitment.
  d Abreu was also a politician and a minister in the government.
  e However, it seems that there are always individuals whose lives are changed.

48 Unit 4 Cultural Transformation

🎧 **17** **JOSE ANTONIO ABREU** trained and worked as an economist for many years, but his dream was to have a life in music. He fulfilled that dream, first through individual performance, but later, and more importantly, by founding *El Sistema*. *El Sistema* is an innovative program for teaching music to children from diverse social backgrounds. It has been so successful that an orchestra that is part of the program, the Venezuelan National Youth Orchestra, has been named among the five leading orchestras in the world. (1) _____ .

When he first started the orchestra, Abreu had managed to get 50 music stands for the 100 children he was expecting to come and rehearse. In the end, only 11 showed up. What was he going to do? Give up? Try to get more children involved? In fact, he went several steps further, and promised those 11 students that he would turn the orchestra into a world leader! So apart from this fierce ambition, how did it happen?

(2) _____ . It pays for instruments and teaching for over 500,000 young musicians who are involved in the program and also provides monthly grants to older students as a reward for their hard work. It also pays for performances and teaching younger children in the program. Private companies often sponsor local groups and parents also raise funds for tours.

However, money is not the only factor in its success. (3) _____ . New students can start from as young as three, but students and their parents must agree to a strict set of rules and attend classes and rehearsals for between one and four hours a day, up to six days a week. Teachers may visit parents to help them understand the hours required to improve and how to support their children.

While discipline is important, the musical training also emphasizes fun, team spirit, physical expression, and the value of performance. Students start in a choir and work on rhythm and percussion, before moving on to playing the recorder, and then finally choosing their instrument at the age of seven. (4) _____ .

El Sistema is seen by many people from low-income families as a way to stay in education and escape poverty. It can present opportunities to travel via tours within Venezuela and abroad. (5) _____ . No wonder many other countries have looked to copy the program.

Setting up a "sistema" is not a straightforward process, and there have been mixed results. (6) _____ . As one parent from the Scottish Sistema put it, "My son was struggling, and I was worried he was going to drop out of school and end up hanging out with the wrong kids. *El Sistema* has made a huge difference. He's gained confidence, learned discipline, and he's definitely back on track."

f Yet, 40 years ago, such an idea seemed a long way off.
g Lessons are mainly conducted as a group, with all the class working towards performing a piece in front of an audience.

4 Read about *El Sistema* again. Answer the questions.

1 How many children went to Abreu's first rehearsal? How many participate now?
2 How old are children when they choose a musical instrument?
3 How much do they practice?
4 Why do other countries like *El Sistema*?

5 Work in pairs. Discuss the questions.

1 Have you ever learned how to play a musical instrument? How good were / are you?
2 If you gave up playing a musical instrument, why?
3 If you still play a musical instrument, how much do you practice? Do you ever perform?
4 What kind of music do you listen to? What do you like about it?

6 Work in pairs. Look at the adjective-noun collocations in Activity 1 again. Tell each other what was said about them in the article. Check your answers.

CRITICAL THINKING Understanding and evaluating ideas

> If you want to copy a successful idea or make use of what you have learned in a new context, you need to understand all the factors that made the idea a success and evaluate how far they can be applied in a new context.

7 Work in groups. Discuss the different factors you read about that help make *El Sistema* a success.

8 Work as a class. Discuss:

1 Are all the factors you discussed in Activity 7 possible in your country? Why?
2 Are there any factors that you think are not necessary? Why?
3 Would *El Sistema* work in your country? Why?

9 MY PERSPECTIVE

Would you like to participate in a program like *El Sistema*? Why?

The Guggenheim Museum contributed to the "Bilbao Effect."

4C High Hopes

GRAMMAR Future forms 2

1 Look at the Grammar box. Then look at the sentences in each set. Which sentence in each set does not show the future in the past?

a *was / were going to*
  1 Before the election, the mayor said he **was going to** make changes.
  2 I **was going to** enter a painting competition but didn't finish in time.
  3 I fell asleep in the car when we **were going to** the gallery.

b *would*
  1 I **would** really like to go to the Edinburgh Festival next year.
  2 They thought it **would** bring a lot of investments into the city.
  3 If we did more cultural activities here, I'm sure we **would** attract more tourists.

c *was / were + present participle*
  1 The show **was starting** in a matter of minutes, so we had to rush.
  2 I couldn't hear the movie because the people behind me **were talking**.
  3 I only bought two tickets because I thought your brother **wasn't coming**.

> **The future in the past**
>
> **a** My son was struggling, and I was worried he **was going to** drop out of school and end up hanging out with the wrong kids.
> **b** He went several steps further and promised those 11 students that he **would** turn the orchestra into a world leader!
> **c** Abreu had managed to get 50 music stands for the 100 children he thought **were coming** to rehearse.

Check the Grammar Reference for more information and practice.

2 Complete the first parts of the sentences using *was / were going to* and these verbs. Then match them with the second parts of the sentences.

be	cost	get	hold	play	rain

  1 They said the building _____ something like $35 million,
  2 The forecast did say it _____ a bit,
  3 We _____ tickets for the concert next month,
  4 They told us the band _____ on stage around nine,
  5 I thought they _____ all their hits,
  6 When they announced they _____ the World Cup here,

  a but they just played loads of new stuff. They were absolutely terrible.
  b but it literally sold out in seconds. I couldn't believe it.
  c loads of people were actually against it.
  d but it cost way more than that.
  e but we had to wait for hours. It must've been midnight before they came on.
  f but it just poured all day.

3 PRONUNCIATION Contrastive stress

  a Listen to how the quantity words in the second part of the sentences are stressed to emphasize the contrast with previous plans or predictions. 🎧 18
  b Practice saying the complete sentences from Activity 2.

4 Read about the Bilbao Effect. What is it? Which of the italicized parts are grammatically incorrect? Correct them.

By the 1990s, the city of Bilbao in northern Spain was no longer the industrial center it once was and the future (1) *was looking* bleak. It was hard to see how new jobs (2) *was going to be* created or what could be done to ensure things (3) *improve*. Local authorities decided to invest over $1 billion in the hope that a new focus on culture (4) *would attract* visitors. The money (5) *was going to be spent* on transportation, bridges, parks, libraries, and the remarkable Guggenheim Museum, designed by Frank Gehry. Once people saw what the building (6) *was looking like*, excitement grew. When it opened, the authorities (7) *were expecting* around 300,000 visitors in the first year, but by the end of that year it had attracted a million! The impact on the city has been even more dramatic than people hoped it (8) *was*, so it's no wonder other cities are now desperate to copy what has become known as the "Bilbao Effect"!

5 **MY PERSPECTIVE**

Think of three possible reasons why the "Bilbao Effect" might not work in another city.

6 Listen to three people describing cultural events they went to. Answer the questions. 🎧 19

1 What event did each person go to?
2 How did they feel about it? Why?

7 Think of places or cultural events you have been to. Plan what you want to say, using the language below. Then share your experiences in groups.

It was much / way… than I thought it would be.

I wasn't expecting it to be very…, but it was actually…

It was nowhere near as good as I was expecting.

I was expecting it to be pretty… but it was actually very…

8 Work in pairs. Look at the Grammar box. Answer the questions.

1 What is the form of the future perfect? What is the form of the future perfect continuous?
2 Which form do we use to emphasize the duration of an activity before a certain point in the future?
3 Which form do we use to emphasize completed actions by a certain point?
4 Which word shows a point in the future?

> **The future perfect**
>
> Use the future perfect to show the time in the future by which something will be complete.
>
> *It **will** soon **have been running** for 70 years, and over 10 million people **will have seen** it.*

Check the Grammar Reference for more information and practice.

9 Complete the sentences with the future perfect or future perfect continuous form of the verb.

1 By the end of next year, the band _____ (play) together for 30 years!
2 By the end of this course, I _____ (study) English for ten whole years!
3 I can't talk now. I'll call you after five. I _____ (finish) school by then.
4 He's originally from Peru, but by June he _____ (live) in Canada for ten years.
5 This museum _____ soon _____ (be) open for a whole century.

10 **CHOOSE** Choose one of the following activities.

- Find out about a new development in your town or country. Why was it built? Has it been a success?
- List ten things that will have happened in your life by the time you are 30. Then work in pairs. Which are the most or least likely to happen?

The Zubizuri (Basque for "white bridge") stretches across the Nervion River in Bilbao.

> "...that's the power that public space can have to transform how people experience their city and interact with each other."
>
> **ROBERT HAMMOND**

Read about Robert Hammond and get ready to watch his TED Talk. ▶ 4.0

AUTHENTIC LISTENING SKILLS

Recognizing words you know

Sometimes you may not recognize words in fast speech because you expect to hear the full form. For example, in a dictionary *with* is shown as /wɪθ/, but in fast speech it may sound more like /wɪ/.

1 Look at the Authentic Listening Skills box. Then listen and complete the extracts from the TED Talk. 🎧 20

1. And by 1980, the last train rode. It was a train _____ .
2. I first read about it in the *New York Times*, in an article _____ demolished.
3. And _____ we were the only two people that were sort of interested in the project.
4. And that's really where we started... the idea coalesced around... let's make this a park, and _____ this wildscape.

2 Listen to the extracts again. Which of the words were the most difficult to hear? 🎧 20

3 Say each sentence twice, slowly the first time—with a gap between each word—then faster, linking the words in each part of the sentences together.

WATCH

4 Work in pairs. Discuss the questions.

1. Where you live, are there any old buildings, industrial places, or pieces of land that are no longer used? Do you know when or why they stopped being used?
2. Do you know of any old buildings or places that used to be used for one purpose, but are now used for a different purpose? Do you like the change?
3. What's your favorite public space? Why? How often do you go there?

5 Watch Part 1 of the talk. Choose the correct options. ▶ 4.1

1. In the old days, the freight line trains:
   a. used cowboys to protect the goods they were carrying.
   b. were pulled by horses.
   c. caused several fatal accidents.
2. As time went by:
   a. more freight started being transported by road.
   b. the line was mainly used to transport meat.
   c. people in the neighborhood wanted it demolished.
3. At the community board meeting, Robert:
   a. offered to volunteer to help preserve the High Line.
   b. realized he was in a small minority.
   c. knew a writer from the *New York Times*.
4. The main inspiration for the project came from:
   a. the spectacular views of Manhattan.
   b. the industrial architecture of the line.
   c. the way nature had started reclaiming the abandoned space.

6 Watch Part 2 of the talk. Why were the following mentioned? ▶ 4.2

1. 9/11
2. 100 million
3. 20 years and 250 million
4. half a billion
5. three

7 Work in groups. Robert Hammond explains that a special study was designed to show whether the High Line would add value to the city. Discuss:

- how the creation of a park on the High Line might add value to the local area.
- how demolishing the High Line might add value to the area.
- who you think would benefit most in each case—and which plan of action is better.

8 Watch Part 3. Are the sentences *true* or *false*? ▶ 4.3

1 Twice as many people as expected used the High Line last year.
2 Architects have taken inspiration from the High Line.
3 Some parts of the High Line have been elevated to a higher level.
4 Robert Hammond doesn't really like the design.
5 He believes the space encourages people to behave in ways they wouldn't normally.

9 **VOCABULARY IN CONTEXT**

a Watch the clips from the TED Talk. Choose the correct meanings of the words and phrases. ▶ 4.4

b Work in pairs. Discuss the questions.
1 What different ways of reducing the number of people who get *run over* can you think of?
2 What problems might arise if ancient *relics* are found in a construction area?
3 Who do you usually talk to if you need to *figure out* what to do about a problem? Why?

4 Which ideas do you think your town or city would really *get behind*? Why?
- Free art gallery and museum entrance for everyone
- Spending more money on public art
- Official areas for young people to put up street art
- Free art materials for all schoolchildren
- Displaying work by local poets on public transportation

CHALLENGE

Work in pairs. Make a list of all the activities you think Friends of the High Line had to do at each stage to transform the abandoned rail line into a park. Think about:

- events and meetings.
- money.
- people.
- the law.

Work with another pair of students. Then use some of the phrases below to discuss:

- what personal qualities are needed to help change a neighborhood in this way.
- which of these qualities you think you have.
- how you could develop these kinds of qualities and skills.

I think you'd need to be very… if you were going to…

You'd have to be a very… kind of person if you wanted to…

I'd like to think I'm fairly…

I'd be lying if I said I was…

The best way to get better at… would be to…

4E What's the plan?

SPEAKING

Useful language

Making suggestions

Do you feel like going to…?

I was wondering if you'd like to go to…?

Rejecting suggestions

To be honest, it's not really my kind of thing.

Doesn't really sound like my kind of thing, I'm afraid.

Suggesting alternatives

OK. Well, in that case, how about going to…?

OK. Well, if you'd rather, we could always go to…

1. Choose the options that are true for you. Then work in pairs and explain your choices.

   1 I usually go out to meet friends *four or five times a week / two or three times a week / maybe once a week*.
   2 I *hardly ever / sometimes / often* go out with my parents.
   3 I prefer going out *alone / with one or two close friends / with a big group*.
   4 When it comes to deciding where and when to meet, *I let other people decide / we generally try to reach a group decision / I basically like to take charge*.
   5 I mostly like going to *the same place / different kinds of places*.
   6 When I go out with friends, *I like to plan everything in advance / I'm happy to just go with the flow and see what happens*.
   7 I *often / rarely / never* go to cultural events like concerts, exhibits, and plays.

2. Listen to two friends making plans. Answer the questions. 🎧 21

   1 What different cultural events do they mention?
   2 What do they decide to do in the end?
   3 Why are the other ideas rejected?
   4 Where and when do they arrange to meet? Why?

3. Listen to the two friends again. Complete the sentences by adding two or three words in each blank. 🎧 21

   1 I was wondering. Do you _____ somewhere with me tomorrow?
   2 Where did you have _____ ? Anywhere in particular?
   3 OK. What _____ is it? I'm not really into art, so…
   4 How about _____ this band that are playing in the park tomorrow night?
   5 What about just going to see a film? Would you be _____ that?
   6 Let's _____ the later one—but meet a little bit earlier.
   7 I'll book tickets _____—just to _____ .

4. Work in pairs. Make plans to go to a cultural event. Make sure you:

   - use real places or events that are local to you.
   - reject at least one suggestion and explain why.
   - arrange where and when to meet.
   - use language from Activity 3 and the Useful language box.

Some festivals and events that attract a lot of people like this color run sometimes require a large cleanup operation.

WRITING A *for* and *against* essay

5 Work in pairs. Look at this essay title. Think of two reasons why you might agree with the statement in the title, and two reasons why you might disagree.

Building a new museum would boost tourism in the area and benefit the whole community

6 Read the essay on page 150. Does the writer agree with the statement in the essay title? Why?

7 **WRITING SKILL** Introducing arguments

Work in pairs. Look at the essay on page 150 again. Use the Writing strategy box to identify each of the three stages of the introduction. Answer the questions.

1. How does the writer stress the importance of the subject?
2. What phrase is used to introduce an opposing point of view?
3. How does the writer signal a disagreement?

8 Complete the sentences, which give a weak argument, with these words.

| believed | claimed | common | seen | sometimes | supposedly |

1. It is _____ said that art is a mirror of society. In fact,…
2. Creativity _____ belongs to the world of the arts. In reality, though,…
3. It is widely _____ that music can help to connect young people from different backgrounds. However,…
4. It is often _____ that comedy works best when it's cruel. However,…
5. Museums are sometimes _____ as being of no interest to young people. However,…
6. One _____ argument against more focus on the arts in schools is that they do not make students more employable. In reality,…

9 Work in pairs. Complete the second sentences in Activity 8 to show how each of the arguments could be seen as weak.

10 Choose one of the options and write a *for* and *against* essay of 250 words.

a. Argue the opposite point of view to the student essay you read on page 150.
b. Write an essay on one of these titles:
What our city needs is a big new concert hall
We should not host a festival because the cleanup is too expensive
New technologies have had a very negative effect on our cultural lives

---

Writing strategy

Opening paragraph

When writing the opening paragraph of a *for* and *against* essay:
- show the reader you know why the subject is relevant.
- give what you feel is a weak argument or point of view.
- say why you disagree and give your own opinion.

Useful language

Showing relevance

Over recent years,… has become increasingly important.
…is getting better and better / worse and worse at the moment.
Over the last few years, there has been a dramatic increase / drop in…

Introduce an opposing view

It is sometimes said that…
It is often claimed that…

Say why we disagree

…but, in fact,…
In reality, though,…
However,…

5 It's Not Rocket Science

IN THIS UNIT, YOU...

- learn about and discuss different life hacks.
- read about why humans are curious.
- learn about brain research.
- watch a TED Talk about science being for everyone.
- design and write about an experiment.

5A Life Hacks

VOCABULARY Science in action

1 Work in groups. Discuss the questions.

1 In what ways has science made life easier or better in your lifetime?
2 Can you think of two mysteries science has yet to solve?
3 Which scientists have you heard of? Why are they famous?
4 What personal qualities are most important if you want to be a scientist? Why?

2 Work in pairs. Do you understand the words in bold? Use a dictionary, if necessary.

1 **design** an experiment
2 **conduct** research
3 **form** a hypothesis and **prove** it
4 **put** a substance in water and **heat** it **up** to help it **dissolve**
5 **create** a chemical reaction that **releases** a gas
6 **track** students' progress
7 **record** the results of an experiment and **analyze** them
8 **write** a report and **add** references at the end
9 **place** something under a microscope
10 **reward** hard work
11 **get rid of** a chemical
12 **submit** an assignment

3 Work in pairs. Do the actions in Activity 2 happen in your science classes at school? Who does each activity? Give examples.

We don't really design experiments at school. We just follow the ones in the textbook or do what the teacher tells us to do.

4 Complete the phrases. Add verbs from Activity 2 that are commonly used with each set of words.

1 …a theory / …an opinion
2 …samples / …the results
3 …an operation / …a survey
4 …chemicals into the atmosphere / …an animal
5 …an essay / …it before the deadline
6 …their effort / …her for her work
7 …the movement of birds / …your progress

5 Work in pairs. Compare your answers in Activity 4. Then think of one more word or phrase to go with each verb. Use a dictionary, if necessary.

6 Look again at your completed phrases in Activity 4. Who might perform each action? Why?

7 MY PERSPECTIVE

Work in groups. Discuss the questions.

1 What science experiments have you done at school that you enjoyed?
2 Have you ever designed an experiment yourself? If yes, what for? If no, why not? What experiment would you like to design?

Taylor Wilson is the youngest person ever to produce a type of energy called *nuclear fusion*. He did it by building a reactor in his parents' garage.

LISTENING

8 Work in pairs. Read the definition. Then tell each other any life hacks you know for:

1 smartphones.
2 computers / computer games.
3 the home.
4 food and drink.

Life hack /laɪf hæk/ *noun* [countable]
A simple solution or a piece of advice that helps you solve a problem, save time, or improve how something works.

9 Listen to an extract from a radio show called *Life Hacks*. Answer the questions. 🎧 22

1 What four life hacks are mentioned?
2 What problems do the life hacks help solve?

10 Correct the false information in each sentence. Then listen again to check your ideas. 🎧 22

1 Marie bought herself a phone for her birthday.
2 Marie's a morning person.
3 It's best to put the paper cup right next to your bed.
4 The cup throws the sound around the room.
5 The app alters your sleep patterns.
6 Phones can be charged faster on airplanes.
7 Spicy food increases the temperature in your mouth.
8 The chemical in chilies is easily dissolved with water.

11 Complete the extracts with three words in each blank. Then listen again to check. 🎧 22

1 Well, I _____ this lovely new smartphone.
2 And of course it works better as an alarm if the cup _____ far away from your bed, as then _____ to get up to turn it off.
3 The cup channels the sound in one direction, whereas normally _____ around all over the place.
4 _____ to track your sleep patterns and wake you up during light sleep rather than deep.
5 If your _____ and you need it done ASAP, then what you need to do is put it in airplane mode.
6 An email has _____ to me by Maxine, who's suggested a hack for anyone out there who likes a spicy curry from time to time.

12 MY PERSPECTIVE

Which of the four life hacks do you think is:

- the most useful? the least? Why?
- the easiest to understand from a scientific point of view? the hardest? Why?

GRAMMAR Passives 1

13 Work in groups. Look at the Grammar box. Then answer the questions.

1 What tense are each of the passive forms in Activity 11?
2 Why is the passive used in each case?
3 Identify the object(s) in the sentences in the Grammar box. Are the objects direct or indirect? What do they refer to?

58 Unit 5 It's Not Rocket Science

The passive

The passive is made by using a form of the verb *be* + past participle.

a *I was recently given this lovely new smartphone.*
b *An email has just been sent to me by Maxine.*

Check the Grammar Reference for more information and practice.

14 Complete the blog entry with the correct passive forms.

If you're making a list of the most important inventions ever, the internet should (1) _____ (place) right at the top! Our lives (2) _____ completely _____ (transform) since the first web page (3) _____ (create) in 1990. It could even (4) _____ (say) that the internet is the ultimate life hack! Of course, various linked systems of computers (5) _____ (use) for some time before the birth of the world wide web, and early versions of what was to become the web (6) _____ regularly _____ (test) throughout the 1970s and 80s. Today, though, it's rare to meet someone who has no interest in (7) _____ (connect). For many young people, that means more than 20 hours a week online! Indeed, the internet has become so essential to our lives that some argue it is like air, and that everyone should (8) _____ (give) free access to it.

15 PRONUNCIATION Stress in passives

When using the passive, greater stress is placed on the main verb and less stress is placed on the auxiliary verb.

a Look at the completed blog entry in Activity 14. Which word is stressed in each passive construction?
b Work in pairs. Practice reading the blog entry in Activity 14 with the correct stress.

16 Work in pairs. Discuss the questions.

1 Do you agree that the internet is the most important invention ever? Why?
2 What other inventions would you put near the top of the list? Why?

17 Underline the passives in the descriptions. Can you name the things described?

1 The name is taken from Tagalog, a language that's spoken in the Philippines, where it was used as a weapon for hundreds of years. It was first produced as a toy in California in the 1920s.
2 It is thought that it was first produced in Mocha, Yemen, over a thousand years ago. It's now consumed all over the world—particularly in the morning.
3 It was first invented in Ancient China over 2,000 years ago for use in government, but wasn't introduced into Europe until the 11th century.
4 You've probably been asked to type letters into one of these when using the web. They're used to prevent spam and were invented by TED speaker Luis Von Ahn from Guatemala.

18 Work in pairs. Write a description of something like in Activity 17. Use the passive. Then work with another pair of students. Can they correctly guess what is being described?

People have created more original ways to use cups as loudspeakers.

Unit 5 It's Not Rocket Science 59

5B Curiosity, Cats, and Kids

VOCABULARY BUILDING

Adjective endings

Adjectives can sometimes be recognized by their endings. Common adjective endings include:

-ous: curious, tremendous, previous
-able: reliable, treatable, adaptable
-ive: effective, innovative, imaginative
-ful: beautiful, hopeful, helpful
-al: practical, electrical, social

1 Work in pairs. Think of a noun that each adjective in the Vocabulary Building box often goes with. Use a dictionary, if necessary.

2 Choose four pairs of words from Activity 1. Write a sentence for each pair.

*Research needs to have **practical applications**.*

3 Choose the correct options.

It is often thought that (1) *innovation / innovative* in science comes from the labor of (2) *curiosity / curious* geniuses: the kinds of individuals who work in isolation, find (3) *pleasure / pleasurable* in exploration, and who don't worry too much about the (4) *practicality / practical* applications of their findings. While it is true that the (5) *use / useful* of many new discoveries is not always immediately clear, you only have to look at the results of scientific work conducted by teams to see that it is a (6) *social / society* process and involves far more (7) *cooperation / cooperative* than is often imagined. (8) *Collaborative / Collaboration* can not only help to speed up scientific work; it can also enhance the quality of the work and help share knowledge amongst a wider group of individuals.

4 MY PERSPECTIVE

Work in pairs. Answer the questions.

1 What are the advantages and disadvantages for scientists or researchers working on their own, as part of a small team, and in a much bigger team?
2 How do you prefer to work? Why?

READING

5 Read the article about curiosity. Which sentence is the best summary of the main point?

a Technology can help us become more curious, but it can also kill our curiosity.
b It's more important than ever to make sure kids learn to be curious.
c Social media doesn't help us know people better.
d We run the risk of becoming less curious if we're not careful.

6 Work in pairs. Which statements do you think the writer would likely agree and disagree with? Refer to the article to explain why.

1 Parents should make sure kids don't experiment too much.
2 You can't create anything new unless you recognize the limits of your understanding.
3 The people funding scientific research should demand clear outcomes.
4 Humans are basically programmed to ask why.
5 You don't get a full picture of people from the way they present themselves online.
6 We need to share ideas with like-minded people if we are to develop our curiosity.

7 Work in groups. Do you agree with the statements in Activity 6? Why?

CRITICAL THINKING Asking critical questions

To check ideas and deepen understanding, ask questions about statements or research. For example:

Research has shown that curiosity is just as important as intelligence in determining how well students do at school.

The starting points for thinking critically about this statement might be:

How is student success measured? In what subjects?

How are curiosity and intelligence measured? How different are they?

Can you be intelligent without being curious, and vice versa?

Can you be successful at school without one of these characteristics?

Is curiosity important for doing well in a job? What kind of jobs?

8 Work in pairs. What are two questions you would ask if you wanted to think critically about each statement?

1 Hard work is more important for success than either curiosity or intelligence.
2 There is some evidence that bees can think like humans.
3 It has been shown that you can only learn seven words in a language lesson.

9 Compare your ideas in Activity 8. How many of the questions can you already answer? What is the best question to explore each statement?

Back to the future?

Curiosity allows us to embrace unfamiliar circumstances, brings excitement into our lives, and opens up new possibilities. But how curious are we in the 21st century?

Curious explorers make their way through Rising Star Cave in South Africa.

🎧 **23** Perhaps you've heard the old saying "curiosity killed the cat." It's a phrase that's often used to warn people—especially children—not to ask too many questions. Yet it's widely agreed that curiosity actually makes learning more enjoyable and effective. In fact, research has shown that curiosity is just as important as intelligence in determining how well students do in school.

Curiosity also allows us to embrace unfamiliar circumstances, brings excitement into our lives, and opens up new possibilities. Being curious requires us to be both humble enough to know we don't have all the answers, and confident enough to admit it. Asking the questions that help us bridge the gap between what we already know and what we'd like to know can lead us to make unexpected discoveries.

In science, basic curiosity-driven research—conducted without pressure to produce immediate practical results—can have unexpected and incredibly important benefits. For example, one day in 1831, Michael Faraday was playing around with a coil and a magnet when he suddenly saw how he could generate an electrical current. At first, it wasn't clear what use this would have, but it actually made electricity available for use in technology, and so changed the world.

Unsurprisingly, there are chemical and evolutionary theories to explain why humans are such curious creatures. When we become curious, our brains release a chemical called dopamine, which makes the process of learning more pleasurable and improves memory. It is still not known why learning gives us such pleasure, but one theory is that we may have developed a basic need to fight uncertainty—the more we understand about the world around us, the more likely we are to survive its many dangers!

However, curiosity is currently under threat like never before—and perhaps the biggest threat comes from technology. On one level, this is because technology has become so sophisticated that many of us are unable to think too deeply about how exactly things work anymore. While it may be possible for a curious teenager to take a toaster apart and get some sense of how it works, how much do you understand about what happens when you type a website address into a browser? Where does your grasp of technology end and the magic begin for you?

In addition to this, there's the fact that we all now connect so deeply with technology, particularly with our phones. The more we stare at our screens, the less we talk to other people directly. To make matters worse, all too often we accept the images of people that social media provides us with, and then feel we know enough about a person not to need to engage further with them.

The final—and perhaps most worrying—way in which technology stops us from asking more has to do with algorithms, the processes followed by computers. As we increasingly get our news via social media, algorithms find out what we like and push more of the same back to us, meaning that we end up inside our own little bubbles, no longer coming across ideas that challenge our pre-existing beliefs. Perhaps the real key to developing curiosity in the 21st century, then, is to rely less on the tech tools of our age.

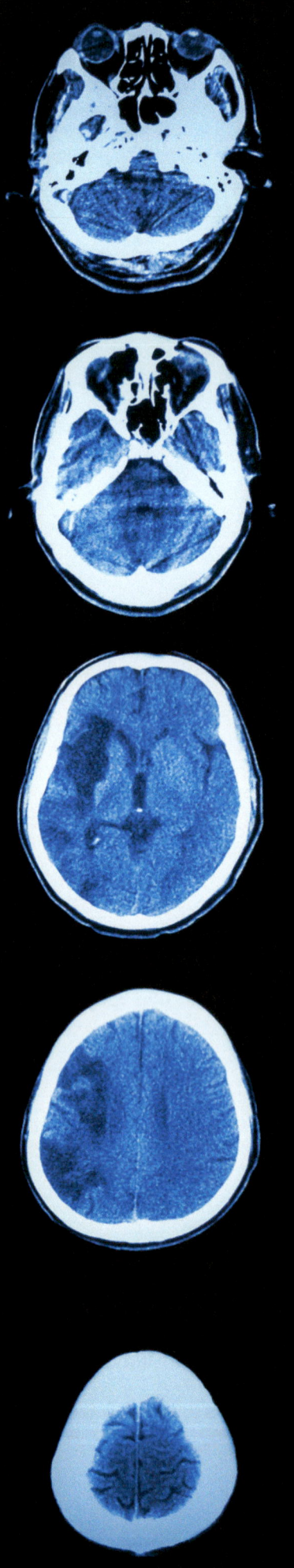

5C Mind-blowing!

GRAMMAR Passives 2

1 Work in groups. Look at the Grammar box. Do you believe the sentences are true? Explain why using these phrases.

I'm absolutely sure.
I'm not sure but, if I had to guess, I'd say…
I read about it recently. / We did it in class.
I remember hearing about it.
I've got a feeling it's a myth / it's a trick question.

> **Passive reporting verbs**
>
> **a** The heart was believed to be the center of intelligence until the Middle Ages.
> **b** It is claimed that computer training programs can limit the effects of aging on the brain.
> **c** Einstein's brain was said to be bigger than average, which explains his intelligence.
> **d** It is estimated that the human brain is about 75 percent water.
> **e** It is well known that most of the time we only use ten percent of our brain capacity.
> **f** Exercising is thought to create chemicals that reduce your ability to think.
> **g** The part of the brain called the hippocampus is known to be connected with our sense of direction.
> **h** It has been generally accepted that creative people have a dominant right brain.

Check the Grammar Reference for more information and practice.

2 Listen and find out which sentences in the Grammar box are true. How many did you get right? 🎧 24

3 Work in pairs. Look at the Grammar box again and:

1 identify the whole passive reporting pattern in the sentences that begin with *It*.
2 identify the form of the verb that follows the passive forms in sentences that do not begin with *It*.
3 discuss what you notice about the different patterns.

4 Write sentences about the brain using these notes and the passive.

1 The brain / estimate / contain…around 12 percent fat.

   The brain is estimated to contain around 12 percent fat.

2 It / once / think / the brain / become…fully mature by the time children were six.
3 The brain / now / know / develop…most during the teenage years.
4 It / once / believe / the brain's networks / become…fixed as we aged.
5 Brain training activities / claim / improve…listening skills and memory.
6 It / sometimes / say / brain size / affect…intelligence.
7 It / still / not really know…why we dream while we sleep.
8 Brain transplants / generally accept / be…impossible.

5 Work as a class. Discuss how you think research into the brain is carried out.

6 Choose the correct options to complete the article about brain research. Does the article cover the ideas you thought of in Activity 5?

Our understanding of the brain has changed with developments in science, surgery, and medical technology. For example, as new technologies were invented, the brain was thought (1) *to be / that it is* like a mechanical watch or telephone communication. More recently, it (2) *has been described / describes* as a computer.

After Galen proved that the brain was the center of intelligence, it was generally assumed that different parts of the brain (3) *to control / controlled* certain senses and functions of the body. However, the brain could only really (4) *understand / be understood* from the outside by studying animal brains and dissecting human bodies. Knowledge increased as a result of surgery where a patient had a tumor removed from their brain and the resulting physical change meant that functions could be mapped to the part of the brain that had been operated on. This mapping came about as much through failed operations as successful ones. Now, operations (5) *sometimes conduct / are sometimes conducted* while the patient is awake and talking. If a part of the brain (6) *touched / is touched* and it affects one of the patient's senses, he or she can tell the surgeon!

Since the late 1970s, medical technology, such as MRI scanning, (7) *has allowed / has been allowed* safe research into the brain without the need for surgery or X-rays. MRI uses powerful magnets and computer imaging to see high blood flows in different parts of the brain that (8) *believe / are believed* to show brain activity. If people (9) *have / is* their brains scanned while doing various thinking activities, researchers think they can (10) *identify / be identified* more accurately how the brain works. One result of this research is to show the limits of the brain-computer comparison. For example, it is now understood that memories are not stored in one place, but are the result of activity in many parts of the brain.

> **Causative *have* and *get***
>
> **a** *Scientists can do research into the brain by using scanners.*
> **b** *Research into the brain can be done (by scientists) by using scanners.*
> **c** *To get the research done, scientists used a brain scan.*

Check the Grammar Reference for more information and practice.

Since the late 1970s, medical technology, such as MRI scanning, has allowed safe research into the brain without the need for surgery or X-rays.

7 Look at the Grammar box. Then complete the explanation.

- In the first sentence, _____ is the object of the verb *do*.
- In the second sentence, *research* becomes the _____ of the passive structure *can be done*.
- In the third sentence, we use the structure *get* + something + _____ so we can make the person affected by an action (scientists) the subject of the sentence.

8 Write normal sentences in the passive, based on these sentences.

1 They had their brains scanned while they were singing.
2 The hospital is having a new MRI scanner installed.
3 The scientists had their research evaluated.
4 I'm going to have my examination later.
5 My dad had his head examined when we were in the hospital.

9 Work in pairs. Complete the sentences in as many different ways as you can. Use a dictionary, if necessary.

1 The patient had _____ scanned.
2 I had _____ examined.
3 They should have _____ tested.
4 The scientists are having the laboratory _____ .
5 I'm going to have my injury _____ .
6 The research center is going to have _____ .

10 CHOOSE

Choose one of the following activities.

- Write a set of sentences like the ones in the first Grammar box. Share your facts.
- Discuss ways in which the brain could be compared to:
  – a city.   – a computer.
  – an orchestra. – a spider's web.
- Write about one of these experiences.
  – a time you had to have something scanned or tested
  – a time something in the news proved to be wrong

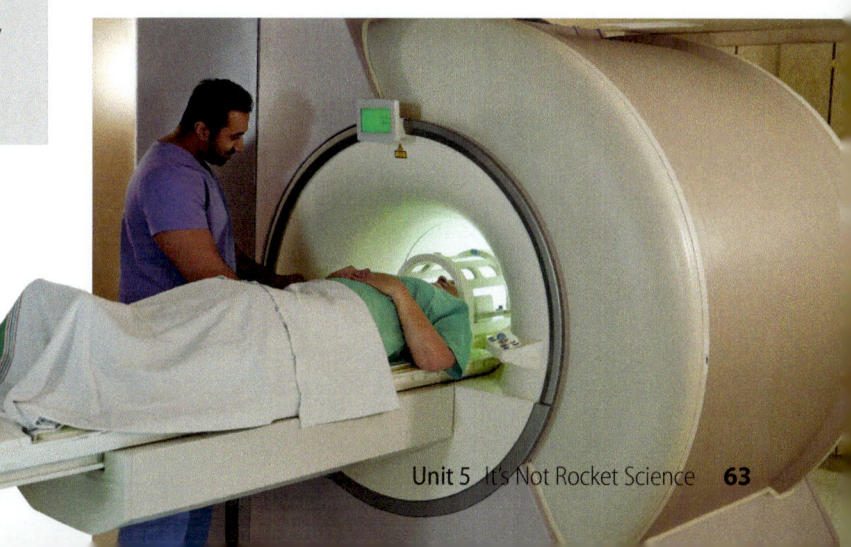

5D Science is for everyone, kids included

> " Play is one of the only human endeavors where uncertainty is actually celebrated. Uncertainty is what makes play fun. "
>
> **BEAU LOTTO**

Read about Beau Lotto and Amy O'Toole and get ready to watch their TED Talk. ▶ 5.0

AUTHENTIC LISTENING SKILLS

Fillers

You can use words and phrases like *right*, *all right*, and *you know* to ask for agreement, to check that people are understanding, or as a filler while we pause or move on to the next point.

So, this game is very simple. All you have to do is read what you see. **Right?**

1 Look at the Authentic Listening Skills box. Listen to the extract. Identify where Beau adds *right* or *all right*. 🎧 25

What are you reading? There are no words there. I said, read what you're seeing. It literally says, "Wat ar ou rea in?" That's what you should have said. Why is this? It's because perception is grounded in our experience. The brain takes meaningless information and makes meaning out of it, which means we never see what's there, we never see information, we only ever see what was useful to see in the past. Which means, when it comes to perception, we're all like this frog. It's getting information. It's generating behavior that's useful.

2 Practice reading aloud the extract in Activity 1 in a similar style to Beau.

WATCH

3 Work in groups. Discuss the questions.

1. Are you good at science? Why?
2. In what ways do you think science is similar to play?
3. Have you ever asked someone a question about science that they could not answer? What was it?

4 Put the sentences (a–h) in order. The first and last are given.

1. Perception is grounded in our experience.
   a. These are the exact same ways of being you need in order to be a good scientist.
   b. If perception is grounded in our history, it means we're only ever responding according to what we've done before.
   c. Uncertainty is what makes play fun. It opens possibility and it's cooperative.
   d. The question "why?" is one of the most dangerous things you can ask, because it takes you into uncertainty.
   e. But actually, it's a tremendous problem, because how can we ever see differently?
   f. So what is evolution's answer to the problem of uncertainty? It's play.
   g. So if you add rules to play, you have a game. That's actually what an experiment is.
   h. Now… all new perceptions begin in the same way. They begin with a question.
10. So armed with these two ideas—that science is a way of being and experiments are play—we asked, can anyone become a scientist?

5 Watch Part 1 of the talk. Check your order of the sentences in Activity 4. ▶ 5.1

6 What does Beau not mention when he talks about uncertainty making play fun?

a. Play is adaptable to change.
b. Play is cooperative.
c. Play opens up possibility.
d. Play is unrewarding.

64   Unit 5   It's Not Rocket Science

7 Watch Part 2 of the talk. Are the sentences *true*, *false*, or *not stated*? ▶ 5.2

1 None of the questions the children thought of had ever been studied before.
2 The children wanted to research if bees adapt their behavior to solve problems like humans do.
3 Bees are one of the most intelligent insects.
4 The experiment required bees to recognize the correct color to get a reward.
5 There were several ways for the bees to solve the puzzle the children set up.
6 The results of the experiment were surprising.
7 Beau wrote the journal article.
8 The paper was rejected by the publisher because it was written in the wrong style.

8 Watch Part 3 of the talk. Answer the questions. ▶ 5.3

1 How did the research finally get published?
2 What was the reaction to the research?
3 What were two lessons that Amy learned?

9 Amy says that changing the way a person thinks about something can be easy or hard. Explain why you think it would be easy or hard to change the way people think about:

- what they eat.
- what they watch on TV.
- where they shop.

10 MY PERSPECTIVE

Did the TED Talk change your views about science and scientists at all? In what way?

11 VOCABULARY IN CONTEXT

a Watch the clips from the TED Talk. Choose the correct meanings of the words and phrases. ▶ 5.4

b Work in pairs. Talk about:
- a time you received a *reward* for doing something.
- a time you regret *not bothering* to do something.
- an interesting or possible *link* that scientists have discovered in recent times.
- a time you had to *adapt* to a new situation.
- people you think should be given more of *a voice*.

CHALLENGE

Beau and Amy do not explain much about how the experiment worked, apart from showing the one pattern of flowers. Work in groups. Discuss how you would:

- give rewards to bees for going to "good flowers."
- identify which bees are going to which flowers.
- train the bees to learn the pattern of one color surrounded by another.
- check that the bees aren't just "smelling" the good flowers.
- check that the bees aren't just choosing the good flowers by color.
- check that the bees aren't just choosing the flowers in the middle.

Read the paper about Blackawton Bees and see exactly how the children set up the experiment and what they discovered. It's available on the TED website.

5E Conducting Experiments

Useful language

Staging

The first thing we'd need to do is…

We'd also need to make sure that we (didn't)…

I suppose then we should…

Preparing research questions

I wonder if / how / why…

It'd be good to know what / whether…

We'd need to try to figure out…

Hypothesizing

I'd expect the results to show…

I'd imagine that the data would probably reveal…

I would / wouldn't have thought it would be possible to prove that…

SPEAKING

1. Work in pairs. Look at the questions. Discuss why it might be useful to know the answer to each of them. What do you think the answers are?

   1. How much does homework improve exam results?
   2. Do goldfish only have a ten-second memory?
   3. How many words can you learn in an hour?
   4. Does going out with wet hair cause colds or the flu?
   5. Do boys get more attention in class? If so, why?
   6. Are people who listen to pop music happier?
   7. What is the quickest way to have people board a plane?

2. Work in groups. If you were going to design an experiment for a question like one of those in Activity 1, what steps would you need to complete?

3. Listen to a short lecture on how to design experiments. Note the six main steps. Then compare your answers with a partner. Use the light bulb experiment to explain each stage. 🎧 26

4. As a class, discuss why you think:

   1. certain kinds of hypotheses are easier to prove than others.
   2. proving a hypothesis wrong can be an important step towards learning.
   3. it's important to record in detail how experiments are set up and conducted.
   4. proving a hypothesis right in the way described could be seen as insufficiently scientific.

5. Work in pairs. Design an experiment to:

   a. find the answer to a question in Activity 1.
   b. see if one of the life hacks you learned about earlier actually works.
   c. test another life hack you have heard about.

   Use some of the language in the Useful language box. Decide:
   - how you would set the experiment up.
   - what kind of data you would record.
   - what points of comparison you would need.
   - what you would expect the results to prove.

6. Work with another pair. Explain the design of your experiment. Can your partners see any way in which it could be improved?

How can you find out if goldfish really have a ten-second memory?

WRITING A scientific method

7 WRITING SKILL Describing a process

Work in pairs. How do you think writing about a process is different from telling a story? Is the guidance typical of stories or scientific reports?

1. You avoid using personal pronouns, such as *I*, *he*, or *she*.
2. You use a wide variety of words and descriptive language.
3. You use a lot of passive sentences.
4. You write steps in the order they happened.
5. You define words you think your reader may not know.
6. You use idioms and colloquial language.
7. You summarize what you are going to tell people at the beginning.
8. You explain the reason for doing something.
9. You may add a diagram of what you are describing.
10. You have a final sentence or comment that summarizes the point of the text.

8 Read about the process that was completed in preparation for the Blackawton Bee experiment on page 151. Which of the features in Activity 7 can you identify?

9 Look at the Useful language box. Use the language and these verbs to retell the process in the diagram on this page. Then look at the process on page 151 and check how well you did.

let into	paint	pick up	place	put into
release	remove	return	turn off	warm up

10 Write a method like the one on page 151, describing:

- one of the experiments you designed in Activity 5.
- an experiment you have conducted at school.
- a famous historical experiment that you are interested in.

Useful language

Introducing the process

The experiment aimed to show that…
The purpose of the experiment was to find out if…
The diagram illustrates the process used to…
Figure one shows how…

Linking steps

First of all,…
Before starting the experiment,…
The bees were then released…
Once the bees had been released…
After being released, the bees…
Finally,…

Explaining the steps

*They were marked **to** identify them.*
*They were marked **in order to** identify them.*
*They were marked **so that** they **could** be identified.*
In order to do this,…

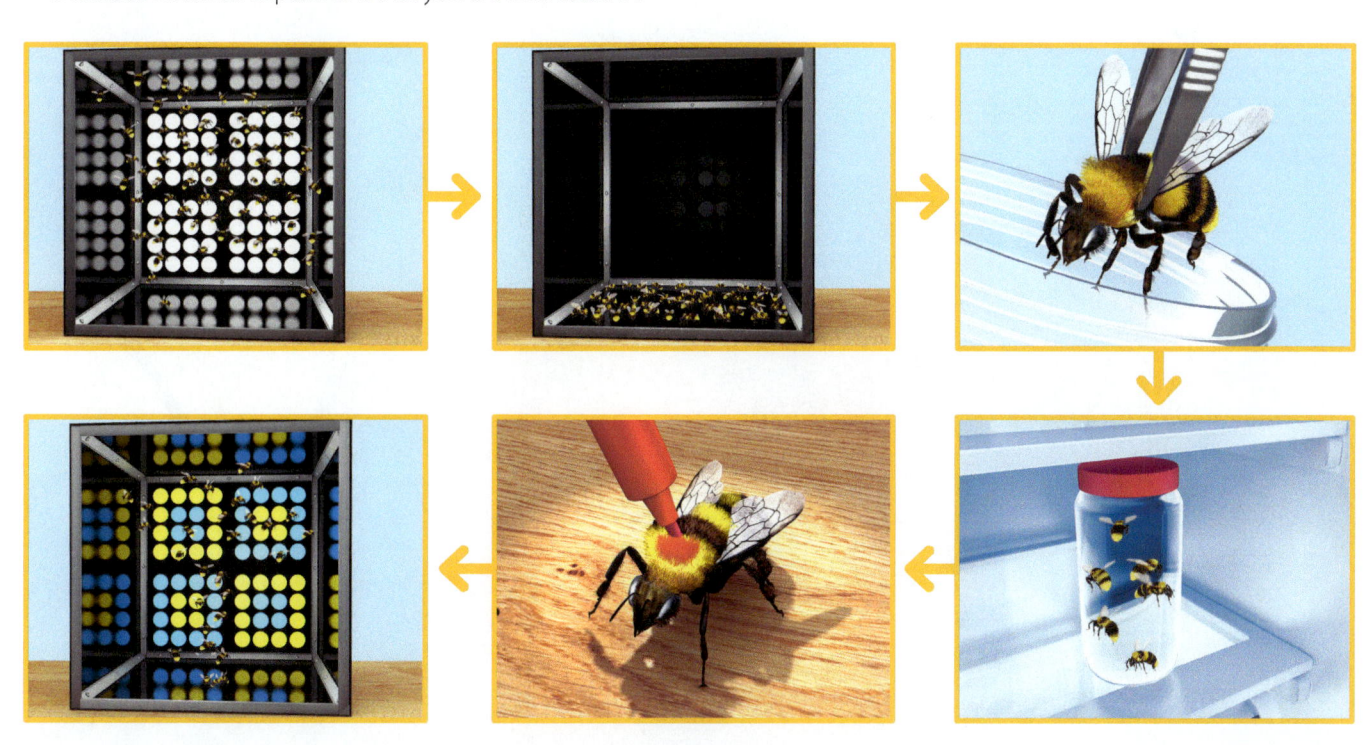

6 Adapt to Survive

IN THIS UNIT, YOU...

- discuss evolution and conservation.
- read about an endangered animal.
- learn about mysterious occurrences.
- watch a TED Talk about where camels come from.
- write a solution to a problem.

The flag-footed bug has evolved to hide among leaves and flower petals.

6A Evolution and Conservation

VOCABULARY Endangered species

1 Work as a class. Discuss the questions.

1 What is evolution? What is conservation?
2 What reasons are there for a species to adapt? What characteristics about a species might change?

2 Complete the article about Madagascar with these words.

| adapted | breed | conservation | died out | endangered | extinct |
| habitat | hunting | risk | saved | species | survival |

Madagascar is an island famous for its biodiversity. Evolution has created thousands of unique (1) _____ that have (2) _____ to life on the island. In fact, scientists have discovered more than 600 new animals since the beginning of this century. However, while it may seem that wildlife is doing well, many animals and plants are in fact at (3) _____ because tropical forests are being destroyed to make farmland. Eighty percent of Madagascar's human population live in poverty and depend on basic farming for (4) _____ . The silky sifaka is one of the most (5) _____ animals. There are only around 250 left in the wild. A (6) _____ program is trying to preserve its (7) _____ and prevent people from (8) _____ it. The national dog of Madagascar, the Coton de Tulear, was (9) _____ from extinction, and now people (10) _____ it in several countries. The Madagascan Elephant Bird wasn't so lucky. It became (11) _____ in the 17th century. It was three meters tall and may have (12) _____ because people stole its huge eggs, which were big enough to feed a family.

3 Work in pairs. Discuss the questions.

1 What endangered species do you know?
2 Why are they endangered?
3 How are they being protected?
4 What animals have become extinct? Why?
5 What arguments can you think of for and against conservation?

4 Match each word with the correct group of collocations.

| benefit | consequence | conservation | gene |
| habitat | risk | species | survival |

1 bring a lasting… / a potential… / be of… *benefit*
2 …of the fittest / its long-term… / ensure its…
3 at… of extinction / a high… / reduce the… of disease
4 work in nature… / be involved in a… group / improve energy…
5 an endangered… / a… of bird / discover a new…
6 destroy their… / preserve their… / lose its natural…
7 pass on their…s / in its…s / find a… for cancer
8 as a… / have serious…s / consider the…s

5 Look through the collocations in Activity 4. Underline any phrases that are new to you. Write an example sentence for each of the new phrases.

Unit 6 Adapt to Survive 69

LISTENING

6 Listen to the interview with a conservationist. Who mentions these points—the interviewer (I), the conservationist (C), or both (B)? 🎧 27

1 Most animals have died out.
2 Conservation goes against evolution.
3 Genetic changes through evolution do not make a species more perfect.
4 Animals can't choose to adapt to a new environment.
5 Human activity is increasing the number of extinctions.
6 We must protect endangered species because we can.
7 Conservation is expensive.
8 Humans may become extinct sooner rather than later.

7 What reasons for possible human extinction did you hear in the interview? Listen again and check. 🎧 27

8 Work in pairs. Discuss the questions.

1 Do you like television shows about the natural world? What was the last one you saw? What was it about?
2 Have you studied anything about conservation at school? What other things did you learn?
3 Would you like to be a conservationist? What might be good or bad about the job?
4 Have you ever taken action to protect something? What did you do?

GRAMMAR Modals and meaning

9 Look at the Grammar box. Then compare the first and second sentence in each item below. Notice the changes in the use of modals. What is the difference in meaning?

1 You might stop weak species from going extinct.
  You will stop weak species from going extinct.
2 Maybe we shouldn't interfere.
  We must not interfere.
3 "The survival of the fittest" can suggest evolution is a kind of competition.
  "The survival of the fittest" suggests evolution is a kind of competition.
4 If that habitat disappeared for whatever reason, they'd easily die out.
  When the habitat disappears, the animals die out.
5 Will you leave it there?
  Could you leave it there?

> **Modals and meaning**
>
> A modal (*would*, *will*, *may*, *might*, *could*, *can*, *should*, *shall*, *must*) adds a general meaning to another verb to show a speaker's attitude or intention.
>
> *The first thing that **will strike** people is…*
> = I am certain it strikes people.
>
> *The first thing that **should strike** people is…*
> = I believe it strikes people, but I'm not certain.
>
> Other meanings are: certainty, uncertainty, obligation, permission, suggestion, possibility, and frequency (habit).

Check the Grammar Reference for more information and practice.

Baobab trees in Madagascar have adapted to survive in places where there is little rainfall. Their wide trunks can store large amounts of water.

10 Read about National Geographic explorer Cagan Sekercioglu. What similarities can you find with what you heard in the interview? Think about:

1. the rate of extinction.
2. the importance of conservation.
3. what happens to animals that adapt and then face a sudden change.

Growing up in Turkey, Cagan Sekercioglu was once taken to a child psychologist because he (1) <u>constantly brought</u> small animals and insects <u>back</u> to his house. Fortunately, it didn't end his interest in wildlife, and now he's a professor of biology working to protect birds in countries such as Costa Rica, Australia, Ethiopia, the United States, and Turkey. He says (2) <u>losing 25 percent of all bird species this century is a possibility</u>, and that whatever happens to birds (3) <u>is certain to happen</u> to other animals and even people. The question is not if (4) <u>it's better for us to do something</u> about it, but when (5) <u>are we going to decide to do something</u> and (6) <u>what are we going to decide to do</u>?

In Costa Rica, he's found that species (7) <u>sometimes become</u> endangered because the area of forest they live in shrinks as it becomes surrounded by agriculture. The birds are so well adapted to a certain part of the forest that they (8) <u>refuse to</u> move, even when bigger areas of forest (9) <u>are possibly</u> close by. Cagan says (10) <u>it's essential that conservationists work</u> with local people to improve the situation by explaining to farmers why (11) <u>they're better off encouraging</u> bird diversity. For example, if farmers encourage birds to live on their land, (12) <u>the birds will eat</u> insects that destroy their crops, which could possibly increase farmers' profits.

11 Rewrite the underlined parts in Activity 10 using modals. Use each modal in the Grammar box at least once.

12 Write nine sentences about yourself, using a different modal in each sentence. Your teacher will read the sentences to the class. Guess who the person is.

13 **MY PERSPECTIVE**

Make a list of animals, habitats, jobs, languages, customs, activities, or skills that are at risk of dying out. Would you try to preserve any of them? Why?

6B Tree Life?

VOCABULARY BUILDING

Compound nouns

We often use two or more nouns together to create a new meaning. The words in compound nouns can be joined together, or they can be separated using a space or hyphen. The first noun acts like an adjective. It describes the type of thing, its use, the material it is made from, or other aspects of the second noun, such as where it is found.

Bookstores are dying out in our country because people are buying books online.

Ice ages caused the extinction of many species.

1 Choose the correct forms to complete the sentences.

1. We often go skiing in the *Olympic Mountains / Mountain Olympics*, north of here.
2. On average, there is 20 centimeters of *rainfall / fallrain* here in March.
3. Many environmental charities run *campaign social media / social media campaigns*.
4. Scientists believe there might be many *sea creatures / creature seas* that still have not been discovered.
5. I really like our *teacher science / science teacher*. She brings the subject to life.
6. I avoid all *animal products / product animals*. I don't even wear *shoe leather / leather shoes*.

2 Work in groups. Starting with these compound nouns, how many other compound nouns can you create by changing one word each time? Use a dictionary, if necessary.

farm animal	leather shoes	rainfall	science teacher

ice age: ice cream; cream cheese; cheesecake

READING

3 Choose one animal from these categories that you are familiar with, and one that you would like to learn more about.

farm animals	pets	sea creatures	wild animals

4 Work in groups. Compare the animals you chose. Explain your choices.

5 Work in pairs. Look at the photo on page 73 and discuss the questions.

1. Where do you think this animal is found?
2. What is unusual about it?
3. How do you think the photographer was able to get the shot?

6 Read the article from a website on page 73 to check your ideas in Activity 5. What else do you learn about questions 1 and 2 in Activity 5?

7 Which statements are supported by the article? Underline the parts of the article which helped you make your decisions.

1. The tree octopus is the most endangered creature in the United States.
2. Washington State is one of the wettest places in the US.
3. The tree octopus may provide clues about how early sea creatures adapted to live on land.
4. The animals often live in small groups.
5. Many companies that cut down trees in the forests are not doing enough to protect octopuses.
6. Octopuses are affected by pollution.

8 Work in groups. Discuss the questions.

1. Did you know about the tree octopus before? If not, what surprised you most?
2. Should people care about the tree octopus? Why?

9 Look at the source for the article. Do you think it is reliable? What other sources could you check to make sure the information is accurate?

10 Listen to a news extract about the tree octopus story. Answer the questions. 🎧 29

1. Why is the story mentioned?
2. What do the findings seem to suggest?

CRITICAL THINKING Assessing information

You will often see information or read something that is unfamiliar. You need to do further reading to check the information is accurate and from a reliable source.

11 Work in pairs. Discuss the questions

1. Why do you think so many people believe this story?
2. Looking back, is there anything in the story that should have made you more suspicious?

12 MY PERSPECTIVE

Work in groups. What are the consequences of fake news stories?

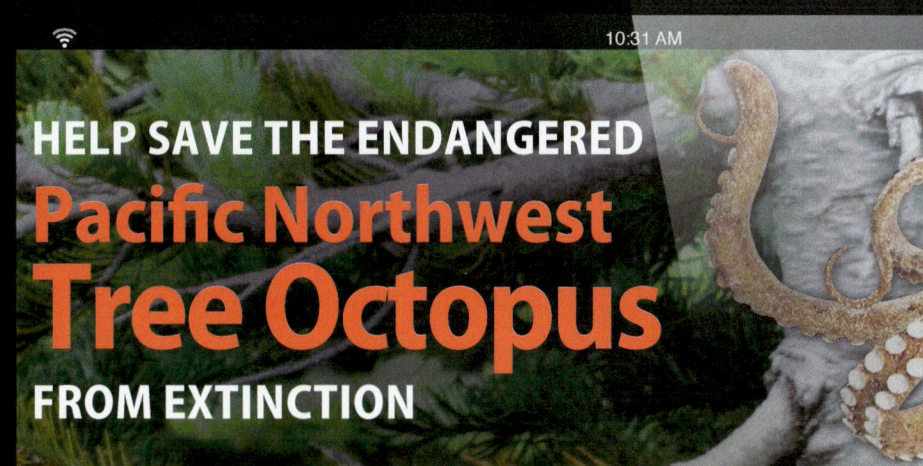

HELP SAVE THE ENDANGERED
Pacific Northwest Tree Octopus
FROM EXTINCTION

ABOUT | HELP | FAQs | SIGHTINGS | MEDIA | ACTIVITIES | LINKS

🎧 28 About

The Pacific Northwest tree octopus (*Octopus paxarbolis*) is only found in the forests of Washington State, on the eastern side of the Olympic Mountains, in the United States.
5 These creatures reach an average size of between 30 and 35 centimeters and live for around four years. They are unusual in that they live both in water and on land, a fact made possible by the very high amounts of
10 rainfall in this part of the United States.

Possessing the largest brain of any octopus, the tree octopus explores its surroundings by touch and sight. Some scientists believe that the way it has adapted to life in the forest
15 mirrors the way early life forms adapted to life away from the water. Although they are not social animals like humans, they can still show emotions by changing their skin color: red indicates anger and white, fear. Normally,
20 though, they are a green-brown color that matches their surroundings.

Every spring, tree octopuses leave their homes and travel to the coast to breed. Males soon return to the forest, while females
25 lay their eggs underwater. The young then spend their first month or so floating near the shore before moving out of the water and beginning their adult lives in the forest.

Source: http://zapatopi.net/treeoctopus/

Why it is endangered

Although the tree octopus is not yet on the
30 official list of endangered animals, it should be, as numbers are now seriously low. It faces many threats: trees in Pacific-Northwest forests are constantly being cut down; new roads have cut off access to water; the growth
35 of local towns has introduced house cats into the region, which hunt the octopuses; and pollution is getting worse. Immediate action needs to be taken to stop the tree octopus from becoming extinct.

Become an activist

40 Here are some things you can do to help protect the last few tree octopuses:

- Write to the government to say you are worried and that you feel the tree octopus should be given special protection and
45 included on the Endangered Species List.

- Write to celebrities, asking them to talk in interviews about the dangers facing the tree octopus.

- Let the world know about the tree
50 octopus: tell your family and friends.

- Tell people not to buy products made by companies that don't protect the tree octopus when cutting down trees.

- Start an online campaign! Encourage
55 people to sign a petition.

6C Mysterious Changes

GRAMMAR Modals and infinitive forms

1. Listen to three people. What did they change their minds about? Why? 🎧 30

2. Listen to the people again. Complete the sentences. 🎧 30

   1a I _____ attention when I read about it.
   1b All the links about the different kinds of tree octopuses go to the same page. I really _____ that.
   1c Even my little brother _____ me that the photos were fake.
   2a I mean, you _____ me how cruel it was, and I honestly _____ .
   2b I don't know, but if it was that, it _____ an impact because I've been vegan for quite some time now.
   3a I _____ touch one or pick one up if the chance had arisen.
   3b I _____ certainly _____ about owning one, that's for sure.
   3c Our favorite is a python called Monty. We _____ him for three years this November.

3. Look at the sentences in Activity 2. Answer the questions.

   1. Which sentence describes a period leading up to a future point?
   2. Are the other sentences about the past, the present, or the future?
   3. Which modal emphasizes that an action was in progress at the same time as another?

   Modals and infinitive forms

   Modals can be followed by different kinds of infinitive forms.

   I **can't see** it.
   We **should be doing** more to help.
   It **wouldn't have made** any difference.
   You **can't have been listening** properly.
   More attention **must be paid** to this issue.
   The eggs **must have been moved** from the nest.

   Check the Grammar Reference for more information and practice.

4. Work in groups. Look at the Grammar box. Does each pair of sentences have the same meaning? Discuss any differences.

   1a They must not have been serious.
   1b They must have been joking.
   2a I should have helped him.
   2b I would have helped him.
   3a It must have been really interesting.
   3b It was really interesting.
   4a I guess that might have been the reason.
   4b I guess that could have been the reason.
   5a You shouldn't have texted me.
   5b You shouldn't have been texting me.
   6a It should have arrived by now.
   6b It will have arrived by now.

Mount Merapi erupts in Indonesia. Volcanic gases are made up of many different gases, including methane.

Unit 6 Adapt to Survive

5 PRONUNCIATION Weak form of *have*

When the sentences in Activity 4 are said slowly and carefully, *have* is often pronounced differently than how it is pronounced in fast speech.

a Listen to each sentence from Activity 4. Notice how *have* changes its sound in fast speech. Repeat what you hear. 🎧 31

b Work in pairs. Practice reading the sentences in Activity 4 slowly and quickly.

6 Complete the summary using the modals and the correct form of the verbs in parentheses. Make one modal negative.

Reported sightings of the Loch Ness Monster (1) _____ soon _____ (will / go on) for a century! In 1933, a man named George Spicer reported seeing something that looked like a plesiosaur, a kind of long-necked marine dinosaur. Some people think such a creature (2) _____ very easily (could / survive) in the quiet Scottish waters, away from people, while others are convinced that Spicer (3) _____ (must / lie) or that he (4) _____ (might / see) a piece of wood covered in green water plants. Most scientists question the whole story and claim that a creature like this (5) _____ (can / live) in the loch* for so long without any real human contact. If it was real, they say, it (6) _____ (would / capture) by now—or at least caught on film. Others, though, suspect that the monster (7) _____ (might / develop) special skills that help it to hide from those hunting it. Even today, true believers can be found on the shores of the loch trying to spot a beast that (8) _____ (should / die out) 65 million years ago.

loch *a Scottish word for a lake.*

7 Work in pairs. Read the two paragraphs about mysteries of the natural world. Then discuss what you think happened. Use modals where necessary.

The Great Dying
Around 250 million years ago, long before dinosaurs roamed the Earth, about 95 percent of all species were suddenly wiped out. This was by far the biggest mass extinction the world has ever seen. The event—widely known as the Great Dying—came close to ending all life on the planet. Everything alive today comes from the five percent of species that survived back then.

The Bloop
The Bloop was an extremely low and very powerful underwater sound first detected at points across the vast Pacific Ocean by NOAA, the National Oceanic and Atmospheric Administration. The Bloop was significantly different from other previously recorded sounds and many theories emerged to explain the mysterious noise.

Dinogorgon became extinct a quarter of a billion years ago, long before dinosaurs roamed the Earth.

8 Read about what really happened. Student A: read about the Great Dying; Student B: read about the Bloop. See if you guessed correctly. Then report back to your partner.

Student A: The Great Dying
Many theories to explain the Great Dying have been put forward—everything from asteroids from space hitting Earth to huge volcanic eruptions. Volcanoes did in fact play a part in the event. At the time, Siberian volcanoes were erupting almost constantly, sending out huge quantities of a gas called methane. This resulted in the oceans and the atmosphere being poisoned and so many species dying out.

Student B: The Bloop
Theories put forward to explain the Bloop ranged from the sensible to the strange. Some people thought the noise must be from an unknown deep-sea creature while others thought it could be mermaids or voices from a lost city. In the end, it turned out that the sound was actually made by an icequake. A large mass of ice in Antarctica was slowly breaking up and was picked up by NOAA.

9 CHOOSE

Choose one of the following activities.

- Work in groups. Prepare a short presentation about a mystery you have read about or know. Include at least four different modals.
- Write a story about something you regret doing—or not doing. Include at least four different modals.
- Work in pairs. Write a conversation between two people about an influential or inspiring person. Include at least four different modals.

Unit 6 Adapt to Survive   75

6D You have no idea where camels really come from

> ❝ I've learned that, actually, a lot of scientists are historians, too. They make sense of the past. ❞
>
> **LATIF NASSER**

Read about Latif Nasser and get ready to watch his TED Talk. ▶ 6.0

AUTHENTIC LISTENING SKILLS

Understanding fast speech

In quick speech, it can be difficult to hear individual words because words get shortened or sound as one.

1 Look at the Authentic Listening Skills box. Then listen to these extracts from the TED Talk where people speak quickly. Try to write down what you hear. 🔔 32

1 … she thought it was just a splinter of wood, because _____ at the Fyles Leaf Bed before—prehistoric plant parts.
2 How certain were you that you had it right, like… that _____ , like?
3 … something like a cow or a sheep. But _____ . It was just too big.
4 … you're going to have different body sizes. _____ , so they're actually functionally like giraffes.
5 And, as a historian, you start with an idea _____ .

WATCH

2 Work in groups. Do you think the sentences are *true* or *false*? Why?

1 Camels have been around for about a million years.
2 The first camels were only found in North America.
3 Giraffes and llamas are in the same family as camels.
4 The hump on a camel's back contains water.
5 Camels have evolved to walk on sand.

3 Work in pairs. Write down as many other facts about camels as you can. Then compare your ideas with another pair of students. Do any of the other pair's facts surprise you? Why?

4 Watch Part 1 of the talk. Complete the summary with one to three words in each blank. ▶ 6.1

One day in 2006, Natalia Rybczynski was digging at a site less than (1) _____ south of the North Pole when she found a strange object. To begin with, she thought it was a piece of (2) _____ . She collected more fragments over the next four years and eventually used a (3) _____ to find out that it was a (4) _____ of a huge mammal. When they cut a piece off one fragment, they (5) _____ collagen, which is a substance found in bones and which (6) _____ in the ice. A couple of years later, she sent the fragments to a colleague who had invented a technique called (7) _____ , which can identify an animal from a bone. They discovered it was a(n) (8) _____ million-year-old camel and that it must have weighed (9) _____ , which is (10) _____ than camels today.

5 Watch Part 2 of the talk. Check your answers from Activity 2. Correct the false answers. ▶ 6.2

Camels have been around longer than a million years. According to Latif, they have been around for 45 million years.

TEDTALKS

6 Watch Part 2 of the talk again. Choose the correct options. ▶ 6.2

1 Scientists believe that at first, camels were only found in *hot places / cold places*.
2 They also believe that 40 million years ago, there were around *20 / 24* different species of camels.
3 They say that some early camels were as small as *dogs / rabbits*.
4 They also say that one branch of camels became *llamas / giraffes*.
5 Some scientists believe that a camel's hump helped it to survive long *walks / winters*.
6 It is believed that three and a half million years ago, the weather was significantly *warmer / cooler* than today.

7 Watch Part 3 of the talk. Which sentence best summarizes the point Latif is making? ▶ 6.3

a It's important to change your mind about things.
b Scientists should also study history.
c Much of what we think we know might be wrong.
d Camels are well suited to different environments.

8 What discoveries or news have you heard about the natural world recently? Think about:

- archaeology.
- new or lost species.
- the sea.
- medical advances.

9 VOCABULARY IN CONTEXT

a Watch the clips from the TED Talk. Choose the correct meanings of the words and phrases. ▶ 6.4

b Work in pairs. Discuss the questions.

1 Have you ever experienced *hitting a wall*? Why? How did you overcome it?
2 What scientific theories still have no *proof*?
3 What good *spots* do you know to:
   - have a picnic?
   - see wildlife?
   - hang out with friends?
   - watch the world go by?
4 What things would you be *willing* or *unwilling* to do to be successful in life?

CHALLENGE

Think of a time in your life when you have had to rethink what you thought you knew about something—or someone.

- What did you use to believe? Why?
- What caused you to rethink your beliefs?
- Did you develop your new ideas quickly or slowly?
- How do you feel about the thing or person now?

Work in groups. Tell each other your experiences. Ask and answer questions about the changes. Decide who experienced the biggest change.

6E Finding a Solution

SPEAKING

1 Work in pairs. Look at the photo and discuss the questions.

1 Where do you think the photo was taken? Who might the man be?
2 How would you feel if you were the man in the photo?

2 Read the opening lines of six different anecdotes. Which sounds most interesting to you? What would you ask about it?

a I once saw a polar bear in a zoo. It was really sad.
b I almost stepped on a scorpion once.
c My brother once tracked a group of gorillas in Africa.
d When I went to the city, I saw lots of foxes in the street.
e Where my grandma lives, there are vultures. We once climbed up to their nests.
f I hate cows. I was chased by some once. It was really scary!

3 You are going to tell an anecdote about a time you encountered some kind of wild animal—big or small. Make notes using these questions and think of a sentence you will say to start the anecdote to get people interested.

- When did it happen? How old were you?
- Where was it?
- What happened?
- What was the animal doing?
- How did it make you feel?
- Did it have an effect on you afterwards?

4 Work in pairs. Tell your anecdotes. Your partner should show interest and ask questions to help you.

Speaking strategy

Telling anecdotes

Anecdotes are short real-life stories. When we want to tell an anecdote, we often give a very short summary of what we are going to say. We might also add a comment or say how we felt in order to make it sound interesting.

Useful language

Responding to anecdotes

If the listener is interested, they will say things like:
Really? Why was that?
Wow! What happened?
Really? They have foxes there?

Some people have a special connection with animals.

WRITING A problem-solution essay

5 Tigers are endangered in the wild. Do you think having them in zoos and parks is good for their survival? Why? What other things might help them?

6 **WRITING SKILL** Topic sentences

Read the essay about how people can help to protect tigers on page 151. Put the topic sentences in the correct order as they might appear.

a The author J.A. Mills suggests we should strengthen rules about domestic tigers.
b Finally, we should work closely with local people.
c According to the WWF (World Wildlife Fund), there are only about 4,000 tigers left in the wild.
d Countries have to work together to protect the habitat.

7 In the essay, the writer refers to various organizations and people. Answer the questions.

1 Why does the writer do this?
2 Do you think they are good sources to reference? Why?
3 What other information would be good to know? What other sources could you look for?

8 Work in pairs. Choose one of the animals or things from your list that are at risk of dying out (page 71, Activity 13). Find out more and take notes on three big problems it faces. Then think of ways to tackle these problems and help save it.

9 Work on your own. Using your notes, write a problem-solution essay.

- In the first paragraph, outline the problems and say you will suggest solutions. Then tackle each problem in a subsequent paragraph. Use the writing model on page 151 as a guide if you need to.
- Find two or three sources that you can add to your essay to give it greater authority. Decide how you want to use them and where to place the sources. Use the Useful language box to help you.

10 Exchange your essay with your partner. Read your partner's work and comment on:

- the structure and the strength of the argument.
- the use of sources.
- the use of language.

Writing strategy

Topic sentences

It is good to start a new paragraph with a topic sentence—a sentence that explains what the paragraph is about.

Useful language

Naming sources

According to [name / organization / book, etc.],…
The [job title], [name], *says that…*
I agree with [job title], [name], *when she/he says that…*

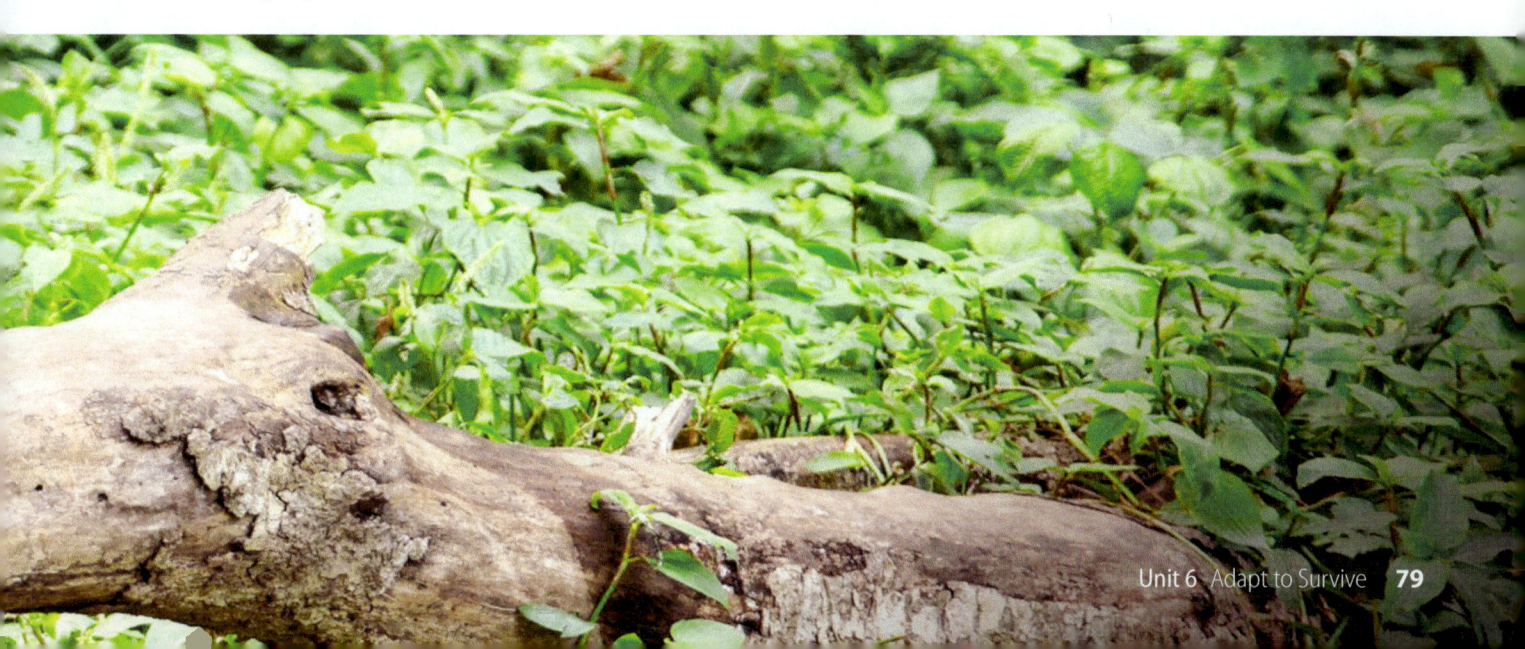

7 Outside the Box

IN THIS UNIT, YOU...

- discuss the importance of creativity.
- read about creativity tests.
- imagine alternative outcomes to situations.
- watch a TED Talk about making up new words.
- come up with creative approaches.

The members of the band A-WA are three Israeli sisters who mix traditional Yemenite music with modern electronic dance music.

7A Rules of Creativity

VOCABULARY Breaking the mold

1 Work in pairs. How many different words based on the root word *create* can you think of? Think of at least two collocations for each.

create   *create a group, create excitement*

2 Complete the sentences with words based on the root word *create*. You can use the same word more than once.

1 Everyone should learn a musical instrument in their spare time to encourage _____ .
2 Students have not needed to learn facts since the _____ of the internet.
3 You need to study a lot and copy other people before you can be _____ yourself.
4 There aren't many people who actually _____ something completely new.
5 Watching a lot of television kills people's _____ .
6 People who can think _____ do better in school.

3 Identify the collocations with the different forms of *create* from Activity 2. Were they the same as the ones you thought of in Activity 1?

4 Work in pairs. Do you agree with the sentences from Activity 2? Why?

5 Complete the phrases with these pairs of words. Use a dictionary, if necessary.

approaches + solution	comes up with + adapts
invents + follows	makes up + writes
obeys + breaks	writes + scores

1 someone who does what he is told and _____ the rules or someone who _____ them
2 someone who _____ a test or someone who _____ highly on a test
3 someone who _____ a new word or someone who _____ word definitions
4 someone who comes up with a wide variety of _____ to a problem or someone who analyzes things and comes up with a simple _____
5 someone who _____ something or someone who _____ a set of rules to make something
6 someone who _____ new ways of doing things or someone who _____ existing ways of doing things

6 MY PERSPECTIVE

Work in pairs. Which person in each phrase in Activity 5 do you think is more creative? Explain your ideas.

LISTENING

7 Listen to an extract from a podcast. Which sentence best summarizes the main point? 🎧 33

a You can only be truly creative if you think like a child.
b The best monsters are usually created by children.
c Schools could do more to encourage creativity.
d In the future, there will be lots of new kinds of jobs.

8 Listen again. Choose the correct options. 🎧 33

1 *The Monster Engine*:
   a exists across a range of different formats.
   b has only been around for a few years.
   c was created by Dave Devries and his children.

2 Dave Devries started working on *The Monster Engine*:
   a to make one of his relatives happy.
   b because he illustrates comic books.
   c after being inspired by a young child.

3 Sir Ken Robinson claimed that:
   a drawing cartoons makes you more creative.
   b if you're creative, you're more likely to do well in the future.
   c people will need to work harder in the next 20 or 30 years.

4 The speaker thinks that, at its heart, creativity is about:
   a playing games.
   b listening to young people more.
   c not giving up and learning from mistakes.

9 Work in groups. Discuss whether you agree with the statements.

1 It's sometimes useful to see the world like a child.
2 Jobs will be very different in the future.
3 Skills are more important than knowledge.
4 Trying and failing are important parts of the creative process.

GRAMMAR First, second, third, and mixed conditionals

10 Work in pairs. Look at the Grammar box. Discuss which forms you see in the *if* clauses and result clauses in each of the four sentences.

> ### First, second, third, and mixed conditionals
>
> **First conditionals**
> a *If you're in school today, you'll probably start working sometime in the 2020s.*
>
> **Second conditionals**
> b *If these drawings were painted more realistically, they would look amazing.*
>
> **Third conditionals**
> c *If Dave Devries hadn't spent a day with his niece back in 1998,* The Monster Engine *would never have happened.*
>
> **Mixed conditionals**
> d *If their schools had encouraged unusual ways of seeing the world, lots of adults would be more creative.*

Check the Grammar Reference for more information and practice.

11 Which kind of conditional sentences do we use to talk about:

1 an imaginary past situation and an imaginary present result?
2 an imaginary situation and result now or in the future?
3 an imaginary situation and result in the past?
4 a possible situation and result now or in the future?

Dave Devries applies color and shading to children's artwork (right) to bring their pictures to life.

12 Complete the conditional sentences by using the correct forms of the verbs in parentheses.

Many people think of creativity as chance Eureka moments.* The mathematician and inventor who coined the term *Eureka*, Archimedes, discovered that the weight of an object floating on water is the same as the amount of water it displaces. He made this discovery by chance. If he (1) _____ (pay) more attention to the amount of water in his bathtub, he (2) _____ (not step) into it and spilled water over the side. Apparently, we (3) _____ (not have) penicillin today if Alexander Fleming (4) _____ (be) a bit neater and washed his petri dishes before he went on vacation. On his return, he discovered the penicillin mold had killed bacteria on the dishes. What (5) _____ (our world / be) like now without these discoveries?

The book *Inside the Box* by Drew Boyd and Jacob Goldenberg suggests that such moments are rare and if we (6) _____ (rely) on these "methods," we would not get very far. In fact, the authors say, most inventions come from following a limited set of rules. The rules can help failing schools and companies; if they (7) _____ (integrate) the rules into their teaching and product development, they (8) _____ (become) more successful. The implication of their argument is that it's not all up to luck.

Eureka moment *sudden understanding of a previously unknown solution to something*

13 Work in pairs. Read the situations. How many conditional sentences can you come up with to talk about:

- the different outcomes and how the situations could have been avoided?
- what could be done next?

Situation 1

Some schoolchildren were waiting outside before lunch. There was snow on the ground. The teacher who usually supervises the children arrived late because of a meeting. The students were pushing each other and playing around. Two students slipped on the ice and one ended up in the hospital. The treatment cost a lot of money. The parents complained, but the school says that students have to wait outside because a health and safety report explained that there was not enough space inside. Therefore, it was dangerous to line up inside.

Situation 2

Last year, the teacher who usually helps students with study skills lost her job because the school was trying to save money. Since then, one of the best students in the school has gotten into trouble because she copied an essay from the internet. She is worried this will ruin her chances of going to a good college. She says she did it because she was under a lot of pressure from her parents and did not have anyone to go to for advice.

14 Work with another pair of students. Compare your ideas from Activity 13. Who thought of the most conditional sentences? Who has the main responsibility for the outcomes in both situations?

Unit 7 Outside the Box

7B Testing Times

VOCABULARY BUILDING Noun forms

1 Look at these pairs of words. How are the nouns formed from verbs and adjectives?

Verb	Noun	Adjective	Noun
analyze	analysis	concerned	concern
assess	assessment	intelligent	intelligence
conclude	conclusion	flexible	flexibility
know	knowledge	fluent	fluency
publish	publication	logical	logic
vary	variety	useful	usefulness

2 Choose the correct words from Activity 1 to complete the sentences.

1 I know a lot of words in English, but I need to become more _____ in using them!
2 My main _____ when I do anything in English is not to make any mistakes.
3 I got a good grade in the last _____ I did for English.
4 I'd like to write a novel and _____ it myself.
5 I like to do things in a(n) _____ order, from A to B to C.
6 The _____ in my study schedule allows me to study when I feel most productive.
7 I don't think exams are a(n) _____ demonstration of how much people know.

3 Work in pairs. Which sentences in Activity 2 are true for you? What do you think they say about you? Which sentences do you think are signs of creativity? Why?

4 Work in groups. Think of other *verb* / *noun* and *adjective* / *noun* combinations that follow the patterns in Activity 1.

READING

5 Work in groups. Discuss the questions.

1 What do you think it means to be creative?
2 Do you think creativity is only connected to the arts?
3 How important is creativity these days? Why?
4 Do you think it is possible to assess levels of creativity?
5 Who is the most creative person you know? Why?

6 Read about a set of tests commonly used to assess creativity. Think about the questions as you read.

1 What do the tests involve?
2 Does the author think they are good tests of creativity?

7 Work in pairs. Answer the questions and discuss your ideas. Then read about the tests again to check.

1 When were the tests first published?
2 How are the tests scored?
3 How are divergent and convergent thinking different?
4 Why were people worried about children's test scores in the United States?
5 What are the possible causes for the drop in test scores?
6 How does problem-based learning encourage creativity?

8 Look at the four examples of divergent thinking tasks in lines 11–22. Work in groups to complete one.

9 Compare your results from Activity 8 with a partner. Use the questions to evaluate their creativity. What do you think the questions tell you about a person's creativity?

1 How many logical solutions are there to the task?
2 How original are the solutions?
3 How well can the solutions be explained?

CRITICAL THINKING Fact and opinion

> **Facts** are statements that are true. **Opinions** are statements showing what people believe.

10 Read the statements about Torrance's *Tests of Creative Thinking*. Do they present *facts* or *opinions*? Does each fact or opinion support the value of the tests as a test of creativity? Why?

1 Torrance found that people often scored very differently on the different parts of the tests.
2 Torrance believed you could teach creativity. The tests were originally teaching tools.
3 The tests give the idea that creativity is all one thing. Fail the tests and you are not creative.
4 Torrance collected information about adults' creative success by asking them to fill out a form to report what they had achieved creatively.
5 Learning to solve one problem rarely helps to solve another kind of problem.
6 It's difficult to see how the tests measure creativity in science or mathematics.

11 MY PERSPECTIVE

Work in pairs. Discuss the questions.

1 Would you like to use the problem-based way of learning? Why?
2 How is creativity encouraged in your school?

Testing Creative Thinking

🎧 **34** It is now over 50 years since the first publication of E.P. Torrance's *Tests of Creative Thinking*, which continue to be used worldwide as standard assessments of creativity.

The tests typically consist of "divergent thinking" tasks—the ability to generate a wide variety of solutions that are then scored on fluency, flexibility, originality, and how fully explained they are. For example:

- Ways to improve: What could you do to make a toy truck more fun to play with?

- Imagine consequences: How would the world be different if everyone had an eye in the back of their head?

- Alternative uses: How many unusual uses for a brick can you think of?

- Make drawings from a shape: Turn the Xs into pictures people might be surprised by. The X can be in any part of the picture. Add details to tell complete stories and give each picture a title.

Some question if the tests fully assess creativity because they say creativity is about originality and usefulness. Creativity not only requires divergent thinking but also "convergent thinking," where you find one single solution that you feel is the best for the problem you are trying to solve.

Torrance followed the lives of children who first took his tests to see if they predicted creative achievements as adults. Analyses of these studies suggest they do. In fact, his tests are better at judging future creative success than intelligence tests. This is why they are frequently used to identify top managers in business and children for special educational programs. It is also why there was concern in the United States when the magazine *Newsweek* reported that children's scores on the tests were falling.

Some have argued that this drop is because of children's lifestyles: too many video games, too much TV, and too little freedom to make choices. Others have suggested that education in the United States has become too focused on exam results, so teachers use fewer creative activities and favor more traditional learning. This is in contrast to countries with a history of more traditional activities, like China and its emphasis on memorization and drills. These countries are doing the opposite, and encouraging creativity through techniques such as problem-based learning.

Problem-based learning involves setting a genuine problem, such as reducing noise in a school library or deciding on a week of meals for an athlete. In reaching a conclusion, students have to do research across several subjects and be creative in the fullest sense. No doubt Torrance would have approved if he was still alive.

One of the tests for creative thinking involves making drawings from a shape.

Unit 7 Outside the Box 85

Do you ever wish you were a better dancer?

7C If only…

GRAMMAR Wish, if only, would rather

1 Work in pairs. Look at the Grammar box. Discuss which of the statements are true for you.

> **Wish, if only, would rather**
> a I wish I could draw better.
> b I wish I was a better dancer.
> c I wish my parents hadn't forced me to learn Latin.
> d I sometimes wish my classmates wouldn't make so much noise.
> e I wish I didn't have to take art classes.
> f I'd rather not get any homework.
> g My parents would rather I studied something else in college.
> h If only I had an eye in the back of my head!
> i I often say to myself, "If only I'd spent more time thinking about this before I started."
> j If only I wasn't sitting here now!

Check the Grammar Reference for more information and practice.

2 Look again at the sentences in the Grammar box and find examples of:
1 the simple past.
2 the past forms of *can* and *will*.
3 the past continuous.
4 the past perfect.

3 Which sentences in the Grammar box refer to:
1 a wish about a present situation?
2 a wish about a past situation?
3 a wish or preference for someone to do something differently in the present or the future?

4 Complete the exchanges using correct forms of the verbs in bold.

1 **have to**
   A Don't you ever wish you _____ sleep? Imagine what you could do with all those extra hours.
   B Stop it! You're making me tired!

2 **hear**
   A I wish I _____ that song. I can't get it out of my head now.
   B I know. It's incredibly catchy, isn't it?

3 **hate**
   A With those grades, maybe you should study medicine.
   B Yeah, if only I _____ the sight of blood or needles! Honestly, I could never work as a doctor.

4 **finish**
   A Should we stop now and do the rest tomorrow?
   B I'd rather we _____ it today. It will bother me all night if we leave it.

5 have + be
   A You four should start a band. You could be really big!
   B Yeah, if only we _____ the money to buy equipment—and could come up with ideas!
   A You have lots of good ideas! I wish I _____ as creative as you!

6 be + relax
   A I wish you _____ there. You would've loved it.
   B Yeah, I know. I wish my parents _____ and let me go out more.
   A Well, maybe next time.

5 **PRONUNCIATION** Elision of consonants *t* and *d*

> When people talk fast, they often leave out the final consonant when the next word starts with a consonant.
>
> *I'd get bored* will often sound like *I-ge-bored.*

a Look at the phrases with *wish*, *if only*, and *I'd rather* in Activity 4. Which final consonants do you think might disappear?
b Listen to the phrases and repeat them. 🎧 35

6 We often add comments to statements with *wish*, *if only*, and *would rather*. Match the statements (1–5) with the pairs of follow-up comments (a–e). Does each comment refer to an imagined consequence (IC) or the actual situation (AS)?

1 I wish you'd told me earlier. c
2 If only he was taller.
3 I'd rather we didn't talk now.
4 I wish they would do more to help.
5 I wish I didn't have to go.

a People might hear.
   I need to think more carefully about it.
b The place is a mess.
   We could get things done a lot faster.
c It would've saved me a lot of effort. IC
   I don't have time to do it now. AS
d I don't really like meetings.
   Unfortunately, he's expecting me to be there.
e He could have become a model.
   He probably would make the basketball team.

7 Work in pairs. Look again at the sentences that are true for you in Activity 1. Add comments, like in Activity 6.

8 Read the poem. What do you think happened?

Regrets

I wish I could tell you how I really feel
And say what's on my mind.
I wish I hadn't done what I did
Or had thought before I acted.
I wish I was spending my time with you
Instead of sitting here all alone.

9 **CHOOSE** Choose one of the following activities.

- Write a poem similar to the one in Activity 8 about regrets. Write it from the perspective of another person, such as a student, a teacher, or an athlete.
- Write a list of eight sentences like those in the Grammar box for your classmates to discuss.
- Write five things you would wish for if anything was possible. Discuss your ideas with a partner.

   I wish money grew on trees.

Do you ever wish you were taller?

Unit 7 Outside the Box

> **"Everybody who speaks English decides together what's a word and what's not a word."**
>
> **ERIN MCKEAN**

Read about Erin McKean and get ready to watch her TED Talk. ▶ 7.0

AUTHENTIC LISTENING SKILLS

Speeding up and slowing down speech

Speakers often vary the speed of their speech in order to maintain people's interest, as well as for other specific reasons. For example, they may speak more quickly when they are saying very common phrases, making jokes, or making comments that are not important. They may speak more slowy when they are starting their speech, emphasizing something important, or thinking of what to say next.

1 Look at the Authentic Listening Skills box. Then listen to the opening of Erin's talk. Identify where her speech slows down and speeds up. 🎧 36

I'm a lexicographer. I make dictionaries. And my job as a lexicographer is to try to put all the words possible into the dictionary. My job is not to decide what a word is; that is your job. Everybody who speaks English decides together what's a word and what's not a word. Every language is just a group of people who agree to understand each other. Now, sometimes when people are trying to decide whether a word is good or bad, they don't really have a good reason. So they say something like, "Because grammar!" I don't actually really care about grammar too much—don't tell anybody.

2 Work in pairs. Compare your answers from Activity 1. Practice reading the paragraph using the same kind of speech patterns as Erin.

WATCH

3 Work in pairs. Discuss the questions.

1. Which dictionaries do you use? Why?
2. Do you know how dictionaries are made? How?
3. Do you like learning new words in English? in your own language? Why?
4. Have you seen or heard any new words recently? Where? What do they mean?
5. Have you ever made up a new word? What was it? What does it mean?

4 Watch Part 1 of the talk. Match the excerpts from the talk (a–e) with these notes (1–3). ▶ 7.1

1. New words
2. The unconscious natural grammar rules that live inside our brains
3. The grammar of "manners," known as usage

a. "Because grammar!"
b. "This is a wug, right? It's a wug. Now… there are two…"
c. "…take a hoodie, don't forget to obey the law of gravity."
d. "Can you wear hats inside?"
e. "No! No. Creativity stops right here, whippersnappers."

5 Work in pairs. Compare your ideas from Activity 4 and explain the point Erin was making in each excerpt.

6 Look at these notes about six ways to make new words. Watch Part 2 of the talk. Complete the notes. ▶ 7.2

Erin gives six ways to create new words in English:
1 _____ : using words from another language, e.g. *kumquat* and *caramel*.
2 Compounding: putting two words together, e.g. _____ .
3 _____ : putting parts of two words together, e.g. _____ .
4 Functional _____ : e.g. using a noun as a verb, e.g. _____ .
5 Back formation: _____ a part of the word to create a new one, e.g. _____ .
6 Acronym: taking the first letter of several words, e.g. _____ .

7 Watch Part 3 of the talk. The purpose of her talk is to: ▶ 7.3

a explain her job and what is important about it.
b argue that words are more important than grammar.
c encourage people to create words and contribute to her online dictionary.
d argue that it is important to break rules to be more creative.
e explain different ways new words are formed and disappear from use.

8 VOCABULARY IN CONTEXT

a Watch the clips from the TED Talk. Choose the correct meanings of the words. ▶ 7.4

b Work in pairs. Discuss the questions.
1 What did your parents teach you about *manners*? Do you think good *manners* are important?
2 Why might someone be *heartbroken*? What would you do or say for him or her?
3 What do you do to *edit* your essays before you hand them in? Do you get anyone else to help?
4 Give an example of a time when it was difficult to *get your meaning across*. Did you succeed?
5 What movies or books *grabbed* your attention right at the beginning? How? Did they keep your attention?

9 MY PERSPECTIVE

Work in groups. Discuss the questions.

1 Why do you think these groups of people might invent new words? Is it always to aid in communication?

| poets | politicians | scientists | teenagers |

2 Why do you think some words disappear from use?
3 If you are learning English, do you think it's OK to create new words? Why?
4 How might knowing how to make new words help you to develop your English?

CHALLENGE

Work in groups. How many examples of the six different ways of forming words can you think of?

- borrowing
- blending
- back formation
- compounding
- functional shift
- acronyms

Unit 7 Outside the Box 89

7E Creative Solutions

Useful language

Raising concerns
I don't see how that would work.
The issue with that is…
If we did that, wouldn't…?

Suggesting a better approach
Wouldn't it be better to…?
If you ask me, I think we should…

Giving reasons
That way you could…
That allows / enables…
If we do that,…

SPEAKING

1 Work in groups. Look at the photo and discuss the questions.

1 In what ways is this class similar to and different from yours?
2 How many ways of improving your learning environment can you think of? Which two ways would make the biggest difference to the teacher and the learners? Why?

2 Read the situations (a–c). As a class, choose the situation you want to resolve. Then work in groups and:

1 discuss what additional facts you would like to find out about the situation.
2 use divergent thinking to make a list of as many different ways of approaching the situation as you can.
   a Your town or city wants to attract more tourists. It is planning to spend a lot of money on advertising, but no decisions have yet been made about how best to sell the town or city—or what kind of advertisements might work best.
   b This year, a lot less money is going to be available for your school. The school will need to continue offering a great education to students while spending up to 50 percent less. No decisions have yet been made on what changes will need to be made.
   c Your English class has been given some money to make an app or a website to help current and future students deal with their biggest problems. No decisions have yet been made about what should go on the app or website.

3 Exchange the list you made in Activity 2 with another group of students. Then use convergent thinking and the expressions in the Useful language box to:

- discuss the difficulties there might be with each of the ideas.
- decide what the best approach would be—and why.

4 Each group should now choose one person to present their approach to the class. Listen to each group and decide who has the best solution.

High school students in a robotics class build a robot to enter into a competition.

WRITING A report

5 Look at the report on page 152. Identify the two suggestions made by students for reducing external noise in the school library. Can you think of any other possible solution?

- a Install two sheets of glass in each window to stop 75 percent of the water coming in from outside.
- b Install two sheets of glass in 75 percent of the windows to reduce the noise coming in from outside.
- c Install two sheets of glass in each window to reduce the noise coming in from outside.
- d Fill the space between two sheets of glass with water to reduce the noise by 75 percent.

6 **WRITING SKILL** Cohesion

Look at the Writing strategy box. Find examples of how to structure reports in the model on page 152.

7 Work in pairs. Rewrite the sentences using the sentence starters in bold.

1 I guess we could invest in some new, heavier curtains.
   We might consider _____ .

2 It would be much better if we moved the library to another room.
   I would strongly recommend _____ .

3 Maybe we could play quiet music to cover the noise from outside.
   We would suggest _____ .

4 If we put more plants in the library, they would stop some of the sound.
   I propose _____ .

8 Write a short report about the situation your class chose in Activity 2.
- Follow the guidance in the Writing strategy box.
- Make your recommendations using some of the language in Activity 7.

Writing strategy

Structuring reports

Begin with a title to show what the report is about.

Make the aim of the report clear in the introduction.
The purpose of this report is to…
The report will also make recommendations on…

Have clear paragraphs and add subheadings to each paragraph.

Use full forms (*it is*, *they will*, etc.) instead of contractions, like *it's* and *they'll*.

Make recommendations.
We believe that the best solution to this problem would be to…
Perhaps we could also consider…

Avoid expressing personal feelings or opinions.

Unit 7 Outside the Box

8 Common Ground

IN THIS UNIT, YOU...

- talk about interpersonal and intercultural communication.
- read about four different subcultures from around the world.
- learn about different ways of tackling discrimination.
- watch a TED Talk about what is meant by "normal."
- write a complaint.

A *kunik* is a traditional Inuit greeting between family members and loved ones.

8A Cultural Crossings

VOCABULARY Identity and communication

1 Work in groups. Look at the photo and discuss the questions.

1 Could this be a typical scene where you are from? Why?
2 How do you normally greet the people in the box? Does it vary at all? Does everyone in the group greet each other in the same way? Why?

friends	friends' parents	sales associates
teachers	visitors from another country	your parents

2 MY PERSPECTIVE

In addition to greetings, are there any rules you think it would be important for a foreign visitor to your country to know? Do you *always* follow these rules?

3 Complete the sentences with these pairs of words.

awkward + compliment	be offended + implied
conscious + discrimination	discourage + reaction
misunderstanding + work it out	response + negative comments

1 If my friends have a(n) _____ or a big argument, I'm good at helping them _____ .
2 I usually feel a bit _____ if someone pays me a(n) _____ or praises what I've done.
3 I would _____ if someone _____ that I looked older than I really am.
4 I think the best _____ to things like _____ is to challenge them.
5 If someone tries to _____ me from doing something, my initial _____ is to want to do it more!
6 I think I'm pretty _____ of how to avoid _____ .

4 Work in pairs. Read the sentences in Activity 3 aloud. Are they are true or false for you? Why?

5 Complete the collocations with the correct forms, based on the word families.

1 pay me a big **compliment** / _____ me on my work / be very **complimentary** about it
2 _____ against young people / fight **discrimination** / **discriminatory** rules
3 avoid _____ people / a negative _____ / a **stereotypical** person
4 took _____ at what he said / didn't mean to **offend** anyone / use _____ language
5 respond _____ to questions / an **awkward** silence / a sense of **awkwardness** in social settings
6 _____ the instructions / a silly **misunderstanding**

6 Choose five of the collocations from Activity 5. Write example sentences that are true for you.

Unit 8 Common Ground 93

LISTENING

7 Work as a class. Discuss the questions.

1 How might you define *intercultural communication*?
2 In what situations is it necessary to be considerate of other cultures?

8 Work in pairs. What can cause communication to break down in these situations? What might you do if this happens? How could you avoid it?

| greeting people | making plans |
| ordering food | trying to get somebody's attention |

9 Listen to an interview about travel and intercultural communication. What is normal for people from these countries that may be different elsewhere? 🎧 37

| China | Germany | Russia | US |

10 According to the conversation, are the sentences *true*, *false*, or *not stated*? Listen again and check your answers. 🎧 37

1 Stacey's parents are diplomats.
2 The German girl who Stacey spoke to was deliberately rude to her.
3 If a Russian person smiles at another Russian they don't know, they may be seen as untrustworthy.
4 Stacey's Korean friend was confused by people in the United States asking "How're you doing?"
5 In Chinese, a common greeting can be translated as *Have you eaten*?
6 Intercultural communication courses are effective.

GRAMMAR Reported speech

11 Look at the Grammar box. Try to complete the sentences. Listen again and check your ideas. 🎧 37

> **Reported speech**
>
> a I asked a German girl from my class if she _____ the train station.
> b And I thought, "That _____ rude."
> c I said I _____ something and _____ go back to school.
> d That evening I told my dad what had happened and he said that I _____ be so sensitive.
> e A Russian friend told me their parents kind of _____ them from smiling at strangers. There _____ a Russian proverb that says, "Laughter for no reason is a sign of stupidity."

Check the Grammar Reference for more information and practice.

12 Match the sentences in the grammar box to these points.

1 The sentence includes the actual words that were spoken or thought.
2 The sentence includes advice or instruction the speaker was given.
3 The sentence includes a question (or plan) about an action in progress at the time.
4 The sentence includes a statement about a previous action and consequence.
5 The sentence includes a statement about something which is still generally true.

13 Look at sentences a–c in the Grammar box. What happens to the tenses when we report speech? Why?

14 Complete the responses to the statements that are correcting misunderstandings.

1. **A** We're meeting on Tuesday.
   B Really? I thought you said we _____ on Thursday!
2. **A** I got a B on my science essay.
   B Oh, that's pretty good! I thought you said you _____ a D!
3. **A** I'm interested in seeing the new *Star Wars* movie.
   B Really? I thought you told me you _____ interested!
4. **A** I'll bring you all the stuff you need next week.
   B You don't have it? I thought you _____ it today.
5. **A** I'm going to my dance class later.
   B I didn't know you _____ dancing. How long have you been doing that?
6. **A** We have to leave at 11 o'clock.
   B I thought we _____ leave at 12 o'clock.

15 PRONUNCIATION Stress for clarification

a Work in pairs. Listen to the exchanges from Activity 14. Notice how we stress the corrections. Then practice the exchanges. 🎧 38

b Work in pairs. Take turns saying the sentences. Your partner should respond with something they had misunderstood.
1. Are you coming to my birthday party on Saturday?
2. We went to Mexico on vacation last summer.
3. My mom works at a hospital near here.
4. I can't stand that band.
5. Sorry, I can't come out tonight. I have to study.

16 Think of two situations when you might hear these expressions. How might they possibly have different meanings or interpretations?

1. I've been waiting here forever.

Someone in a line advising someone not to wait.

Someone you had arranged to meet being very annoyed because you were late.

2. Don't be silly!
3. Are you going to eat that?
4. What did you do that for?
5. You'll be sorry.

17 Use your ideas from Activity 16 to tell a short story. Report what was said, how you replied, and what you did next.

I went to buy tickets for a concert, but when I got to the theater there was a huge line. Someone there said they'd been waiting forever, so I decided to forget it and just went home.

18 MY PERSPECTIVE

Choose one of these situations. Spend a few minutes planning how to explain what happened. Include some reporting. Then work in pairs. Tell your partner your story.

- A compliment someone paid you or you paid someone else
- A misunderstanding or argument you once had or saw
- A conversation you wish you hadn't overheard

Is eating with your hands normal where you are from? It is in Ethiopia.

Unit 8 Common Ground 95

8B I Am Who I Am

VOCABULARY BUILDING

Compound adjectives

Compound adjectives are made up of more than one word. As with single-word adjectives, it is important to learn not only the meanings, but also the nouns that they most commonly describe.

1 Match these compound adjectives with their meanings.

cost-effective	deep-rooted
heartbroken	highly respected
like-minded	long-lasting
open-minded	two-faced
well-mannered	worldwide

1 sharing tastes, interests, and opinions
2 dishonest and not to be trusted
3 admired by lots of people because of qualities or achievements
4 willing to consider new ideas and ways of thinking
5 existing or happening everywhere
6 behaving in a polite way
7 firmly fixed; strong and hard to change
8 providing good value for the amount of money paid
9 continuing for a long period of time
10 extremely sad and upset

2 Complete the sentences with compound adjectives from Activity 1.

1 She achieved _____ fame when a video she posted online went viral.
2 Everybody around here knows she does good work. She's a _____ figure.
3 My little brother was absolutely _____ when his team lost the championship game!
4 The problems are too _____ for there to be any real hope of a quick fix.
5 If you only ever spend time talking to _____ people, you don't get to hear different points of view.

3 Work in groups. Use five of the adjectives in Activity 1 to describe people or things from your own experience.

My dog died last year, which left me heartbroken.
I bike almost everywhere. It's the most cost-effective way of getting around.

READING

4 Work in pairs. Look at the photo showing a subculture.* Predict:

1 where the subculture originated.
2 what members of the subculture have in common.
3 what kind of music—if any—is associated with this subculture.

subculture *a group of people within a larger cultural group who share the same interests*

5 Read the article and find the answers to the questions in Activity 4 for all of the subcultures mentioned.

6 What reasons for joining subcultures are mentioned in the article? What downside is mentioned?

7 Which of the four subcultures:

1 is more of a virtual than real-world phenomenon?
2 became known worldwide thanks to a music video?
3 is a combination of the ultra-modern and the old?
4 includes members who identify with animals?
5 can trace its origins back the furthest?
6 involves a form of recycling?
7 rejects a common belief about their characteristics?
8 involves regional rivalries?

CRITICAL THINKING Understanding other perspectives

Learning to think more critically sometimes requires us to suspend our own judgment and instead to try to see things from other points of view.

8 Work in groups. For each of the four subcultures mentioned in the article, decide:

1 what the appeal might be for those who get involved.
2 what common ground might exist with other groups.
3 what concerns parents might have.
4 which are common—or have some kind of local equivalents—where you live.

9 MY PERSPECTIVE

The article is written from the point of view of someone who is not involved in any of the subcultures mentioned. Do you think people who are part of the subcultures might want to change any of the details? Why?

A PLACE TO BE

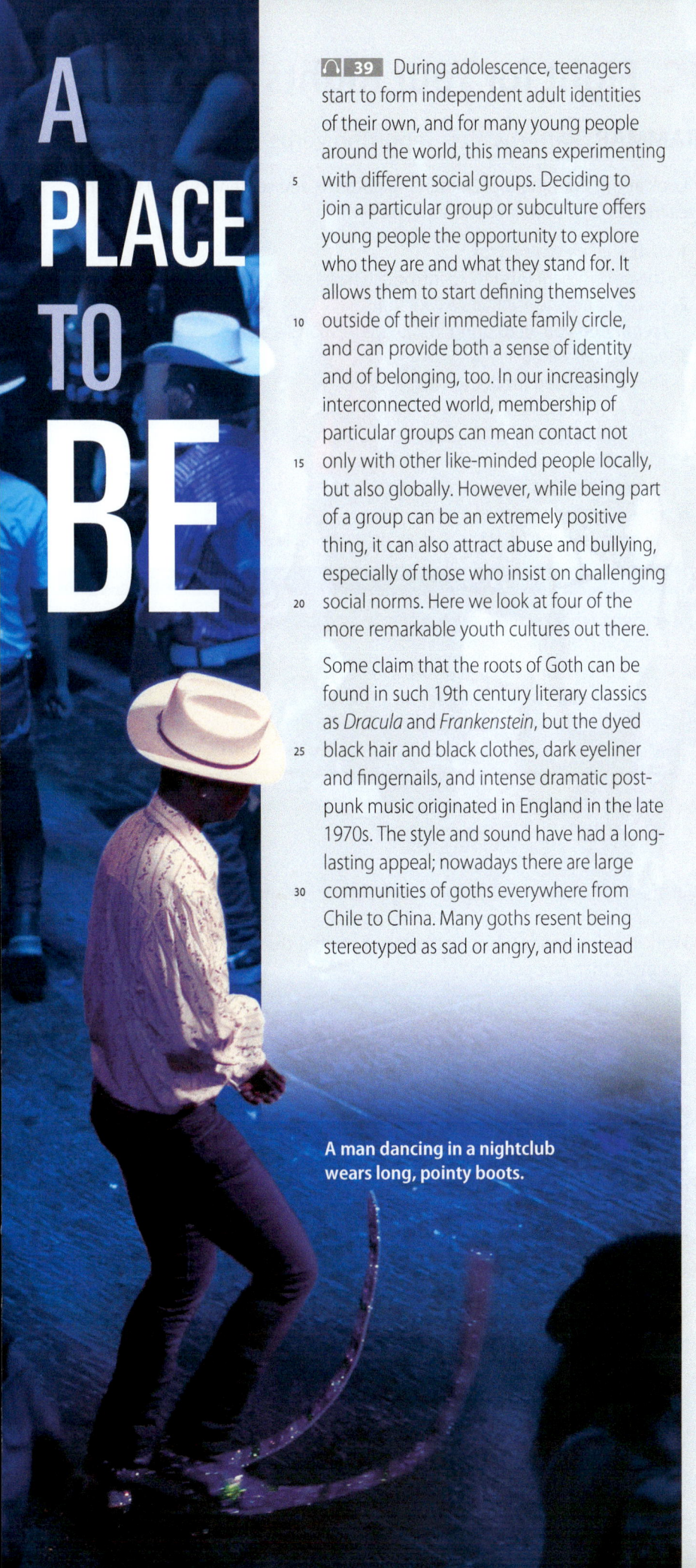

🎧 39 During adolescence, teenagers start to form independent adult identities of their own, and for many young people around the world, this means experimenting with different social groups. Deciding to join a particular group or subculture offers young people the opportunity to explore who they are and what they stand for. It allows them to start defining themselves outside of their immediate family circle, and can provide both a sense of identity and of belonging, too. In our increasingly interconnected world, membership of particular groups can mean contact not only with other like-minded people locally, but also globally. However, while being part of a group can be an extremely positive thing, it can also attract abuse and bullying, especially of those who insist on challenging social norms. Here we look at four of the more remarkable youth cultures out there.

Some claim that the roots of Goth can be found in such 19th century literary classics as *Dracula* and *Frankenstein*, but the dyed black hair and black clothes, dark eyeliner and fingernails, and intense dramatic post-punk music originated in England in the late 1970s. The style and sound have had a long-lasting appeal; nowadays there are large communities of goths everywhere from Chile to China. Many goths resent being stereotyped as sad or angry, and instead see themselves as romantic, creative, open-minded, and able to find beauty in what others may see as dark or ugly.

Over recent years, a far more localized subculture has been developing in Mexico, where a style of music known as *Tribal Guarachero* has evolved, complete with its own remarkable fashions. More commonly known just as *Trival*, the hugely popular sound mixes traditional regional folk music with electronic dance. Young fans often identify themselves by combining futuristic elements with a basic farmworker look… and wearing extremely long, pointy boots when dancing, often competitively against groups from other local towns. Believe it or not, some items of footwear have apparently reached five feet in length!

Of course, subcultures that develop in a particular area can spread like wildfire in a matter of moments these days, thanks to the internet. This is what's happened with the Scraper Biker subculture. Originally the obsession of a small group of young people in the San Francisco Bay area, scraper bikes are simply ordinary bicycles that have been modified by their owners, typically with decorated wheels and bright body colors. Much of the decoration is done very cheaply, using tinfoil, reused cardboard, candy wrappers, and paint! The craze went global after a hip-hop video featuring these creations went viral. Scraper bikes can now be seen in cities all over the world.

If the internet helps some subcultures grow, for others it's their main home. Otherkin—people who identify to some degree as non-human—have a massive online presence that's growing all the time. While some otherkin believe themselves to actually be, say, dragons or lions or witches or foxes, others simply feel special connections to certain creatures—and have found a space within which to explore these feelings.

It seems that, whatever you're going through and whatever your own personal enthusiasms, there's a worldwide community out there just waiting for you to find it—and to assure you that you belong!

A man dancing in a nightclub wears long, pointy boots.

Unit 8 Common Ground

Iceland was the first European country to elect a female president. Vigdis Finnbogadottir was elected in 1980.

8C Fight for Your Rights

GRAMMAR Patterns after reporting verbs

1 Look at the Grammar box. Match the patterns and sentences (1–6) with the examples (a–f) that have the same pattern.

1 verb + infinitive (with *to*)
   The government **intends to introduce** new laws to tackle the problem.
2 verb + someone + infinitive (with *to*)
   I **reminded you all to bring** in your permission slips.
3 verb + preposition + *-ing*
   They **apologized for doing** what they did.
4 verb + (*that*) clause
   She **argued (that)** things really need to change.
5 verb + *-ing*
   He **denied answering** the question.
6 verb + someone + (*that*) clause
   He **promised me (that)** he'd never do anything like that again.

Patterns after reporting verbs
a *Deciding to join a particular group offers young people the opportunity to explore who they are.*
b *Many goths resent being stereotyped as sad or angry.*
c *Some claim that the roots of Goth can be found in 19th century literary classics.*
d *There's a worldwide community out there just waiting to assure you that you belong!*
e *It allows them to start defining themselves outside of their immediate family circle.*
f *It can also attract abuse and bullying of those who insist on challenging social norms.*

Check the Grammar Reference for more information and practice.

2 Work in pairs. Decide which patterns in Activity 1 these verbs use. Some verbs use more than one pattern.

acknowledge	advise	agree	be accused
be blamed	convince	imagine	invite
persuade	pretend	state	suggest

3 Choose the correct options.

Many governments have been criticized (1) *of / in / for* turning a blind eye to racism. Some have even been accused (2) *of / for / from* encouraging it when it suits them. However, the Bolivian government recently announced (3) *to launch / launching / that it's launching* an app designed to encourage citizens (4) *that they should report / to report / reporting* any incidents of racism or discrimination that they encounter. The app is called No Racism. Reports can be submitted 24 hours a day. The government has promised (5) *responding / for responding / to respond* to all complaints and take legal action, where appropriate.

4 Complete the report with the correct forms of the verbs. Add prepositions where necessary.

It was recently announced that Iceland (1) _____ (be) now the best place in the world to be female. However, young Icelandic women have previous generations to thank (2) _____ (fight) for their rights. On October 24th, 1975, fed up with their status as second-class citizens, 90 percent of all women in the country refused (3) _____ (work). Their goal was to remind men that the success of the nation (4) _____ (depend) women and to urge them (5) _____ (accept) greater equality. They threatened (6) _____ (continue) their general strike until changes were made. Men listened, and within five years the country had become the first to elect a female president, Vigdis Finnbogadottir. Iceland can now claim (7) _____ (have) one of the highest proportions of female politicians—over 40 percent—in Europe. In the spring of 2017, a law was passed (8) _____ (require) employers to prove that their companies are free from gender-based salary discrimination.

5 Work in pairs. Look at the ideas for tackling gender inequality. Discuss:

- how they might change things.
- which you think are good ideas. Why?
- other ways in which things could be improved.

a Encourage stores to stop selling toys aimed at either boys or girls.
b Demand that companies employ an equal number of female and male bosses.
c Insist on mothers and fathers getting equal amounts of parental leave when they have children.
d Advise schools to ensure that both boys and girls do school subjects such as cooking and woodwork.
e Force schools to have equal numbers of men and women in photos on the walls.
f Persuade parents to discuss images of men and women in the media with their children.

6 Complete the short news article with the correct forms of these pairs of linked verbs.

| accuse + discriminate | agree + examine | decide + make |
| deny + be | force + change | insist on + have |

A 13-year-old girl in South Africa has been (1) _____ schools three times because of her hair. Zulaikha Patel has (2) _____ her current school, Pretoria High School for Girls, of _____ against black students through its uniform policies that (3) _____ students _____ a "neat, conservative appearance." Angry that this was being interpreted as meaning that she couldn't wear her hair in her natural afro style, she launched a silent protest, which attracted the attention of the national media. The school (4) _____ discriminatory in any way, but (5) _____ its policies before (6) _____ whether or not _____ any significant changes.

7 CHOOSE

Choose one of the following activities.

- Think of conversations you have had—or heard—recently. Use some of the reporting verbs from pages 98 and 99 to describe what they were about.

- Work in pairs. Write a news report about one of these topics. Use at least four reporting verbs.
  – an incident of discrimination
  – a protest
  – a new project that's trying to change things

- Work in groups. Tell each other about a time that:
  – you intended to do something, but then didn't. Explain why you didn't do it.
  – you refused to do something. Why?
  – someone famous was accused of doing something bad.
  – you had to apologize for doing something.
  – someone powerful acknowledged they'd done something wrong.

Zulaikha Patel and her classmates are fighting for rights that go beyond the style of their hair. They are standing up against racism.

8D Why I keep speaking up, even when people mock my accent

> **"** Normal is simply a construction of what we've been exposed to, and how visible it is around us. **"**
>
> **SAFWAT SALEEM**

Read about Safwat Saleem and get ready to watch his TED Talk. ▶ 8.0

AUTHENTIC LISTENING SKILLS

Just

Just has several meanings—*only, simply, exactly, soon, recently*—and is also used to emphasize a statement or soften a request, to make it sound smaller or more polite.

1 Look at the Authentic Listening Skills box. Listen to these extracts from the TED Talk and add *just* in the correct place. 🎧 40

1 I had to grunt a lot for that one.
2 I sat there on the computer, hitting "refresh."
3 This was the first of a two-part video.
4 I could not do it.
5 If I stutter along the way, I go back in and fix it.
6 And the year before, that number was about eight percent.
7 Like the color blue for Ancient Greeks, minorities are not a part of what we consider "normal."

2 Work in pairs. Discuss each meaning of *just* in Activity 1. Then practice saying the sentences.

WATCH

3 Work in pairs. Discuss the questions.

1 In what ways do people make fun of others?
2 In what ways might people react to being made fun of?
3 Why do you think people make fun of others?

4 Watch Part 1 of the talk. Are the sentences *true* or *false*? ▶ 8.1

1 People have sometimes joked, "Have you forgotten your name?" because of Safwat's stutter.
2 Safwat is interested in video games.
3 The video Safwat posted only got negative feedback.
4 The negative comments were mainly about Safwat's stutter.
5 The incident led Safwat to do more voice-overs in order to prove his critics wrong.
6 In the past, Safwat used video and voice-overs to become more confident in speaking.
7 Safwat practiced to improve his voice and accent to sound more normal.

5 Work as a class. Read the conclusion of Safwat's talk. Discuss the questions.

The Ancient Greeks didn't just wake up one day and realize that the sky was blue. It took centuries, even, for humans to realize what we had been ignoring for so long. And so we must continuously challenge our notion of normal, because doing so is going to allow us as a society to finally see the sky for what it is.

1 How do you think the Ancient Greeks and the color of the sky might be related to what you have talked about and seen so far?
2 What do you think Safwat means by "the sky," with regard to society today?

TED TALKS

6 Put the sentences in order. The first one is given. Then watch Part 2 of the talk and check your answers. ▶ 8.2

1 Few colors are mentioned in ancient literature. Why?
   a In the same way, narrators with strong accents are not part of people's "normal."
   b People discriminate because they don't "see" or relate to people who are different from themselves.
   c Should Safwat accept or challenge ideas of normality?
   d Blue was "invisible" and not part of ancient people's "normal," unlike red.
   e Minorities are not part of society's "normal," like the color blue wasn't for the Greeks.
   f One theory is that colors weren't named or "seen" until people could make them.
   g This is why Safwat has gone back to using his voice in his work.
   h People learn not to relate to minorities because there are few images of minorities in books.
   i People's ideas of "normal" can lead to discrimination, such as offering fewer interviews to people with black-sounding names.

7 MY PERSPECTIVE

How do you feel about your own accent in English? Would you like to change it at all? What would be a "normal" accent for you?

8 VOCABULARY IN CONTEXT

a Watch the clips from the TED Talk. Choose the correct meanings of the words and phrases. ▶ 8.3

b Work in pairs. Tell each other about:
   - something *humorous* you have seen or read recently.
   - a time you felt a bit *self-conscious*.
   - a time you took *a big step*.

CHALLENGE

Work in groups. You are going to discuss a video you could make about ONE of these topics. Choose a topic and follow the steps (1–5).

- Challenge the idea of what is "normal."
- Raise awareness of discrimination.
- Discourage bullying.
- Show how different groups share experiences, likes, and dreams.
- Encourage people to do activities with different groups of people.

1 Decide on one aspect of the topic to focus on.
2 Think of two or three different messages for the campaign.
3 Brainstorm some ideas to illustrate these messages.
4 Choose the best idea and develop it further.
5 Share your idea with the rest of the class.

8E Teenage Kicks

Useful language

Identify yourself

As a… / someone who…
Speaking as…
If you look at it from… point of view…

Agree or disagree

I totally support it.
I'm in favor.
I'm (totally) for / against the idea.
It's crazy.
I don't get it.

Challenge ideas and assumptions

Just because…, (it) doesn't mean…
…are we supposed to…?

Give examples

I mean, …

Just hanging out?

SPEAKING

1 Work in pairs. Look at the photo and discuss the questions.
   1 Where was the photo taken?
   2 What are the people doing? What else might they do?
   3 How do you think others might react to these people? Why?

2 Listen to five people giving opinions about a policy. What do you think the policy is about? 🎧 41

3 Listen to the five people again. 🎧 41
   1 Who is speaking in each case?
   2 Are they for or against the policy? Why?

4 Complete the sentences by adding two words in each blank—contractions count as one word. Then listen again and check your answers. 🎧 41
   1 We've lost some stock recently, which I think might be _____ .
   2 I mean, where else are we _____ go? Or are we just _____ to hang out at all?
   3 As _____ goes there pretty often, I _____ the idea.
   4 _____ one or two misbehave _____ they all do. _____ , adults shoplift and cause problems, too.
   5 If I look _____ from my grandpa's _____ view, I can kind of understand it.

5 Work in pairs. Look at the statements. Which ones are normal in your country? Which ones do you agree or disagree with? Why? Use some of the expressions in the Useful language box to discuss them.
   1 Teenagers shouldn't hang out without a responsible adult around.
   2 Everyone should wear a school uniform.
   3 Boys and girls should be educated separately.
   4 Men are better at certain subjects or in certain jobs than women.
   5 You can only get a good job if you go to college.
   6 Students need to do lots of homework to succeed.

6 Work in groups. Choose a role. Discuss the statements in Activity 5 in your role. Then think about the statements from a different perspective.

businessperson   parent   politician   teacher

WRITING A complaint

7 One of the speakers in Activity 2 mentioned negative stereotypes about teenagers in the media. What stereotypes do you think you fit? How does that make you feel? Why?

8 Do you think there are any stereotypes in the media about these groups of people? Are they positive, negative, or neither?

boys	businesspeople	girls
old people	people from your country	students

9 Read the complaint on page 152 and answer the questions.

1 Who is the person writing to and why?
2 How does she feel? Why?
3 What does she want to happen? Why?

10 WRITING SKILL Using appropriate tone

Work in pairs. Read the complaint on page 152 again. Discuss the questions.

1 Does the writer follow the advice in the Writing strategy box?
2 What other details could the writer give, if any?
3 Do you think complaints are worth writing? Why?

11 Work in groups. Think of reports, policies, rules, TV programs, or movies you know about. Discuss the questions.

1 Have you read or seen anything that you thought was untrue, unfair, or stereotyped people?
2 What was the problem?
3 Who was responsible?
4 How could it have been changed?

12 Write a complaint about one of the ideas you discussed in Activity 11. Follow the structure of the writing model on page 152. Try to use some of the language from this unit.

Writing strategy

When we write to complain about something, we:

- say what the general problem is in the first sentence.
- give details of the problem (including times and examples).
- explain more about how the problem has affected us.
- ask for some kind of action.
- sometimes say what we will do next if we are unsatisfied with the response.

The writing is more effective if it:

- is polite.
- is fairly formal.
- uses linking words such as *however* and *while*.

9 Lend a Helping Hand

IN THIS UNIT, YOU…

- talk about natural disasters and technology that helps to deal with them.
- read about how the United Nations gives a voice to young people.
- learn about local community action and dealing with crime.
- watch a TED Talk about helping people recover after a disaster.
- write a letter of application for a volunteer position.

Rescuers evacuate local people from their homes in China.

9A In Times of Crisis

VOCABULARY Dealing with disaster

1 Work in pairs. Look at the photo and discuss the questions.

1 What do you think has happened?
2 What do you think the three main challenges in this area would be at this time?
3 What would be needed to help people overcome these challenges?

2 Check that you understand these pairs of words. Use a dictionary, if necessary. Then complete the series of events following an earthquake.

appealed + aid	blocked + supplies
debris + task	earthquake + devastation
infrastructure + flee	launched + evacuate
rise + crisis	shortages + limited

1 The _____ struck coastal areas just after midnight and caused widespread _____ .
2 Much of the _____ was damaged or destroyed, and thousands of people started to _____ the worst-affected areas.
3 As the number of injuries continued to _____ , it became clear that a humanitarian _____ was starting to unfold.
4 There were food _____ and a _____ amount of clean drinking water.
5 The government _____ to the international community for _____ .
6 The roads were _____ , so they had to use helicopters to drop _____ to people.
7 They _____ a relief effort and started to _____ people from the disaster zones.
8 They finally managed to clear the _____ and started the huge _____ of rebuilding.

3 Work in pairs. Discuss the questions.

1 In addition to earthquakes, what else can cause **widespread devastation**?
2 What kind of systems form the **infrastructure** of a town or city?
3 What else might there be **shortages of** after a disaster?
4 What else might **rise** after a natural disaster?
5 What kind of **aid** can the international community provide in crises?
6 How is **debris** usually cleared?
7 How are people usually **evacuated from disaster zones**?
8 What other reasons are there that roads may be **blocked**?

4 Think about a natural disaster you know about and prepare to discuss it. Write notes on:

- what happened, where, and when.
- the immediate impact of the disaster.
- the relief effort involved—and how effective it was.
- the biggest challenges.

5 Work in groups. Discuss your notes from Activity 4. Try to use some of the language from Activity 2.

Unit 9 Lend a Helping Hand   **105**

When a powerful earthquake struck Nepal in 2015, Patrick Maier's team used drones to take photos of the affected areas.

LISTENING

6 Listen to the first part of a radio program. Find out: 🎧 42

1. what the disaster was, where it happened, and when.
2. what the impact of the disaster was.

7 Work in groups. Discuss the questions.

- Had you heard about the disaster described in Exercise 6 before? Do you know anything more about it and how the country is now?
- How do you think social media, maps, and photographs, such as the one above, could help in this situation?

8 Listen to the second part of the radio program about how Patrick Maier first used an online mapping technology called Ushahidi in Haiti. Answer the questions. 🎧 43

1. How did he get information to update the online maps on Ushahidi?
2. How did this information help the people affected by the disaster?
3. How else has Ushahidi helped people elsewhere in the world?

9 Work in pairs. Try to remember what was said about the following. Then listen again and check your ideas. 🎧 43

1 Christine Martin	5 helicopters
2 Kenya	6 world attention
3 Haitian roots	7 Russia
4 one million	8 a smartphone

10 Patrick Maier calls the work he does *crisis mapping*. In recent years, crisis mappers have started using more technological tools in their work. How might these tools be useful to them? Can you think of anything else that might help?

3D modeling technology	artificial intelligence
drones	GPS
hashtags	satellites

Hashtags might be useful for crisis mappers because they can use social media to see where the most requests for aid are coming from.

GRAMMAR Relative clauses

11 Look at the Grammar box. Answer the questions.

1. What are the relative pronouns in each sentence?
2. When do you think each one is used?
3. Defining relative clauses qualify nouns and tell us exactly which thing, person, or place is being referred to. Which sentences include them?
4. What is the difference between the defining relative clauses in the sentences you just identified and the others?
5. In which sentence can the relative pronoun be left out? Why?
6. Look at sentence *d*. Where does the preposition go in relation to the verb? How else could you write this clause?

Relative clauses

a *The earthquake that struck Haiti measured seven on the Richter scale.**
b *The devastation which it caused was simply staggering!*
c *The country, which has long been one of the poorest in the world, struggled to cope.*
d *The seaport, which supplies would normally have been delivered to, was also unusable.*
e *Watching all of this in his Boston home was Patrick Maier, who decided that he had to do something to help.*
f *Maier, whose girlfriend was doing research in Haiti at the time, came up with the idea of using technology to create an interactive online map.*
g *He had to reach out for volunteers, many of whom had Haitian roots and were very happy to help.*
h *Helicopters were able to drop tents and food to desperate people whose homes had been destroyed and evacuate people who were trapped or injured.*

Richter scale *a scale for measuring the size of an earthquake*

Check the Grammar Reference for more information and practice.

12 Complete the summary with a relative pronoun in each blank. Can any of the blanks contain a different word or be left blank? If so, which ones? Explain your choices.

The year 1945 was an important one for Europe. Some people see it as the year (1) _____ the modern world started. Europe was in a mess, the kind of mess (2) _____ is almost impossible for people today to imagine. Six years of war had devastated the continent. Tens of millions had died; millions more had been forced to move from the places (3) _____ they had previously lived—and life was unbelievably hard for those (4) _____ had survived. The majority of the survivors were women and children (5) _____ husbands and fathers had been killed or imprisoned. Nobody had anything (6) _____ they could sell, and men with weapons wandered the land, taking whatever they wanted. How was the task of rebuilding achieved?

Well, most importantly, Harry Truman, (7) _____ was then President of the United States, put into place systems (8) _____ were intended to help all states regarded as allies. In 1947, the US Secretary of State, General George Marshall, (9) _____ name was given to the plan, announced massive amounts of aid for war-torn countries, much of which was to be used for reconstruction. The Marshall Plan ran for over ten years and paid for the rebuilding of infrastructure, (10) _____ provided employment and sped up the return of normal life.

13 Work in pairs. Add relative clauses to the sentences.

1 Crisis mapping has been used in many countries.
2 At 4:35 AM local time, the hurricane hit the coastal town.
3 The International Red Cross and Red Crescent have over 50 million volunteers.
4 Donations have now topped ten million dollars.
5 People are taking shelter in the local school.

14 MY PERSPECTIVE

Work in groups. Discuss the questions.

1 Have any disasters affected your country? In what way?
2 Did there need to be any rebuilding after the disaster(s)? How was this done?

Unit 9 Lend a Helping Hand 107

9B Future Leaders

Shouting Out for the Young

At the UN Youth Assembly, young people discuss UN policies from a youth perspective.

VOCABULARY BUILDING

the + adjective

We sometimes talk generally about groups of people using *the* + adjective.

*These days, **the young** face many challenges that didn't exist in the past.*

1 Work in pairs. Discuss whether you agree or disagree with the sentences.

1 The old need to listen to the young more.
2 There is one set of rules for the rich and another for the poor.
3 The loud and outgoing get too much attention.
4 Only the brave or the stupid would believe they could change the world.
5 Only the best get to the top.

2 Write your own sentence starting *Only the*. Then share your idea with the class and discuss what it means.

READING

3 Look at the photo and discuss the questions.

1 Who do you think the people are?
2 Would you like to take part in something like this?
3 Do you think young people can change policies in these areas? Why?

the world   your country   your school   your town

4 Read the article quickly. Write a one-sentence summary. Then work in pairs and discuss your summaries.

5 Read the article again. Find:

1 someone who started a trend.
2 an organization that provides aid.
3 someone who created a record.
4 someone who showed determination.
5 someone who founded an organization.
6 a country that has changed a law to benefit children.

Unit 9 Lend a Helping Hand

🎧 44 Almost half of the world's seven billion citizens are under the age of 25, and they have huge potential to shape the countries they live in. A few countries, such as Argentina, have tried to empower their youth by giving them the right to vote at the age of 16, but it still seems that in many places young people's opinions are often overlooked or simply not heard. However, one organization that has a long history of giving a voice to young people is the United Nations (UN).

In 1946, the UN created a fund called UNICEF to support the millions of children affected by World War II, thanks to the leadership of the Polish medical scientist Ludwik Rajchman. The fund distributed aid without discrimination because, as its director Maurice Pate said, "There are no enemy children." One of those helped by the fund was seven-year-old Dzitka Samkova from Czechoslovakia, as it was known then. She painted a picture of five dancing girls as a thank you and it was turned into a greeting card, the first of many such cards sold to raise money for millions more children.

Having campaigned on behalf of young people, UNICEF also had a key part in the creation of the UN's Convention on the Rights of the Child (CRC) in 1989, now signed by more countries than any other convention. The 54 articles of the CRC declare different rights connected to housing, health, the economy, culture, and politics, including such things as the right to a safe home, the right to play and rest, and a child's right to choose their own friends.

In recent years, the UN has opened up new ways to address Article 12 of the CRC, which states that children have the right to give their views, and for adults to listen and take them seriously. UNICEF's Voices of Youth website brings together young bloggers and activists working on development issues to share their ideas and successful projects for change in a huge range of countries, from Sierra Leone to the Philippines. Using online discussion boards as a "meeting place," the initiative provides a space for youngsters who care.

The UN also established the Youth Assembly in 2002 and a network of Youth Observers. Since starting, the assembly has brought around 20,000 people between the ages of 16 and 28 from over 100 countries to its headquarters in New York. Through workshops, panel discussions, and networking events, these young people discuss UN policies from a youth perspective. The assembly also helps to build friendships across different cultures and give political experience to those who can bring change for children. One of its graduates, Ahmad Alhendawi of Jordan, became the UN Secretary General's first ever representative for youth and the youngest ever senior official in the UN.

Of course, the Youth Assembly and its delegates are only a tiny number of those three and a half billion young people, but they are important role models. It can be easy to find reasons not to act, but as Nicol Perez, a youth observer to the UN General Assembly says, "I have a voice, and I'm going to use it. I'm going to shout it out till somebody hears me."

---

7 an online initiative that brings together politically active people.
8 a place where young people help to decide how things are done in the world.
9 a document that states the rights of children.

6 In your opinion, how influential were these people from the article? Put them in order from most influential to least influential. Then work in small groups. Compare your answers and discuss your choices.

Ahmad Alhendawi	Dzitka Samkova
Ludwik Rajchman	Maurice Pate
Nicol Perez	Voices of Youth bloggers

CRITICAL THINKING Detecting bias

Even though articles give a lot of factual details, the way that the arguments are organized and the vocabulary that is used can show if the writer has an underlying opinion.

7 What do you think the author's general opinion is about the UN and young people? Why?

8 Identify the words and phrases in the opening paragraph which reveal the author's opinion. How does the structure of the paragraph reinforce these opinions?

9 Rewrite the first paragraph so that it is neutral. Change words and the structure of the paragraph. Remove words or phrases as necessary.

10 Work in groups. Discuss ideas you have to achieve these UN 2030 goals. Then share your ideas as a class.

- End poverty in all its forms everywhere.
- Ensure inclusivity and equality for all and promote lifelong learning.
- Achieve gender equality.
- Make cities inclusive, safe, resilient, and sustainable.

Unit 9 Lend a Helping Hand

Malala Yousafzai is a young activist for female education. She spoke at the United Nations on her 16th birthday.

9C Community Service

GRAMMAR Participle clauses

1 Identify all the relative clauses that are correct and could have the same meaning as the corresponding reduced clause in the Grammar box.

1 The UN created a fund
   a who is called UNICEF.
   b which was called UNICEF.
   c that is called UNICEF.

2 The fund supported millions of children
   a who were affected by World War II.
   b which affected World War II.
   c that had been affected by World War II.

3 The CRC declares different rights
   a where connected to housing, health, the economy and politics.
   b which the UN connected to housing, health, the economy and politics.
   c which are connected to housing, health, the economy and politics.

4 The Voices of Youth website brings together young bloggers and activists
   a who work on development issues.
   b who have been working on development issues.
   c that are working on development issues.

> **Reduced relative clauses**
>
> a *In 1946, the UN created a fund (1) called UNICEF to support the millions of children (2) affected by World War II.*
> b *The 54 articles of the CRC declare different rights (3) connected to housing, health, the economy, culture, and politics, (4) including such things as the right to a safe home and the right to play.*
> c *The Voices of Youth website brings together young bloggers and activists (5) working on development issues to share their ideas.*

Check the Grammar Reference for more information and practice.

2 When do we use an *-ing* participle and when do we use an *-ed* participle to shorten a relative clause?

3 Read about some research findings and projects available to young people. Fill in the blanks with the correct participle of each verb.

Research has found that the number of young people (1) _____ (involve) in dangerous behavior has fallen greatly over recent years. In fact, youths are actually far more likely to be victims of crime rather than criminals. Yet most people think that the amount of youth crime and antisocial behavior is getting worse. The suggestion is that this may be because media reports still focus on youngsters (2) _____ (misbehave), (3) _____ (ignore) the many community projects (4) _____ (reduce) crime. These community projects involve such things as cafes (5) _____ (set up) for teenagers to meet after school, community gardens (6) _____ (teach) teens about sustainability, and a "time bank" (7) _____ (design) by young people (8) _____ (allow) them to earn rewards for doing volunteer work.

4 Work in pairs. Discuss the questions.

1 Do you think the research explained in Activity 3 would produce similar results in your country? Why?
2 How are community projects successful in reducing crime and antisocial behavior?

5 PRONUNCIATION *-ing* forms

a Listen to the statements. Note the pronunciation of the /ŋ/ sound. 🎧 45
b Practice repeating the statements. 🎧 45

> **Adverbial participle clauses**
>
> **a** *Having campaigned* on behalf of young people, UNICEF also had a key part in the creation of the UN's Convention on the Rights of the Child (CRC) in 1989.
> **b** *Using* online discussion boards as a "meeting place," the initiative provides a space for youngsters who care.

Check the Grammar Reference for more information and practice.

6 Look at the sentences in the Grammar box. Choose the correct options.

1 The subject of the participle clause is *the same as / different from* the subject of the verb in the main clause.
2 The present participle (*Using*) shows the action happened *at the same time as / before* the action in the main clause.
3 A perfect participle (*Having campaigned*) shows the action happened *at the same time as / before* the action in the main clause.

7 Complete this story about a foolish criminal by choosing the correct options.

(1) *Having walking / Walking* home from school one day with a friend, we came across a man on his bike. He started asking us where we were going and what phones we had. We just ignored him, but then he blocked us, (2) *shouted / shouting* at us to give him our phones. (3) *Not wanting / Wanting* to get into a fight, we handed them over and he biked off. (4) *Returned / Having returned* home, I told my mom what had happened and we reported the incident to the police.

A week or so later, (5) *arresting / having arrested* someone, the police asked us to go and see if we could identify him. Unfortunately, it wasn't the man who had robbed us. We left kind of frustrated. But then, two days later, my friend's mom got a WhatsApp message from my friend's stolen phone! The robber had actually sent her a message, (6) *thinking / thought* it was his own mom—and he had his picture on the account he was using!

Even after (7) *having seen / seeing* the evidence against him, the robber still tried to tell the police he was innocent! I think he was hoping we wouldn't go to court, but (8) *faced / facing* with us actually giving evidence, he changed his mind and pleaded guilty.

8 Do the participle clauses in Activity 7 add information about time, reason, or method? Can you rewrite them with words like *because*, *after*, *while*, etc.?

9 MY PERSPECTIVE

What other stories about failed crimes or foolish criminals have you heard?

10 CHOOSE

Choose one of the following activities.

- On your own, write a story about a failed crime or a foolish criminal.
- Work in pairs. Think of six different ways you could promote young people and their issues.
- Work in pairs. Using participle clauses, describe four other trends using similar patterns to the examples in Activity 5. Then, in groups, discuss why these trends are happening.

The number of young people playing sports has fallen a lot.

Young people volunteer to serve food to less fortunate people in their community.

9D (Re)touching Lives through Photos

> " We take photos constantly. A photo is a reminder of someone or something, a place, a relationship, a loved one. "
>
> **BECCI MANSON**

Read about Becci Manson and get ready to watch her TED Talk. ▶ 9.0

AUTHENTIC LISTENING SKILLS

Intonation and completing a point

We often use a rising intonation to show we are going to add an idea and a falling intonation to show that our point is complete. This pattern is common in lists and contrasts.

1 Look at the Authentic Listening Skills box. Then listen to Becci. Practice saying the extract yourself. 🎧 46

A photo is a reminder of someone or something, a place, a relationship, a loved one. They're our memory-keepers and our histories, the last thing we would grab and the first thing you'd go back to look for.

2 Decide where you might use a rising intonation and where you might use a falling intonation in these extracts from the TED Talk. Practice saying them.

1 We make skinny models skinnier, perfect skin more perfect, and the impossible possible.
2 We pulled debris from canals and ditches. We cleaned schools. We de-mudded and gutted homes.

WATCH

3 Work in groups. Tell each other about—and show each other, if you can—photos that remind you of special people, places, or times in your life.

4 Watch Part 1 of the talk. Find an example of where Becci: ▶ 9.1

1 makes a joke about her profession.
2 defends her profession.
3 gives an example of an unpleasant job she did.
4 had an initial moment of realization.
5 felt a sense of pride.
6 had a positive reaction from her contacts.

5 Work in pairs. Tell each other about:

- things you've lost or broken and wish you still had.
- things you're good at repairing.

6 Watch Part 2 of the talk. Are these statements *true*, *false*, or *not stated*? ▶ 9.2

1 The little girl in the first photo didn't survive the tsunami.
2 Before long, Becci and her team were scanning photos every other day.
3 Some of the people who brought photos were unfamiliar with the technology Becci was using.
4 The kimono in the photo took months to retouch.
5 Photos would only get retouched once their owners had come forward.
6 The lady who brought the family portraits already had extra copies.
7 Both of the lady's children were caught in the waves when the tsunami reached land.
8 All of the photos Becci and her team retouched were returned to their owners.
9 Becci and her team needed new printers.

7 MY PERSPECTIVE

Work in pairs. Discuss the questions.

1 Why do you think the response to Becci's request for help on social media was so high?
2 What other causes do you think might receive a high response on social media? Why?

8 Watch Part 3 of the talk. Which sentence is the best summary of the main point Becci makes? ▶ 9.3

a Everyone loves taking photos.
b Photographs are the most important things most people own.
c Both survivors and volunteers involved in the project benefited in a major way.
d Without photos, we wouldn't be able to remember our past that well.

9 Work in pairs. Which of these statements do you think are lessons from the talk? Do you agree with them?

1 Our differences matter, but our common humanity matters more.
2 In times of crisis, individuals can make a difference in ways that governments cannot.
3 We don't think enough about the psychological and emotional side of recovery after disasters.
4 It's important to feel that the work you do has a positive impact on society.
5 Some people volunteer because they feel guilty about how lucky they've been.
6 Countries shouldn't be expected to deal with large-scale disasters on their own.

10 VOCABULARY IN CONTEXT

a Watch the clips from the TED Talk. Choose the correct meanings of the words and phrases. ▶ 9.4

b Work in pairs. Tell each other about:
- a film, book, photo, or piece of art that *struck a chord* with you.
- three places around *the globe* you'd love to visit.
- a time you remember watching a major news story *unfold*.

CHALLENGE

Work in groups. Look at the situations (1–3). Thinking about both the immediate and the longer-term future, list what you think are the most important things that could be done in each situation by:

- the local government.
- other governments around the world.
- NGOs (Non-Governmental Organizations).
- volunteers on the ground.
- individuals in other places around the world.
- you.

1 A remote Pacific island has been hit very badly by flooding caused by global warming. Whole villages have been washed away and land has been lost to the sea.
2 A humanitarian crisis is developing in a country that has been devastated. There's a shortage of food and medicine, with children and old people being particularly at risk.
3 A big fire has destroyed dozens of homes in a town near you, leaving over a hundred people homeless and causing serious environmental damage.

9E Give It a Try

Useful language

Countering possible opposition
Now, I know what you might be thinking.
I realize there's a perception that…
I'm obviously not denying that…

Listing
To begin with, consider the fact that…
On top of that,…
Let's not forget that…
And finally, it's important to note that…

SPEAKING

1. Work in pairs. Look at these jobs. Discuss how they might be useful in a crisis or disaster. How might they generally be good for society?

actor	banker	chemistry teacher
computer programmer	photo retoucher	plastic surgeon
politician	street cleaner	

2. Work in pairs. Which job in Activity 1 do you think each sentence describes? Do you agree?

   1 They are often criticized for creating fake images, but they can also help restore things that are very precious to people.
   2 Some people say they're only motivated by greed and self-interest, but they generate jobs, and businesses couldn't work without them.
   3 Without them, we'd be surrounded by piles of trash and dirt.
   4 They can bring a huge amount of joy to millions of people.
   5 They can transform the lives of people who have been injured.
   6 They are fundamental to the technological world.
   7 Yes, they can be corrupt and lie, but they can also be a huge force for good.
   8 They don't just have knowledge, they have the ability to pass it on.

3. Listen to a student explain a job she thinks is important for society. Answer the questions. 🎧 47

   1 What job is she talking about?
   2 What reasons does she give?

4. Work in pairs. Answer the questions.

   1 What did the student mention before listing positive aspects of the job? Why?
   2 Which aspects of her argument do you agree and disagree with? Explain why.

5. Work in groups. Discuss which person or job in Activity 1 is best suited to help in a crisis. Follow these steps.

   1 Give each person in the group a job to defend.
   2 Spend some time preparing what you'll say. Use the Useful language box.
   3 Take turns presenting your arguments.
   4 Discuss who is the best person to help in the crisis.
   5 Vote to choose the best person for the job.

After an oil spill, people volunteer to help with the clean-up operation which can involve helping wildlife.

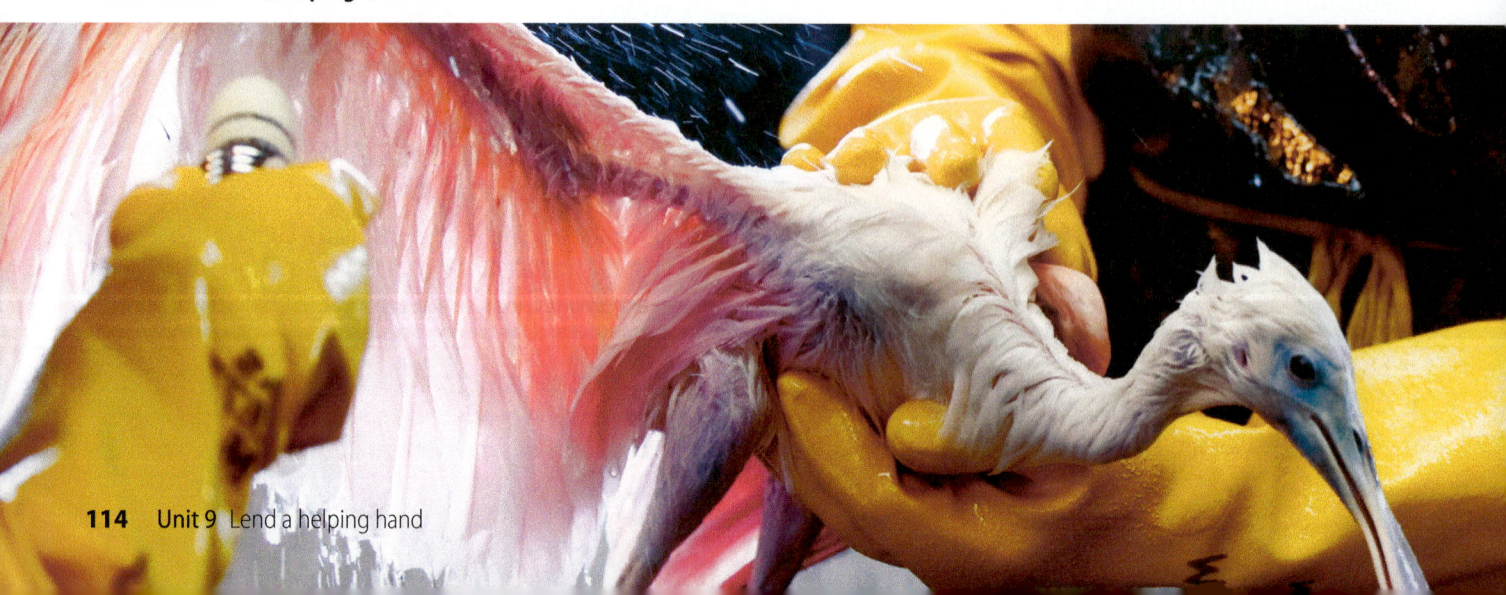

WRITING A letter of application

6 Read the advertisement. Discuss the questions.

> Spend your winter vacation this year doing something different. We're looking for volunteers between the ages of 16 and 21 to rebuild a school in Belize that was destroyed in a hurricane last year. You will learn traditional building methods to provide a great space where learning can take place. For more details, write and tell us who you are and what you would bring to the project.

1. What do you think daily life for volunteers on this project would involve?
2. What problems might they face?
3. What kind of skills do you think would be required to do this work?
4. How do you think any volunteers who take part might benefit?
5. Would you be interested in doing something like this? Why?

Useful language

Introducing subjects that you want to discuss
In terms of my experience, I have…
With regard to my degree, I have…
As far as language skills go, I can…

Explaining your suitability
I feel I would be suitable because…
I'm prepared to…
I feel confident that I'd be able to…

7 WRITING Structuring an application

If you were writing in response to an advertisement, decide how you would order each of these features. Compare your ideas with a partner.

a Refer to the ad that you saw
b List the skills and abilities you have
c Describe who you are and where you are from
d Outline your plans for the future
e Explain why you are writing

8 Work in pairs. Read the letter of application on page 153. Which order did the writer choose? Do you think this person would be a suitable volunteer? Why?

9 Complete the sentences by adding the correct prepositions from the letter.

1. I'm writing _____ response to your recent letter.
2. Please send me more information _____ the post.
3. Please send details _____ how to apply.
4. I'm currently _____ my last year of high school.
5. _____ terms of my experience, I have a part-time job.
6. _____ addition, I have experience working with animals.
7. I feel that I would be suitable _____ the post.
8. I look forward _____ hearing from you soon.

10 Look at the advertisement. List the skills and abilities you have that might make you a suitable volunteer.

> Spend your summer in Mexico helping to preserve some of the world's most endangered species by participating in wildlife volunteer projects. Depending on where you're placed, you may care for animals, conduct research, or help with community programs. You may also be asked to teach basic English to local guides. You may find yourself working with dolphins or even jaguars. Contact us for details and to let us know why you'd be a great fit for our team.

11 Write letter of application in response to the advertisement in Activity 10. Use the Useful language box to help you.

10 Life-changing

IN THIS UNIT, YOU...

- talk about recovering from illnesses and accidents.
- read about the fight against superbugs.
- learn how medical advances have changed lives.
- watch a TED Talk about redefining yourself after a life-changing moment.
- write a story about overcoming something.

The da Vinci surgical system allows surgeons to carry out difficult procedures by looking at a screen.

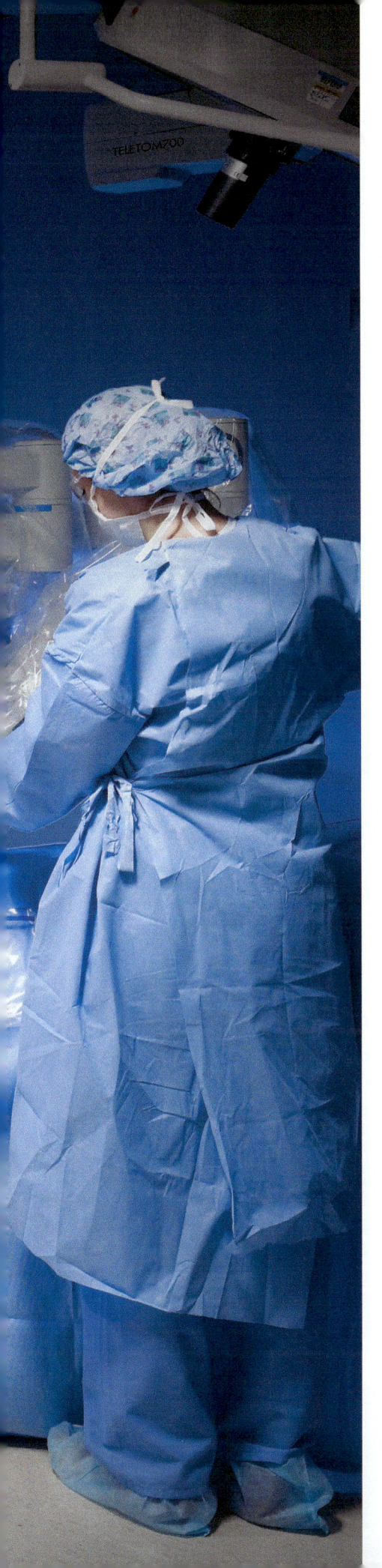

10A Road to Recovery

VOCABULARY Illness and injury

❶ **Look at the photo. Discuss the questions.**

1 What do you think is happening?
2 What do you think has happened to the patient?
3 How might an operation like this have been carried out in the past?

❷ **Complete the sentences with the words in bold.**

1 action / health / leg
   I slipped on the stairs and broke my *leg*, so I was out of *action* for a while, but I'm back to full *health* now.

2 cure / drugs / symptoms
   There's no for it, but she takes to control the, and she leads a fairly normal life.

3 injury / operation / physical therapy
   It was quite a serious wrist, but thanks to the and all the I had, it's almost as good as new.

4 detected / made / spread
   Luckily, they the cancer early before it to his lungs, and he a full recovery.

5 bleeding / damage / intensive care
   They managed to stop the, but he was in for days. Thankfully, it didn't leave any permanent brain.

6 normal / therapy / stroke
   He couldn't really speak after the, but he had a lot of speech, and he's more or less back to now.

7 lost / think / slammed
   I the tip of my finger after I it in a car door. To be honest, I hardly about it now.

8 car accident / waist / wheelchair
   He started playing basketball after he was left paralyzed from the down in a.

9 antibiotics / chest / prescribed
   She said I just had a infection and nothing life-threatening! She me some, and it cleared up after a week.

10 feel / had / keep down
    I an upset stomach, and I could hardly any food. It was horrible, but I a lot better now.

❸ **Work in groups. Look at your completed sentences in Activity 2. Find:**

1 eight parts of the body.
2 at least five nouns that are medical problems.
3 four adjectives describing illnesses or injuries.
4 at least five phrases which show that someone has recovered from something.

❹ **Work in pairs. Discuss the questions.**

1 Have you ever broken any bones? What happened?
2 When was the last time you had a day off of school due to illness? Why?
3 What do you do to recover from an illness? Are you a good patient?
4 What stories have you heard of people recovering from illnesses or injuries? What happened?

Unit 10 Life-changing 117

LISTENING

5 Listen to Jaime and Clara talking about movies. Answer the questions. 🎧 48

1 What four movies do they talk about?
2 What is the connection between the movies?
3 What doubts do they have about recommending the first three movies?

6 Work in pairs. Complete the sentences with three words in each blank. Listen again and check your answers. 🎧 48

1 He was in the _____ and no one could help because he hadn't told anyone where he was going.
2 It is horrible, but they managed to film it in a way which isn't _____ .
3 It's the same with that film about the guy who had a stroke and was left completely paralyzed and _____ .
4 It's based on his book which he actually _____ by only moving his eye.
5 Yeah, it is incredible, but, sorry the movie didn't _____ me.
6 This is about Frida Kahlo, the Mexican artist who _____ all her life after a terrible bus accident.

7 Work in pairs. Discuss the questions.

1 Have you seen any of the movies Jaime and Clara talked about? If yes, what did you think of them? If not, would you like to see them? Why?
2 Can you think of any other movies that could fit the same category as those discussed? Are they based on true stories? What happened?

8 MY PERSPECTIVE

Think again about what you do when you are recovering from something. Answer the questions.

1 Would these stories inspire you to act differently? Why?
2 What things might you do to overcome challenges you face?

GRAMMAR Expressing past ability

9 Look at the Grammar box and answer the questions.

1 What forms of the verb follow *could*, *manage*, *able*, and *succeed in*?
2 How do you make negatives in the past with *could*, *able*, and *manage*?
3 Which sentences describe a general ability / inability?
4 Which sentences describe success in a task in the past?

> **Expressing past ability**
>
> a He couldn't move his arm.
> b No one could help.
> c She managed to deal with that pain in the end and was able to turn it into incredible art.
> d She succeeded in becoming a world-renowned artist.
> e He was unable to speak.
> f They weren't able to do anything about it.
> g I didn't manage to see it when it was playing in theaters.

Check the Grammar Reference for more information and practice.

Frida Khalo managed to deal with her pain and turn it into art that is admired by people all around the world.

10 Work in pairs. Are all the sentence endings in 1–3 correct? Explain those that are incorrect.

1 After I recovered from the illness,
  a I could see perfectly well in front of me, but I couldn't see anything to the side.
  b I was able to see perfectly well in front of me, but I wasn't able to see anything to the side.
  c I managed to see things perfectly well in front of me, but I didn't succeed to see anything to the side.

2 Following the accident,
  a she couldn't walk to begin with, but she could learn again since then.
  b she was unable to walk to begin with, but she's been able to learn again since then.
  c she wasn't able to walk, but she's managed to learn again since then.

3 He wrote a book about his experiences
  a and managed to get it published.
  b and succeeded in getting it published.
  c and could get it published.

11 Discuss how you think the paralyzed man Clara and Jaime talk about managed to dictate his book. Then read the summary and find out what happened.

Although his mind was working perfectly, his thoughts were locked inside him. He (1) *couldn't move* a muscle in his body. He (2) *couldn't make* a sound or even see clearly. So how did the ex-actor and magazine editor Jean-Dominique Bauby write a whole book? Well, first the nurses started communicating with him by asking a question and saying "yes" or "no." Bauby (3) *was able to indicate* his answer by blinking the only part of his body he (4) *could move*—his left eye. Then his speech therapist invented a way of arranging the alphabet in the order of the most frequent letters in French. She pointed to each letter, and Bauby blinked at the correct one so (5) *she was able to spell* the word. Claude Mendible, an editor, then took up the job of writing with Bauby. Together, they (6) *managed to complete* a 120-page book about Jean-Dominique's life and his experience of "locked in" syndrome. After its publication, Bauby's memoir became a bestseller.

12 Rewrite the italicized words in Activity 11 using these words at least once.

able	could	managed	succeeded	unable

13 **PRONUNCIATION** Stress on auxiliaries

> Stress is sometimes added to the verbs *be* or *have* to emphasize that something is true—especially when clarifying or contrasting with another viewpoint.

a Listen and repeat the sentences. 🎧 49

b Complete these sentences with your own ideas. Then work in pairs. Practice saying the sentences.
  1 It is an amazing story, but _____ .
  2 I have heard of the story, but _____ .
  3 I am happy to be here. It's just _____ .
  4 It was a difficult situation, but _____ .

14 Work in pairs. Think of an inspiring story about someone who survived an accident or managed to deal with an illness. Think about:
- who it happened to and how old they were.
- how the accident happened or the person got sick.
- what the consequences were.
- how they survived and recovered.
- what the lessons from the story are.

15 Tell your stories to each other in groups or as a class.

10B The Battle against Bacteria

VOCABULARY BUILDING

Dependent prepositions

Certain verbs, adjectives, and nouns are often followed by specific prepositions, which we call *dependent*, because their choice depends on the particular word and its meaning. There are no fixed rules about which dependent prepositions go with which words, so it is important to pay attention to them as you learn them.

She was **diagnosed with** a rare eye disease.

I'm **allergic to** nuts.

The drug offers at least some **protection from** disease.

1 Complete the sentences with the correct prepositions. Use a dictionary, if necessary.

1. I would love it if more time was **devoted** _____ physical education at school.
2. I would be very **capable** _____ living on my own on a desert island.
3. Most fast food advertising is **aimed** _____ children.
4. We're all **exposed** _____ far too much air pollution.
5. A lot is done to raise **awareness** _____ health issues—especially among young people.
6. Any **investment** _____ health care has to be a good thing.
7. I think I have a good **chance** _____ living until I am 100.
8. It's natural for people to be **resistant** _____ change.
9. I can't remember the last time I needed a **prescription** _____ anything.

2 Work in pairs. Do you agree or disagree with the sentences in Activity 1? Why?

READING

3 Work in groups. Look at the title of the article you are going to read. Then discuss:

- how you think some of the words in bold in Activity 1 might be connected to the story.
- what, if anything, you know about the discovery of antibiotics.
- why antibiotics are important and how you think they may have changed medicine.
- what you think antibiotics are generally used for.
- what the "apocalypse" in the title might refer to—and how it might be avoided.

4 Read the article. Find out what the "antibiotic apocalypse" is and how it can be avoided.

5 Read the article again. Which of the points below are not made?

a. Airplane cabins provide perfect conditions for bacteria to multiply.
b. New forms of old diseases are now proving fatal.
c. The WHO doubts that the worst-case scenario will happen.
d. The possibility of resistant bacteria has been known since the early days of antibiotics.
e. Technology is contributing to the overuse of antibiotics.
f. Agricultural uses of antibiotics increase the likelihood that deadly superbugs will develop.
g. Hosam Zowawi is developing a way of treating bacterial infections faster.
h. The slower the recognition of resistant bacteria, the greater the risk of superbugs spreading.

6 MY PERSPECTIVE

Work in pairs. Discuss the questions.

1. Had you heard about the battle against bacteria before? If yes, did you learn anything new?
2. How does the article make you feel? Scared? Optimistic? Determined to change things? Or something else? Why?

CRITICAL THINKING Thinking through the consequences

The consequences of an action are the results or effects that the action produces. One element of reading critically is being able to see possible consequences of actions mentioned in a text.

7 Work in groups. How many possible consequences of these actions can you think of?

1. Drug-resistant diseases spread as a result of international air travel.
2. Antibiotics can no longer be used in hospitals.
3. Online sites selling antibiotics are closed down.
4. The use of antibiotics in farming is banned.
5. The government decides to greatly increase investment in medical research.

Avoiding the Antibiotic Apocalypse

🎧 50 This may sound like the stuff of nightmares or of terrifying science-fiction movies, but according to the World Health Organization (WHO) the threat of an "antibiotic apocalypse" is very real, and many experts fear that it's only a matter of time before we see the emergence of a superbug—a very powerful type of bacteria that normal drugs cannot kill—capable of wiping out huge numbers of people.

Perhaps most disturbing of all is the fact that this potential disaster has been predicted for many decades. In fact, the earliest warnings came from Sir Alexander Fleming, the Scottish doctor and bacteriologist who in 1928 discovered the world's first antibiotic substance—penicillin.

Like many groundbreaking scientific finds, the discovery of penicillin was largely accidental. Its importance wasn't realized for at least another ten years, and mass production didn't start until the 1940s. However, there's no doubting the fact that it changed medical practices beyond all recognition. Infections that had previously been fatal were now treatable.

In the speech he made when accepting the Nobel Prize for his work, Fleming warned that bacteria could easily become resistant to antibiotics if regularly exposed to concentrations insufficient to kill them. He went on to express his fears that penicillin would end up being so widely used that such changes were inevitable. Worryingly, this is precisely what happened!

Antibiotics are now regularly prescribed for such non-life-threatening illnesses as sore throats, colds, and ear infections, and if doctors refuse their requests, many patients turn to the internet for their desired medication. On top of this, a large percentage of all antibiotics sold are now being used in farming. They are, for instance, often given to healthy animals to ensure rapid weight gain. Given all of this, it's no surprise that more and more bacteria are evolving a resistance.

One man determined to overcome this challenge is the Saudi microbiologist Hosam Zowawi, who has devoted a considerable portion of his time to developing a test that's able to identify bacteria in hours rather than days, allowing doctors to act more quickly and efficiently, and slowing the potential spread of any deadly infections. Zowawi is also very actively involved in campaigns designed to raise public awareness of the risks of antibiotic overuse.

In addition to reducing the use of antibiotics, there are many other ways that the situation is now being addressed. For instance, in the Netherlands, the government has started putting pressure on farmers to reduce the amount of antibiotics given to animals. Elsewhere, there's a growing understanding of the need to address the underlying conditions that allow new diseases to spread, which, in turn, leads to better trash collection, better drainage, and better housing. Finally, we're starting to see increased investment in research aimed at finding the new antibiotics that could be the penicillin of tomorrow.

E. coli **infections make up a large percentage of antibiotic-resistant infections.**

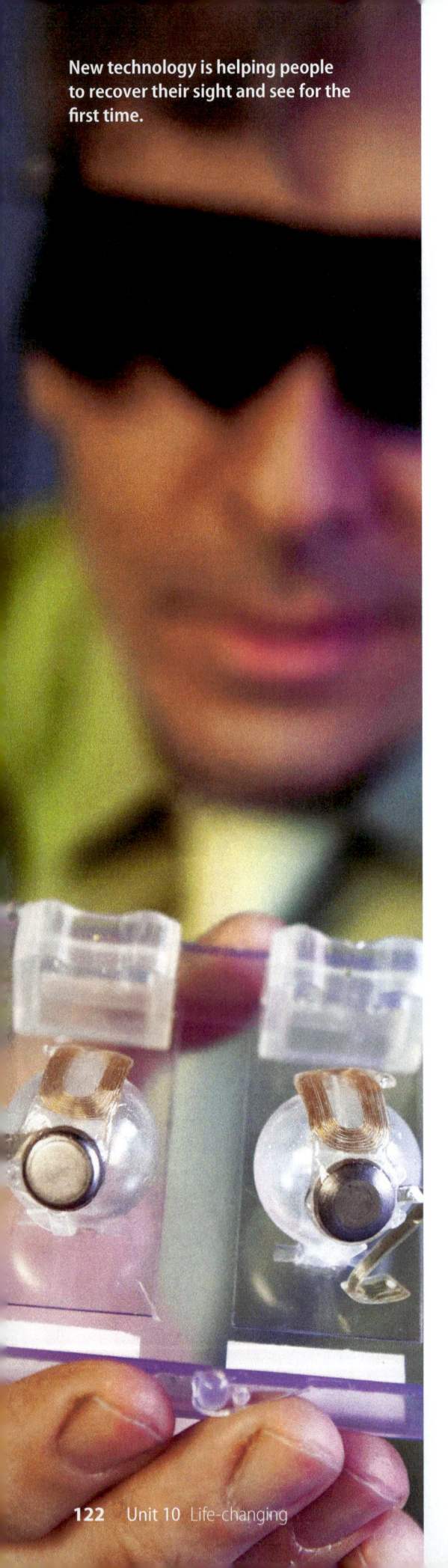

New technology is helping people to recover their sight and see for the first time.

10C Medical Advances

1 Work in groups. The photos show different ways that technology is helping to improve vision. Discuss what you think each picture shows and how it might work.

2 Listen to an extract from a radio program. Find out: 🎧 51

1 which of the photos is being discussed.
2 if the technology is expensive.

3 Work in pairs. Can you explain how the technology works using these words? Listen again and check your answers. 🎧 51

| camera | cells | chip | electrical signals |

4 MY PERSPECTIVE

Work in pairs. Think of as many different ways to fund medical research and treatments as you can. Then discuss these questions with another pair of students.

1 What is the best way to fund medical research and treatment?
2 How might a health service decide when a treatment is too expensive?
3 How might a health service decide between two very expensive treatments?

GRAMMAR Emphatic structures

5 As well as pronunciation grammar can also be used to add emphasis. Look at the Grammar box and answer the questions.

1 How is emphasis added in sentences *a* and *b*?
2 What adverbs are used in sentences *c* and *d* to introduce the point being emphasized?
3 What happens to the order of the words that follow these adverbs?

> **Emphatic structures**
>
> **a** *While surgical options did exist before, none were nearly as effective.*
> **b** *While each bionic eye does cost a lot, reports from users have been incredibly positive.*
> **c** *We're all used to hearing news about terrible things, but rarely do we hear much about exciting new developments.*
> **d** *When Second Sight started experimenting, little did they know that they were on their way to revolutionizing the treatment of blindness!*

Check the Grammar Reference for more information and practice.

6 Rewrite the sentences in a more emphatic style, using the words in parentheses.

1 Some doctors read research about new medicine, but too many just accept what big drug companies tell them. (do)
2 While caffeine increases energy levels, in large doses it can actually prove fatal. (does)

3 In the old days, doctors sometimes removed arms or legs without using any painkillers! (did)
4 When the patient started having terrible headaches, she didn't know it was because a spider was living in her ear. (little)
5 No research suggests that there is anything unhealthy about a vegetarian diet. (in no way)
6 Doctors didn't often cut people open in the days before penicillin. (rarely)
7 You don't fully become an adult until the age of 24. (only after)
8 In the Middle Ages, doctors were never in doubt that releasing blood from the body kept people healthy. (at no time)
9 Plastic surgery didn't become very popular until the 1980s, despite having been around for over 200 years before then. (not until)
10 People in the United States do less exercise than anyone else in the world. (nowhere)

7 PRONUNCIATION Adding emphasis

Do / Does / Did is usually stressed in sentences where it has been added for emphasis. Negative adverbs are also usually stressed when they introduce a point to be emphasized.

a Listen and check your answers in Activity 6. Then listen again and note the way stress is used to add emphasis. 🎧 52
b Practice saying each sentence in an emphatic way. Which of the ideas most and least surprised you? Why?

8 Complete the short article by adding one word in each blank.

There are 39 million blind people in the world. But (1) _____ do people realize that perhaps half of those affected by blindness could be cured, simply by removing the cataract* which causes it. Many people (2) _____ already have surgery to remove cataracts. In fact, it is a very common operation in many countries, and only very (3) _____ does the patient fail to recover good sight. However, until recently the procedure (4) _____ cost quite a lot and was too expensive for sufferers in developing countries. That was until Dr. Sanduk Ruit, a doctor from Nepal, created a new system for conducting cataract surgery. (5) _____ only did he manage to reduce the cost of the operation to around 25 dollars per patient, he reduced the time it took and developed a production-line approach. In fact, (6) _____ in the world do they conduct the operation more efficiently and successfully than in Nepal. The result makes a huge difference to thousands of lives. Not only (7) _____ the operation bring sight back, it (8) _____ brings back the ability to farm and do similar work, which in turn helps to reduce poverty.

cataract *a medical condition which causes the lens of the eye to become cloudy, resulting in blurred vision*

9 CHOOSE Choose one of the following activities.

- On your own, find out about an amazing development in medical history. Write a summary of your findings, explaining what happened, when, and why it was important.
- Work in pairs. Decide what you think the biggest health risk facing your country is. Think of five ways it could be tackled.

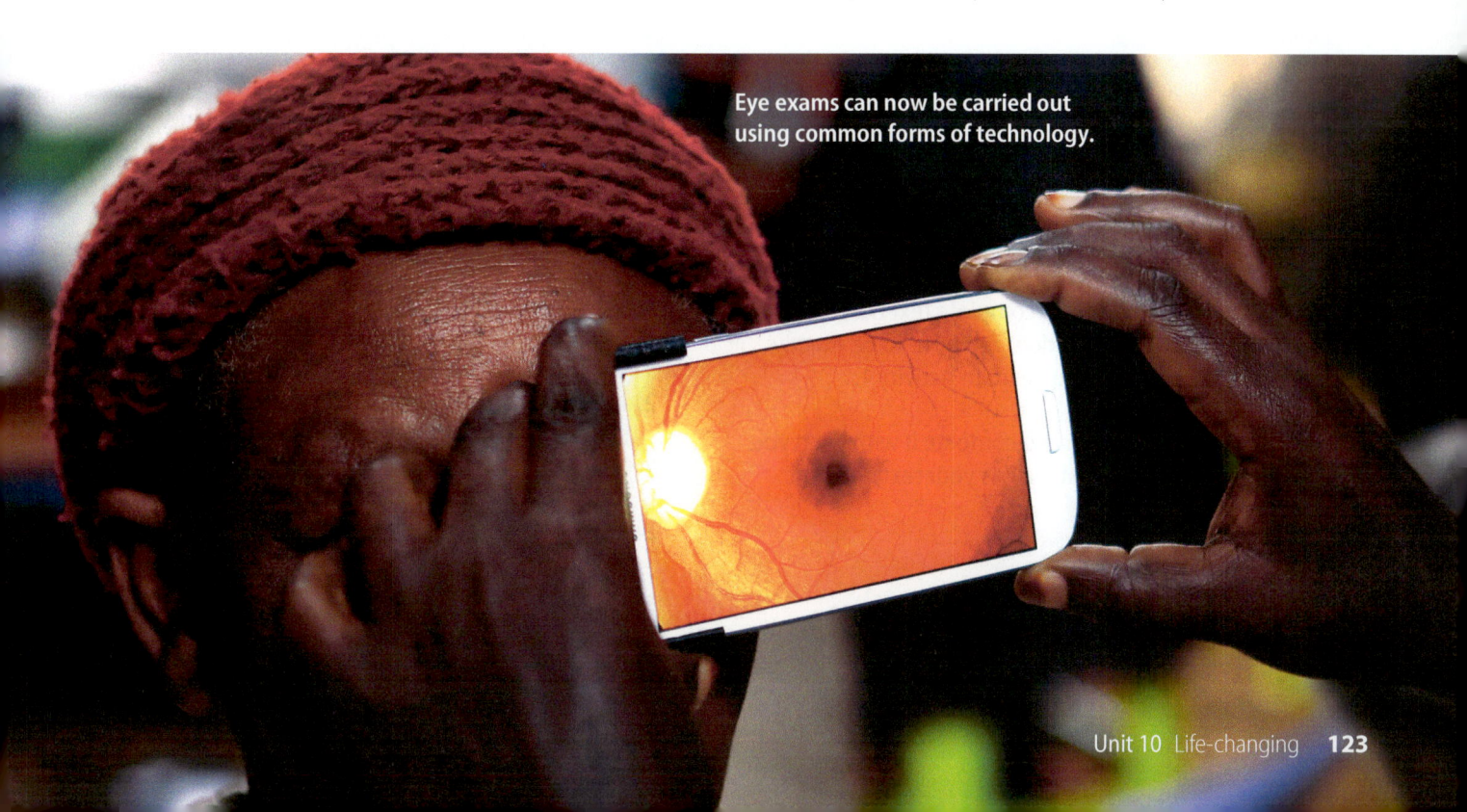

Eye exams can now be carried out using common forms of technology.

> **When you let go of what you are, you become what you might be.**
>
> **JANINE SHEPHERD**

Read about Janine Shepherd and get ready to watch her TED Talk. ▶ 10.0

AUTHENTIC LISTENING SKILLS

Collaborative listening

Fast speech can be difficult to understand. Focus on what you did hear. Think about the context and what you know about the subject or situation to guess what might have been said. If you are with someone, compare what you heard; you may have heard different things.

1 Look at the Authentic Listening Skills box. Then work in groups. Listen to the extract from the beginning of Janine's talk. 🎧 53

- Student A: Listen and note the nouns and things you hear.
- Student B: Listen and note the verbs and actions you hear.
- Student C: Listen and note whatever you want.
- Student D: Listen carefully without taking notes.

2 Work in your groups. Write a complete text based on your combined notes. Your text does not have to be exactly the same as the extract you heard in Activity 1.

3 Listen to the extract again and compare it with what you wrote in Activity 2. In what ways is your text different from the extract? 🎧 53

WATCH

4 Watch Part 1 of the talk. Are the sentences *true* or *false*? ▶ 10.1

1 The accident took place at the time of the Olympics.
2 The vehicle that hit Janine was going fast.
3 Janine's bike helmet protected her head from any damage.
4 Janine had an out-of-body experience as she was fighting for her life.
5 Janine had no movement below her waist after the operation.
6 The doctor said the result of the operation meant that Janine would eventually be as good as new.

5 Work in pairs. Watch Part 2 of the talk. Take notes on what you hear and compare. ▶ 10.2

6 Work in pairs. Complete the sentences together. Then watch Part 2 of the talk again and check your answers. ▶ 10.2

1 Janine did not know what the other people in the spinal ward _____ .
2 Janine felt the friendships she made there were unusual because they were _____ .
3 The other people in the ward shared their hopes and _____ rather than have _____ .
4 When Janine left the ward and first saw the sun again, she felt _____ for her life.
5 The head nurse had told Janine she would _____ , but she did not believe her.
6 Janine wanted to give up because she was in _____ .

124 Unit 10 Life-changing

TEDTALKS

7 Look at these phrases. How do you think they are connected? What new activity and job do you think Janine took up?

buttons and dials	get a license
learn to navigate	pass a medical
sense of freedom	slide up on the wing
take the controls	teach other people

8 Watch Part 3 of the talk. Was your answer to Activity 7 correct? ▶ 10.3

9 Work in pairs. Explain what happened to Janine using the phrases in Activity 7.

10 Watch Part 4 of the talk. What do you think Janine's message is? Discuss your idea with a partner. ▶ 10.4

11 **VOCABULARY IN CONTEXT**

a Watch the clips from the TED Talk. Choose the correct meaning of the words and phrases. ▶ 10.5

b Work in pairs. Discuss the questions.
1 What might be something that is difficult to *grasp*? Have you ever experienced this?
2 Do you think it is good to get *out of your comfort zone*? Why? Have you ever been in that situation? What happened?
3 Do any of your friends or family have a *nickname* you like? Why do they have it?

12 Work in pairs. Discuss the questions.
1 Did you enjoy Janine's talk? Why?
2 Do you think you could have overcome something like Janine's experience? Why?
3 What judgments do people make when they meet people for the first time?
4 Have your friends ever helped you overcome a problem or difficulty? How?
5 Is there something you would like to do but have not? What's stopping you?

CHALLENGE

Work in pairs. Discuss what challenges these situations might create for a person and what opportunities might be created. Then work with another pair of students and put your challenges in order from the most difficult to the easiest. Discuss your reasons.
- Having a serious accident like Janine's.
- Moving to a new country because of a parent's job.
- Failing your final exams at school.
- Going to college in a new city.

Unit 10 Life-changing

10E Getting Better

Speaking strategy

Developing the conversation

When we respond to news, we don't just show sympathy or surprise. We often add a follow-up comment or a question to keep the conversation going.

You're joking! When did he do that?
Poor guy. So is he OK?

Useful language

Reporting stories / news
Apparently,…
I heard (that)…

Expressing surprise
You're kidding!
Oh no!

Responding to good news
Wow! That's great!
Awesome!

Showing sympathy
Poor guy
He must be fed up!

Passing on a message
Say "hi" from me.
Tell him to get well soon.
Tell her I'm thinking of her.

SPEAKING

1. Work in pairs. What would you say or ask if you heard that someone you knew:
   - got good grades on their exams?
   - was moving from where they live?
   - had been kicked out of school?
   - was sick or had an accident?

2. Listen to two conversations between friends. Answer the questions. 🎧 54
   1. Who are they talking about? Why?
   2. What happened to the person they are talking about?

3. Which of the phrases in the Useful language box did you hear in each conversation? Listen again and check. 🎧 54

4. Work in pairs. Take turns saying the sentences below. Your partner should respond and add a follow-up question or comment.
   1. Apparently, he'll have to have an operation.
   2. Her mom said she was grounded.*
   3. I saw him yesterday and he said he was feeling a lot better.
   4. Apparently, it's a really bad cold. He's going to be out all week.
   5. Did I tell you? My older sister's going to have a baby!

   grounded *not allowed to go out as a punishment for doing something wrong*

5. Practice having conversations based on your ideas in Activity 1. Use the Useful language box to help you.

WRITING A success story

6. Work in groups. Can you think of a time you overcame one of the following? Tell each other your success stories.

| a difficulty | disgust | a fear |
| an illness | an inability | an opponent |

7. Work in pairs. Student A: read the story on this page. Student B: read the story on page 153. Then tell each other:

1 which of the things mentioned in Activity 6 each writer overcame.
2 what the writer finally managed to do.

I looked down at the water and the waves crashing against the rocks. My legs immediately started to shake. Someone shouted "Come on Yasine, you can do it!" I was on an adventure vacation. This is what I had wanted to do—walking, climbing, camping—and now here I was doing these things and I couldn't move. I wanted to be anywhere else but here. We were doing a walk along a narrow coastal path, but it had become less and less like a path and more like a cliff we had to climb along. We finally came to a point where we had to hold on to a rock and jump over a small gap to get to the rest of the path. Everyone else had done it and I was the last one. It wasn't far—not much more than a few feet. But I just couldn't do it. I was sure I was going to fall. I was stuck. The rest of the group then started to shout together, "You can do it! You can do it!" I grabbed the rock and leapt to the other side. I made it! Everyone cheered. I had finally managed to do it and it felt like I was champion of the world.

8 Read the story that you did not read in Activity 7. Can you find these features in either text? Compare your findings.

1 An interesting opening sentence that grabs the reader's attention
2 Inversion to make part of the story more emphatic
3 Examples of direct speech
4 Descriptive verbs that make the story more exciting

9 WRITING SKILL Using descriptive verbs

Complete each sentence with the correct form of these descriptive verbs.

creep	grab	leap	peer
rush	scream	slam	stare

1 They _____ me to the hospital and we got there just in time!
2 I _____ the top of the table and pulled myself up.
3 "Watch out!" she _____ as the motorcycle came speeding towards me.
4 I could hear a strange noise, but as I _____ into the darkness, I couldn't see anything!
5 When I heard the scream, I _____ out of my chair and ran into the kitchen to see what the problem was.
6 I _____ at the letter in complete amazement! I just couldn't believe my eyes!

10 Write a story of between 200 and 250 words about overcoming something. Use the phrase *I finally managed to…* somewhere in the story.

Have you ever overcome a fear?

Useful language

Explaining how you felt before you succeeded

I was absolutely terrified.
I was sure I was going to fall / fail / lose!
I'd tried absolutely everything.
I was ready to just give up.

Explaining how you felt in the end

It was the best day / one of the best days of my life.
It was a moment I'll never forget.
It was a truly memorable experience.
It was a day that changed my life.

UNIT 1 GRAMMAR REFERENCE AND PRACTICE

PRESENT AND PAST FORMS

Simple present

The simple present describes things that are generally true, habits, or permanent states.

I **miss** my host family.

The simple present also describes things scheduled to happen at a particular time in the future.

We **arrive** at seven in the morning and then **leave** the following evening.

Present continuous

The present continuous describes actions seen as temporary, in progress, or unfinished.

We**'re talking** about study-abroad programs.

The present continuous is also used to talk about things in the future that one has arranged to do with other people.

I**'m meeting** some friends on Sunday.

Simple past

The simple past is used to describe finished actions in the past, especially when there is one finished action after another.

I **spent** six months in Berlin in 2015. Then I **came** home.

Past continuous

The past continuous is used to emphasize an action in progress around a time in the past.

I **was** actually **thinking** about canceling my trip before I left.

Past perfect

The past perfect emphasizes that one thing happened before a particular point in the past.

I**'d** never **left** Argentina.

Past perfect continuous

The past perfect continuous (*had been* + *-ing*) is the preferred form for talking about something in progress over a period of time *up to* or *before* a particular point in the past. However, the past perfect can also be used in most of these cases.

I**'d been wanting** to go there for ages.

Remember that some "state" verbs that do not express action are not used in continuous forms.

USED TO AND WOULD

To talk about habits, regular actions, or events in the past, use *used to* and *would*. The simple past can also be used. Often, these habits or events no longer happen.

Would is more common than *used to*. *Used to* is often used to start a topic, and then *would* or the simple past is used to give extra details.

I **used to do** it all the time when I was a student going home to visit friends… Often, when you **went** to some hitching spots, **you'd have to line up** behind several others already waiting for a ride… I often argued with my parents about the dangers of hitchhiking and **I would tell them** about all the amazing experiences I'd had.

Used to or the simple past (not *would*) are used to describe past states existing over a period of time.

Hitchhiking **used to be** / **was** / ~~would be~~ so common when I **was** / **used to be** / ~~would be~~ a student.

Describe individual past events and situations with the simple past only. Do not use *used to* or *would*.

I also **spent** / ~~used to spend~~ / ~~would spend~~ one summer hitching around South America.

To form negatives, use *didn't* to show the past tense. Notice that *use to* is used in negatives.

People **didn't use to worry** about sharing their space.

It is common to form negatives using *never* instead of *didn't*. Notice that *used to* is used to indicate the past tense in this case.

People **never used to worry** about sharing their space.

When asking questions, use the auxiliary *did* to show the question is in the past tense. Notice that *use to* is used in questions.

Did you **use to go** there?

There is no present form of *used to*. The adverb *usually* or the verb *tend to* is used.

People **don't** ~~used to~~ **usually** hitchhike now.

128 Unit 1 Grammar Reference

1 Choose the correct option.

I (1) *was going / went* on a student exchange to France recently. I (2) *was staying / stayed* with a French boy named Olivier and his family for three weeks over Easter. I (3) *had / was having* an amazing time there. They (4) *were taking / took* me skiing for ten days, which was incredible! I (5) *didn't go / hadn't been* before, but (6) *I'd been taking / I was taking* lessons to get myself ready, so I wasn't completely clueless when I got there. Over the next few weeks, both my skiing and my French (7) *had improved / improved*. The only bad thing about the trip was that while we (8) *had been staying / were staying* in the mountains, I got really sick. I don't know if it was food poisoning or what, but I (9) *felt / had felt* really bad. Olivier (10) *has been coming / is coming* here in July. I'm a little worried because I can't take him to do exciting things like skiing! Most of the time here, (11) *I just hang out / I'm just hanging out* with my friends. (12) *I still look / I'm still looking* forward to seeing him, though.

2 Complete the sentences. Use the past perfect continuous form of the verb if appropriate. If not, use the past perfect.

1 My sister _____ (talk) about doing a student exchange for years, so it's great that she finally went.
2 We _____ (know) each other for years before we decided to travel together.
3 I got really badly sunburned. I _____ (lie) around on the beach all day and just forgot to put sunscreen on!
4 I _____ (see) a lot of the country during my time there, but that was my first time in the capital.
5 This was my third time in the city. I _____ (enjoy) it the other two times but didn't have much of a feel for it yet.
6 They were so nice. We _____ (stay) in a B&B, but they said we could sleep at their place.

3 Complete the text about HitchBot with *would*, *used to*, or the simple past.

HitchBot was a special robot designed by scientists at two Canadian universities as an experiment to see how humans react to robots. They (1) _____ send the robot on hitchhiking trips with instructions to try to visit certain places along the way. They (2) _____ leave the robot at the side of the road, and when someone pulled up to see what it (3) _____ (be), the robot (4) _____ read a message explaining what it wanted to do. The driver then had to pick up the robot, put it in their car, and then leave it by the side of another road to be picked up by someone else. The vast majority of people (5) _____ (treat) the robot well and it (6) _____ (complete) four trips in Canada, Holland, Germany, and the United States.

4 Rewrite each sentence using *used to* or *would* and the word in bold.

1 My grandparents usually came on vacation with us when I was younger. **come**
My grandparents _____ on vacation with us when I was younger
2 In the past, most workers only had one day a week off. **work**
In the past, most workers _____ six days a week.
3 In the 19th century, women usually traveled with someone. **travel**
Women _____ on their own in the 19th century.
4 My hair's a lot longer now. **have**
I _____ shorter hair.
5 My dad gave up playing soccer professionally because he got injured. **to be**
My dad _____ a professional soccer player until he got injured.

5 Complete each pair of sentences with the correct form of the verb in bold, and a pronoun. Use the adverb in parentheses, if given. Put one sentence in a past form and the other in a present form.

leave
1a When I went to Mexico in 2016, it was the first time _____ my country. (ever)
1b _____ ? You've hardly seen the city. (already)

get used to
2a I was in the UK for almost nine months, but I can't say I _____ the food. (ever)
2b It's taken a while, but _____ speaking in Spanish. Hopefully, I'll be fluent by the time we leave. (slowly)

stay
3a I was a little worried because _____ with a host family before, but it was fine. (never)
3b Where _____ on your study-abroad trip next year?

get
4a We took a wrong turn back there. _____ way off the beaten path.
4b We went to seven cities in four days, so _____ a feel for the places. (hardly)

UNIT 2 GRAMMAR REFERENCE AND PRACTICE

PRESENT PERFECT FORMS AND SIMPLE PAST

Present perfect

The present perfect is used:
- to introduce or list experiences connected to a present situation / discussion.
- to refer to a completed event within a period of time including now.
- to talk about the duration of something that is still true now.

*Most successful entrepreneurs **have failed** at least once.*
*Entrepreneurs **have always needed** the confidence to recover from failure.*

The present perfect continuous is used:
- to talk about duration of activities that are still true now.
- to emphasize the process (not the completed action).

*The number of entrepreneurs **has been growing** over the last few years.*
*Kickstarter **has been running** for several years now.*

The continuous form is preferred when talking about duration, but the simple form can also be used with no difference in meaning.
*The number of entrepreneurs **has been growing** over the last few years.*
*The number of entrepreneurs **has grown** over the last few years.*

The simple form is usually used when talking about a completed action, while the continuous form is usually used to emphasize the process. This is why the simple form is preferred with specific amounts.

*Since it started, Kickstarter **has** ~~been raising~~ **raised** two billion dollars.*
*He's ~~been starting~~ **started** ten different companies over the last fifteen years.*

Simple past

The simple past is used:
- to tell a story of completed events.
- with time phrases that show completed time.
- to talk about the duration of completed events.

*D'Aloisio's first investor **contacted** him via email from Hong Kong.*
*She **wrote** for ten years without success.*

VERB PATTERNS (-ING OR INFINITIVE WITH TO)

The -ing form is commonly used with the following verbs.

admit	avoid	can't stand	consider
delay	enjoy	finish	keep
mind	miss	practice	recommend

The infinitive with *to* is commonly used with the following verbs.

agree	arrange	decide	expect
fail	hope	intend	need
offer	plan	promise	refuse

Objects before -ing and to

Some verbs can have an object before an -ing form or an infinitive with *to*.

catch sb/sth -*ing*	discover sb/sth -*ing*	feel sb/sth -*ing*
find sb/sth -*ing*	got sb/sth -*ing*	hear sb/sth -*ing*
imagine sb/sth -*ing*	leave sb/sth -*ing*	mind sb/sth -*ing*
notice sb/sth -*ing*	remember sb/sth -*ing*	see sb/sth -*ing*

advise sb/sth *to*	allow sb/sth *to*	ask sb/sth *to*
beg sb/sth *to*	cause sb/sth *to*	challenge sb/sth *to*
convince sb/sth *to*	dare sb/sth *to*	expect sb/sth *to*
force sb/sth *to*	get sb/sth *to*	hire sb/sth *to*
invite sb/sth *to*	order sb/sth *to*	pay sb/sth *to*
permit sb/sth *to*	prepare sb/sth *to*	remind sb/sth *to*

Negatives can be made using *not*.
*I hate **not having** a cell phone with me.*

Verbs with two objects

These verbs are commonly followed by two objects.

ask	book	bring	build
buy	cook	find	get
give	lend	make	owe
pass	save	show	tell

With most verbs that can be followed by two objects, the order of the objects can be reversed if *for* or *to* is put in front of the person / group of people. The preposition used depends on the initial verb.

*Can you **email me the report** sometime today, please?*
*Can you **email the report to me** sometime today, please?*

130 Unit 2 Grammar Reference

1. Do the time phrases show a completed time (a), a time period that includes now (b), or both (ab)?

   a The company's profits rose _____ .
   b The company's profits have been rising _____ .

   1 over the last five years
   2 last year
   3 in 2015
   4 in the past few months
   5 since they found a different distributor
   6 when we did the marketing campaign
   7 for a long time
   8 over the last year

2. Complete the summary with one word in each space.

   Madison Forbes has (1) _____ loved drawing and design, and (2) _____ 2010, she's been turning her designs into a successful business called Fishflops, which produces flip flops with Madison's cute sea characters on them. She came up with the name in 2006—(3) _____ she was just eight years old—and, with the help of her father, (4) _____ up the business, which now sells to clothing stores like Nordstrom as well as to the Association of Zoos and Aquariums (AZA). Over the (5) _____ few years, they have also started producing shoes and T-shirts, and the company has (6) _____ several million dollars in sales—not that Madison has been (7) _____ a life of luxury with the profits; instead, she (8) _____ saved most of the money to pay for college. The company also gives to several charities, and a portion of the AZA sales goes to protect endangered animals.

3. Explain the use of these verb forms from Activity 2.

   1 Madison Forbes has always loved drawing…
   2 She's been turning her designs into a successful business…
   3 She came up with the name…
   4 They have also started producing shoes…
   5 The company has made several million dollars in sales…
   6 Not that Madison has been living a life of luxury…

4. Are the sentences correct (C) or incorrect (I)? Correct the incorrect sentences.

   1 I need to practice giving this presentation before class.
   2 We've almost finished to raise the money we need.
   3 Have you considered to pay someone who can do it?
   4 I'm going to keep to write to them until I get an answer!
   5 He admitted sending thousands of spam emails.
   6 I'd recommend to report it. It doesn't look right.
   7 I tried to get a better deal, but they basically just refused negotiating.
   8 That report needs checking before you send it.

5. Complete the sentences with the correct form of the verbs.

   1 I can't imagine him _____ (post) something like that! It's so out of character.
   2 I accidentally downloaded a virus and it caused the whole system _____ (crash).
   3 Our teacher always forces us _____ (speak) in English in class.
   4 I got some bad feedback on my project. It left me _____ (feel) very upset.
   5 We'd like to remind you _____ (change) your password within the next two weeks.
   6 Websites _____ (play) music while they load is so annoying!
   7 I can still remember begging my parents _____ (buy) me my first Xbox!
   8 They caught him _____ (try) to access the school's online records.
   9 If I could, I'd hire someone _____ (take) my science exam so I didn't have to study for it.
   10 I just can't see them _____ (win). They have too many players injured.

6. Look at each first sentence. Add three words to complete each second sentence so that it has a similar meaning to the first.

   1 My parents didn't let me use social media until I was 16.
   My parents never allowed _____ social media when I was younger.
   2 That video really made me think. Online companies have so much power over us!
   That video really got _____ how much power online companies have!
   3 I warned her about sending her details, but she didn't listen!
   I begged _____ send her personal details, but she didn't listen.
   4 Every time you enter the site, they make you change your password.
   Every time you enter the site, they _____ change your password.
   5 That video is amazing. How could anyone not like it?
   I can't imagine _____ that video! It's so amazing!
   6 Don't let me forget how terrible that site is!
   _____ to use that site again! It's awful!

Unit 2 Grammar Reference 131

UNIT 3   GRAMMAR REFERENCE AND PRACTICE

DETERMINERS

Determiners are words used before nouns. They have two main functions:

- to show which noun is being referred to.
- to show how much / how many of something.

Articles

The indefinite article is used:

- before nouns when they are one of several, when it is not important which one is meant, or when something is mentioned for the first time.
- to say what people or things are / were.

The definite article is used:

- before nouns when it is thought to be clear which thing or things is / are meant.
- before superlative adjectives.
- as part of some fixed expressions.

No article is used:

- before uncountable nouns.
- with plural nouns to talk about things in general.
- after prepositions in many expressions with places.
- before the names of most cities, countries, continents, street names, airports, or stations.

Quantifiers

Quantifiers are determiners that show *how much* or *how many* of something. Some can only be used with uncountable nouns or plural countable nouns.

Both is used to talk about two people and / or things.

Either and *neither* are followed by singular countable nouns. They are used before a noun to talk about two choices or possibilities. *Neither* is a negative, so it is not used with *no* or *not*.

Every and *each* are used only with singular countable nouns. Sometimes it is not important which word is used, but generally:

- *each* is used to focus on individual things in a group, or to list two or more things.
- *every* is used to talk about a group or to list three or more things.
- *all* is used to talk about the whole of something. *All* is followed by uncountable or plural nouns.
- *any* is used in positive sentences when it is not important to specify the exact person or thing, because what is being said applies to everyone or everything.
- when quantifiers are used with pronouns, *of* is added after the quantifier.

COMPARATIVES AND SUPERLATIVES

Comparatives and superlatives can be made with adjectives, adverbs, or nouns.

To emphasize that something is "less than," the comparative form *…not as X as…* is often used.

*Their training was **not as hard as** it is now.*

Size differences can be shown by modifying the comparative with a number or measurement, or a modifier.

*On average, shot putters are now **two and a half inches taller** and **130 pounds heavier** than they were in the past.*

***Over a thousand more people** have run sub-four-minute miles since Bannister did it.*

Big difference	much / a lot / a great deal / far	better more efficient
Small difference	a little / slightly	

We can also add modifiers to "not as" comparatives.
   not nearly as fast   not nearly as many
   not quite as good   not quite as much

Remember, *many* and *few* go with countable nouns, and *much* and *little* go with uncountable nouns.

The pattern *the more… , the more…* can be used to show how two or more changes happen together or affect each other.

Comparative	Clause remainder	Comparative	Clause remainder
The longer and thinner	*your legs are,*	*the more energy-efficient*	*they are to swing.*

Look at the box to see how situations now are compared with the past.

Athletes are training harder and more intelligently than	*they used to do.* *before.* *in the past.* *they did before.*
Elite shot-putters now are two and a half inches taller than	*they were in the past.* *they used to be.* *40 years ago.*

132 Unit 3 Grammar Reference

1 Choose the correct option.

1. Mia Hamm started playing soccer when she was living in *the Italy / Italy*. Later, when she was in *the junior high school / junior high school*, she played on *the boys' team / boys' team*.
2. Hamm has done a lot to promote *a women's / the women's / women's* soccer.
3. To tell you *the truth / truth / a truth*, I'm not really interested in *motorcycles / the motorcycles*, but I admire Valentino Rossi. He has *charm / a charm / the charm* and *a lovely personality / lovely personality / the lovely personality*.
4. Jesse Owens was born in *the Alabama / Alabama* in 1913. He was *the youngest / youngest / a youngest* of ten children, and his father was *farmer / the farmer / a farmer*.
5. As *the teenager / teenager / a teenager*, Owens helped his family by delivering *the groceries / groceries* and working in *a shoe repair shop / shoe repair shop / the shoe repair shop*.
6. Susi Susanti now runs *company / the company / a company* selling *the badminton rackets / badminton rackets*. She imports *a material / the material* for *rackets / the rackets* from Japan, and they're then produced in China.

2 Choose the correct option. In some cases, both may be correct.

1. There's *not much / only a few* difference between the two teams.
2. I have *almost no / hardly* interest in sports, to be honest.
3. *Very few / Not many* talented young athletes actually become successful.
4. I've never really had *no / any* talent for sports.
5. I don't have *very much / very little* respect for most soccer players.
6. *A lot of / Most* medals we win at the Olympics are in long-distance running.
7. When the World Cup is on, I usually try to watch *all / every* game.
8. I couldn't see much because there were *a lot of / so many* people in front of me.

3 Complete the sentences with these determiners.

| all | any | both | each |
| either | every | neither | no |

1. I like the fact that you can play the game anywhere. _____ special equipment is needed.
2. Mia Hamm was named FIFA's World Player of the Year in _____ 2001 and 2002.
3. _____ his school nor his family had the money to send Jesse Owens to the 1932 Olympics.
4. My brother can name _____ player who's played for the team in the last ten years!
5. I admire _____ athlete who works hard and has a good attitude.
6. It's a very close game. _____ team could win, but I still think Brazil looks stronger.
7. _____ my friends are really into boxing, but I can't stand it!
8. There's a website that shows you how much _____ player earns.

4 Complete each second sentence so that it has a similar meaning to the first sentence, using the word in bold and two or three extra words.

1. This season they have scored 65 goals and we've only scored 30.
   This season they've scored _____ we have. **far**
2. Usain Bolt actually ran only slightly faster than Jesse Owens.
   Jesse Owens _____ as Usain Bolt. **fast**
3. I used to play basketball a lot, but I hardly ever play now.
   I don't play basketball _____ I used to. **much**
4. No one has ever won as many gold medals in swimming for her country as she has.
   She is our _____ ever. **successful**
5. If you continue to play, your injury will only get worse.
   The _____ worse your injury will get. **longer**
6. The number of professional athletes has increased dramatically.
   There _____ athletes in the past. **far**

5 Complete the comparatives using your own ideas.

1. I'm slightly _____ than _____ .
2. I'm nowhere near _____ .
3. Young people these days are far more _____ .
4. There _____ as _____ as there _____ in the past.
5. I _____ than I used to.
6. _____ , the more successful you will be.

UNIT 4 GRAMMAR REFERENCE AND PRACTICE

FUTURE FORMS 1

Be going to + verb is usually used to talk about what has already been planned. Unless an adverb like *probably* is used, it means it is a definite plan.

They'**re going to** build a new museum in our town.
I**'m going to** stay in tonight and study.

The present continuous is also often used, particularly with plans and arrangements involving other people.

I'**m meeting** a friend of mine later.

Sometimes *will* is used to talk about scheduled plans.

The coach **will arrive** at nine and **will take** everyone to the museum, where the tour **will start** at ten.

Will + infinitive is usually used at the moment of making a decision.

A: What's your flight number?
B: I don't know. I'**ll check** later and I'**ll send** you a text with it.

Will is usually used to make promises, threats, refusals, etc. (see Unit 6).

Will or *be going to* can be used to talk about predictions. Unless an adverb like *probably* or *possibly*, or an introductory verb such as *think* or *guess* is used, they both mean the speaker is certain about their prediction. *May / might* can also be used to show less certainty.

Certain	Less certain
It'**s going to create** jobs.	It'**s possibly going to create** jobs.
It'**s going to be** a disaster.	It'**s probably going to be** a disaster.
They'**ll go** over budget.	They'**ll probably go** over budget. / I think they'**ll go** over budget.
They **won't get** many visitors.	They **might not get** many visitors.

The future continuous is used to emphasize that an action is ongoing / unfinished in relation to a particular point in time or a second future action. The future continuous is *will be + -ing.* (*Be going to be + -ing* is also used.)

It's going to create jobs, and they'**ll be employing** local artists.

When a future time clause is used, the verb is in the simple present or present perfect.

But what about once it'**s been completed**?

Be about to is sometimes used to talk about a plan, arrangement, or prediction concerning what is going to happen in the immediate future. *Just* is sometimes added to emphasize it is the next thing planned.

We'**re about to** hold a community festival.
He'**s just about to** leave, but if you rush you might catch him before he does.

FUTURE FORMS 2

The future in the past

When the future is talked about as seen from a time in the past, *was / were going to*, *would* as the past tense of *will*, and the past continuous can all be used.

My son was struggling, and I was worried he **was going to** drop out of school and maybe end up hanging out with the wrong kids.

He went several steps further and promised those 11 students that he **would** turn the orchestra into a world leader!

Abreu had managed to get 50 music stands for the 100 children he **was expecting** to come and rehearse.

Future perfect

The future perfect is formed using *will / won't* + *have* + past participle.

Soon, over 10 million people **will have seen** it.

The future perfect emphasizes actions completed by a certain time.

I'll call you after six. I'**ll have finished** work by then. (= already finished before six)

The future perfect continuous is formed using *will / won't* + *have been* + *-ing*.

It'**ll** soon **have been running** for 70 years.

The future perfect continuous emphasizes an ongoing action that is taking place in the present and will continue up until a point in the future.

By the end of this course, I **will have been studying** English for ten whole years!

The future perfect is usually accompanied by a time reference such as *before the weekend*, *by Thursday*, etc.

1 Complete the sentences using the two future forms in bold and the verbs in parentheses. Decide which form is the best for each space.

present continuous / *be going to*
The festival _____ (be) great because some of my favorite bands _____ (play).
The festival *is going to be* great because some of my favorite bands *are playing*.

1 simple present / *will*
   What do you think you _____ (do) after you _____ (leave) school?
2 simple present / future continuous
   Let's hope that when we _____ (have) the concert outside, it _____ (not / rain).
3 present perfect / *going to*
   They _____ (start) the project once they _____ (raise) enough money.
4 present continuous / present perfect
   We _____ (go) on a school trip to Hong Kong after we _____ (finish) all our exams.
5 *will* / future continuous
   I _____ (not do) much this weekend, so I _____ (show) you around the city, if you want.
6 present perfect / *be about to* / *will*
   I'm sorry, the movie _____ (start). I _____ (call) you when it _____ (finish).

2 Complete the second sentences using 3–5 words—including the words in bold—so that they have the same meaning as the first sentences.

I'll come over to your house after I have finished my homework. **am**

I'll come over to your house, but *I am going to finish* my homework first.

1 The tickets are going to sell out immediately. **soon**
   The tickets will sell out almost _____ gone on sale.
2 First they're going to repair the houses, and then they'll paint them. **before**
   They're going to repair the houses _____ them.
3 They need to raise a lot of money so they can complete the project. **to**
   If _____ the project, they have to raise a lot of money.
4 I don't think that the project will be a failure. **should**
   The project _____ .
5 I could meet you when I go shopping in town on Saturday. **be**
   I _____ in town on Saturday, so I could meet you then.

3 Complete the summary with these words.

expected   going   than   wasn't   were   would

In many ways, Sheffield and Bilbao are similar. By the 1990s, both were post-industrial cities wondering how they were (1) _____ to cope in the coming years. Like the Guggenheim, the National Centre for Popular Music was (2) _____ to be a landmark building that (3) _____ boost tourism in the city. Bosses at the Centre (4) _____ hoping for 400,000 visitors a year, but numbers were far lower (5) _____ expected, with only around 140,000 showing up in the first 12 months. People soon realized that the center on its own (6) _____ going to be enough to transform the city, and it closed down before even reaching its second birthday.

4 Complete the second sentences using the words in parentheses and 1–3 additional words.

1 I had high hopes for it, but it was actually sort of a letdown.
   It wasn't as good as _____ (thought) be.
2 I had high expectations, but it totally exceeded them.
   It was even better than _____ (expecting) to be.
3 They ended up with three million visitors—far more than initially expected.
   They _____ (hoping) to get around a million visitors, but ended up with three times that!
4 I'd planned to go out and meet some friends, but in the end I was too tired.
   I _____ (going) to go out and meet some friends, but in the end I was too tired.
5 I hadn't planned to return yet, but I ran out of money.
   I _____ (stay) longer, but I ran out of money.

5 Choose the correct option.

1 Hurry up! The movie will *start* / *have started* by the time we get there, if we don't get moving!
2 *I'm going* / *I will have gone* to a concert tomorrow night, so can we meet on Friday instead?
3 *I'm helping* / *I'll have helped* a friend with something tomorrow, but *I'll have finished* / *I'm finishing* by five, so I'll call you then.
4 *I'll have been living* / *I'm going to live* here for the last five years in July.
5 I read somewhere that by the time you're 60, you will have *been sleeping* / *slept* for twenty years!

Unit 4 Grammar Reference 135

UNIT 5 GRAMMAR REFERENCE AND PRACTICE

PASSIVES 1

The passive is used to focus on who or what an action affects. The passive is also used when it is unclear or unimportant who performs an action. The passive is formed using *be* + a past participle.

Simple present

The cup **is** then **left** far away from your bed.
The machines **are exported** all over the world.

Present continuous

If your phone **is being** charged…
The wrong questions **are being** asked.

Present perfect

I **have** just **been sent** an email by Maxine.
It **has been designed** to track your sleep patterns.

Simple past

I **was** recently **given** this lovely new smartphone.
We **were** only **told** about it at the last minute.

Past continuous

There was a power outage while the experiment **was being carried out**.
They **weren't being produced** in Mexico, so I saw an opportunity.

Past perfect

I wanted to produce them, but a patent **had** already **been taken out**.

After modals

You'**ll be forced** to get up.
It **would be thrown** around all over the place.

After prepositions

I'm scared of **being asked** questions I can't answer.

Some verbs have two objects: the <u>direct object</u> and an **indirect object**.

My parents gave **me** <u>a great new smartphone</u>.
Maxine sent **me** <u>an email</u>.

A passive sentence can be made in two ways when there are two objects.

I was recently given <u>this great new smartphone</u>.
<u>A new smartphone</u> was given **to me**.
I have just been sent <u>an email</u> by Maxine.
<u>An email</u> has just been sent **to me** by Maxine.

PASSIVES 2

Passive reporting verbs

A passive structure is often used to report general knowledge, beliefs, and assumptions. There are two common patterns after the passive.

The brain	is thought	to have over 12,000 miles of blood vessels.
	was believed	to be controlled by four different elements or "humors."
	is estimated	to weigh six and a half pounds.
	is known	to recover from serious damage.
It	is thought	(that) the brain works like a watch.
	is claimed	(that) the brain is like a computer.
	is assumed	(that) people know what they are doing.
	is well known	(that) smoking causes cancer.

In the second pattern, *it* is impersonal. It is there because in English sentences with a verb need a subject.

Causative *have* and *get*

Have / *get* + something + past participle is a passive construction, similar in meaning to the sentences in **b**. However, with this structure the person or thing that causes the action or is affected by the action can be brought in (*I* and *My brother* in the sentences in **c**). This structure is used to show that someone else does something for or to the subject.

a Someone stole my bag. The hairstylist dyed my brother's hair.
b My bag was stolen. My brother's hair was dyed.
c I **had** my bag stolen. My brother **got** his hair dyed.

Causative *get* is usually:

- less formal and uncommon in writing.
- used when the subject is the cause of the action. (My brother paid the hairdresser to dye his hair.)

1 Complete the sentences with the correct active or passive form of the verbs in parentheses.

1. Language (1) _____ obviously _____ (exist) for many thousands of years before writing (2) _____ (invent), but the existence of written records really (3) _____ (mark) the beginning of history as we know it. The earliest writing (4) _____ (find) in part of what (5) _____ now _____ (call) Iraq.

2. The printing press (1) _____ often _____ (call) one of the most important inventions of all time. Of course, books (2) _____ (produce) before Johannes Gutenberg (3) _____ (present) his first creation to the world, but always by hand! Before too long, thousands of books (4) _____ (print) and (5) _____ (distribute) all over Europe.

3. If you're worried about your phone (1) _____ (steal), here's a helpful hack. A special app can (2) _____ (install) so that you can (3) _____ (track) the phone if it's lost or stolen. You'll also be able to see if the phone (4) _____ (use). It can even (5) _____ (wipe) clean remotely, to stop criminals from (6) _____ (get) hold of your data.

4. The first self-driving car only (1) _____ (hit) the road very recently, but it's quite possible that cars as we know them will soon (2) _____ (replace) by this new model. Over recent years, much of the research into these cars (3) _____ (fund) by Elon Musk, a TED speaker who (4) _____ (start) lots of different companies. Thousands of self-driving cars (5) _____ already _____ (build)—and they (6) _____ (get) more sophisticated.

2 Complete each sentence by making these verbs with two objects into the passive.

---
award Ahmed Zewail the Nobel prize in Chemistry
give me it
give us some tricky questions
~~show the queen one of the first telephones~~
teach us how to do it
---

1. In January 1878, one of the first telephones _was shown to the queen_ by its inventor, Alexander Graham Bell.
2. In 1999, the Nobel prize in Chemistry _____ , who was the first Egyptian to receive the prize.
3. The science test was sort of a nightmare because we _____ !
4. I can type very fast because we _____ in elementary school.
5. I had my watch stolen, and I was really upset because it _____ by my grandparents.

3 Complete each pair of sentences using the word in bold. One sentence should be in the active form and the other should be in the passive form.

1. **accept**
   a. It _____ now that increases in global temperatures are due to human activity.
   b. Most scientists _____ that we need to take action to reduce global warming.
2. **not know**
   a. We _____ exactly how many stars there are in the solar system.
   b. It _____ exactly how stars were first formed.
3. **think**
   a. Some researchers _____ that it could be possible to live on Mars.
   b. Mars _____ to have water under its surface.
4. **believe**
   a. In the past, many diseases _____ to be caused by having too much blood in the body.
   b. Doctors in the past _____ that they could cure diseases by removing blood from the body.

4 Complete the short report with one word in each space.

The government is (1) _____ air quality tested because high levels of pollution (2) _____ thought to (3) _____ increasing. The government is also having research (4) _____ in schools to try to find out whether air pollution is having any effect on students' performance. Air pollution is known (5) _____ affect health and is estimated to (6) _____ thousands of deaths each year. (7) _____ is also claimed (8) _____ it affects the development of the brain and young people's intelligence, but more research is needed to determine if there is a clear link.

UNIT 6 GRAMMAR REFERENCE AND PRACTICE

MODALS AND MEANING

Modals never change their form. They go with normal verbs and are followed by the infinitive without *to* form of those verbs. Modals add meaning to verbs. A phrase or normal verb can sometimes be used instead of a modal.

Will/would

Will is used to express that something is certain or sure to happen, and to express promises, offers, habits, and refusals.

*The first thing that **will** strike people…*

Would is used to express that something is theoretically certain to happen, to report as the past form of *will*, and to express a habit in the past.

*If the habitat disappeared, they**'d** die out.*

Should/shall

Should is used to express a good or better idea, or if something is expected to happen in the future.

***Should** we be trying to conserve these species?*

Shall is used to ask for and give suggestions, or to make offers about a current or future situation.

*What **shall** we do about it?*

Can/could

Can expresses ability and permission. It is also used if something is only possible sometimes and factually possible (or not, in the negative).

*They **can** be difficult to see in the wild.*

Could is used to express past ability / inability, if something happened sometimes, or is theoretically possible. *Could* is also used in polite requests.

*I **couldn't** swim until I was in my twenties.*

may/might/must

Might is used if something is uncertain but possible.

*You **might** stop weak species from going extinct.*

May is also used if something is uncertain but possible, and for permission.

*These changes **may** bring benefits.*

Must is used if something is necessary and if the speaker is sure of something based on experience.

*These changes **must** bring benefits.*

Have can sometimes behave as a modal.

*You **have** to go to school.*

MODALS AND INFINITIVE FORMS

Modals can be followed by different kinds of infinitive forms.

To talk about actions generally, use a modal + the infinitive without *to* form.

*As you **can see**, it does look quite professional.*

To talk about actions in progress or extended over time, use a modal + *be* + *-ing* (the continuous infinitive without *to*).

*We **should be doing** more to protect them.*

To talk about the past in general, use a modal + *have* + past participle (the perfect infinitive without *to*).

*You **could have (could've) told** me how cruel it was and I honestly **wouldn't have cared**.*

To emphasize that an action was in progress when another thing happened, use a modal + *have been* + *-ing* (the perfect continuous infinitive without *to*).

*I **can't have been paying** attention when I read about it.*

Modals can also be used with passive forms.

*More **should be done** to reduce the suffering of animals.* (= generally)

*I got really sick after eating that meat. It **can't have been** cooked properly.* (= in the past)

1 Choose the correct option.

Juliana Machado Ferreira is a conservation biologist who is trying to stop illegal wildlife trade in Brazil. People in Brazil (1) *will / shall* often keep wild birds as pets, but Machado says they (2) *shouldn't / couldn't*. Taking animals from nature (3) *can / should* have a terrible impact on the habitat and other animals there. For example, if a large proportion of the wild birds that are captured are female, this (4) *might / will* inevitably reduce future populations. The birds (5) *may / would* also be predators for other animals or consume particular plants, so a reduction in the bird numbers (6) *can / can't* have an impact on the rest of the ecosytem. She believes the public (7) *must / might* be educated about these effects. In the past, she has worked with the police to help return birds to their original habitat. The problem is that they (8) *could / shall* be from any number of different places, so Machado used a genetic test to determine where the birds (9) *might / will* be from. She developed her ideas at the US Fish and Wildlife Service Forensics Laboratory. She got an internship there because she (10) *would / could* write regularly to them asking if she (11) *would / could* become a volunteer until eventually they said yes! And now Juliana shows the same determination in her work. She has a very varied work life but, in the next few years, she (12) *may / can* spend more time in her home office. She also says that if she (13) *can / could* talk to her younger self, she (14) *would / should* tell herself to learn something about finance and marketing. This is because she is now in a management position, and students aren't taught how to deal with money in biology classes.

2 Choose the best self-follow-up comment to each question.

1 Would I ever do it?
   a Only if I had no other option.
   b Of course I can.
2 Shall I do it for you?
   a I still haven't decided.
   b It's no trouble.
3 Must I do it?
   a It'll be fun.
   b Can't someone else?
4 Should I really do it?
   a There's no other option.
   b I'm not sure it'll improve things.
5 Will I do it at some point?
   a I still haven't decided.
   b I don't mind if you don't want to.
6 Can I do it?
   a I'd really like to try.
   b I might not.

3 Choose the correct option.

1 New research has shown that there *can't / might* once have been a creature similar to a unicorn.
2 I can't believe how little he ate. He *can't be feeling / can't have been feeling* very hungry.
3 I can't believe you thought that story was true. You *should / must* have checked it on some other sites!
4 I'm not surprised his parents were angry. He *shouldn't have had / shouldn't have been having* snakes without telling them!
5 Surely there *would / will* have been more in the papers about the tree octopus if it were true.
6 I'm guessing that you *might / should* have heard about the tree octopus, right?
7 We promise that any cat you buy from us *will have been being / will have been* thoroughly checked by a vet.
8 You *shouldn't have scared / shouldn't scare* the dog. He *wouldn't / couldn't* have barked at you otherwise.

4 Complete the rewrite for each sentence. Use the best modal and two or three other words in each space.

1 It's just not possible for the Loch Ness monster to have survived that long without being found.
   The Loch Ness monster _____ that long without being found. It's impossible.
2 It's possible that Loch Ness was once connected to the ocean.
   Loch Ness _____ connected to the ocean.
3 I can't believe I didn't realize the movie was a fake. I'm so stupid. I really _____ the movie was a fake.
4 If there really was a monster, why aren't there more photos of it?
   People _____ more photos of the monster if it really existed!
5 It's impossible to get near the loch now without being filmed by security cameras.
   By the time you get to the edge of the loch, you _____ by security cameras.
6 There's no way he was telling the truth about what he saw.
   If you ask me, he _____ about what he saw.
7 Loch Ness is only 10,000 years old. Plesiosaurs died out 60 million years ago.
   Loch Ness _____ around when plesiosaurs still existed.
8 I swear I saw something. Honestly, if only I'd had my camera with me!
   I _____ my camera with me. I _____ what I saw if I'd had it.

UNIT 7   GRAMMAR REFERENCE AND PRACTICE

FIRST, SECOND, THIRD, AND MIXED CONDITIONALS

First conditional

First conditionals describe possible results of real situations now or in the future.

If you're in school today, *you'll* probably start working sometime in the 2020s.

I'm going to take the test again *if I fail*.

Second conditional

Second conditionals describe imaginary situations and results now or in the future.

If these drawings **were painted** more realistically, they **would look** amazing.

I wouldn't joke about it *if I were you*.

Third conditional

Third conditionals describe imaginary situations and results in the past.

If she'd wanted pictures, *she'd have told* us.

If he hadn't spent that day with his niece, the Monster Engine **would never have happened**.

Mixed conditional

Mixed conditionals describe imaginary past situations and imaginary present results.

If their schools had encouraged unusual ways of seeing the world, lots of adults **would be** more creative.

I wouldn't be here now *if she hadn't helped* me.

Other modals can also be used in the result clauses of conditional sentences.

If I do OK on my exams, I **might / may try** *to study fine art in college.*
= Maybe I will study fine art.

If I get really good grades, I **can go** *and study abroad.*
= It will be possible for me to study abroad.

If he had been a little taller, he **could have become** *a really great basketball player.*
= It would have been possible for him to become a great player.

WISH, IF ONLY, WOULD RATHER

Wish, *if only*, and *would rather* all introduce hypothetical ideas—things that a speaker wants to be true, but sees as impossible. As with conditional sentences, past forms of verbs are used to talk about hypothetical events.

The simple past, the past continuous, *could*, and *would* are used to hypothesize about present situations.

The simple past is used when hypothesizing about general situations or states.

I wish I **was** *better with words.*

I wish I **was** *as creative as her / him.*

I wish I **didn't have** *to take art classes.*

If only I **had** *an extra eye in the back of my head!*

I'd rather the teacher **didn't give** *homework.*

The past continuous is used to hypothesize about an action or specific situation happening now.

If only I **wasn't sitting** *here now!*

I wish I **was doing** *something else. This is boring.*

Could is used to hypothesize about an ability we want.

I wish I **could draw** *better.*

I wish I **could help** *you, but I just can't.*

Would is used to hypothesize about a habit or behavior we want to stop (or start).

I sometimes wish my classmates **wouldn't make** *so much noise.*

I wish she **would speak** *slower. I can't understand anything she says.*

The past perfect is used to hypothesize about the past and express regrets.

I wish my parents **hadn't forced** *me to learn an instrument.*

*I often say to myself, "If only I'**d spent** more time thinking about this before I started."*

Note that, where the subject of *would rather* is the same as the verb that follows it, an infinitive without *to* is used.

I'd rather **you did** *it.*

I'd rather **do it** *myself.*

1 Choose the correct option.

1 If you *will want / want* to study abroad, you'll need to save some money first.
2 I wouldn't play this instrument well if my dad *hadn't helped / doesn't help* me when I first started.
3 If I *would have / had* more time, I'd love to learn how to paint with watercolors.
4 It's your fault! If you hadn't been late, everything *would've been / was* fine.
5 The test's next week and you *don't / are not going to* do well if you don't work more!
6 If we hadn't changed things when we did, the situation *would / will* be worse now.
7 It might not have worked if we *tried / had tried* it that way.
8 If I spoke to my mother like that, she really *won't / wouldn't* be happy!

2 Complete the sentences with the correct form of the verbs in parentheses.

1 If I _____ (not ask) lots of questions when I was at school, I wouldn't be a scientist now.
2 If you _____ (create) a culture that encourages creativity, people will be happier.
3 I don't think I _____ (start) painting if my parents hadn't encouraged me.
4 If I _____ (be) fluent in English, life would be so much easier!
5 Just think! Things _____ (be) very different today if ways of writing hadn't developed.
6 If you don't practice, you _____ (never get) better at it.
7 I _____ (not do) that if I was you.
8 If it _____ (not be) so noisy in the exam room, I would've done better.

3 Make conditional sentences based on the information below.

1 They only realized how talented she was after giving all the children tests to assess creativity levels.

   They wouldn't have realized how talented she was if they hadn't given all the children tests to assess creativity levels.

2 Follow the rules or fail the course. It's your choice!
3 I can't really play this. I haven't practiced recently.
4 Some colleges don't value creativity. That's why they don't really help students develop it.
5 She didn't obey the rules when she started her business. That's why she's successful today.
6 Creativity in children is like anything else: encourage it or be prepared for it not to grow.

4 Choose the correct options.

1 A This is taking too long to do.
   B Yeah, sorry. I thought it was a good idea at the time, but I wish I *hadn't suggested / didn't suggest* it now.
2 A Shall I ask my mom or dad if they can take us there?
   B I'd rather we *go / went* on our own.
3 A I'd like to study abroad somewhere.
   B Me too. If only I *can / could* speak Chinese! I'd love to go to Shanghai.
4 A I wish the teacher *would / wouldn't* make us copy everything from the book.
   B I know. It's a little boring, isn't it?
5 A Did you go to the gig yesterday?
   B No, but I wish I *had / did*. I heard it was great.
6 A If only I *didn't have to / wouldn't have to* leave. I'd love to talk more.
   B Don't worry. I need to be home before 12, anyway.

5 Complete each second sentence so that it has a similar meaning to the first sentence, using the word given and three extra words.

1 I'm afraid we can't do anything more to help. **only**
   If _____ more to help.
2 My brother is so negative. It's really annoying. **would**
   I wish my brother _____ about things.
3 I wanted to walk here, but we took the car. **rather**
   I _____ the car at home.
4 We should have done a better analysis of the problem. **wish**
   I _____ the problem better.

6 Complete each sentence with one word. Contractions count as one word.

1 A Is it OK if I put some music on?
   B I'd rather you _____ . I'm trying to study.
2 A Do you want to go to the mall?
   B I'd rather _____ somewhere else. I don't like the stores there.
3 A I wish we _____ asked someone to help us.
   B Really? I'd rather _____ to do it myself first, even if I make a mistake.
4 A I'd rather you _____ this a secret between us. It's a bit embarrassing.
   B Don't worry. I'd rather _____ knew what happened! If _____ I could forget it myself!

GRAMMAR REFERENCE AND PRACTICE

REPORTED SPEECH

When an anecdote or story is told, what people said is often reported. This can be done with:

- direct speech.

*She said, "I **love** you," and then he said, "**Will** you marry me?"*

- indirect speech.

*She said she **loved** him, and he then asked (her) if she'**d** marry him.*

- a mixture of the two.

*She said, "I **love** you," and then he asked if she'**d** marry him.*

When reporting with indirect speech, follow the normal rules of tenses within a story. This often involves a tense backshift from direct speech. Look at the direct and indirect speech used to report statements about:

- a situation or action at the time it was said / thought.

I said, "I need to go back to school."
*I said I **needed** to go back to school.*

- an action in progress at the time it was said.

She said, "I'm going to the station."
*She said she **was going** to the station.*

- an action further back in time before it was said.

He said, "I've forgotten my money."
*He told me **he'd forgotten** his money.*

- a plan or prediction for the future at the time it was said.

I asked and they said, "We'll try!"
*They said they **would** try.*

When the statement being reported is still true, present and other tenses can be used, as they apply to now.

*Miriam told me to tell you she'**ll be** late.*
= She's not here yet, so she still will be late.
*He told me he'**s never had** tea.*
= As far as I know, he still hasn't had tea.

When correcting a misunderstanding, the backshift is preferred because the misunderstanding is no longer true, but it is not essential.

A: We are meeting at 10.
B: I thought we **were** meeting at 11.

In indirect reporting of questions the normal word order of a statement is used.

*I said, "**What are you doing** here?"*
*I asked her **what she was doing** there.*
*I thought, "**Why did you ask** that?"*
*I wondered **why she'd asked** me that.*
*She said, "**Do you need** any help?"*
*She asked **if I needed** any help.*

Remember that when what was said is reported, different words must be used for times or places if what is being reported has finished, is no longer true, and / or was in a different place.

*They said, "Can we wait until **tomorrow**?"*
*They asked if they could wait until **the next day**.*
*He said, "I talked to her **yesterday**."*
*He said he'd talked to you **the day before**.*
*I told them, "I was here **last Tuesday**!"*
*I told them I'd been there **the previous Tuesday**.*

Other useful time phrases for reporting:

today	that day
now / immediately	at that moment / right away
tomorrow	the next day
next week	the next week / the following week
last week	the week before / the previous week

PATTERNS AFTER REPORTING VERBS

Notice the patterns that often go with particular verbs.

verb + infinitive (with *to*): agree; arrange; claim; decide; intend; offer; pretend; promise; refuse; threaten

verb + *-ing*: admit; avoid; consider; continue; deny; imagine; resent; recommend; suggest

verb + (*that*) clause: acknowledge; announce; argue; claim; confess; declare; deny; insist; recommend; state

verb + someone + (*that*) clause: assure; convince; notify; persuade; promise; remind; tell; warn

verb + someone + infinitive (with *to*): advise; ask; encourage; force; invite; persuade; remind; tell; urge; warn

verb + preposition + *-ing*: accuse somebody of; admit / confess to; apologize for; blame somebody for; criticize somebody for; forgive somebody for; insist on; thank somebody for

1 Choose the correct option.

A few years ago, a Chinese friend of my parents asked if I (1) *want / wanted* to visit (2) *the following summer / this summer* to spend time with their daughter, who was my age. It was a great opportunity, so I agreed to go. I had to fill out a long visa application. My father and I took it to the Chinese embassy, and they told us to come back (3) *next week / the next week* to pick up the visa. When we went back, there was a long line for some reason. My dad explained to the security people that we had been (4) *here / there* (5) *the previous week / last week* and we were just picking up a visa, but he was told that we (6) *have to / had to* line up like everyone else. So we stood there and started chatting with the man in front of us. He asked my dad where (7) *I was / was I* going, and it turned out it was the same place where he lived. "What (8) *were / are* you doing there?" he asked. My dad told him I (9) *was going to / will* stay with a friend of his from college. Then the man asked, "What college?" When my dad told him, the man said one of his best friends (10) *had been / be* at the same college a few years before. He said his friend's name, and it was actually my dad's friend, too! It was an amazing coincidence!

2 Complete the story with the verbs in parentheses and the correct modals, verb forms, or tenses.

Yesterday, I was trying to get to sleep when I heard my dog barking. I got up and my dog was there with some paper in his mouth. I told him (1) _____ (let) it go. I pulled, and the piece of paper tore. I suddenly realized it was my math homework and asked my mom (2) _____ (come) and take a look. When she saw what had happened, she just laughed. I said it (3) _____ (be not) funny and I (4) _____ (have to) do it all over again, but my mom said it (5) _____ (be) too late. She promised she (6) _____ (write) a note to the teacher in the morning and said I (7) _____ (not worry). However, the next morning my mom got a call from work before I got up. They told her someone (8) _____ (call) in sick and asked her if she (9) _____ (go) in early. She completely forgot about the note. So of course, in my math class, when the teacher asked why I (10) _____ (not do) my homework and I explained, he didn't believe me! His exact words were, "Do you (11) _____ (think) I was born yesterday?" But I swear that (12) _____ (be) exactly what happened!

3 Complete the second sentences so they have a similar meaning to the first. Use two to five words, including the correct form of the verb in bold.

1 My mom said I should write to the TV company and complain about it.
My mom *suggested writing* to the TV company to tell them how I felt. **suggest**

2 They said that they'd meet me to explain their decision.
After I complained, they _____ me and explain their decision. **agree**

3 I felt terrible for what I said, so I wrote to say sorry.
I wrote them a letter _____ for such awful things. **apologize**

4 Of course, they reject all accusations and claim that they're in the right.
Naturally, they _____ anything wrong. **deny**

5 The goal of the rule was prevention of discrimination.
The rule _____ discrimination. **intend**

6 There has been a lot of pressure on the school to change its dress code.
The school _____ its dress code. **urge**

7 He knew what the rules were, but he decided to ignore them!
He basically just _____ the rules! **refuse**

8 They have an employment policy that prioritizes total gender equality.
The school _____ an equal number of male and female teachers. **insist**

4 Which two options are possible in each sentence?

1 My parents *advised / recommended / urged* my sister to complain to her boss about it.
2 He's been *blamed / accused / criticized* for not employing enough staff from minority backgrounds.
3 We've been trying to *tell / warn / state* them that there will be problems if things don't change!
4 I read online that she'd *admitted / apologized / denied* sending racist emails.
5 They've *avoided / promised / refused* to tackle the problem.
6 He was *arguing / telling / insisting* that nothing will change unless people take direct action.

5 Rewrite each sentence in Activity 4 using one of the verbs with a different verb pattern.

1 *My parents **recommended** that my sister complain to her boss about it.*

Unit 8 Grammar Reference

UNIT 9 GRAMMAR REFERENCE AND PRACTICE

RELATIVE CLAUSES

Relative clauses add information after nouns. Different relative pronouns are used depending on the nouns being qualified or on the information that follows.

Defining and non-defining clauses

Some relative clauses explain exactly what the thing or person is (defining), and some just add extra information that may be of interest (non-defining).

With defining relative clauses:
- commas are not used.
- the relative pronoun can be left out when it is the object of the relative clause.

The devastation (which) it caused was simply staggering!

With non-defining relative clauses:
- the clause is separated from the rest of the sentence by commas.
- *that* isn't used as a relative pronoun.
- the relative pronoun is never left out.

The country, which has long been one of the poorest in the world, descended into chaos.

A relative clause can start with a preposition + *which / whom*. However, this is rather formal in English and the preposition is usually placed at the end of the clause.

Where or *when* can also replace a preposition + *which*.

*Crisis mapping brought about change in the place **in which / where** I was born.*

PARTICIPLE CLAUSES

A relative clause is often reduced by using a participle construction.

Past participle clauses reduce relative clauses which use a passive verb, whichever tense is used.

*The UN created a fund **called** UNICEF.*
*= The UN created a fund **which was called** UNICEF.*

Present participle clauses reduce relative clauses which use an active verb, whichever tense is used.

*The CRC declares different rights **including** things such as the right to a safe home.*
*= The CRC declares different rights, **which include** things such as the right to a safe home.*

Adding *not* to the participle can make a negative.

*Students **not wearing** the correct uniform will be punished.*

Adverbial participle clauses

Participle clauses add information about the time or reason / method connected to the main clause. The subject of both clauses must be the same.

***Having campaigned** on behalf of young people, UNICEF also had a key part in the creation of the UN's Convention on the Rights of the Child (CRC) in 1989.*
*= **After UNICEF had campaigned** on behalf of young people, UNICEF also had a key part in the creation of the UN's Convention on the Rights of the Child (CRC) in 1989.*

***Using** online discussion boards as a "meeting place," **the initiative** provides a space for youngsters who care.*
*= **The initiative uses** online discussion boards as a "meeting place" through which **the initiative** provides a space for youngsters who care.*

***Having seen** the robbery, I had to go to court to give evidence.*
*= **Because I had seen the robbery** I had to go to court to give evidence.*

-ing participles are more common in this kind of clause, but *-ed* participles can also be used with passives.

***Faced** with a robber in the street, I would give them whatever they wanted.*
= If I was faced with a robber in the street, I would give them whatever they wanted.

The present participle shows that an action happens or happened more or less at the same time as the action in the main clause.

***Working** as a policeman, my dad sees a lot of really scary things.*
= My dad is a policeman and while he's at work, he sees a lot of really scary things.

A perfect participle (*having* + *-ed*) shows that the action happened before the action in the main clause.

***Having just closed** the door, I realized I didn't have my keys.*
= I had just closed the door when I realized I didn't have my keys.

1 Complete the sentences with these relative pronouns.

| none of whom | most of which | that | where |
| which | which is | when | who | whose |

1 One of the first major events to utilize crisis mapping was the 2010 Haiti earthquake, _____ killed and injured hundreds of thousands of people.
2 Technology is particularly relevant in places _____ official government is limited, or no longer fully functions.
3 More than 40 percent of the population now receives some form of international aid, _____ is food assistance.
4 Many local people, _____ lands have been ruined by illegal mining, are now turning to technology to tackle the problem.
5 The plane crashed in thick fog with 87 people on board, _____ is thought to have survived.
6 The volunteers, _____ come from all across the region, quite literally put roads, buildings, and highways onto the map.
7 The amount of data available via social media increased dramatically in October, _____ the flooding reached the capital.
8 Online mapping _____ relies on volunteers with varying skills to interpret satellite images obviously has its limitations.

2 Rewrite the sentences in a more informal manner with the prepositions at the end of the clauses. Leave out the relative pronouns where appropriate.

1 The town in which we were staying narrowly missed being hit by the hurricane.

The town we were staying in narrowly missed being hit by the hurricane.

2 It's an achievement of which we are all very proud.
3 The following day, a second, smaller earthquake hit the town from which the aid was being distributed.
4 As we fled the city, we encountered an elderly man with whom my son insisted we share our food.
5 The roads out of the west of the city, from where many thousands fled, were largely blocked by debris.
6 The experience varies wildly, depending on the charity with which we're working.
7 On her arrival, Ms. Kuti, with whose approach I totally agreed, took control of the situation.
8 The book to which you're referring was the very first on the subject to be published.

3 Rewrite the following sentences using a participle clause.

1 The policeman who dealt with my case was very helpful.
The policeman _____ my case was very helpful.
2 The man who was arrested after the incident last night has not been charged.
Police have not charged the man _____ the incident last night.
3 The number of young people who are not working or in school is rising.
There has been a rise in the number of young people _____ or in school.
4 The number of people who have personally experienced a crime has actually gone down.
The number of people _____ a crime has actually gone down.
5 I think that children who are exposed to lots of violent movies often become violent themselves.
I think that children _____ lots of violent movies often become violent themselves.
6 Anyone that the train strike tomorrow will seriously affect can stay home.
Anyone seriously _____ by the train strike tomorrow can stay at home.

4 Reduce the underlined clauses.

Police are searching for a man (1) <u>who has been accused</u> of attempting to rob a bank in Vienna today. A man wearing a bright red scarf (2) <u>which was wrapped</u> around his face approached a cashier and told her he wanted money. (3) <u>Because she didn't realize</u> that the man was actually demanding money, the clerk simply said that she didn't deal with cash transactions, (4) <u>and at the same time directed</u> him to the next counter. Apparently, (5) <u>because he was put off</u> by the long line at the next counter and the clerk's calm reply, the man dropped the box he was carrying and ran off. (6) <u>After she had seen</u> the man run off, the cashier suddenly realized what had happened. (7) <u>Because they were concerned</u> that the box looked suspicious, the bank called the police and evacuated the building. The package was found to be harmless and the robber pretty useless.

GRAMMAR REFERENCE AND PRACTICE

EXPRESSING PAST ABILITY

Could, be able to, and *managed to* describe ability or inability to do something when talking about specific situations or telling stories.

Could expresses that something was possible in a specific situation. *Couldn't* shows it wasn't possible to do something in a specific situation.

He **couldn't move** his arm because it was trapped by a rock.

Could can also be used with other words related to negatives.

No one could send for help.
All he **could** do was wait.
I was so nervous I **could hardly** say a word.

To talk about a specific ability to do something at a particular time in the past, use *was / were able to* rather than *could*.

She managed to deal with the pain, and in the end, **was able** to turn it into great art.

Negatives can be made with *not able to, unable to,* or *couldn't*.

I wasn't able to / was unable to / couldn't feel or say anything, I was in such shock.

Be able to is also used with other tenses and modals, where *could* is not possible.

At least ~~we've could~~ **we've been able to** agree on one movie.

Could usually describes a general ability in the past while *manage to* emphasizes an ability to do something that was difficult. It isn't usually used to talk about general ideas or senses.

When it rained, he ~~could catch~~ **managed to catch** some water to drink.

Manage to often goes with words and phrases such as *finally / in the end / eventually*.

Manage to can be used in a negative sentence in a similar way to *couldn't*.

I looked for a long time, but I **didn't manage to / couldn't** find it.

Sometimes *succeed in + -ing* is used instead of *manage to*, but *manage to* is far more common.

She **succeeded in making** it as a professional.
= She **managed to make** it as a professional.

EMPHATIC STRUCTURES

Stressing an auxiliary verb like *is* or *have* adds emphasis. When there is no auxiliary verb available to stress, as with verbs in the simple present and simple past, emphasis can be added by putting *do / does / did* before an infinitive.

It **did make** a huge difference to my quality of life, having the implant.

Emphasis is often added in this way to contradict what someone has said, or to contrast two opposing ideas.

While **surgical options did exist before**, none were nearly as effective.

Emphasis can also be added by starting a clause with a negative adverb or phrase (*rarely, not only,* etc.) and then using inversion (changing the order of the subject and verb, as in questions).

We're all used to hearing news about terrible things, but **rarely do we hear** much about exciting new developments.

When Second Sight started experimenting, **little did they know** that they were on their way to revolutionizing the treatment of blindness!

Only after the Second World War **were antibiotics** more widely available to the general public.

Note that inversion is far more common in academic, literary, or journalistic writing, though it is also used in more formal speech or to make stories more dramatic.

1 Complete the article about Aron Ralston with one word in each space.

If the story of Aron Ralston's escape from a canyon was remarkable, what happened next is no less so. Immediately after freeing himself, he still had to return to safety. With only one arm and still bleeding, he (1) _____ to get down a 65-foot cliff and then walk several miles in the burning sun. Luckily, he met a family walking in the valley who (2) _____ able to give him something to eat and drink and then look for help. Then, a helicopter which was out searching for him was (3) _____ to pick him up. This all happened within four hours and saved his life. Following the accident, the park authorities (4) _____ only remove the rock that had trapped Aron's arm by using a machine and several men. While medics were (5) _____ to save Aron's arm, he otherwise made a full recovery and returned to full fitness. Amazingly, since then he's (6) _____ able to do pretty much all the things he did before the accident. He has since rafted down the Grand Canyon, skied down a volcano in Ecuador and, in 2011, (7) _____ in climbing all the mountains in Colorado that are over 14 thousand feet. He also now works as a motivational speaker.

2 Correct the error underlined in each sentence. You may need to change, add, and remove words.

1 I twisted my ankle very badly, but I still <u>manage walk</u> home. It was really painful, though.
 I twisted my ankle very badly, but I still *managed to walk* home. It was really painful, though.
2 Following physical therapy, Janine Shepherd <u>were able walk</u> again with the help of a stick.
3 Doctors have been looking for a cure for motor neuron disease, but they <u>couldn't find</u> one yet.
4 After years of research, scientists believe they have finally <u>succeeded the development</u> a treatment for diabetes which avoids the need to inject insulin.
5 I wish I <u>could meet</u> my grandfather before he died. He sounded like an amazing person.

3 Rewrite the second sentences using the word in bold and the correct form of *could, be able to, manage to,* or *succeed in*.

1 Bethany Hamilton became a world champion surfer despite losing her arm in an accident. **becoming**
 Bethany Hamilton lost her arm in an accident but still _____ a world champion surfer.
2 Luckily, we stopped the bleeding and he was fine. **stop**
 We _____ the bleeding and he was fine.
3 After the accident, it was only because of the surgery that he didn't lose his eyesight. **save**
 He damaged his eye in the accident, but the surgeon _____ his eyesight.
4 She lost most of her hearing after the accident, but she seems to be back to normal now. **hear**
 She's recovered really well, considering she _____ a thing after the accident.

4 Make complete sentences by matching the halves.

1 While they **do** remove the immediate pain,
2 I **do** think that medical research is incredibly important,
3 Don't get me wrong. The operation **did** help,
4 Only after several tests **did they**
5 At no time during my stay in the hospital **did I**
6 Nowhere else in the world **do you**
7 Let's be clear about this. In no way **does this development**
8 We read a lot about medical developments, but rarely **do we**

a think I wouldn't make a complete recovery.
b hear about the psychological advances in managing disease.
c but I don't see why it can't all be privately funded.
d diagnose the problem.
e find so many 100-year-olds as in Okinawa, Japan.
f drugs are not the only solution and can create problems of their own.
g mean the disease has been cured, but it's a step in the right direction.
h just not as much as I was hoping it would.

5 Complete the sentences with these words.

at no time	little	not only
not until	only	rarely

1 What made things even worse was the fact that _____ did doctors ever admit they'd made a mistake.
2 In the days before antibiotics, only very _____ did children survive serious lung infections.
3 _____ after the Second World War did penicillin become widely available.
4 When the doctor first suggested it, _____ did I realize that the treatment was actually centuries old.
5 _____ do we need a massive increase in investment, but we also need to rethink the way we educate the young about physical and mental well-being.
6 _____ in this country do people go bankrupt from trying to pay their medical bills!

INFINITIVE	SIMPLE PAST	PAST PARTICIPLE
arise	arose	arisen
beat	beat	beaten
become	became	become
bend	bent	bent
bet	bet	bet
bite	bit	bitten
blow	blew	blown
break	broke	broken
breed	bred	bred
bring	brought	brought
broadcast	broadcast	broadcast
build	built	built
burn	burned	burned
burst	burst	burst
cost	cost	cost
cut	cut	cut
deal	dealt	dealt
dig	dug	dug
dream	dreamed	dreamed
fall	fell	fallen
feed	fed	fed
fight	fought	fought
flee	fled	fled
forget	forgot	forgotten
forgive	forgave	forgiven
freeze	froze	frozen
grow	grew	grown
hang	hanged/hung	hanged/hung
hide	hid	hidden
hit	hit	hit
hold	held	held
hurt	hurt	hurt
keep	kept	kept
kneel	knelt	knelt
lay	laid	laid
lead	led	led
lend	lent	lent
let	let	let
lie	lay	lain
light	lit	lit
lose	lost	lost
mean	meant	meant

INFINITIVE	SIMPLE PAST	PAST PARTICIPLE
misunderstand	misunderstood	misunderstood
must	had to	had to
overcome	overcame	overcome
rethink	rethought	rethought
ring	rang	rung
rise	rose	risen
sell	sold	sold
set	set	set
shake	shook	shaken
shine	shone/shined	shone/shined
shoot	shot	shot
shrink	shrank	shrunk
shut	shut	shut
sink	sank	sunk
slide	slid	slid
smell	smelled	smelled
spell	spelled	spelled
spend	spent	spent
spill	spilled	spilled
split	split	split
spoil	spoiled	spoiled
spread	spread	spread
stand	stood	stood
steal	stole	stolen
stick	stuck	stuck
strike	struck	struck
swear	swore	sworn
tear	tore	torn
throw	threw	thrown
upset	upset	upset
wake	woke	woken
win	won	won

UNIT 1 A review

When writing reviews, it is common to use relative clauses beginning with *which* in order to express personal comments or beliefs.

1. Wu and Ting Ting were incredibly welcoming and did everything that they could to make me feel at home, although during the stay I was often left to my own devices because they were busy working. I had a lovely big room, my own TV, and a desk to study at. I was a little far from my school, though, which wasn't ideal.

2. I can't complain about the place as a whole. There were plenty of rides, which kept the kids satisfied, but given that the price for a family of four for the day was $195, it's just not worth it. Not when you realize that Fantasyland is cheaper. What's more, the lines are longer than at Fantasyland, as it is packed with locals. If it hadn't been as full, and we'd actually been able to go on more than three rides in seven hours—and it was less expensive—it might have been worth it. As it is, though, I'd skip it and go to Fantasyland instead.

3. After I'd checked in and been given my key, I found that my room wasn't much bigger than a shoebox! Feeling that this wouldn't work for a four-night stay, I went back down to the front desk and asked for a larger room. They then tried to charge me €40 per night to upgrade to a suitable room, which was ridiculous. We finally agreed on €9 per night for the upgrade. On top of that, parking was €15 a day! Terrible place with terrible service. They're trying to make as much extra money as they can. I'm scared to ask for another pillow, which is necessary since the bed only has one!

4. If you like to see and be seen, then grab yourself one of the outdoor seats here, order a coffee, sit back, and enjoy! Looking out over the main square, and close to the museum and the market, this is a great people-watching spot—and it does great breakfasts, lunches, and snacks as well, which is perfect if you're feeling hungry. I can't recommend it enough.

UNIT 2 A persuasive article

Young Entrepreneur Trying to Turn a Nightmare into a Dream Business

Have you ever spent hours working on a project and saved it to your flash drive only to then lose your drive and all your work? You know you should have backed it up, but it's easy to forget, isn't it? And then you have to explain it to your teacher or boss. Awful! Well, all that might soon be a thing of the past thanks to the bright idea of a 16-year-old entrepreneur from Northern Ireland.

Mason Robinson has invented a piece of software that automatically backs up your work to the cloud when you save your work to a flash drive. As Mason says, "It has a unique aspect in saving people's work twice!"

He developed the *i-save USB* idea as part of a summer project at a local science park. Now he is trying to raise two thousand dollars through a Kickstarter campaign to improve the product and distribute it.

So why don't you support Mason to make his business dreams a reality and, at the same time, end the nightmare of lost homework and research?

Grab the reader's attention by asking a have you ever… *question to stimulate a shared experience.*

Present factual information related to the solution.

Persuade the reader to continue reading by saying that you will present a solution.

Provide a reason why the reader should take action in the final paragraph.

UNIT 3 A survey

Start reporting findings by referring the reader to the source of results and explaining the aim of the investigation.

This bar chart shows the results of a survey carried out on 50 people aged between 13 and 55. The aim of the survey was to find out levels of participation in exercise in the four weeks before the interview.

Explain the most important statistics related to your aim.

During this time, 68 percent of those interviewed walked for health and recreation, about one in six biked, and over half did some kind of sport. As can be seen from the chart, the most popular sports during this month were swimming and diving, with almost 15 percent of those asked trying it at least once. This was followed closely by various health and fitness activities.

Account for the results and explain how one might make the statistics more reliable.

Obviously, these results were determined to at least some degree by the weather. If the survey were to be repeated in the summer rather than the winter, we might, for instance, expect the popularity of soccer and golf to increase.

You may choose to give a further description of interesting findings.

Among the people who did not take part in any exercise during the month in question, the main reasons given for not participating were lack of time, cost, and general poor health.

UNIT 4 A *for* and *against* essay

In the opening paragraph of a for and against essay, demonstrate why the subject is relevant now.

Over recent years, tourism has become more important to the local economy. As the area attracts more tourists, it is only natural that local officials should be thinking about ways of promoting the region further. It has been claimed that the creation of a new museum would boost visitor numbers. However, I believe that such a plan would not have as positive an impact as other possible options.

Introduce your opposing argument or point of view by using the passive, and signal you disagree by using words or phrases like however. Then provide your own opinion.

State the advantages of the topic first and follow this with the limitations.

One argument in favor of a big new museum is that it would put the region on the map and draw in visitors, who would then spend money on accommodation, transportation, and food. In addition to this, it would create jobs—initially in construction, and then within the building. Finally, museums are often seen as being good for the wider community as they help educate people.

However, a museum would be expensive. It might be better to spend that money on other areas of the local community. Local schools and hospitals could be improved greatly if a similar sum of money were made available, and this would benefit a wider range of people. In addition, it is worth asking how many local people would actually visit a new museum. There is already a small museum in town and it is almost always empty.

In conclusion, while a new museum might bring limited benefits and lead to the creation of some jobs, other choices are preferable. Investment in vital facilities may not bring more tourists, but would create a more skilled, healthier, and happier society.

Finally, take notice of both sides of the argument and state your position.

UNIT 5 A scientific method

When writing a scientific method, start by introducing the process.

Words linking the steps of the process are used.

Use phrases like *in order to* to explain why certain steps were taken in the process.

The Blackawton Bee Experiment

The experiment aimed to discover if bees could think in the same ways as humans. The experiment was carried out using a large transparent box called the Bee Arena. The arena contained colored circles representing flowers which had small holes in them that could be filled with sugar water to attract the bees. Before the experiment was started, the bees were marked individually to identify them. In order to do this, forager bees (bees that fly around looking for and collecting pollen) were let into the bee arena. Once all the bees were inside the arena, the lights were turned off in order to make them stop flying. The bees were then picked up using tweezers and put into a pot with a lid. The pot was then placed in a fridge so that the bees would fall asleep. Once they had fallen asleep, the bees were removed from the pot one at a time and painted with different colored dots. Finally, the bees were returned to the pot and warmed up before being released back into the bee arena.

UNIT 6 A problem-solution essay

Use topic sentences to start each paragraph. These sentences introduce and express the main idea of the paragraph.

Refer to sources to strengthen your argument.

How can we help save tigers?

(1) _____ Tigers are hunted and sold for their fur and other parts. They are losing the habitats they live in and they are shot by local people because they kill farm animals. In this essay, I will suggest solutions to these three problems.

(2) _____ In the US, there may be over 9,000 tigers that are kept as pets, for example. They are sold easily, and Mills says that can encourage the trade of wild tigers because people want "the real thing."

(3) _____ Tigers do not recognize borders, so the area they live in can be in more than one country. According to takepart.com, several countries met and agreed to take action together to save tigers. It has had some success, but they could do more.

(4) _____ National Geographic Explorer Krithi Karanth says that sometimes farmers cannot earn enough money to survive because of wildlife destroying their crops and animals. We need to compensate them so they do not take revenge on endangered species like tigers.

Writing Bank 151

UNIT 7 A report

Use the title to show what the report is about.

Improving Learning in the Library

Purpose

Explain the purpose of the report in the introduction.

The purpose of this report is to find out why so much external noise can be heard in the school library. The report will also make recommendations on how to reduce noise and create a better atmosphere to study in.

Background

Students frequently complain about the noise in the school library and many choose not to use the space at all.

Subheadings are added to each paragraph.

Methods of Investigation

In order to better understand the issues, we visited the library twice and read about how sound travels through different materials. We then explored a range of possible solutions before making our own models, which we used to test our ideas.

Findings

The library windows face a public space and, even when closed, let too much noise through. This problem is made worse by the fact that the curtains in the room are made from a thin material that does not stop sound in any way.

Finish a report by making recommendations, if necessary.

Recommendations

To solve this problem, we would recommend installing two panes of glass in each window. Perhaps we could also consider filling the space between the glass with water. This would prevent up to 75 percent of the outside noise from entering the room.

UNIT 8 A complaint

Say what the general problem is in the first sentence and give details about the problem—including examples—in the first paragraph.

Dear Sir or Madam,

I am writing to complain about the recent reporting on the issue of immigration in your paper. In your reports, you frequently suggest that migrants who come to this country are looking for benefits and are involved in crime. While there are obviously unemployed people or criminals among the migrant population, official statistics show that there is a larger percentage among people who were born here. You have also used language such as "swarm" and "flood," which suggests migrants are not human and are a dangerous problem.

Explain how the problem has affected you.

As the granddaughter of an immigrant, I find use of this language very upsetting and I think that if a paper uses it, it often makes other people feel they can say similar things. My grandfather worked hard to make a home here. And for me it *is* my home, but your reporting makes me feel I am not a normal citizen.

Complete a complaint by asking for some kind of action.

I am not saying you should stop campaigning for immigration controls. Everyone has a right to their point of view. However, I would like you to stop using these stereotypes and generalizations to make your point. Migrants are all individuals like us—just born in a different place.

Sincerely,

Maria Asare

UNIT 9 A letter of application

Start a letter of application by referring to the advertisement or posting that you saw.

Explain who you are, where you are from and your plans for the future.

Explain any skills and abilities you have which would make you suitable for the job.

Dear Sir or Madam,

I am writing in response to your advertisement looking for volunteers to rebuild a school in Belize. I would be very grateful if you could send me more information about this opportunity and details of how to apply.

My name is Melanie Gleich and I am 17 years old. I am from Aachen in Germany. I am currently in my last year of high school and will be taking my final exams next spring. I hope to then go on to study Spanish and Latin American Studies in college.

In terms of what I would bring to the project, I already have a good level of both Spanish and English, and having traveled widely, I am used to being around people from other cultures. I am also prepared to get my hands dirty and help out in any way I can. I do a lot of sports and would say I have a good level of fitness, so I feel confident that I would be able to cope with the manual labor.

In addition, I have some experience in both gardening and farming because my grandparents live on a farm and I usually spend the summers helping out there. I am also an excellent team player and like to think I possess good social skills.

I hope you feel I am suitable for the post and look forward to hearing from you soon.

Yours sincerely,

Melanie Gleich

Explain why you are writing.

UNIT 10 A success story

When writing success stories, it is customary to explain how you felt before you succeeded.

Explain how you felt after succeeding.

"Stop!" my teacher whispered loudly. "Look over there." I had been dreading this moment—almost hoping we wouldn't find one. But there it was—a python lying in the grass. I hated snakes. I'd never even touched one. My usual reaction would have been to run away screaming, but I had no choice this time. It was a field trip for my biology class, and not only did we have to look for them, we had to catch one too!

There was a group of us. I had to put a special stick at the back of its head while my teacher and other students got hold of it. At least this way I wouldn't have to touch it. We had practiced lots of times with a plastic snake at school. We crept nearer. My hands started to sweat; my heart started beating like a drum. The snake didn't move. And then it all happened in a flash! I put the stick behind its neck and the others leapt over and grabbed it.

As the others held the snake down and measured it, I forced myself to touch it. I finally managed to do it! Little did I know how nice they actually felt! That day changed my life. Rather than being disgusted by snakes, I became fascinated by them, and now I plan to do lots of research on them.

Use descriptive verbs to make the story more exciting.

Writing Bank 153

UNIT 1

accessible (adj)	/æk'sɛsəbəl/
anxiety (n)	/æŋ'zaɪəti/
B&B (n)	/'bi ən 'bi/
ban (v)	/bæn/
basically (adv)	/'beɪsɪkli/
be up for (phr v)	/bi 'ʌp ˌfɔr/
break down (phr v)	/'breɪk 'daʊn/
budget (n)	/'bʌdʒɪt/
cause (v)	/kɔz/
come across (phr v)	/'kʌm ə'krɔs/
come down to (phr v)	/ˌkʌm 'daʊn tu/
community (n)	/kə'mjunɪti/
culture shock (n)	/'kʌltʃər ˌʃɒk/
date back (phr v)	/'deɪt 'bæk/
deal (n)	/dil/
decline (n)	/dɪ'klaɪn/
established (adj)	/ɪ'stæblɪʃt/
evaluate (v)	/ɪ'vælju,eɪt/
extensive (adj)	/ɪk'stɛnsɪv/
fluent (adj)	/'fluənt/
food poisoning (n)	/'fud ˌpɔɪzənɪŋ/
genuinely (adv)	/'dʒɛnjuɪnli/
get a real feel for (phr v)	/ˌgɛt ə 'riəl 'fil fɔr/
get used to (the food) (phr v)	/ˌgɛt 'juzd tu/
grand (adj)	/grænd/
hang out (phr v)	/'hæŋ ˌaʊt/
hiking (n)	/'haɪkɪŋ/
honesty (n)	/'ɒnɪsti/
host family (n)	/'hoʊst ˌfæməli/
ideal (adj)	/aɪ'diəl/
incredibly (adv)	/ɪn'krɛdəbli/
independence (n)	/ˌɪndɪ'pɛndəns/
individual (n)	/ˌɪndɪ'vɪdʒuəl/
influence (v)	/'ɪnfluəns/
investment (n)	/ɪn'vɛstmənt/
keep in touch (idiom)	/'kip ɪn 'tʌtʃ/
left to (your) own devices (idiom)	/'lɛft tu (yər) 'oʊn dɪ'vaɪsɪz/
legal (adj)	/'ligəl/
lie around (phr v)	/'laɪ ə'raʊnd/
look after (phr v)	/'lʊk 'æftər/
look back (phr v)	/'lʊk 'bæk/
major (adj)	/'meɪdʒər/
media (n)	/'midiə/
move on (phr v)	/'muv 'ɒn/
necessarily (adv)	/ˌnɛsə'sɛrəli/
negotiate (v)	/nɪ'goʊʃi,eɪt/
opt (v)	/ɒpt/
overseas (adv)	/'oʊvər'siz/
participant (n)	/pɑr'tɪsəpənt/
perspective (n)	/pər'spɛktɪv/
pick up (phr v)	/'pɪk 'ʌp/
reinforce (v)	/ˌriɪn'fɔrs/
reliability (n)	/rɪˌlaɪə'bɪlɪti/
reputation (n)	/ˌrɛpjə'teɪʃən/
resource (n)	/'risɔrs/
restriction (n)	/rɪ'strɪkʃən/
revolution (n)	/ˌrɛvə'luʃən/
ridiculous (adj)	/rɪ'dɪkjələs/
robbery (n)	/'rɒbəri/
roots (n)	/ruts/
rush (v)	/rʌʃ/
servant (n)	/'sɜrvənt/
sights (n)	/saɪts/
simply (adv)	/'sɪmpli/
spread (v)	/sprɛd/
standard (n)	/'stændərd/
stare (v)	/stɛər/
step out (phr v)	/'stɛp 'aʊt/
strongly (adv)	/'strɔŋli/
trip up (phr v)	/'trɪp 'ʌp/
turn out (phr v)	/'tɜrn 'aʊt/
tutor (n)	/'tutər/
upgrade (n)	/'ʌp,greɪd/
upgrade (v)	/ʌp'greɪd/
vice versa (adv)	/'vaɪsə 'vɜrsə/
wealth (n)	/wɛlθ/
welcoming (adj)	/'wɛlkəmɪŋ/
worry (n)	/'wɜri/

UNIT 2

(a) matter (of) (idiom)	/(ə)'mætər (əv)/
adapt (v)	/ə'dæpt/
aspect (n)	/'æspɛkt/
assume (v)	/ə'sum/
attach (v)	/ə'tætʃ/
automatically (adv)	/ˌɔtə'mætɪkli/
backup (n)	/'bæk,ʌp/
banking (n)	/'bæŋkɪŋ/
bargain (n)	/'bɑrgɪn/
barrier (n)	/'bæriər/
be based (phr v)	/bi 'beɪst/
beg (v)	/bɛg/
businessperson (n)	/'bɪznɪs,pɜrsən/
campaign (n)	/kæm'peɪn/
capable (adj)	/'keɪpəbəl/
climate change (n)	/'klaɪmɪt ˌtʃeɪndʒ/
code (n)	/koʊd/
confirm (v)	/kən'fɜrm/
corporate (adj)	/'kɔrpərɪt/
cut down (phr v)	/'kʌt 'daʊn/
data (n)	/'deɪtə/
demonstrate (v)	/'dɛmən,streɪt/
detect (v)	/dɪ'tɛkt/
discourage (v)	/dɪs'kɜrɪdʒ/
distant (adj)	/'dɪstənt/
distribute (v)	/dɪ'strɪbjut/
distribution (n)	/ˌdɪstrə'bjuʃən/
diverse (adj)	/dɪ'vɜrs/
edit (v)	/'ɛdɪt/
email (n)	/'i,meɪl/
entrepreneur (n)	/ˌɒntrəprə'nʊər/
executive (adj)	/ɪg'zɛkjətɪv/
expand (v)	/ɪk'spænd/
export (v)	/'ɛkspɔrt/
failure (n)	/'feɪljər/
filter (n)	/'fɪltər/
fund (n)	/fʌnd/
fund (v)	/fʌnd/
gender (n)	/'dʒɛndər/
go too far (idiom)	/'goʊ ˌtu 'fɑr/
guarantee (n)	/ˌgærən'ti/
handle (v)	/'hændl/
harvest (v)	/'hɑrvɪst/
illegal (adj)	/ɪ'ligəl/
impressive (adj)	/ɪm'prɛsɪv/
inbox (n)	/'ɪn,bɒks/
infect (v)	/ɪn'fɛkt/
intrigue (v)	/ɪn'trig/
invent (v)	/ɪn'vɛnt/
investor (n)	/ɪn'vɛstər/
knock on the head (idiom)	/'nɒk ɒn ðə 'hɛd/
leadership (n)	/'lidər,ʃɪp/
market (v)	/'mɑrkɪt/
network (v)	/'nɛt,wɜrk/
origin (n)	/'ɔrɪdʒɪn/
out of hand (idiom)	/'aʊt əv 'hænd/
post (v)	/poʊst/
potential (n)	/pə'tɛnʃəl/
pressure (n)	/'prɛʃər/
profile (n)	/'proʊfaɪl/
profit (n)	/'prɒfɪt/
publisher (n)	/'pʌblɪʃər/
put together (phr v)	/'pʊt tə'gɛðər/
raise money (phr v)	/'reɪz 'mʌni/
reality (n)	/ri'ælɪti/
recover (v)	/rɪ'kʌvər/
risk (n)	/rɪsk/
scam (n)	/skæm/
social media (n)	/'soʊʃəl 'midiə/
solar (adj)	/'soʊlər/
source (n)	/sɔrs/
spam (n)	/spæm/
statement (n)	/'steɪtmənt/
store (v)	/stɔr/
strategy (n)	/'strætɪdʒi/
summarize (v)	/'sʌmə,raɪz/
supplier (n)	/sə'plaɪər/
tribe (n)	/traɪb/
turn up (phr v)	/'tɜrn 'ʌp/
victim (n)	/'vɪktɪm/
wealthy (adj)	/'wɛlθi/

UNIT 3

accelerate (v)	/æk'sɛlə,reɪt/
advance (n)	/æd'væns/
agree with (phr v)	/ə'gri ˌwɪð/
amount (n)	/ə'maʊnt/

anticipate (v)	/ænˈtɪsəˌpeɪt/
athletic (adj)	/æθˈlɛtɪk/
attitude (n)	/ˈætɪˌtud/
awareness (n)	/əˈwɛərnɪs/
billion (n)	/ˈbɪljən/
brand (n)	/brænd/
bronze (adj)	/brɒnz/
captain (v)	/ˈkæptən/
championship (n)	/ˈtʃæmpiənˌʃɪp/
change the face of (idiom)	/ˈtʃeɪndʒ ðə ˈfeɪs əv/
closely (adv)	/ˈkloʊsli/
compete (v)	/kəmˈpit/
conquer (v)	/ˈkɒŋkər/
debt (n)	/dɛt/
determine (v)	/dɪˈtɜrmɪn/
elite (adj)	/ɪˈlit/
energetic (adj)	/ˌɛnərˈdʒɛtɪk/
entire (adj)	/ɛnˈtaɪər/
essentially (adv)	/ɪˈsɛnʃəli/
establish (v)	/ɪˈstæblɪʃ/
evolution (n)	/ˌɛvəˈluʃən/
evolve (v)	/ɪˈvɒlv/
expense (n)	/ɪkˈspɛns/
fade away (v)	/ˈfeɪd əˈweɪ/
fame (n)	/feɪm/
formal (adj)	/ˈfɔrməl/
forward (n)	/ˈfɔrwərd/
funding (n)	/ˈfʌndɪŋ/
gardening (adj)	/ˈgɑrdnɪŋ/
glory (n)	/ˈglɔri/
goal (n)	/goʊl/
greatly (adv)	/ˈgreɪtli/
hold (a record) (v)	/hoʊld/
host (v)	/hoʊst/
injury (n)	/ˈɪndʒəri/
instantly (adv)	/ˈɪnstəntli/
intensively (adv)	/ɪnˈtɛnsɪvli/
junk food (n)	/ˈdʒʌŋk ˌfud/
largely (adv)	/ˈlɑrdʒli/
long-term (adj)	/ˈlɔŋˌtɜrm/
marathon (n)	/ˈmærəˌθɒn/
medal (n)	/ˈmɛdl/
muscle (n)	/ˈmʌsəl/
nation (n)	/ˈneɪʃən/
participate (v)	/pɑrˈtɪsəˌpeɪt/
pay off (phr v)	/ˈpeɪ ˈɔf/
percentage (n)	/pərˈsɛntɪdʒ/
personality (n)	/ˌpɜrsəˈnælɪti/
popularity (n)	/ˌpɒpjəˈlærɪti/
positive role model (phrase)	/ˈpɒzɪtɪv ˈroʊl ˌmɒdl/
preferably (adv)	/ˈprɛfərəbli/
principle (n)	/ˈprɪnsəpəl/
psychological (adj)	/ˌsaɪkəˈlɒdʒɪkəl/
quote (n)	/kwoʊt/
ranking (n)	/ˈræŋkɪŋ/
real passion (phrase)	/ˈriəl ˈpæʃən/
recreation (n)	/ˌrɛkriˈeɪʃən/
represent (v)	/ˌrɛprɪˈzɛnt/
role model (n)	/ˈroʊl ˌmɒdl/
roughly (adv)	/ˈrʌfli/
schedule (n)	/ˈskɛdʒul/
season (n)	/ˈsizən/
select (v)	/sɪˈlɛkt/
set (a new record) (v)	/sɛt/
set up (v)	/ˈsɛt ˈʌp/
shrink (v)	/ʃrɪŋk/
slightly (adv)	/ˈslaɪtli/
slow down (phr v)	/ˈsloʊ ˈdaʊn/
smash (v)	/smæʃ/
specialize (v)	/ˈspɛʃəˌlaɪz/
specific (adj)	/spəˈsɪfɪk/
spirit (n)	/ˈspɪrɪt/
stamina (n)	/ˈstæmɪnə/
status (n)	/ˈsteɪtəs/
subsequently (adv)	/ˈsʌbsɪkwəntli/
subway (n)	/ˈsʌbˌweɪ/
suit (v)	/sut/
sum (n)	/sʌm/
surface (n)	/ˈsɜrfɪs/
tackle (v)	/ˈtækəl/
target (n)	/ˈtɑrgɪt/
technique (n)	/tɛkˈnik/
technological (adj)	/ˌtɛknəˈlɒdʒɪkəl/
tend to (phr v)	/ˈtɛnd tu/
terminal (n)	/ˈtɜrmɪnl/
throughout (prep)	/θruˈaʊt/
top (adj)	/tɒp/
vast (adj)	/væst/

UNIT 4

actual (adj)	/ˈæktʃuəl/
authority (n)	/əˈθɔrɪti/
behind (prep)	/bɪˈhaɪnd/
boost (v)	/bust/
carnival (n)	/ˈkɑrnɪvəl/
choir (n)	/kwaɪər/
claim (v)	/kleɪm/
comedy club (n)	/ˈkɒmɪdi ˌklʌb/
commitment (n)	/kəˈmɪtmənt/
confidence (n)	/ˈkɒnfɪdəns/
construction (n)	/kənˈstrʌkʃən/
costume (n)	/ˈkɒstum/
creation (n)	/kriˈeɪʃən/
creativity (n)	/ˌkrieɪˈtɪvɪti/
demolish (v)	/dɪˈmɒlɪʃ/
desperate (adj)	/ˈdɛspərɪt/
discipline (n)	/ˈdɪsəplɪn/
diverse social background (col)	/dɪˈvɜrs ˈsoʊʃəl ˈbækˌgraʊnd/
dramatic (adj)	/drəˈmætɪk/
duration (n)	/dʊˈreɪʃən/
economist (n)	/ɪˈkɒnəmɪst/
economy (n)	/ɪˈkɒnəmi/
emphasize (v)	/ˈɛmfəˌsaɪz/
engagement (n)	/ɛnˈgeɪdʒmənt/
expression (n)	/ɪkˈsprɛʃən/
factor (n)	/ˈfæktər/
fatal (adj)	/ˈfeɪtəl/
festival (n)	/ˈfɛstɪvəl/
figure out (phr v)	/ˈfɪgjər ˈaʊt/
found (v)	/faʊnd/
foundation (n)	/faʊnˈdeɪʃən/
fulfill (v)	/fʊlˈfɪl/
gallery (n)	/ˈgæləri/
gang (n)	/gæŋ/
generate (v)	/ˈdʒɛnəˌreɪt/
hard work (col)	/ˈhɑrd ˈwɜrk/
impact (n)	/ˈɪmpækt/
income (n)	/ˈɪnkʌm/
industrial (adj)	/ɪnˈdʌstriəl/
initially (adv)	/ɪˈnɪʃəli/
innovative (adj)	/ˈɪnəˌveɪtɪv/
inspiration (n)	/ˌɪnspəˈreɪʃən/
lead to (phr v)	/ˈlid tu/
leading orchestra (col)	/ˈlidɪŋ ˈɔrkɪstrə/
literally (adv)	/ˈlɪtərəli/
low income (adj)	/ˈloʊ ˈɪnkʌm/
mayor (n)	/ˈmeɪər/
minister (n)	/ˈmɪnɪstər/
minority (n)	/mɪˈnɔrɪti/
mixed results (phrase)	/ˈmɪkst rɪˈzʌlts/
museum (n)	/mjuˈziəm/
official (adj)	/əˈfɪʃəl/
organizer (n)	/ˈɔrgəˌnaɪzər/
parade (n)	/pəˈreɪd/
physical (adj)	/ˈfɪzɪkəl/
poverty (n)	/ˈpɒvərti/
pride (n)	/praɪd/
private company (col)	/ˈpraɪvɪt ˈkʌmpəni/
process (n)	/ˈprɒsɛs/
professional (n)	/prəˈfɛʃnl/
public art (col)	/ˈpʌblɪk ˈɑrt/
redevelopment (n)	/ˌridɪˈvɛləpmənt/
rehearse (v)	/rɪˈhɜrs/
reject (v)	/rɪˈdʒɛkt/
relic (n)	/ˈrɛlɪk/
remarkable (adj)	/rɪˈmɑrkəbəl/
rhythm (n)	/ˈrɪðəm/
run over (phr v)	/ˈrʌn ˈoʊvər/
sell out (phr v)	/ˈsɛl ˈaʊt/
signal (v)	/ˈsɪgnl/
skilled (adj)	/skɪld/
stand for (phr v)	/ˈstænd fɔr/
straightforward process (col)	/ˌstreɪtˈfɔrwərd ˈprɒsɛs/
strict set (col)	/ˈstrɪkt ˈsɛt/
struggling (adj)	/ˈstrʌgəlɪŋ/
supposedly (adv)	/səˈpoʊzɪdli/
take charge (phr v)	/ˈteɪk ˈtʃɑrdʒ/
theater (n)	/ˈθiətər/
venue (n)	/ˈvɛnju/
violence (n)	/ˈvaɪələns/
vital (adj)	/ˈvaɪtl/
volunteer (n)	/ˌvɒlənˈtɪər/
widely (adv)	/ˈwaɪdli/

Word Lists

WORD LISTS

UNIT 5

alter (v)	/ˈɔltər/
arm (v)	/ɑrm/
assignment (n)	/əˈsaɪnmənt/
beautiful (adj)	/ˈbjutəfəl/
belief (n)	/bɪˈlif/
bother (v)	/ˈbɒðər/
browser (n) /	/ˈbraʊzər/
bubble (n)	/ˈbʌbəl/
bulb (n)	/bʌlb/
capacity (n)	/kəˈpæsɪti/
chemical (n)	/ˈkɛmɪkəl/
circumstance (n)	/ˈsɜrkəmˌstæns/
conduct (v)	/kənˈdʌkt/
consume (v)	/kənˈsum/
cooperation (n)	/koʊˌɒpəˈreɪʃən/
cooperative (adj)	/koʊˈɒpərətɪv/
curiosity (n)	/ˌkjʊəriˈɒsɪti/
deadline (n)	/ˈdɛdˌlaɪn/
determining (adv)	/dɪˈtɜrmɪnɪŋ/
discovery (n)	/dɪˈskʌvəri/
dissolve (v)	/dɪˈzɒlv/
dominant (adj)	/ˈdɒmɪnənt/
downwards (adv)	/ˈdaʊnwərdz/
effective (adj)	/ɪˈfɛktɪv/
electrical (adj)	/iˈlɛktrɪkəl/
embrace (v)	/ɛmˈbreɪs/
engage (v)	/ɛnˈgeɪdʒ/
evidence (n)	/ˈɛvɪdəns/
function (n)	/ˈfʌŋkʃən/
genius (n)	/ˈdʒiniəs/
grasp (n)	/græsp/
helpful (adj)	/ˈhɛlpfəl/
hopeful (adj)	/ˈhoʊpfəl/
identify (v)	/aɪˈdɛntəˌfaɪ/
imaginative (adj)	/ɪˈmædʒənətɪv/
increasingly (adv)	/ɪnˈkrisɪŋli/
innovation (n)	/ˌɪnəˈveɪʃən/
innovative (adj)	/ˈɪnəˌveɪtɪv/
intelligence (n)	/ɪnˈtɛlɪdʒəns/
journal (n)	/ˈdʒɜrnl/
labor (n)	/ˈleɪbər/
lid (n)	/lɪd/
link (n)	/lɪŋk/
listener (n)	/ˈlɪsənər/
make matters worse (phrase)	/ˈmeɪk ˈmætərz ˈwɜrs/
mark (v)	/mɑrk/
mature (v)	/məˈtʃʊər/
mechanical (adj)	/mɪˈkænɪkəl/
medical (adj)	/ˈmɛdɪkəl/
mode (n)	/moʊd/
movement (n)	/ˈmuvmənt/
myth (n)	/mɪθ/
network (n)	/ˈnɛtˌwɜrk/
place (v)	/pleɪs/
pleasurable (adj)	/ˈplɛʒərəbəl/
pleasure (n)	/ˈplɛʒər/
practical (adj)	/ˈpræktɪkəl/
previously (adv)	/ˈpriviəsli/
ray (n)	/reɪ/
reaction (n)	/riˈækʃən/
reference (n)	/ˈrɛfərəns/
release (v)	/rɪˈlis/
researcher (n)	/rɪˈsɜrtʃər/
return (v)	/rɪˈtɜrn/
reward (n)	/rɪˈwɔrd/
sample (n)	/ˈsæmpəl/
scan (n)	/skæn/
social (adj)	/ˈsoʊʃəl/
society (n)	/səˈsaɪəti/
sophisticated (adj)	/səˈfɪstɪˌkeɪtɪd/
submit (v)	/səbˈmɪt/
substance (n)	/ˈsʌbstəns/
surgeon (n)	/ˈsɜrdʒən/
surgery (n)	/ˈsɜrdʒəri/
surround (v)	/səˈraʊnd/
survey (n)	/ˈsɜrveɪ/
theory (n)	/ˈθɪəri/
threat (n)	/θrɛt/
transform (v)	/trænsˈfɔrm/
transparent (adj)	/trænsˈpærənt/
tremendous (adj)	/trəˈmɛndəs/
ultimate (adj)	/ˈʌltəmɪt/
uncertainty (n)	/ʌnˈsɜrtənti/
use (n)	/jus/
useful (adj)	/ˈjusfəl/
voice (n)	/vɔɪs/

UNIT 6

administration (n)	/ədˌmɪnəˈstreɪʃən/
agriculture (n)	/ˈægrɪˌkʌltʃər/
alarming (adj)	/əˈlɑrmɪŋ/
anger (n)	/ˈæŋgər/
animal product (n)	/ˈænəməl ˌprɒdəkt/
arise (v)	/əˈraɪz/
assess (v)	/əˈsɛs/
breed (v)	/brid/
camp (n)	/kæmp/
capture (v)	/ˈkæptʃər/
catch on (phr v)	/ˈkætʃ ˈɒn/
characteristic (n)	/ˌkærɪktəˈrɪstɪk/
chase (v)	/tʃeɪs/
clue (n)	/klu/
compensate (v)	/ˈkɒmpənˌseɪt/
concern (n)	/kənˈsɜrn/
consequence (n)	/ˈkɒnsɪˌkwɛns/
conservation (n)	/ˌkɒnsərˈveɪʃən/
constantly (adv)	/ˈkɒnstəntli/
cure (n)	/kjʊər/
die out (v)	/ˈdaɪ ˈaʊt/
diversity (n)	/dɪˈvɜrsɪti/
domestic (adj)	/dəˈmɛstɪk/
emotion (n)	/ɪˈmoʊʃən/
endanger (adj)	/ɛnˈdeɪndʒər/
ensure (v)	/ɛnˈʃʊər/
equivalent (adj)	/ɪˈkwɪvələnt/
extinct (adj)	/ɪkˈstɪŋkt/
fake (adj)	/feɪk/
feature (n)	/ˈfitʃər/
fox (n)	/fɒks/
gene (n)	/dʒin/
genetic (adj)	/dʒəˈnɛtɪk/
growth (n)	/groʊθ/
habitat (n)	/ˈhæbɪˌtæt/
historian (n)	/hɪˈstɔriən/
hit a wall (idiom)	/ˈhɪt ə ˈwɔl/
hunt (v)	/hʌnt/
indicate (v)	/ˈɪndɪˌkeɪt/
influential (adj)	/ˌɪnfluˈɛnʃəl/
inspire (v)	/ɪnˈspaɪər/
interfere (v)	/ˌɪntərˈfɪər/
mammal (n)	/ˈmæməl/
mass (adj)	/mæs/
misunderstanding (n)	/ˌmɪsʌndərˈstændɪŋ/
mysterious (adj)	/mɪˈstɪəriəs/
overcome (v)	/ˌoʊvərˈkʌm/
polar bear (n)	/ˈpoʊlər ˌbɛər/
proof (n)	/pruf/
psychologist (n)	/saɪˈkɒlədʒɪst/
purely (adv)	/ˈpjʊərli/
put forward (phr v)	/ˌpʊt ˈfɔrwərd/
rainfall (n)	/ˈreɪnˌfɔl/
rate (n)	/reɪt/
rethink (v)	/riˈθɪŋk/
reveal (v)	/rɪˈvil/
revenge (n)	/rɪˈvɛndʒ/
save (v)	/seɪv/
science teacher (n)	/ˈsaɪəns ˌtitʃər/
sea creature (n)	/ˈsi ˌkritʃər/
short-term (adj)	/ˈʃɔrtˈtɜrm/
shorten (v)	/ˈʃɔrtn/
significantly (adv)	/sɪgˈnɪfɪkəntli/
social media campaign (n)	/ˈsoʊʃəl ˈmidiə kæmˌpeɪn/
species (n)	/ˈspiʃiz/
sponsor (v)	/ˈspɒnsər/
spot (n)	/spɒt/
strengthen (v)	/ˈstrɛŋkθən/
sudden (adj)	/ˈsʌdn/
surroundings (n)	/səˈraʊndɪŋz/
survival (n)	/sərˈvaɪvəl/
survive (v)	/sərˈvaɪv/
suspect (v)	/səˈspɛkt/
suspicious (adj)	/səˈspɪʃəs/
take to (phr v)	/ˈteɪk tu/
unique (adj)	/juˈnik/
unwilling (adj)	/ʌnˈwɪlɪŋ/
willingness (n)	/ˈwɪlɪŋnɪs/
wipe out (phr v)	/ˈwaɪp ˈaʊt/

WORD LISTS

UNIT 7

additional (adj)	/əˈdɪʃənl/
alternative (adj)	/ɔlˈtɜrnətɪv/
analysis (n)	/əˈnæləsɪs/
analyze (v)	/ˈænəˌlaɪz/
approach (n)	/əˈproʊtʃ/
assessment (n)	/əˈsɛsmənt/
bacteria (n)	/bækˈtɪəriə/
break (v)	/breɪk/
brick (n)	/brɪk/
combination (n)	/ˌkɒmbɪˈneɪʃən/
come up with (phr v)	/ˈkʌm ˌʌp ˌwɪð/
commonly (adv)	/ˈkɒmənli/
concerned (adj)	/kənˈsɜrnd/
conclude (v)	/kənˈklud/
conclusion (n)	/kənˈkluʒən/
contribute (v)	/kənˈtrɪbjut/
create (v)	/kriˈeɪt/
creative (adj)	/kriˈeɪtɪv/
creatively (adv)	/kriˈeɪtɪvli/
demonstration (n)	/ˌdɛmənˈstreɪʃən/
desire (v)	/dɪˈzaɪər/
detailed (adj)	/ˈditeɪld/
displace (v)	/dɪsˈpleɪs/
electrocute (v)	/ɪˈlɛktrəˌkjut/
external (adj)	/ɪkˈstɜrnəl/
extreme (adj)	/ɪkˈstrim/
flexibility (n)	/ˌflɛksəˈbɪlɪti/
flexible (adj)	/ˈflɛksəbəl/
fluency (n)	/ˈfluənsi/
follow (v)	/ˈfɒloʊ/
format (n)	/ˈfɔrmæt/
freedom (n)	/ˈfridəm/
functional (adj)	/ˈfʌŋkʃənl/
genuine (adj)	/ˈdʒɛnjuɪn/
get (your) meaning across (phrase)	/ˈgɛt (jər) ˈminɪŋ əˌkrɔs/
grab (v)	/græb/
heartbroken (adj)	/ˈhɑrtˌbroʊkən/
imaginary (adj)	/ɪˈmædʒəˌnɛri/
implication (n)	/ˌɪmplɪˈkeɪʃən/
integrate (v)	/ˈɪntɪˌgreɪt/
intelligent (adj)	/ɪnˈtɛlɪdʒənt/
know (v)	/noʊ/
knowledge (n)	/ˈnɒlɪdʒ/
learner (n)	/ˈlɜrnər/
lifestyle (n)	/ˈlaɪfˌstaɪl/
logic (n)	/ˈlɒdʒɪk/
logical (adj)	/ˈlɒdʒɪkəl/
make up (phr v)	/ˈmeɪk ˌʌp/
manners (n)	/ˈmænərz/
measure (v)	/ˈmɛʒər/
needle (n)	/ˈnidl/
obey (v)	/oʊˈbeɪ/
original (n)	/əˈrɪdʒənl/
outcome (n)	/ˈaʊtˌkʌm/
preference (n)	/ˈprɛfərəns/
publication (n)	/ˌpʌblɪˈkeɪʃən/
publish (v)	/ˈpʌblɪʃ/
realistically (adv)	/ˌriəˈlɪstɪkli/
recommendation (n)	/ˌrɛkəmɛnˈdeɪʃən/
rely on (phr v)	/rɪˈlaɪ ˌɒn/
resolve (v)	/rɪˈzɒlv/
safety (n)	/ˈseɪfti/
score (v)	/skɔr/
sketch (n)	/skɛtʃ/
solution (n)	/səˈluʃən/
stimulate (v)	/ˈstɪmjʊˌleɪt/
supervise (v)	/ˈsupərˌvaɪz/
task (n)	/tæsk/
treatment (n)	/ˈtritmənt/
truly (adv)	/ˈtruli/
usage (n)	/ˈjusɪdʒ/
usefulness (n)	/ˈjusfəlnɪs/
variety (n)	/vəˈraɪəti/

UNIT 8

abuse (n)	/əˈbjus/
accuse (v)	/əˈkjuz/
acknowledge (v)	/ækˈnɒlɪdʒ/
apparently (adv)	/əˈpærəntli/
appropriate (adj)	/əˈproʊpriɪt/
associate with (phr v)	/əˈsoʊʃiˌeɪt ˌwɪð/
assumption (n)	/əˈsʌmpʃən/
assure (v)	/əˈʃʊər/
awkward (adj)	/ˈɔkwərd/
awkwardness (n)	/ˈɔkwərdnɪs/
belong (v)	/bɪˈlɔŋ/
breakdown (n)	/ˈbreɪkˌdaʊn/
bully (v)	/ˈbʊli/
campaign (v)	/kæmˈpeɪn/
cardboard (n)	/ˈkɑrdˌbɔrd/
citizen (n)	/ˈsɪtəzən/
classic (n)	/ˈklæsɪk/
combine (v)	/kəmˈbaɪn/
compliment (v)	/ˈkɒmpləˌmɛnt/
conscious (adj)	/ˈkɒnʃəs/
conservative (adj)	/kənˈsɜrvətɪv/
cost-effective (adj)	/ˈkɔst ɪˌfɛktɪv/
criticize (v)	/ˈkrɪtɪˌsaɪz/
decoration (n)	/ˌdɛkəˈreɪʃən/
deep-rooted (adj)	/ˈdipˈrutɪd/
define (v)	/dɪˈfaɪn/
deliberately (adv)	/dɪˈlɪbərɪtli/
deny (v)	/dɪˈnaɪ/
diplomat (n)	/ˈdɪpləˌmæt/
discriminate (v)	/dɪˈskrɪməˌneɪt/
dishonest (adj)	/dɪsˈɒnɪst/
elect (v)	/ɪˈlɛkt/
element (n)	/ˈɛləmənt/
elsewhere (adv)	/ˈɛlsˌwɛər/
encounter (v)	/ɛnˈkaʊntər/
enthusiasm (n)	/ɪnˈθuziˌæzəm/
equality (n)	/ɪˈkwɒlɪti/
experiment (v)	/ɛkˈspɛrəˌmɛnt/
fed up (phr v)	/ˈfɛd ˌʌp/
fingernail (n)	/ˈfɪŋgərˌneɪl/
firmly (adv)	/ˈfɜrmli/
forget (v)	/fərˈgɛt/
generalization (n)	/ˌdʒɛnərələˈzeɪʃən/
global (adj)	/ˈgloʊbəl/
highly-respected (adj)	/ˈhaɪli rɪsˈpɛktɪd/
humorous (adj)	/ˈhjumərəs/
identity (n)	/aɪˈdɛntɪti/
ignore (v)	/ɪgˈnɔr/
immigrant (n)	/ˈɪmɪgrənt/
incident (n)	/ˈɪnsɪdənt/
insist on (v)	/ɪnˈsɪst ˌɒn/
intense (adj)	/ɪnˈtɛns/
interpret (v)	/ɪnˈtɜrprɪt/
invisible (n)	/ɪnˈvɪzəbəl/
like-minded (adj)	/ˈlaɪkˈmaɪndɪd/
long-lasting (adj)	/ˈlɔŋˈlæstɪŋ/
make fun (phr v)	/ˈmeɪk ˈfʌn/
massive (adj)	/ˈmæsɪv/
misbehave (v)	/ˌmɪsbɪˈheɪv/
misunderstand (v)	/ˌmɪsʌndərˈstænd/
modify (v)	/ˈmɒdɪˌfaɪ/
norm (n)	/nɔrm/
notion (n)	/ˈnoʊʃən/
obsession (n)	/əbˈsɛʃən/
offended (adj)	/əˈfɛndɪd/
open-minded (adj)	/ˈoʊpənˈmaɪndɪd/
phenomenon (n)	/fəˈnɒmɪˌnɒn/
policy (n)	/ˈpɒləsi/
praise (v)	/preɪz/
presence (n)	/ˈprɛzəns/
pretend (v)	/prɪˈtɛnd/
proportion (n)	/prəˈpɔrʃən/
protest (n)	/ˈproʊtɛst/
racism (n)	/ˈreɪsɪzəm/
react (v)	/riˈækt/
refresh (v)	/rɪˈfrɛʃ/
regional (adj)	/ˈridʒənl/
response (n)	/rɪˈspɒns/
self-conscious (adj)	/ˈsɛlfˈkɒnʃəs/
shopkeeper (n)	/ˈʃɒpˌkipər/
sort (it) out (phr v)	/ˈsɔrt (ɪt) ˈaʊt/
statistic (n)	/stəˈtɪstɪk/
stereotype (n)	/ˈstɛriəˌtaɪp/
stock (n)	/stɒk/
two-faced (adj)	/ˈtuˌfeɪst/
well-mannered (adj)	/ˈwɛlˈmænərd/

UNIT 9

absence (n)	/ˈæbsəns/
affect (v)	/əˈfɛkt/
aid (n)	/eɪd/
ally (n)	/ˈælaɪ/
appeal (v)	/əˈpil/
assistance (n)	/əˈsɪstəns/
block (v)	/blɒk/

care for (phr v)	/ˈkɛər ˌfɔr/
coastal (adj)	/ˈkoʊstl/
convention (n)	/kənˈvɛnʃən/
cope (v)	/koʊp/
corrupt (adj)	/kəˈrʌpt/
crisis (n)	/ˈkraɪsɪs/
debris (n)	/dəˈbri/
delegate (n)	/ˈdɛlɪgɪt/
devastation (n)	/ˌdɛvəˈsteɪʃən/
disaster (n)	/dɪˈzæstər/
donation (n)	/doʊˈneɪʃən/
earthquake (n)	/ˈɜrθˌkweɪk/
edit (n)	/ˈɛdɪt/
evacuate (v)	/ɪˈvækjuˌeɪt/
flee (v)	/fli/
frustrate (v)	/ˈfrʌstreɪt/
give (sth) a go (phr v)	/ˈgɪv ə ˈgoʊ/
global warming (n)	/ˈgloʊbəl ˈwɔrmɪŋ/
globe (n)	/gloʊb/
graduate (n)	/ˈgrædʒuɪt/
greed (n)	/grid/
headquarters (n)	/ˈhɛdˌkwɔrtərz/
homeless (adj)	/ˈhoʊmlɪs/
housing (n)	/ˈhaʊzɪŋ/
humanity (n)	/hjuˈmænɪti/
imprison (v)	/ɪmˈprɪzən/
inclusive (adj)	/ɪnˈklusɪv/
infrastructure (n)	/ˈɪnfrəˌstrʌktʃər/
initiative (n)	/ɪˈnɪʃətɪv/
interactive (adj)	/ˌɪntərˈæktɪv/
joy (n)	/dʒɔɪ/
launch (v)	/lɔntʃ/
limited (adj)	/ˈlɪmɪtɪd/
neutral (adj)	/ˈnutrəl/
on behalf of (phr v)	/ˌɒn bɪˈhæf əv/
on the ground (phrase)	/ˌɒn ðə ˈgraʊnd/
overlook (v)	/ˌoʊvərˈlʊk/
panel (n)	/ˈpænl/
portrait (n)	/ˈpɔrtrɪt/
precious (adj)	/ˈprɛʃəs/
programmer (n)	/ˈproʊgræmər/
psychological (adj)	/ˌsaɪkəˈlɒdʒɪkəl/
realization (n)	/ˌriələˈzeɪʃən/
reconstruction (n)	/ˌrikənˈstrʌkʃən/
recovery (n)	/rɪˈkʌvəri/
relief (n)	/rɪˈlif/
reminder (n)	/rɪˈmaɪndər/
remote (adj)	/rɪˈmoʊt/
representative (n)	/ˌrɛprɪˈzɛntətɪv/
restore (v)	/rɪˈstɔr/
right (n)	/raɪt/
rise (v)	/raɪz/
satellite (n)	/ˈsætlˌaɪt/
scale (n)	/skeɪl/
senior (adj)	/ˈsinjər/
shelter (n)	/ˈʃɛltər/
shortage (n)	/ˈʃɔrtɪdʒ/
skip (v)	/skɪp/
staggering (adj)	/ˈstægərɪŋ/
strike a chord (phr v)	/ˈstraɪk ə ˈkɔrd/
supply (n)	/səˈplaɪ/
survivor (n)	/sərˈvaɪvər/
sustainable (n)	/səˈsteɪnəbəl/
the best (n)	/ðə ˈbɛst/
the brave (n)	/ðə ˈbreɪv/
the loud (n)	/ðə ˈlaʊd/
the old (n)	/ði ˈoʊld/
the outgoing (n)	/ði ˌaʊtˈgoʊɪŋ/
the poor (n)	/ðə ˈpʊər/
the rich (n)	/ðə ˈrɪtʃ/
the stupid (n)	/ðə ˈstupɪd/
trap (v)	/træp/
unfamiliar (adj)	/ˌʌnfəˈmɪljər/
unfold (v)	/ʌnˈfoʊld/

UNIT 10

actively (adj)	/ˈæktɪvli/
address (v)	/əˈdrɛs/
aim (v)	/eɪm/
allergic (adj)	/əˈlɜrdʒɪk/
amazement (n)	/əˈmeɪzmənt/
antibiotics (n)	/ˌæntibaɪˈɒtɪks/
apocalypse (n)	/əˈpɒkəˌlɪps/
award (v)	/əˈwɔrd/
bench (n)	/bɛntʃ/
bestseller (n)	/ˈbɛstˌsɛlər/
blindness (n)	/ˈblaɪndnɪs/
blink (v)	/blɪŋk/
cast (n)	/kæst/
category (n)	/ˈkætɪˌgɔri/
cell (n)	/sɛl/
chance (n)	/tʃæns/
cheer (v)	/tʃɪər/
chest (n)	/tʃɛst/
clarify (v)	/ˈklærəˌfaɪ/
clear up (phr v)	/ˈklɪər ˈʌp/
close down (v)	/ˈcloʊz ˈdaʊn/
combine (v)	/kəmˈbaɪn/
comfort zone (n)	/ˈkʌmfərt ˌzoʊn/
concentration (n)	/ˌkɒnsənˈtreɪʃən/
consciousness (n)	/ˈkɒnʃəsnɪs/
considerable (adj)	/kənˈsɪdərəbəl/
contribute (v)	/kənˈtrɪbjut/
convert (v)	/kənˈvɜrt/
darkness (n)	/ˈdɑrknɪs/
deadly (adj)	/ˈdɛdli/
dependent (adj)	/dɪˈpɛndənt/
design (v)	/dɪˈzaɪn/
determined (adj)	/dɪˈtɜrmɪnd/
device (n)	/dɪˈvaɪs/
devote (v)	/dɪˈvoʊt/
diagnose (v)	/ˈdaɪəgˌnoʊs/
dictate (v)	/ˈdɪkteɪt/
disgust (n)	/dɪsˈgʌst/
disturbing (adj)	/dɪˈstɜrbɪŋ/
dose (n)	/doʊs/
drug (n)	/drʌg/
editor (n)	/ˈɛdɪtər/
efficiently (adv)	/ɪˈfɪʃəntli/
expose (v)	/ɪkˈspoʊz/
express (v)	/ɪkˈsprɛs/
extract (n)	/ɪkˈstrækt/
fascinated (adj)	/ˈfæsəˌneɪtɪd/
flash (n)	/flæʃ/
force (v)	/fɔrs/
get out (phr v)	/ˈgɛt ˈaʊt/
gripping (adj)	/ˈgrɪpɪŋ/
heath care (n)	/ˈhɛlθ ˌkɛər/
helmet (n)	/ˈhɛlmɪt/
honor (n)	/ˈɒnər/
house (v)	/haʊz/
inability (n)	/ˌɪnəˈbɪlɪti/
inevitable (adj)	/ɪnˈɛvɪtəbəl/
infection (n)	/ɪnˈfɛkʃən/
insufficient (adj)	/ˌɪnsəˈfɪʃənt/
intensive (adj)	/ɪnˈtɛnsɪv/
keep down (phr v)	/ˈkip ˈdaʊn/
lead (v)	/lid/
lung (n)	/lʌŋ/
make the most of (phrase)	/ˈmeɪk ðə ˈmoʊst əv/
misery (n)	/ˈmɪzəri/
nickname (n)	/ˈnɪkˌneɪm/
optimistic (adj)	/ˌɒptəˈmɪstɪk/
partial (adj)	/ˈpɑrʃəl/
peer (v)	/pɪər/
portion (n)	/ˈpɔrʃən/
precisely (adv)	/prɪˈsaɪsli/
prescribe (v)	/prɪˈskraɪb/
prescription (n)	/prɪˈskrɪpʃən/
procedure (n)	/prəˈsidʒər/
punishment (n)	/ˈpʌnɪʃmənt/
rapid (adj)	/ˈræpɪd/
resistant (adj)	/rɪˈzɪstənt/
respond (v)	/rɪˈspɒnd/
risk (n)	/rɪsk/
run away (v)	/ˈrʌn əˈweɪ/
slam (v)	/slæm/
slide (v)	/slaɪd/
slow (v)	/sloʊ/
stroke (n)	/stroʊk/
sweat (n)	/swɛt/
symptom (n)	/ˈsɪmptəm/
thankfully (adv)	/ˈθæŋkfəli/
therapist (n)	/ˈθɛrəpɪst/
therapy (n)	/ˈθɛrəpi/
think through (phr v)	/ˈθɪŋk ˈθru/
threatening (adj)	/ˈθrɛtnɪŋ/
treat (v)	/trit/
turn to (phr v)	/ˈtɜrn tu/
vision (n)	/ˈvɪʒən/
visual (adj)	/ˈvɪʒuəl/
waist (n)	/weɪst/
ward (n)	/wɔrd/
watch out (phr v)	/ˈwɒtʃ ˈaʊt/

Colégio Bandeirantes

B2

PERSPECTIVES
Combo
Special Edition
for Colégio Bandeirantes

Workbook

NATIONAL GEOGRAPHIC LEARNING

Australia · Brazil · Mexico · Singapore · United Kingdom · United States

NATIONAL GEOGRAPHIC LEARNING

Perspectives Combo Special Edition for Colégio Bandeirantes

Publisher: Sherrise Roehr

Executive Editor: Sarah Kenney

Project Manager: Katherine Carroll

Senior Technology Product Manager: Lauren Krolick

Director of Global Marketing: Ian Martin

Senior Product Marketing Manager: Caitlin Thomas

Sr. Director, ELT & World Languages: Michael Burggren

Production Manager: Daisy Sosa

Senior Print Buyer: Mary Beth Hennebury

Composition: Lumina Datamatics, Inc.

Cover/Text Design: Brenda Carmichael

Art Director: Brenda Carmichael

Cover Design: Raquel Braik Pedreira

Cover Image: © Leonardo Da/Shutterstock.

© 2018 National Geographic Learning, a part of Cengage Learning

ALL RIGHTS RESERVED. No part of this work covered by the copyright herein may be reproduced or distributed in any form or by any means, except as permitted by U.S. copyright law, without the prior written permission of the copyright owner.

"National Geographic", "National Geographic Society" and the Yellow Border Design are registered trademarks of the National Geographic Society
® Marcas Registradas

For product information and technology assistance, contact us at
Cengage Learning Customer & Sales Support, cengage.com/contact

For permission to use material from this text or product, submit all requests online at **cengage.com/permissions**
Further permissions questions can be emailed to
permissionrequest@cengage.com

Perspectives Workbook

ISBN: 978-0-357-46253-9

National Geographic Learning
20 Channel Center Street
Boston, MA 02210
USA

National Geographic Learning, a Cengage Learning Company, has a mission to bring the world to the classroom and the classroom to life. With our English language programs, students learn about their world by experiencing it. Through our partnerships with National Geographic and TED Talks, they develop the language and skills they need to be successful global citizens and leaders.

Locate your local office at **international.cengage.com/region**

Visit National Geographic Learning online at **NGL.Cengage.com/ELT**
Visit our corporate website at **www.cengage.com**

Photo Credits:
2 Lutz Jaekel/laif/Redux, **4** emei/Shutterstock.com, **7** Ersler Dmitry/Shutterstock.com, **8** GoodMood Photo/Shutterstock.com, **14** Rawpixel.com/Shutterstock.com, **16** Fred Turck/Shutterstock.com, **19** chombosan/Shutterstock.com, **20** Juergen Faelchle/Shutterstock.com, **26** Stefan Schurr/Shutterstock.com, **28** (tl) Petr Toman/Shutterstock.com, (bl) grmarc/Shutterstock.com, **31** Leonard Zhukovsky/Shutterstock.com, **38** Kjeld Friis/Shutterstock.com, **40** Anton_Ivanov/Shutterstock.com, **43** Skreidzeleu/Shutterstock.com, **45** Oscity/Shutterstock.com,**52** WilcoUK/Shutterstock.com, **55** Monkey Business Images/Shutterstock.com, **63** Manu M Nair/Shutterstock.com, **64** Photobac/Shutterstock.com, **67** Juan Aunion/Shutterstock.com, **68** Andrew Sutton/Shutterstock.com, **71** (tl1) TPm13thx/Shutterstock.com, (tl2) Nick Fox/Shutterstock.com, (tl3) Kit Korzun/Shutterstock.com, (tl4) Rich Carey/Shutterstock.com, **76** Tupungato/Shutterstock.com, **79** Svitlana-ua/Shutterstock.com, **81** Golubovy/Shutterstock.com, **87** Kzenon/Shutterstock.com, **88** Thoai/Shutterstock.com, **91** bokehart/Shutterstock.com, **100** (cl) VCG/Visual China Group/Getty Images, (cr) Justin Hobson/Shutterstock.com, **103** Oliver Foerstner/Shutterstock.com, **112** Kleber Cordeiro/Shutterstock.com, **115** wawritto/Shutterstock.com, **117** hxdbzxy/Shutterstock.com, **119** (cr) Tomsickova Tatyana/Shutterstock.com, (br) Antonio Guillem/Shutterstock.com.

Text Credits:
4 "Rescuing an Icon", by A.R. William, National Geographic Magazine, August 2015, p.14., **16** "Big Ideas, Little Packages", by Margaret G. Zackowitz, National Geographic Magazine, November 2010, p.24., **16** "Power to the People", by Chris Costas, National Geographic Traveler, August-September 2015, p.18., **28** "To Greeks We Owe Our Love of Athletics", March 1944, p.315., **40** "Street Dreams: Edinburgh Scotland", by Alexander McCall Smith, National Geographic Traveler, February-March 2015, p.11., **52** "Accents and Perception", by Luna Shyr, National Geographic Magazine, June 2011, p.42., **52** "Curiosity and a Cat", by Steve Boyes, National Geographic Magazine, March 2014, p.42., **64** "Baboon Troop Adapts to Survive in Desert", National Geographic Magazine, February 1992, p4., **67** "Shadow Cats", National Geographic Magazine, February 2017, p.104., **76** "Cities are the Key", by Keith Bellows, National Geographic Traveler, May-June 2011, p.26., **79** "A Thing or Two About Twins", by Peter Miller, National Geographic Magazine, January 2012, p.46., **88** "A World Together", National Geographic Magazine, by Erla Zwingle, August 1999, p.12., **88** "Cultures", text from a National Geographic map, 2014. **100** "Tracking a Tornado's Damage from Every Angle", by Daniel Stone, National Geographic Magazine, October 2016, p.22., **103** "Reader Fixes an African Bridge", National Geographic Magazine, October 2002, p32., **112** "The Art of Recovery", by Susan Goldberg, National Geographic Magazine, February 2015., **115** "A Cure in Sight", by David Dobbs, National Geographic Magazine, September 2016, p.30.

Printed in Brazil

Print Number: 01   Print Year: 2019

CONTENTS

1 **Travel, Trust, and Tourism**   2

2 **The Business of Technology**   14

3 **Faster, Higher, Stronger**   26

4 **Cultural Transformation**   38

5 **It's Not Rocket Science**   50

6 **Adapt to Survive**   62

7 **Outside the Box**   74

8 **Common Ground**   86

9 **Lend a Helping Hand**   98

10 **Life-changing**   110

VOCABULARY LIST   122

1 Travel, Trust, and Tourism

1A Cultural Exchange

VOCABULARY Experiences abroad

1 Review Complete the chart with these words.

a bike ride	a taxi	a trip	college
my bus	my train	two hours	work

get to	go for

take	catch

2 Review Complete the sentences with these words.

backpacking	commute	cruise	destination
flight	ride	route	voyage

1 Tim Peake went on a long _____ into space.
2 We need to take a different _____ because there's been an accident.
3 Most people _____ to work by car.
4 You have reached your _____.
5 Could you give me a _____ to work, please?
6 They're traveling on a _____ ship.
7 It was cheap to go _____ around Australia.
8 The earlier _____ gets to the airport at 7:00pm.

3 Read the sentences. Are they logical (L) or illogical (I)?

1 Let's go to all the major sites tomorrow—I want to get off the beaten path! ___
2 I love having a host family stay with me. ___
3 She won't try street food because she's afraid she'll get food poisoning. ___
4 Yumi lost weight in Russia because it took a while to get used to the food. ___
5 Travelers who are outgoing often hang out with the local people. ___
6 Don't wear any expensive jewelry because you might get robbed. ___
7 Ignacio likes to travel so he can lie around the house all day. ___
8 Liu didn't find the people very welcoming and made lots of new friends. ___

4 Choose the correct option (a–d) to complete each sentence.

1 I got huge culture _____ the first time I visited Asia.
   a scare   c fear
   b shock   d clash
2 There wasn't enough time to get a real _____ for the place.
   a look   c feel
   b sight   d emotion
3 She always tries to get off the beaten _____ to escape the tourists.
   a path   c street
   b road   d walk
4 We got _____ outside the hotel.
   a theft   c taken
   b robbed   d stolen

5 Did you hang _____ with any local people?
   a out   c in
   b up   d by
6 I'd prefer to be _____ to my own devices on vacation and not have a guide.
   a used   c taken
   b found   d left

5 Match the two parts of the sentences.

1 I don't find the locals
2 I've never had food
3 It's relaxing to lie
4 The children quickly got used
5 We're staying in
6 I want to see

a poisoning.
b around the house all day.
c all the sights tomorrow.
d the same B&B.
e very welcoming.
f to the different food.

6 Complete the sentences with the correct forms of these verbs.

be	find	get	go	lie	stay

1 I don't want to _____ food poisoning.
2 We're going to _____ with a host family.
3 Let's _____ hiking in the mountains.
4 We'll probably _____ around on the beach most of the week.
5 Did you _____ the locals welcoming?
6 Do you want to _____ left to your own devices?

7 Find the mistake in each sentence and write the correct word.

1 We stayed with a B&B. _____
2 It took a while to get using to the food. _____
3 I found the people really welcome. _____
4 She got food poisoned. _____
5 We were left to his own devices. _____
6 They saw all the sight. _____
7 Have you ever got culture shocking? _____
8 They were robbery the first night. _____

8 Extension Complete the sentences with these words.

amenities	availability	down time	excursion
overbooked	secluded	tourist traps	wander

1 After visiting Cuzco, we went on an amazing _____ to Machu Picchu.
2 The resort was in a very _____ part of the island. It had its own beach!
3 When we got to the hostel, they didn't have any _____. All the beds were taken.
4 What do you like to do when you have _____?
5 He's happiest when he's left to his own devices to _____ around the city.
6 The flight was _____ but no one wanted to give up their seat.
7 The new hotel has all the _____ you want—wifi, large flat-screen television, an excellent restaurant.
8 The guide advised us that the shops on the waterfront are _____.

PRONUNCIATION

9 Listen to the sentences. Does the 'd contraction you hear represent *would* or *had*? 🎧 2

1 a would   b had
2 a would   b had
3 a would   b had
4 a would   b had
5 a would   b had
6 a would   b had
7 a would   b had
8 a would   b had

LISTENING

10 Listen to a short environmental report about the Taj Mahal in India. Match the two parts of the phrasal verbs that you hear. Then practice saying the verbs. 🎧 3

1 pass   a out
2 given   b after
3 took   c up
4 carried   d with
5 stirred   e away
6 came   f on
7 deal   g up
8 looking   h out

11 Listen to the report again. Are the statements true (T) or false (F)? Practice saying the true statements. 🎧 3

1 The Taj Mahal is a tomb for Princess Mumtaz Mahal. ____
2 The princess died having her fourth child. ____
3 The Taj Mahal is made of white ivory. ____
4 The appearance of the building has changed over time. ____
5 Scientists were able to work out the likely cause of the discoloration. ____
6 Human activity has created problems for the building. ____
7 Mike Bergin is a well-known architect. ____
8 The government in Agra acted to help reduce air pollution. ____

12 Choose the correct options. Listen again if necessary. 🎧 3

1 Why was the Taj Mahal built?
   a as a resting place for a princess
   b to attract foreign visitors and boost the economy
   c to hold many of India's finest art masterpieces
2 What city is the closest to the Taj Mahal?
   a Delhi
   b Agra
   c Mumbai
3 What was the original color of the building?
   a brown
   b yellow
   c white
4 How many countries participated in the research?
   a 1
   b 2
   c 3
5 What is an example of a fossil fuel?
   a oil
   b animal waste
   c wood
6 What is Mike Bergen's job title?
   a architectural engineer
   b environmental engineer
   c air quality engineer
7 What kind of fuel did Agra switch many trucks to?
   a propane
   b diesel
   c natural gas

13 Complete the sentences with a word or short phrase. Listen again if necessary. 🎧 3

1 The Taj Mahal is the _____ of Princess Mumtaz Mahal.
2 The building was constructed with _____ marble.
3 The _____ of Agra has been growing rapidly.
4 The Taj Mahal's marble began to _____.
5 Research found two likely causes of the discoloration: _____.
6 The research findings were discussed in the Indian _____.
7 People in Agra have started using _____ to cook with.

4 Unit 1

GRAMMAR Present and past forms

14 Find and correct the mistakes in the sentences. Some sentences have more than one possible correct answer. There are two sentences that are correct.

1 While we were waiting for the bus, I was seeing a poster for tours at the art museum.
_____

2 Melissa wanted to explore the city center while it didn't rain.
_____

3 Enzo shared his photos from Singapore; he was hoping to make his friends jealous.
_____

4 Luis and I were stared at the painting for ten minutes, but we never figured out what it was.
_____

5 Ana was suffering from culture shock because she was being away from home for the first time.
_____

6 The manager offered me a discount when I called to purchase my ticket.
_____

7 While Eva and Eduardo were hanging out at the cafe, Lucas and Rafael were checked the train timetable.
_____

8 We listen to the tour guide's explanation, but my parents were buying postcards.
_____

15 Complete the sentences with the correct forms of the verbs in parentheses.

1 Giovanni _____ (study) English for many years before he _____ (move) to Canada last month.

2 Before we _____ (realize) it, Salma _____ (rush) to the front of the line and bought our tickets.

3 Ali _____ (read) yet another guidebook about New Zealand because she really _____ (want) to visit Auckland next year.

4 Because Amelia _____ (take) a photography course, she _____ (know) exactly which camera to take on her last trip.

5 Before he _____ (visit) the castle, Paul _____ (already, read) several books about its history.

6 Before Jakob _____ (tour) the museum, he _____ (get) a real feel for Athens from walking around its markets.

7 Julia _____ (examine) the painting with great interest because she _____ (study) art history in college many years before.

8 Chen _____ (hike) for eight hours before he _____ (find) a good place to set up his tent.

9 Emma _____ (buy) some more souvenirs while her boyfriend _____ (wait) for his cell phone to charge.

16 Put the words in the correct order to make sentences and questions.

1 ever / Jasmin / abroad / has / traveled
_____?

2 to spend / in / semester / was / Ravi / this / Bologna / planning
_____?

3 is / has / he / Nico / never / scared of / been / because / surfing / the ocean
_____.

4 very / with / has / food / Kari / poisoning / been / sick
_____

5 for / Valparaiso / a / you / get / feel / real / did
_____?

6 happy / devices / to / to / own / her / left / Akita / wasn't / been / have
_____.

7 wanting / Minjoo / Sydney / years / to / for / visit / been / had
_____.

17 Write a sentence about something you are doing, were doing, or had done at the following times.

1 January 1st _____

2 last weekend _____

3 last summer _____

4 10:30 this morning _____

5 9:00 last night _____

6 right now _____

1B A Place to Stay

VOCABULARY BUILDING Phrasal verbs

1 Put the words in the correct order to make sentences and questions.

1 you / make sure / look / your / sister / after / the / at / pool
_____.

2 line / where / we / up / to / get / do / tickets / train
_____?

3 close / to / were / when / down / broke / Las Vegas / we / car / the
_____.

4 hanging / park / at / the / out / amusement / is / fun / lots of
_____.

5 over / where / drivers / pull / on / road / this / can
_____?

6 for / enough / whether / it / to / down / trip / comes / have / I / money / the
_____.

7 airport / the / who / going / is / to / up / him / pick / from
_____?

READING

2 Read the article. Sentences a–g provided here have been removed from the article. Decide which sentence belongs in each place (1–6). One sentence is extra.

1 ____
2 ____
3 ____
4 ____
5 ____
6 ____

a Along these lines, you need to decide what type of lodging you are going to offer.
b Make sure you plan your business with your customer in mind.
c An empty hotel will not stay in business for long.
d Why do people visit this community, and how can your hotel become a part of it?
e How can your hotel make more money than you spend?
f Have you dreamed of opening a hotel of your own somewhere beautiful?
g Next, you need to decide what services your hotel will offer.

3 Do the statements match the information in the article? Is the information true (T), false (F), or not given (NG)?

1 A hotel owner should charge enough for rooms to cover the costs of running the hotel. ____
2 Customers who pay more for rooms will be less concerned about service. ____
3 Offering the right special services to customers can bring more business to a hotel. ____
4 The Philippines offers the best diving in Asia. ____
5 Opening a new hotel can help people living in the local community. ____

4 Find a word from the article that matches each definition.

1 something that doesn't succeed _____
2 to charge less than something is worth _____
3 an amount of money that is charged _____
4 a short pleasure trip _____
5 the feeling of a place _____

Living the Dream

1. Have you ever visited a hotel or B&B so peaceful that you thought about never leaving? (1) You are not alone. Most people have a fantasy of escaping their daily life for a new and exciting adventure, but a few people actually do it. So what does it take to start a small hotel or a B&B? What separates success stories from failures?

2. First, you have to choose a location that will attract plenty of guests. (2) Additionally, those guests need to be willing to pay enough money for their rooms to cover the hotel's costs. Some new hotel owners underprice their rooms, or they open their hotel in a place so far off the beaten path that tourists won't spend enough on lodging to keep the hotel open. Often a hotel's success comes down to being in the right location.

3. (3) Will you have a luxury resort charging high prices or a relaxing hostel where travelers can meet and make friends? (4) For example, travelers paying expensive room rates will expect the highest quality service, while those looking for an informal experience will be more satisfied by a friendly atmosphere than by expensive sheets. Give your customers what they want, and they will come back again and again.

4. (5) Will you have a restaurant? Will you offer excursions like snorkeling trips or guided tours? If so, these services will cost money, and you need to make sure you charge enough to cover the expense. On the other hand, special services can be a major attraction for tourists. When Gabrielle and Matthew Holder left the UK for the Philippines to open their own resort, they chose a site where the diving is fantastic. Tourists travel from around the world to dive in this part of the Philippines, and they are attracted to a resort that offers organized diving tours.

5. Finally, consider the community you are opening your hotel in. (6) Jonathan Baldrey spent three years renovating his hotel in Santo Domingo in the Dominican Republic to reflect the neighborhood's fascinating history. Now it appeals to travelers who want to get a sense of the Dominican Republic's culture when they visit.

6. Whether your dream is to own a luxury hotel or to open a peaceful B&B where you can meet and entertain guests from all over the world, the recipe for success is the same. Do your research, pick the perfect location, work out pricing and costs, and offer the right services and atmosphere for your customers. Do these things, and you too could be living your dream!

1C On the Road

GRAMMAR *Used to* and *would*

1 A word is missing in each sentence. Read the four answer choices and choose the correct option to complete each sentence.

1 I _____ to go to Namibia to visit my family every December.
   a would   c use
   b used   d has

2 When _____ get ready to leave for Namibia, my family would remind me to prepare for the heat—temperatures in northern Namibia can reach 122 degrees Fahrenheit!
   a I'd   c I use
   b I used   d I had

3 When we finally got to Namibia, sometimes _____ go climbing on the Brandberg Mountain.
   a we had   c we used
   b we use   d we'd

4 _____ admire Brandberg's ancient rock paintings.
   a We had   c We used
   b We use   d We'd

5 I _____ to stand for hours and study the ancient artwork.
   a would   c use
   b used   d has

6 Bushman/San hunter gatherers, people who _____ to live in the area more than 2,000 years ago, made this incredible art.
   a would   c use
   b used   d has

7 They _____ make images of things from their everyday life, for example, the jewelry they wore and the animals they must have seen such as giraffes, elephants, and snakes.
   a would   c use
   b used   d has

8 I _____ to imagine a hunter hiding out in the very caves I was visiting, painting the scenes I was seeing so many years later.
   a would   c use
   b used   d has

2 Complete the sentences with these phrases. Use correct capitalization as necessary.

but she used to speak Malayalam
my mother used to live on Kakkathuruthu
she used to paint pictures
used to love eating curries made with coconut and cinnamon
would light lamps and fish in the lagoons
would wear beautiful saris

1 When she was a girl, _____,
   a tiny island in Kerala (a state in southern India).

2 My mother speaks mostly English now, _____
   with her family and friends.

3 _____
   of the many beautiful flowers around her home, such as purple water hyacinths drifting on the lakes.

4 My mother _____,
   served on banana leaves.

5 On Kakkathuruthu, my grandmother and her friends _____
   when they went to the market.

6 At night, fishermen _____.

3 Listen and choose the correct full form for the contracted *'d* form you hear. 🎧 5

1 a They would   b They had
2 a She would   b She had
3 a I would   b I had
4 a we would   b we had
5 a he would   b he had
6 a I would   b I had

Metal pails collect sap on a maple tree.

8 Unit 1

4 Choose the correct option to complete the text.

I live in Vermont, in the United States, and, when I was younger, I (1) *used to help / used to helping* my parents make maple syrup every spring. We (2) *used to love / would love to* pouring the sweet, sticky syrup on everything from pancakes and waffles to ice cream! But making the syrup (3) *would took / took* a lot of work. The cold nights and warm days of spring got the maple trees ready to provide the sap (a thin, sugary liquid stored inside the trees) that we (4) *collected / use to collect* to make our syrup.

To start, we (5) *would pull on / used pull on* our snow boots and warm jackets. Then we (6) *would go / used to* outside and make holes in the trees about an inch deep. Next, (7) *we had hang / we'd hang* buckets on the trees to collect the sap that would drip out of the holes. My grandparents used to have horses to pull the wagon holding the buckets from tree to tree, but we used a tractor. Once we had all the sap gathered, we (8) *would boil / would boiled* it for hours and hours in a special building called a sugarhouse until it (9) *was / used to* sweet, sticky, and golden—it took about 35 gallons of sap to make one gallon of syrup! I (10) *never use to think / used to think* the sugarhouse was like a sauna, with all the heat and steam. Every year, when the syrup (11) *use to be / was* ready, we used to have a big party for all our friends to share the first batch.

5 Put the words in the correct order to make sentences and questions. Use the correct verb form.

1 use / called / be / Constantinople / Istanbul / to
   Istanbul used to be called Constantinople.
2 on / you / post / a / social media / lot / of / to / use / do / photos
   _____?
3 do not / cream / we / to / ice / after / school / use / get
   _____.
4 the / I / TV / would / all / time / watch
   _____.
5 space / use / think / couldn't / people / to / everybody / go / into
   _____.
6 I / to / lot / read / a / of / novels / mystery / use
   _____.
7 use / we / vacations / skiing / never / to / go / on
   _____.
8 hair / your / be / use / did / to / blond
   _____?

6 Read the letter Petra wrote to her grandfather when she studied in Croatia a few years ago. Then write about Petra using *would* and *used to*.

> March 19, 2015
>
> Dear Grandpa,
>
> I love being an exchange student in Croatia! There's so much going on. Every day before class, I meet my friend Lorena for coffee. Then I ride my bike to school, while Lorena goes to her job at the hospital. On Mondays, Wednesdays, and Fridays, I study English and chemistry. On Tuesdays and Thursdays, it's math and history. I study every night at the library, but I never study on weekends.
>
> On weekends, I like to hang out with my friends—sometimes we go snorkelling or hiking. Last weekend, we went to see the ancient city walls in Dubrovnik. And next weekend, I think we're going to Lokrum, a beautiful island with amazing forests.
>
> In your last letter, you asked if I'd been going out to listen to music. Well, my friends and I don't go to concerts because they're too expensive. We usually just enjoy streaming music at home.
>
> Love,
> Petra

While studying in Croatia in 2015…

1 _____
  every day before class.
2 _____
  bike to school.
3 On Mondays, Wednesdays, and Fridays,
  _____.
4 _____
  on Tuesdays and Thursdays.
5 _____
  at the library.
6 _____
  on weekends.
7 _____
  hang out with her friends on weekends.
8 _____
  because they were too expensive.

1D How Airbnb Designs for Trust

TEDTALKS

AUTHENTIC LISTENING SKILLS

1 Listen and complete the extract with the words you hear.

(1) _____ the day after graduating from design school and (2) _____ having a yard sale. And this guy (3) _____ up in this red Mazda and he (4) _____ looking through my stuff. And he (5) _____ a piece of art that I made. And it turns out (6) _____ alone in town for the night, driving cross-country on a road trip before he goes into the Peace Corps.

WATCH ▷

2 Number the statements about Joe's life in order.

____ **a** Joe and Brian build a website and launch their business, Airbed and Breakfast.

____ **b** Now, 785,000 people in 191 countries use Airbnb each day.

____ **c** Joe moves to San Francisco and, after two years, is unemployed.

____ **d** Joe learns that online reviews help to build trust and reduce social bias.

____ **e** Joe suggests to his roommate, Brian, that they host people in their home during a major design conference.

____ **f** Joe hosts his first house guest shortly after finishing design school.

3 Choose the correct option to complete the sentences.

1 Joe *had / used to have* a yard sale when he finished design school.
2 The "Peace Corps guy" *would buy / bought* a piece of art from Joe.
3 Joe and Brian *used to be / would be* roommates in San Francisco.
4 On the old website, people *didn't use to write / would write* negative reviews.
5 In the early days, Joe *would take / had taken* the customer service calls himself.
6 One time, some hosts *used to take / took* their guest to the hospital when he had a heart attack.

7 According to Joe, good design *has helped / used to help* people to overcome their biases.

4 Read the sentence and paragraph provided here. In which place (a–d) could the sentence be added to the paragraph?

This information comes in two forms: information the host shares about themselves and customer reviews.

Joe Gebbia argues that design is able to change the way people relate to one another. (a) By creating hidden guidelines for users, such as the size of a response box, the website encourages people to share just enough information about themselves to create trust, but not so much that people become frightened. (b) Gebbia recognizes that people don't naturally trust strangers and need to learn more about them before opening their homes. (c) Gebbia had to experiment with the review process before arriving at the current format, but he learned that the best approach was to wait until both host and guest had written their reviews before the reviews are revealed. (d) This way, reviewers are not biased by what the other person has written and give more honest feedback.

VOCABULARY IN CONTEXT

5 Match the words and phrases (1–6) with the sentences that illustrate them (a–f).

1 keep in touch ____
2 broke ____
3 rush ____
4 anxiety ____
5 up for it ____
6 trip up ____

a Mark gets so **nervous** when he travels that he has difficulty sleeping.
b Leticia didn't notice how much money she had been spending until she saw **a zero balance** in her bank account.
c When So-Jin first started studying English, the different accents she heard really **confused** her.
d My uncle didn't wake up when his alarm rang, and he had to **hurry** to get to his appointment on time.
e My cousins and I don't live in the same city, but we make sure to **call each other every week** to see how things are going.
f I wanted to see the new movie last night, so I called my friends to see if they were **interested in joining me.**

10 Unit 1

1E Trip Advice

SPEAKING

Useful language

Making suggestions

If sightseeing is their thing, then the best place to go is…

If they want to experience a genuine local night out, I'd suggest trying…

If they're only staying here for a little while, they should probably…

If you ask me, the one place they really have to go to is…

Reacting to suggestions

If they'd rather try something different,… might be worth a shot.

I wouldn't bother going to…, personally.

They'd be better (off) going to…

1 Complete the sentences with these phrases. Then listen to check your answers. 🎧 7

a little while	be better (off)
'd suggest trying	experience a genuine
rather try something	's their thing
the best places	the one place
they should probably	worth a shot
wouldn't bother going	you ask me

If sightseeing (1) _____,
then (2) _____
to go are Lombard Street and the Golden Gate Bridge. If they want to (3) _____ local night out, I (4) _____ Union Square. If they're only staying here for
(5) _____,
(6) _____ see Alcatraz Island.
If (7) _____,
(8) _____ they really have to go to is the beach. If they'd
(9) _____ different, Chinatown might be (10) _____.
I (11) _____ to the wax museum personally. They'd
(12) _____ going to the aquarium or zoo.

2 Match the beginnings (1–8) with the endings (a–h) to make recommendations from a TV travel show about Barcelona. Then listen and check your answers. 🎧 8

Barcelona truly is one of the world's best-loved destinations.

1 If you're only staying here for a little while, ____
2 And if you ask me, ____
   The nature-inspired cathedral designed by Antoni Gaudi is still being built more than 135 years later.
3 If you'd rather try something outside, ____
4 If sports are your thing, then ____
5 Barcelona is famous for its cuisine, but if you want to buy some fresh food, ____
6 You'd be best off going to La Boqueria, ____
7 If you want to experience a genuine local night out, ____
8 Then, head down La Rambla to the Plaça Reial to enjoy some more amazing tapas in one of the many small and friendly cafes, ____

a before finding a club to dance the night away.
b I wouldn't bother going to the supermarkets, personally.
c I'd suggest starting with some traditional tapas in a restaurant in the Raval district.
d one of the last covered markets in Europe, and sampling the wonderful range of food and drink on offer.
e Park Guell will definitely be worth a visit. This sculpted garden is a favorite with locals and tourists alike.
f the best place to go is the Olympic stadium. Home to the 1992 Games, this beautiful stadium also has great views over the city.
g the one place you really have to go to is the Sagrada Familia.
h you should probably hop on the *Bus Turistic* and see all the most famous attractions from an open-top double-decker bus.

3 Some friends from another country are coming to visit your city. Make notes on the best advice and recommendations you can give them for what to do in the area. Use the useful language.

4 Listen to a conversation between a student and a school counselor, and then answer the question. 🎧 9

Question: Make notes on how you would briefly summarize the issue the two speakers are discussing. Then add notes about which solution you recommend and give reasons to explain why. Speak for one minute and record yourself.

Then listen to the sample answer. 🎧 10

WRITING A review

5 Read the extracts from all four reviews. Then give each one a different star-rating, from one (★☆☆☆) to four (★★★★) stars.

1 The outdoor market was one of the highlights of the trip. We enjoyed browsing the stalls and looking at all the local goods and crafts. Unfortunately, they charge higher prices to tourists, but I imagine that happens everywhere. It's still a good place to buy souvenirs, and well worth a visit. ☆☆☆☆

2 The dining area was too dark, and the service was terrible. Our food took a long time to arrive, and when it did, the wrong dish was served to my sister. Also, everything was cold and poorly presented. What's more, it was expensive! I'd skip this restaurant if I were you. ☆☆☆☆

3 The walking tour of the city was a bit disappointing. It was advertised as a one-hour event but it finished after 45 minutes, which was surprising. Some of the sights were cool, but the tour guide didn't really give us much information about them. For $10, it's just not worth it. ☆☆☆☆

4 The three-day art course was the best thing I did all summer! The teacher was excellent and encouraged us all to try new art styles and techniques. I can't believe how much I learned in just a few days. Doing this course gave me so much confidence. I can't recommend it enough. ☆☆☆☆

6 Complete the review with these words and phrases.

arranged	enjoyed
fun	love
On top of that	One other thing was the fact that
recommend	special
what's more	which

Adventure-Break is an organized vacation in Scotland that offers a range of adventure sports and other activities. Two of my friends and I booked an Adventure-Break last month. In the beautiful and wild Scottish countryside, we (1) _____ a variety of outdoor activities, including canoeing, mountain biking, hiking, and even kayaking. It was a memorable experience for all the best reasons! What I particularly like is that everything is (2) _____ for you, (3) _____ is very convenient. You choose your accommodation in advance—camping or staying in a chalet—and the adventure starts as soon as you arrive. (4) _____, they have their own chefs who cook the most delicious meals for everyone. The guides do everything they can to make sure you enjoy your vacation and, (5) _____, they're great (6) _____. You can do as many activities as you want every day. (7) _____ we met lots of people from different countries. We became really good friends with some of them, which was (8) _____. If you like doing outdoor activities and meeting new people, you'll (9) _____ Adventure-Break. I can't (10) _____ it enough!

—Javier Sanchez, Spain

7 Read Javier's review again. Are these statements true (T) or false (F)?

1 Adventure-Break is good for people who enjoy doing sports. ____
2 Javier and his friends went on an Adventure-Break last year. ____
3 Most of the activities are done outside. ____
4 Javier tells us that the Adventure-Break was unforgettable. ____
5 People going on Adventure-Breaks have to find and arrange their own accommodation. ____
6 Adventure-Break participants take turns cooking for each other. ____
7 Javier was impressed with the guides. ____
8 There is no daily limit to the number of activities participants can sign up for. ____
9 Adventure-Break is only available to people from Spain. ____
10 Overall, Javier gives the experience a very positive review. ____

8 You see this announcement on a travel website.

> **Travel reviews wanted**
>
> Have you taken a vacation to a place you found particularly impressive or disappointing? Write us a review saying where you went and explain why. Tell us whether or not you would recommend this place to others. The best reviews will be published on our website.

Write your review.

Review

1 Choose the correct options to complete the email.

> Hi Yumi,
>
> We've just got back! At first, we stayed in a (1) ___. It was in the mountains, and the view (2) ___ my mind. However, I got food (3) ___ in the first week, so we looked for somewhere else to (4) ___ with Airbnb. Next year, I'm (5) ___ camping—then I'll be able to get off the (6) ___ path more and get a better feel for the place.
>
> –Tania

	a	b	c	d
1	B&A	B&B	A&B	B&C
2	blew	rushed	shocked	left
3	poison	poisoner	poisoned	poisoning
4	lie around	stay	live	hang out
5	being	doing	going	getting
6	beat	beating	beats	beaten

2 Complete the words in the sentences. Some of the letters are given for you.

1 It was a real c _____ t _____ shock at first.
2 The locals were so friendly and w _____ c _____.
3 They saw most of the s _____ in the first few days.
4 Sitting by the plane window reduces my a _____.
5 It's too bad that we didn't keep in t _____ after the vacation.

3 Put the words in the correct order to make questions.

1 your / package / Jamaica / tour / meals / did / in / include
_____?
2 about / long / how / at the end of the road / they / known / the private beach / have
_____?
3 rented / who / to / beach / house / their / you
_____?
4 lunch / where / guide / us / the / after / meet / telling / is / to
_____?
5 taken / climb / souvenirs / have / what / as / their / of / trekkers
_____?

4 Match the two parts of the sentences.

1 Every day—well, most days!—___
2 Because I have a meeting tomorrow, ___
3 Yesterday ___
4 My leg hurt while ___
5 By the time my older brother got home, ___
6 When my friend started coming with me to work out, ___
7 When I had classes in the afternoon, ___

a I'd come back from the gym.
b I would go to the gym in the morning.
c I'd already been going to the gym for a while.
d I go to the gym.
e I was running at the gym.
f I'm going to the gym today.
g I went to the gym.

5 Decide if the words in bold are correct or incorrect. Write the correct word(s).

1 When I lived in Costa Rica, I **would go jogging** every morning before breakfast. _____
2 **Did you used** to eat beans for breakfast? _____
3 I **would to want** to study abroad. _____
4 She didn't **would to have** short hair. _____
5 My grandmother **used tell** me stories about when she was growing up in Shanghai. _____
6 Did you **use to ride** your bike to school? _____
7 I **never use to eat** a lot of sugary snacks. _____
8 He didn't **used to study** at the library. _____

2 The Business of Technology

2A Young Business

VOCABULARY Setting up a new business

1 Review Cross out the mistake in each sentence and write the correct word.

1 She is in charge for the marketing team.
   _____
2 I work on the construction industry.
   _____
3 The job market is very competition.
   _____
4 I'm looking for a fully-time job.
   _____
5 Cleaning is not a very well-pay job.
   _____
6 He's responsible at sales.
   _____
7 Farming is a physically demanded job.
   _____
8 Doctors have to work extremely long hour.
   _____

2 Review Complete the sentences with these words.

| charge | flexible | industry | part-time |
| prospects | responsible | stressful | |

1 Are you _____ for the advertising?
2 The job is so _____ I'm not sleeping very well.
3 Our new engineers have excellent career _____.
4 Our manager is in _____ of over 100 people.
5 They want _____ people who don't mind change.
6 It's a _____ job, from 9 to 2.
7 Do you work in the sports _____?

3 Match the words to make phrases connected to business.

1 handle   a a good deal
2 deal with a   b money
3 raise   c stress and pressure
4 put together   d a team of people
5 negotiate   e something new
6 invent   f range of people

4 Do you connect these activities more with people or with products? Complete the table.

distribute   invent   market   meet   negotiate   network

People	Products

5 Choose the correct option (a–d) to complete each sentence.

1 The company needs to _____ another million dollars from the investors.
   a raise
   b deal
   c lend
   d figure

14 Unit 2

2 Don't forget to hand out your business card when _____.
   a inventing
   b networking
   c getting on
   d putting together

3 We _____ a good price with the supplier.
   a managed
   b got on
   c negotiated
   d handled

4 The company was able to _____ from a bad year of sales.
   a redesign
   b accept
   c repair
   d recover

5 I'm responsible for _____ the marketing department.
   a dealing with
   b distributing
   c getting on
   d negotiating

6 The manager _____ together a team of engineers for the project.
   a hold
   b put
   c send
   d manage

6 Complete the sentences with the correct word. The first letter is given for you.

1 Positive comments on social media can r_____ a new company's profile significantly.
2 Remember, you can n_____ anything.
3 The director puts a lot of p_____ on the managers.
4 We're planning to d_____ our products in Europe.
5 How do you plan to m_____ your new product?
6 The t_____ they put together includes sales people in Europe and Asia.
7 The company is based in an o_____ in the city center.
8 It's important to n_____ with people from other companies when you go to a conference.

7 Extension Are the statements true (T) or false (F)?

1 The **founder** of a company has established it. ____
2 If you describe yourself as **proactive**, you enjoy working outdoors. ____
3 To **outsource** means to use suppliers outside your company for goods and services. ____
4 If negotiations are **delicate**, it means they are difficult. ____
5 A **self-starter** is someone who starts new companies. ____
6 A **team player** gets on well with other people at work. ____
7 The **chair** of a meeting is an important piece of furniture. ____
8 A **systematic** employee is good at planning. ____

8 Extension Complete the sentences with these words.

| chair | delicate | founder | outsourced |
| proactive | self-starter | systematic | team player |

1 She isn't a _____ and is difficult to work with.
2 The _____ is going to introduce the speakers.
3 We're having _____ talks with our partners at the moment, so it's a bit risky.
4 I'm not very _____ so the project looks a bit disorganized.
5 The company is looking for a _____ for this role.
6 She is the _____ of the business, which has been going since 2005.
7 The hotel _____ the cleaning to a local company.
8 I'm very _____ and good at making things happen.

PRONUNCIATION

9 Listen to the questions. Does the intonation rise or fall at the end of the question? Practice saying the questions. 🎧 11

1 Isn't there a more secure way to shop online?
_____
2 You fell for an online scam? _____
3 Do you think it's a good idea to post that?
_____
4 Wouldn't it be great to start your own company?
_____
5 What do you want to do with that? _____
6 Wouldn't it be better to help people in need?
_____
7 Haven't you ever had that problem?
_____
8 Why aren't they marketing the product yet?
_____

LISTENING

10 Listen to the speaker. Complete the sentences about the short lecture. 🎧 12

1 Good _____ might save the world one new idea at a time.
2 Designers have always dreamed up _____ goods.
3 New products include _____ roof tiles, electric motorcycles, and more.
4 The _____ Design for Extreme Affordability course is at Stanford University.
5 Some entrepreneurs are taking a look at the concerns of people in _____.
6 Designers are creating products to meet communities' most _____.
7 Problems from health care to _____ water can have affordable, beautifully designed solutions.

orange breasted sunbird

11 Now listen to the description of four innovative products. Match the description with the product. 🎧 13

1 gives hours of safe heat   a Q Drum
2 costs around a dollar   b The Embrace
3 holds almost 13 gallons of water   c Respira
4 stops harmful bacteria and viruses d LifeStraw

12 Listen to the speaker. What is the main idea of her talk? 🎧 14

a the positives and negatives of sustainable eco-tourism
b the benefits brought by conservation entrepreneurs
c the need for entrepreneurs to protect the natural world
d the entrepreneurial spirit of young African people

13 Listen again and choose the correct options. 🎧 14

1 What example does the speaker give of *sustainable eco-tourism*?
   a national parks
   b plant and animal habitats
   c private nature reserves
2 What species does she describe as rare?
   a coral lagoons
   b the Fynbos plant
   c orange-breasted sunbirds
3 Who refers to the area the speaker describes as the "Cape Floral Kingdom"?
   a botanists
   b Lutzeyer
   c natives
4 How did the Lutzeyers raise money for the reserve?
   a they raised the money themselves
   b they used banks in nearby Cape Town
   c they sold the abandoned farms and lands
5 How would you describe the attitude of the local people living near the reserve?
   a unconvinced
   b suspicious
   c supportive
6 What does the speaker describe Grootbos as being part of?
   a a conservation effort
   b a worldwide trend
   c our natural world

16 Unit 2

GRAMMAR Present perfect forms and the simple past

14 Choose the correct options to complete the conversation.

A: What (1) *are you learning / did you learn / have you learned* since starting your own company?

B: The most important thing I (2) *have learned / have been learning / learned* is that you have to be able to deal with failure in this business. But you can learn from failure.

A: When (3) *did you start / have you started / have you been starting* your company?

B: In 2012, my friends and I (4) *have started / started / have been starting* creating what eventually became our app. We had been working on it for two years before we (5) *have decided / have been deciding / decided* to get serious and quit our jobs to work on the app full-time.

A: And how do you define your current success?

B: For me, it (6) *wasn't / hasn't been being / hasn't been* about earning tons of money or having power or influence. I'm successful because I like what I do, and I have fun doing it. When it stops being fun, that's when I'll consider doing something different.

15 Complete the sentences with these words and phrases.

claimed	dreamed
has invented	have been attracting
have failed	have run
have risen	haven't been advertising
made	

1 Companies like ours _____ in print magazines or newspapers.
2 The company's founder _____ that he slept only three hours a night.
3 Many businesses _____ because they _____ out of money.
4 Technology companies _____ the attention of investors for years.
5 The competition _____ an app that works faster than ours.
6 In the late 1990s many people _____ of becoming tech millionaires.
7 Our profits _____ 5% in the last year thanks to automation.
8 We _____ a profit for the first time after three years in business.

16 Complete the article with the correct forms of the verbs in parentheses.

Young Entrepreneurs in India

In recent years, kids in India (1) _____ (make) a difference in important ways. A number of high school students (2) _____ (become) entrepreneurs. Young entrepreneurs, sometimes called "schoolpreneurs," (3) _____ (realize) that starting businesses is important for India's economic development.

Possibly the most famous young technology entrepreneurs in India are Shravan and Sanjay Kumaran, brothers and high school students from Chennai. They (4) _____ (create) GoDimensions in 2011—when they were just 12 and 10 years old. In total, they (5) _____ (develop) seven apps that are available in the Apple App Store and three Android apps for the Google Play Store. People (6) _____ (download) the apps more than 70,000 times! Shravan and Sanjay claim to be the youngest cell phone app developers in India at 16 and 14 years of age. They (7) _____ (give) presentations at a TedX Youth conference in 2015, and plan to donate 15% of their profits to charity.

Fortunately, investors (8) _____ (be) willing to take a risk with young entrepreneurs—they are more interested in good business ideas than in the age of the entrepreneur!

17 Complete the sentences using the correct forms of the verbs in parentheses.

1 For as long as she can remember, people _____ (ask) Leanna Archer what makes her hair look so beautiful.
2 Leanna _____ (decide) to try to sell her all-natural hair product to people she _____ (know).
3 She _____ (put) the special hair product in small containers and _____ (give) samples to her friends and their parents.
4 They _____ (like) it so much, they were willing to pay for it!
5 So Leanna _____ (start) her own hair-care company, Leanna's Essentials, when she _____ (be) just thirteen.
6 Since then, thousands of people _____ (be able) to enjoy Leanna's products.

2B Spreading Fast

VOCABULARY BUILDING Adjective and noun collocations

1 Complete the sentences with these adjectives.

distant	luxury	normal	official
personal	second-hand	well-paid	

1 Be careful with your _____ details so criminals cannot steal your identity.
2 I like to stay at _____ hotels when I travel; they're expensive, but it's worth it.
3 These shoes were only half the _____ price, so I bought them right away.
4 I've been researching online to try to find some of my _____ relatives and get in touch.
5 Has the university sent you your _____ letter of acceptance yet?
6 Jana has got an interesting and _____ job for the summer.
7 I'd like to buy a good _____ car when I graduate.

READING

2 Read the information. Match the information (a–f) with the paragraphs (1–5). Paragraph numbers may be used more than once.

a an example of a successful emotional advertisement ____
b details of advertising fifty years ago ____
c examples of advertisements that used the same marketing strategy ____
d context for how companies can succeed in advertising today ____
e restates information given in other sections ____
f discusses how games and advertising are related ____

3 Complete each sentence with the correct ending based on information from the text.

1 Viral marketing campaigns usually ____
2 Playworld was able to ____
3 Lay's contest to create a new chip flavor ____
4 Chipotle's Scarecrow game ____
5 Emotional responses to advertising content ____
6 A successful advertising campaign ____

a take advantage of the reasons that people share information on social media.
b is appealing to a wide range of people.
c received millions of entries.
d get free advertising by getting communities involved.
e was downloaded thousands of times.
f cause people to share the content with others.

4 Do the statements match the information in the article? Write true (T), false (F), or not given (NG).

1 Companies can make more money through advertising now than they could fifty years ago. ____
2 A company has to understand why people share on social media in order to make a successful advertisement. ____
3 An advertisement that gets an emotional reaction from consumers is less likely to be a success. ____
4 The Dove advertisement was successful because women felt emotionally connected to its message. ____
5 Prizes are more effective than games at getting consumers to share an advertisement. ____

Going Viral

1. Fifty years ago, companies trying to increase awareness of their products knew exactly how to reach consumers. They focused their advertising efforts on television, newspapers, and magazines, and spent time developing creative advertisements that they knew millions of people would see. But today's consumers are flooded with information on a daily basis. In the age of social media, over 4.75 billion pieces of content are added to social media sites every 24 hours. How do companies and their products get noticed? Getting social media users to share content is important to success. Going viral, or having content shared quickly with many users, can make millions of dollars for a company. But how can a company create a viral marketing campaign? It has to understand why people share information and then use that in its advertising.

2. Emotion is a powerful reason that social media users share content. When a user feels a strong connection to an advertisement, whether that emotion is joy, sadness, or even anger, they are much more likely to share that advertisement with others. Take, for example, the advertising campaign about "real women" by the beauty brand Dove. In this advertisement, an artist draws two pictures of a woman without seeing her. One picture is based on that woman's description of herself, and the other is based on a description from someone who knows the woman. The pictures clearly show how the woman is critical of herself while others see her in a much more positive light. This advertisement appealed to the emotions of a diverse range of women, who could relate to its message. It was shared nearly 3.8 million times in a month.

3. But an advertisement doesn't have to be serious to get attention and shares. Some companies have had great success by offering games or prizes to social media users. The fast-food chain Chipotle Mexican Foods released an advertisement called "The Scarecrow" that had both a short film and a free game that users could download. The game had more than 250,000 downloads within four days of its release. This type of advertising is even more effective because a user is reminded of the company every time they open the app to play the game.

4. Social media users also love prizes. The snack food company Lay's increased its sales in the United States by 12% with a viral campaign asking users to create a new flavor of potato chips. The winning flavor, cheesy garlic bread, was selected from almost four million ideas. The playground manufacturer Playworld offered two free playgrounds to users who liked the company's social media page and wrote an essay about why they wanted to bring a playground to their community. Not only did visits to the company's social media page increase significantly, many communities worked together to try to win the playground, and local newspapers and TV news shows covered the contest at no cost to Playworld.

5. For an advertising campaign to succeed today, it has to appeal to people of many ages in many places. The companies producing the most successful advertisements are those that understand the reasons why people share and make their advertisements with those reasons in mind. Advertising is certainly different to what it was fifty years ago, but the profits from a great campaign can still be huge.

2C Tech My Advice

GRAMMAR Verb patterns (-ing or infinitive with to)

1 Choose the correct option to complete the sentences.

1. Nacho won't admit *using / to use* social media.
2. She decided *closing / to close* her social media account.
3. He hopes *receiving / to receive* a letter from the university soon.
4. Esteban needs *planning / to plan* carefully for the future.
5. When a website says it uses cookies, do you agree *continuing / to continue* using it?
6. Her parents want her to delay *using / to use* social media for as long as possible.
7. I didn't intend *offending / to offend* anyone with the post I wrote.
8. Eva refused *accept / to accept* Ivan's friend request on social media.

2 Choose the correct option to complete the sentences.

1. 3-D printing is something experts expect _____ a big role in the future.
   a play
   b to play
   c playing
2. Some people hear about amazing objects made by 3-D printers and start _____ they can make the same things themselves.
   a believing
   b believe
   c to believe
3. 3-D printers allow designers _____ new concepts.
   a to test
   b testing
   c test
4. Experts think _____ human tissue with 3-D printers is a distant possibility.
   a to produce
   b produce
   c producing
5. With 3-D printers, researchers can avoid _____ costly mistakes.
   a make
   b to make
   c making
6. If a student needs _____ a model for a science project, a 3-D printer can be useful.
   a to make
   b making
   c make

3 Are the words in bold correct or incorrect? Correct those that are incorrect.

1. For several decades, robotics companies in Japan have been working toward their ambitious goal—they intend **creating** a perfect humanoid robot. _____
2. They hope, one day, **being** able to make androids look exactly like humans. _____
3. Some scientists are also trying **to give** their androids a personality. _____
4. However, there are people who simply refuse **accepting** a future where robots and humans live and work side by side. _____
5. Other people don't mind **to think** about a future where robots play an important role. _____
6. Personally, I think I would enjoy **to interact** with a robot that can think, act, and relate to humans. _____
7. If asked, I'd certainly agree **to have** an android do chores around my house. _____
8. The question is, will we ever regret **to make** robots so much like humans? _____

4 Complete the conversation using the correct form of the verbs in parentheses. Use verb + -ing or infinitive with to.

A: Have you heard of the Hubble Space Telescope?
B: Yes, I have! It's used (1) _____ (study) our solar system.
A: Do you know how big the telescope is?
B: I know that the Hubble designers dreamed of making a bigger telescope, but they had to compromise. In the end, they managed (2) _____ (design) a smaller telescope that orbits 350 miles above Earth.

A: Did they do a lot of tests before sending it up in space?

B: They did. In fact, one astronaut wanted (3) _____ (guarantee) the telescope could be fixed in space, so he went to the Smithsonian's National Air and Space Museum and practiced (4) _____ (fix) its Hubble replica.

A: What does the Hubble do?

B: Well, one thing is that it allows us (5) _____ (see) stars that are billions of light years from Earth. Hubble researchers are determined (6) _____ (keep) exploring our solar system.

5 Write sentences that are true for you. Use these prompts and verbs with *-ing* or infinitive with *to*.

1 I always try _____

2 I avoid _____

3 Sometimes I miss _____

4 When I finish _____

5 I am considering _____

6 As soon as I can, I hope _____

6 Complete the sentences with the objects and the correct forms of the verbs in parentheses.

1 The teacher asked _____ (me, arrange) a meeting with my parents.
2 Our teacher expects _____ (us, text) each other in English for more practice.
3 My father can't stand _____ (me, check) my phone constantly.
4 Karl watched _____ (her, carry) four heavy bags and didn't offer to help.
5 The neighbors invited _____ (us, swim) in their pool.
6 The airline strike has delayed _____ (me, travel) to Santiago.
7 You can't expect _____ (him, be) happy with the decision.
8 The coach chose _____ (her, play) in the game.

7 Read the sentences. Circle the direct object and underline the indirect object.

1 Can you email me the directions when you can?
2 His aunt gave him money for his class trip.
3 The teacher read the children a story.
4 Can you pass me a pen to write the list?
5 Here, I'll lend you my phone to call him.
6 Veronica bought her parents tickets for the opera.

8 Complete the sentences with direct and indirect objects and/or verbs with *-ing* or infinitive with *to*.

1 They promised _____

2 I don't expect _____

3 It bothers me when people ask me _____

4 I'm going to lend _____

The Business of Technology

2D This is What Happens When You Reply to Spam Email

TEDTALKS

AUTHENTIC LISTENING SKILLS

1 Read statements from James Veitch's TED Talk. Practice reading the responses aloud using intonation and pitch to show surprise. Record and then listen to yourself. 🎧 16

1 We shall be shipping gold to you.
   Response: Shipping gold to me?
2 There's no point doing this at all unless you're shipping at least a metric ton.
   Response: A metric ton?
3 I'm a hedge fund executive bank manager.
   Response: A hedge fund executive bank manager?
4 We're ready for shipping as much gold as possible.
   Response: As much gold as possible?
5 I was in Sainsbury's the other day and there were, like, 30 different varieties.
   Response: 30 different varieties?
6 When we email each other, we need to use a code.
   Response: A code?
7 Send £1,500 via a Giant Gummy Lizard.
   Response: A Giant Gummy Lizard?
8 I am Winnie Mandela, the second wife of Nelson Mandela, the former South African president.
   Response: Winne Mandela?

WATCH ▶

2 Choose the correct option to complete the sentences.

1 James refused *accepting* / *to accept* only 25 kilograms of gold from Solomon.
2 Instead, he offered *to receive* / *receiving* a metric ton of gold.
3 James enjoyed *corresponding* / *to correspond* with Solomon so much that he canceled plans with friends.
4 Apparently, Solomon planned *spending* / *to spend* his earnings on buying property.
5 James doesn't mind to *waste* / *wasting* spammers' time.
6 In corresponding with spammers, James recommends *creating* / *to create* a separate email account.
7 James never agreed *to send* / *sending* money to the person who claimed to be Winnie Mandela.

3 Choose the correct options.

1 What is the main topic of the talk?
   a Gold is a solid investment.
   b Answering spam emails can sometimes be fun.
   c More people should try hummus.
   d Nelson Mandela was an important South African leader.
2 According to James Veitch, what do spammers often do to encourage people to participate in their schemes?
   a They tell you they know where you live.
   b They ask for personal information about you.
   c They share their hopes to make you feel empathy.
   d They offer more money in each email.
3 What does Veitch imply when he says "Don't use your own email address because that's exactly what I was doing at the start and it was a nightmare."?
   a That a spammer will sell your email address to other spammers.
   b That people send a lot of emails at night.
   c That it's dangerous to reveal your real identity.
   d That most people use only one email address.
4 What can be inferred about James Veitch?
   a He thinks spammers don't cause any harm.
   b He wishes he were a bank manager.
   c He enjoys pointing out the absurdity in people's words and actions.
   d He doesn't care about other people.

VOCABULARY IN CONTEXT

4 Match the words and phrases (1–6) with the sentences that show their meaning (a–f).

1 intrigues ____
2 turned up ____
3 matter ____
4 out of hand ____
5 knock it on the head ____
6 gone too far ____

a I will call my brother tonight. We have an important **issue** to discuss.
b Kenneth keeps turning his homework in late, so Sheila told him he needs to **stop that behavior** and start taking his studies seriously.
c Raquel was surprised when her sister **appeared** at her shop one afternoon.
d Jaime was trying to tell jokes, but when nobody laughed, he realized that he had **said something wrong**.
e Jasmine has always enjoyed studying science; biology particularly **interests** her.
f When Gene saw the mess that the children had made, he was upset that the situation had got **out of control**.

2E Investment Opportunity

SPEAKING

Speaking strategy

Persuading
When we are persuading people, we sometimes turn our own experiences and opinions into a negative question to challenge the other person's ideas.
I think it will lose money.
Don't you think it'll lose money?
I'd find it really useful.
Wouldn't you find it really useful?
I have sometimes had that problem.
Haven't you ever had that problem?

1 Listen and complete the useful language with the correct auxiliary verb, then write the original idea. 🎧 17

1 __Do__ n't you think it'll be a mistake?
   I think it'll be a mistake.
2 _____ n't you find it really annoying?
3 _____ n't you ever seen that happen?
4 _____ n't it look weird if you do that?
5 _____ n't that a bad idea?
6 _____ n't we wait five more minutes, please?
7 _____ n't you see her yesterday?
8 _____ n't you finish your homework first?

2 Write a negative question to challenge each of these opinions or ideas using the words in parentheses.

1 I'm going to have another piece of cake.
   (had enough already)
2 Climate change isn't my problem.
   (all responsible / environment)
3 I'm going to buy the latest laptop.
   (wait / a sale)
4 I want to be a famous actor.
   (need / plan B)
5 I'm going to watch movies all day.
   (play / basketball)

3 Look at these situations and decide what your opinions are. Then use negative questions to express your comments on the situations.

1 Your English teacher gives you four pieces of homework in one day.
2 The government is cutting funding to youth projects.
3 Scientists have found a way to change babies' eye color.
4 A friend of yours has found a bag containing $1,000 in the street.
5 A company is considering building a big hotel on a nature reserve.
6 A friend is too lazy to study for their exams.

4 Your school wants to protect itself from cybercrime. Below are some ideas that they are considering and a question for you to discuss. Make notes and then talk about the benefits and drawbacks of these ideas. Record yourself. Remember to use the speaking strategy. Then listen to a sample discussion of the topic. 🎧 18

What are the benefits and drawbacks of these IT security ideas?
- backing up computers every hour
- permanently recording all activity of every user
- only allowing students to use their own devices

WRITING A persuasive article

5 Match the steps for writing a persuasive text (1–4) with the examples (a–d).

1 Grab the reader's attention and stimulate a shared experience. ___
2 Persuade the reader to continue reading by saying that a solution will be provided. ___
3 Present factual information related to the solution. ___
4 In the final paragraph, provide a reason why the reader should take action. ___

a What we can offer you is a happy balance between relaxing under a palm tree and participating in some very worthwhile environmental projects.
b Well, luckily, our team has found a fantastic way to help you live the dream!
c So, why not click <u>here</u> and join one of our *HOLunteering* trips today? You'll be glad you did!
d Have you ever dreamed of going on vacation somewhere exotic… but can't afford it? Trust me, we all have!

6 Read the persuasive text. Then put the information provided here in the correct order.

University students aiming to bring you the ideal sauce

Do you love ketchup but find it a little too sweet? Do you enjoy hot sauce but find it a little too… hot? Most of us do! We've all been served a dish that would be perfect, except that it's missing *something*. Well, problem solved! That something special has finally been developed, you'll be pleased to know, and it has a tantalizing Korean twist.

Theo, Mike, Erica, Ryan and Alex—five classmates at the University of California, Los Angeles (UCLA)—have created K POP, the most exciting and delicious sauce you'll ever taste. K POP Sauce with its winning combination of flavors, including Korean chilli paste and Theo's grandmother's secret ingredient, is simply a condiment like no other.

But the K POP team needs your help. Their Kickstarter goal is to raise enough money to produce K POP Sauce in large quantities, and ship it worldwide.

So, why not support the guys and make a pledge to their Kickstarter campaign? You'll be helping an excellent business get off the ground and giving yourself and the world the delight that is K POP Sauce!

a Says who is involved in developing the product ___
b Points out what the reader's support will accomplish ___
c Establishes the topic with a descriptive title ___
d Explains what the makers of the product need ___
e Lets the reader know a solution has been found ___
f Describes the product ___
g Creates initial interest by describing a shared experience ___
h Invites the reader to get involved ___

7 Read the article. Then listen to the lecture. Write an essay summarizing the points made in the lecture you just heard, explaining how they cast doubt on points made in the reading. 🎧 19

Set up in 2009, the Kickstarter corporation may not be as popular as it once seemed.

People with creative ideas in one of 13 categories, including art, music, and technology, can use Kickstarter to describe their project and appeal for financial support. They set a target amount of money needed and a date by which it must be raised. Any member of the public can access the Kickstarter platform and offer to support an idea. Those who do so are called "backers." If backers pledge enough, that is, promise to donate enough cash to meet the required target within the deadline, then the project is funded. So far so good… or is it? The system certainly has flaws.

Firstly, major celebrities have started using Kickstarter to fund new film ventures or to record new albums. These have been heavily criticized by many who resent already wealthy people potentially taking away opportunities from smaller, unknown artists whose need for Kickstarter is arguably greater.

Secondly, can we really trust Kickstarter projects? Even when projects reach their financial goal, who can guarantee the money won't be used for other purposes? Indeed, it is not unusual for funded projects to soon fail due to poor planning or underestimated needs. This seems like a reckless waste of other people's money.

Lastly, many feel that backers are exploited by the Kickstarter system. No matter how much of their own money they pledge, they receive very little in return. This hardly seems fair, especially as thousands of Kickstarter projects have enjoyed enormous financial success.

Kickstarter may be a good service in some circumstances, but it is far from perfect.

Review

1 Rewrite the sentences. Complete the sentences using the correct form of the word in capital letters. Use two or three words.

1. He works in the Madrid office. BASE
   He _____ the Madrid office.
2. She's working alongside the partners in Asia. DEAL
   She's _____ the partners in Asia.
3. I have to find a good team for the presentation. PUT
   I have to _____ a good team for the presentation.
4. Entrepreneurs can accept failure and quickly move on. RECOVER
   Entrepreneurs can _____ failure quickly.
5. Meditation is useful for dealing with pressure. HANDLE
   Meditation is a good _____ pressure.

2 Complete the sentences with the correct word. The first letter is given for you.

1. The business uses a s _ _ _ _ _ _ _ in China to provide materials.
2. She managed to n _ _ _ _ _ _ _ _ a good pay raise with her manager.
3. They're using online advertising to m _ _ _ _ _ the language school.
4. N _ _ _ _ _ _ _ _ _ is an important part of building professional relationships.
5. Partners help to d _ _ _ _ _ _ _ _ your products in other regions.
6. I'm a social e _ _ _ _ _ _ _ _ _ _ _ working in the field of education.
7. Where is your company b _ _ _ _ ?
8. Successful companies i _ _ _ _ _ _ new things in response to customers' needs.

3 Find and correct the mistakes in these sentences. Two sentences are correct.

1. Organizations that has been using start-up companies to find solutions to social, cultural, or environmental problems are called "social entrepreneurs." _____
2. Traditionally, start-up companies have been measured their success by looking at profits or sales. _____
3. In contrast, social entrepreneurs have worked to end poverty, increase health care, and improve the quality of life. _____
4. Social entrepreneurs have using social networking to reach more people, spread information about their activities, and raise money. _____
5. Kiva.org been lending money to low-income entrepreneurs in 80 countries ($25 at a time) since 2005. _____
6. In 2009, Matt Damon has cofounded Water.org, which works to increase access to safe water and sanitation for people in developing countries. _____
7. For over 12 years, Khan Academy has made education available to people all over the world—for free! _____
8. Since 2000, the Bill & Melinda Gates Foundation is working to increase access to health care and reduce extreme poverty. _____

4 Complete the sentences with the correct form of these verbs. There may be more than one correct answer.

give	link	pick up	see	study

1. Students who like _____ science might be interested in bionics, which is the study of mechanical systems that function like living organisms or parts of living organisms.
2. Scientists have learned it's possible _____ machine and mind.
3. A tiny camera that communicates with her brain allows a blind woman _____ the shapes of trees.
4. A bionic arm can let a person move that arm _____ a fork.
5. Bionics represents a big leap forward. It enables researchers _____ people back a lot of what they've lost.

5 Choose the correct options to complete the sentences. Both forms may be correct.

1. I love *watching* / *to watch* old movies.
2. She advised me *going* / *to go* home because I wasn't feeling well.
3. I fail *seeing* / *to see* how I can help you.
4. I never allow anyone *looking* / *to look* at my homework.
5. Do you avoid *calling* / *to call* your father at work?
6. Did she ask you *going* / *to go* to her house?
7. Tang refuses *using* / *to use* social media.
8. Have you finished *studying* / *to study* for the test?

3 Faster, Higher, Stronger

3A Incredible Achievements

VOCABULARY Describing athletes

1 Review Read the email. Choose the correct options to complete the email.

Hi Juanita,

I just wanted to thank you for (1) _____ me to exercise more. I've been (2) _____ cycling every weekend and I also (3) _____ yoga every morning now. I'm feeling so much better. Are you still (4) _____ hard for the marathon next month? I heard that you (5) _____ your personal best last year and (6) _____ the silver medal. Good for you!

I also wanted to say that it's great that you're going to (7) _____ our charity in the race. All of the runners are (8) _____ an important role in helping us to raise money.

Thank you!

Regards,

Lara

1. a representing   c encouraging
   b achieving   d making
2. a doing   c playing
   b going   d training
3. a do   c play
   b go   d train
4. a going   c doing
   b encouraging   d training
5. a achieved   c had
   b won   d made
6. a beat   c won
   b achieved   d scored
7. a show   c do
   b present   d represent
8. a playing   c doing
   b making   d being

2 Review Circle the odd one out.

1. referee   court   spectator   coach
2. diving   sailing   kick   karate
3. pass   track   rink   court
4. throw   swing   bounce   kick
5. net   diving   court   tennis

3 Choose the correct option to complete the sentences.

1. My brother has a real _____ for cycling.
   a attitude   c role
   b passion   d race
2. Serena Williams is one of the most _____ female tennis players of all time.
   a skilful   c star
   b technique   d great
3. How many goals has Benzema scored in his _____?
   a average   c record
   b game   d career
4. Usain Bolt currently _____ the world record for the 100 metres.
   a wins   c holds
   b sets   d smashes
5. Who _____ the team in Brazil?
   a was captained   c captained
   b did captain   d captain

26   Unit 3

4 Complete the sentences with these verbs.

captained	competed	had
played	scored	smashed
was	won	

1 As a player, he _____ skillful technique.
2 I _____ in a national athletics competition last year.
3 Jenny _____ the star of the team.
4 She _____ a bronze medal in the 100 meter swimming competition.
5 She _____ the existing world record.
6 He _____ the team during the European Championship.
7 He only _____ one goal last season.
8 The whole team _____ a role in winning.

5 Complete the sentences with these words and phrases.

competed in and won	energetic	played a key role
real passion	really great	scored a goal
set	attitude	won

1 Shauna's teammates chose her to be the captain because she has a _____.
2 Tomas is not the greatest player on the team, but he has a _____ for the game.
3 The swimmer _____ a new Olympic record.
4 The defenders _____ in the team's victory over Real Madrid.
5 Ronaldo has _____ in each of his last 12 games.
6 The Australian sailing team _____ a silver medal in the Olympics.
7 She is one of the most _____ coaches in women's basketball today.
8 He _____ the Tour de France last year.

6 Cross out the mistake in each sentence and write the correct word.

1 Young people need a positively role model.
   _____
2 The team won a golden medal.
   _____
3 He was a star of the championship.
   _____
4 He's holding the world record for long jump.
   _____
5 You need to improve your technical.
   _____

7 Extension Complete the table.

Noun	Adjective
	energetic
passion	
	skillful
awareness	
	positive
competition	

8 Extension Write answers that are true for you.

1 What is something you are passionate about?
   _____
   _____

2 Who is the most competitive person you know?
   _____
   _____

3 What are your most important skills?
   _____
   _____

PRONUNCIATION

9 Listen to the sentences. Underline the words that you hear linked together. Then practice saying the sentences. 🎧 20

1 We had the best time at the Olympics!
2 It's far easier than you think it is.
3 She had the fastest time in the race.
4 Soccer isn't as popular in the United States.
5 He's a lot better at it than I am.
6 They're the first team to win two years in a row.
7 We don't play as often as we used to.
8 It's more difficult for me than it was years ago.

A competitor in the show jumping event of the modern pentathlon

LISTENING

10 Listen and choose the correct options. 🎧 21

1 What Greek word means "competition"?
   a athlon
   b penta
   c deca
2 How many events are in the decathlon?
   a 5
   b 10
   c 15
3 What sporting event do the ancient and modern pentathlon have in common?
   a swimming
   b running
   c riding
4 What event is NOT part of our modern pentathlon?
   a shooting
   b fencing
   c wrestling
5 What are athletes awarded for each event in the pentathlon?
   a points
   b medals
   c money
6 Who receives the silver medal?
   a the athlete with the third highest score
   b the athlete with the highest score
   c the athlete with the second highest score

11 Listen to a lecture. Indicate the sports that you hear mentioned. 🎧 22

1 wrestling ____
2 running ____
3 swimming ____
4 javelin throwing ____
5 climbing ____
6 jumping ____
7 horseback riding ____
8 gymnastics ____
9 discus throwing ____
10 boxing ____

12 Listen again. What is the main point that the speaker is trying to make? 🎧 22

a the similarities of the ancient and modern world
b the brutality of human beings not changing over time
c the basic desire of all humans to compete and win
d the enduring influence of Greek culture on athletics

13 Match the words with their definitions. Listen again if necessary. 🎧 22

1 discus ____
2 halteres ____
3 stadion ____
4 sprint ____
5 javelin ____
6 pentathlon ____
7 decathlon ____

a an ancient measure of distance in racing
b a spear-shaped object thrown by an athlete
c an Olympic event with ten events
d a disc-shaped object thrown by an athlete
e an ancient weight made of stone or bronze
f an Olympic event with five events
g a short run at full speed

28 Unit 3

GRAMMAR Determiners

14 Write *a* or *an* in front of the noun phrase.

1 _____ huge crowd of people
2 _____ positive role model
3 _____ average of 15 points
4 _____ world record
5 _____ athlete from Peru
6 _____ decent game
7 _____ absolutely amazing win
8 _____ great attitude
9 _____ injury to her ankle
10 _____ pulled muscle
11 _____ unknown participant
12 _____ winning strategy

15 Circle the correct words to complete the text. Circle *x* if no word is necessary.

Young Olympic Athletes from Rio 2016

Every four years, athletes compete for their countries in the Summer Olympic Games, and young athletes show the world what they can do.

- 18-year-old Yusra Mardini competed for (1) *a / the / x* Refugee Team at (2) *x / every / the* 2016 Rio Olympics. She is a swimmer. She and her family escaped (3) *some / a few / the* war in Syria.
- At the same time, (4) *x / a / a few* sisters Leila, Liina, and Lily Luik are believed to be (5) *those / the / x* first triplets to compete in (6) *an / her / each* Olympics. They called themselves "(7) *his / these / the* Trio to Rio" and competed in (8) *the / those / my* women's marathon—against (9) *all / a / both* team of (10) *x / the / each* German twins! Even though the triplets didn't win (11) *all / any / this* medals, no one will ever forget them.
- 16-year-old Kanak Jha was (12) *that / his / the* youngest Olympian on (13) *some / every / the* entire US team in Rio. (14) *Your / His / These* sport is table tennis. When he was 14, he won (15) *this / neither / the* table tennis World Cup.

16 Complete the sentences with *a, an, the,* or *x* (if no article is needed).

Marjorie Gestring: Young Olympic Gold Medalist

(1) _____ springboard diver from the United States, Marjorie Gestring, was once (2) _____ youngest Olympic gold medalist. At the age of almost (3) _____ 14, she won (4) _____ gold medal for three-meter springboard diving at (5) _____ 1936 Summer Olympics in Germany. (Her exact age was 13 years, 268 days.) She was the youngest person ever to win (6) _____ gold medal (at that time). Today, she's still (7) _____ second youngest gold medalist ever.

Marjorie won (8) _____ major diving competition in 1936 and joined (9) _____ US Olympic diving team.
At the 1936 Olympics, (10) _____ Americans won (11) _____ gold, silver, and bronze medals for springboard diving. After (12) _____ Olympics, Marjorie continued to compete. She became (13) _____ member of (14) _____ International Swimming Hall of Fame.

Today, the youngest gold medal winner is speed skater Kim Yun-mi from South Korea who won (15) _____ gold medal at the 1994 Winter Olympics. She was just 13 years old.

17 Complete the sentences with these words.

a few	a lot	any	both
each	how many	much	some

1 I didn't know _____ about cricket until my friends decided to teach me the rules.
2 At our soccer games, the spectators always scream really loudly for _____ and every goal.
3 _____ points did the winning team get in the first half?
4 We saw _____ people leave the stadium before the end of the game.
5 My friends and I support _____ Real Madrid and Manchester United.
6 It's hard to believe, but _____ of people enjoy watching bowling on TV.
7 Have your friends been to _____ games so far this year?
8 _____ people find it hard to believe that dressage ("horse dancing") is an Olympic sport.

18 Cross out the mistake in each sentence and write the correct word.

1 I really want to learn more about these sport I read about online. _____
2 My younger brother wants to be a athlete when he grows up. _____
3 Do you have some idea how hard it is to run a marathon? _____
4 We don't have a real goal, so just kick the ball between that flags. _____
5 Much of the fans were unhappy when they read that their favorite player had moved to another team. _____
6 Only that most talented athletes can compete at the Olympics. _____
7 We watched the basketball game with both our cousins. _____

3B Think Like an Athlete

VOCABULARY BUILDING Synonyms in texts

1 Complete the sentences using these synonyms for the words in bold.

amounts	elite	establish
money	selected	talents

1 You should make the most of your **abilities** and try to become a professional athlete.
   You should make use of your _____ and try to become a professional athlete.

2 Only **the top** athletes can afford to live in great luxury.
   Only _____ athletes can afford to live in great luxury.

3 The school wants to **set up** a new after-school tennis club.
   The school wants to _____ a new after-school tennis club.

4 No young athlete can rise to the top without the **funding** to train.
   _____ for training is important for young athletes who want to succeed.

5 The **sums** of money made by professional athletes are absolutely amazing.
   Professional athletes make incredible _____ of money.

6 If you want to be **chosen** for the team, you have to practice every day.
   Only those who practice daily will be _____ for the team.

READING

2 Read the article on the opposite page. Then read the introductory sentence for a summary of the article. Choose three of the sentences below to complete the summary.

> Today's top athletes focus on mental as well as physical fitness.

1 Plato believed that mental fitness was more important for success than physical fitness.
2 Although some athletes initially resisted sports psychology, it is now more popular than ever.
3 Athletes in sports that require great focus have had tremendous success with sports psychology.
4 Laurie Hernandez won two medals in the Rio de Janeiro Olympics.
5 Goal setting is important for athletes in some sports and is an effective part of sports psychology.
6 Sports psychology uses breathing, visualization, and the setting of achievable goals to help athletes succeed.

3 Choose the correct option according to the information in the article.

1 According to paragraph 2, which of the following is true of elite athletes?
   a They have been resistant in the past to the idea of using sports psychology.
   b After 1920, they immediately began using sports psychology to train.
   c Their coaches were more open to the idea of using sports psychology than they were.
   d They used sports psychology more in the mid-1900s than they do today.

2 According to paragraph 3, it is NOT true that Simone Biles
   a used sports psychology to help overcome her lack of confidence.
   b used sports psychology to become one of the top athletes in the world.
   c has refused to speak publicly about using sports psychology in her training.
   d inspired her teammate to begin using sports psychology.

3 Which of the following can be inferred about Laurie Hernandez from paragraph 3?
   a She is a better gymnast than Simone Biles.
   b She would never have used sports psychology if not for Simone Biles.
   c Sports psychology helped her to win two Olympic medals.
   d Like Simone Biles, she suffered from a lack of confidence.

4 Write the word from the text that matches each definition.

1 to do better in an activity than others _____

2 to slowly disappear or lose importance _____

3 an activity performed regularly, sometimes as part of a ceremony _____

4 to succeed in reaching a goal _____

5 easy to see or understand _____

Mental Gymnastics

Simone Biles

1. More than 2,000 years ago, the Greek philosopher Plato wrote that "Physical fitness is as important as intellectual fitness." Plato recognized the connection between the body and mind and believed that people should focus on being physically fit as well as being mentally fit. Today's athletes are more physically fit than ever. Everything from an athlete's diet to their training routine to how much they sleep at night is completely planned and controlled. But in the high-pressure world of professional sports, the best athletes often listen to Plato's advice and focus on taking care of their mind as well as their body.

2. The first sports psychology laboratory was founded in Berlin in the early 1920s, and since then, the study and practice of sports psychology has continued to increase. Although most elite athletes are looking for any way to outperform the competition, some were resistant to the idea of seeing a sports psychologist. Athletes have said they didn't want to discuss their fears and they worried about being asked to change their training routines. More importantly, they didn't want to seem "weak" to their competitors. Also, coaches were sometimes concerned about letting someone else control their athlete. But as more and more top athletes have spoken openly about the positive impact of sports psychology, this resistance has begun to fade. For example, after winning a championship in 2010, basketball great Ron Artest appeared on TV to thank his sports psychologist.

3. Almost every sport has athletes that use sports psychology, but athletes in sports that require tremendous focus, like golf, tennis, and gymnastics, use sports psychologists the most. American gymnast Simone Biles is sometimes described as the greatest athlete in the world today. She won five medals at the Olympic games in Rio de Janeiro, and four of them were gold. Biles has been open about how sports psychology has contributed to her success. In 2013, she was struggling with nerves and a lack of confidence. Her father called a sports psychologist, and three years later, Biles was a star of the Olympics. After seeing Biles's dramatic improvement, her teammate Laurie Hernandez started seeing the same sports psychologist. Hernandez won a gold and a silver medal in Rio.

4. So how does sports psychology actually work? Typically, an athlete meets regularly with a sports psychologist who gets to know them and understand their goals. Then the psychologist creates a specific plan for that athlete. This usually includes breathing exercises, visualization exercises—using your imagination to see yourself do something, and goal setting. Before she competes, Laurie Hernandez places one hand on her stomach and breathes deeply. This ritual calms her before she begins. Goal setting usually focuses on specific performance goals, like swimming half a second faster, instead of competitive goals, like winning a medal. By focusing on a specific goal, pressure decreases and the goal seems more achievable.

5. Today's top athletes know what Plato wrote about all those years ago. The body and mind must work together to achieve greatness. The majority of Olympic athletes now use mental training as a major part of their training routine, and the benefits of sports psychology are clear. To compete at the highest level today, your mental game must be as strong as your physical game.

3C Getting Better All the Time

GRAMMAR Comparatives and superlatives

1 Choose the correct option to complete the sentence.

1 There are ____ more baseball players at our school than there are football players.
   a few   **b** little   **c** many   **d** much

2 She spends ____ less time studying than she does practicing soccer.
   a few   **b** little   **c** many   **d** much

3 Busy students have ____ time to participate in sports.
   a few   **b** little   **c** many   **d** much

4 ____ tickets were sold for tonight's game— only 100.
   a Few   **b** Little   **c** Many   **d** Much

5 I keep asking him to join, but he's shown very ____ interest in becoming part of the basketball team.
   a few   **b** little   **c** many   **d** much

6 Very ____ fans were in the stands for this week's game because it was raining and cold.
   a few   **b** little   **c** many   **d** much

7 I couldn't believe I had to pay so ____ money for my tickets to the diving championships. They were expensive!
   a few   **b** little   **c** many   **d** much

2 Complete the sentences using comparatives and the cues in parentheses. There is more than one correct answer for each sentence.

1 The freezer is _____ than the fridge. (cold, big difference)

2 It's _____ today than it was yesterday. (hot, small difference)

3 I have _____ pages to read for my history class than I do for math. (more, big difference)

4 A Lamborghini is _____ than any car I'll ever buy. (expensive, big difference)

5 Joshi gets _____ grades than I do. (good, big difference)

6 It takes _____ to travel to Dubai than it does to get to Sharjah. (long, small difference)

7 I spend a _____ time riding my bike than I do jogging. (more, big difference)

3 Use the information in the two sentences to complete the comparative sentence.

Example: Viktor can lift 285 pounds. Karim can lift 375 pounds. (90 pounds)
Karim can lift *90 more pounds than Viktor can.*

1 The first modern Olympics were held in 1896. The first World Cup football game was held in 1930. (34 years)
The first modern Olympics _____
_____

2 The world record in the women's long jump is about 24.5 feet (7.5 meters). The world record in the men's long jump is about 29.5 feet. (9 meters)
The men's long jump world record is about _____
_____.

3 Approximately 111.3 million people watched the 2017 Super Bowl on TV. There were approximately 70,800 people at the stadium watching the game in person. (more than 111.22 million)
In 2017, approximately 70,800 went to the Super Bowl game, but _____
_____

4 Kai can swim for 60 minutes. Ruby can swim for 45 minutes. (15 minutes)
Kai can swim _____
_____

5 Our team scored nine points. The other team scored four points. (five points)
The other team scored _____
_____

4 Which option is closer in meaning to the original sentence?

1 The more I focus on eating healthily, the more my swimming endurance improves.
   a My swimming endurance improves when I spend more time focusing on eating well.
   b Because my swimming endurance improves, I spend more time focusing on eating well.

2 The more time I practice, the more compliments I get.
   a When I get compliments, I want to spend more time practicing.
   b When I spend more time practicing, I get more compliments.

3 The higher the mountain, the more time it takes to climb.
   a Climbing higher mountains takes slightly less time than climbing lower mountains.
   b It takes more time to climb a higher mountain than a lower mountain.

4 The noisier the concert, the less Gayle wants to go.
   a Gayle prefers going to noisy concerts.
   b If concerts are quite loud, Gayle is less likely to want to go to them.
5 The more challenging the class, the longer I have to study.
   a My classes are challenging before I study.
   b I have to study more for classes that are challenging than for those that are easy.
6 The more beautiful the painting, the more expensive it is.
   a You have to pay more for more beautiful paintings.
   b More expensive paintings aren't more beautiful.
7 The closer we get to Nagasaki, the more excited I am.
   a I'm getting more excited as we get closer to Nagasaki.
   b Because I am more excited, Nagasaki is closer.
8 The more points you score, the more rewards you get.
   a You score more points after you get more rewards.
   b You get more rewards when you score more points.

5 Choose the correct option to complete the sentences.
1 Elite marathon runners are faster these days; in the past, marathon runners were *not as fast / as fast*.
2 More people stream sports on their tablets than five years ago. Five years ago, *not as many / more* people streamed sports on their tablets.
3 Athletes are required to use safer equipment, though in the past, athletes' equipment was *not as safe / as safe* as today.
4 The team's uniforms are a lot more colorful this season, and I think these *not as colorful / more colorful* uniforms look great.
5 A great deal more women play soccer these days. Today there are *as many / more* women playing soccer.
6 Now that I've started practicing with the team, I'm a much better skier. Last year I *wasn't as good / was better* at skiing.
7 A lot fewer people are going to watch the team play. Today there are *not as many / more* people at the games.

6 Are the words in bold correct or incorrect? Correct those that are incorrect.
1 My friend Sahil is **a bit talented than** many Olympic athletes. _____
2 Mount Sanquing in China **is as beautiful** any place on Earth. _____
3 Getting enough sleep **as important as** eating well and exercising. _____
4 This sushi **is slightly better then** the sushi we had last week at the new restaurant near our office. _____
5 Your joke **isn't as funny as** the one Yuri told in class yesterday. _____
6 Oslo, Norway, **is not nearly hot** as Colombo, Sri Lanka. _____
7 Electric cars are **far more efficiency than** cars that use only gasoline. _____
8 Many of the other artists of his time **weren't as innovative as** Picasso. _____
9 The Nile is **the most long** river in Africa. _____

7 Read the information about the 2016 Olympic athletes. Are the statements below true (T) or false (F)?

2016 Summer Olympics Results (partial)			
50km walk (men)			
Rank	Name	Country	Time
1	Matej Toth	Slovakia	3:40:58
5	Wei Yu	China	3:43:00
7	Havard Haukenes	Norway	3:46:43
20km race walk (women)			
4	Antonella Palmisano	Italy	1:29:03
5	Shijie Qieyang	China	1:29:04
6	Ana Cabecinha	Portugal	1:29:23
Long jump (women)			
3	Ivana Spanovic	Serbia	7.08 m
5	Ese Brume	Nigeria	6.81 m
6	Ksenija Balta	Estonia	6.79 m
Hammer throw (men)			
5	Marcel Lomnicky	Slovakia	75.97 m
6	Ashraf Amgad Elseify	Qatar	75.46 m
7	Krisztian Pars	Hungary	75.28 m

1 In the 50km walk, Haukenes was a great deal faster than Toth. _____
2 Haukenes was not nearly as fast as Yu in the 50km walk. _____
3 In the 20km race walk, Palmisano was much faster than Qieyang. _____
4 Cabecinha was over a minute slower than Palmisano in the 20km race walk. _____
5 In the long jump, Brume didn't jump nearly as far as Spanovic. _____
6 Balta jumped nearly as far as Brume in the long jump. _____
7 In the hammer throw, Pars was not quite as good as Lomnicky. _____
8 Pars threw the hammer a bit further than Elseify. _____

3D Are athletes really getting faster, better, and stronger?

TEDTALKS

AUTHENTIC LISTENING SKILLS

1 Listen to the excerpts from David Epstein's TED Talk, and circle the words he uses to mark contrast. 🎧 24

1 **Rather than** the same size as the average elite high jumper, the average elite shot-putter is two and a half inches taller and 130 pounds heavier.
2 So, in sports where large size is prized, the large athletes have gotten larger. **Conversely,** in sports where diminutive stature is an advantage, the small athletes got smaller.
3 These men are seven inches different in height, **but** because of the body types advantaged in their sports, they wear the same length pants.
4 The Kalenjin make up just twelve percent of the Kenyan population **but** the vast majority of elite runners.
5 That's the power that's contained in the human body. **But** normally we can't access nearly all of it.
6 Ultra-endurance was once thought to be harmful to human health, **but now** we realize that we have all these traits that are perfect for ultra-endurance.

WATCH ▶

2 Complete the sentences with a word or short phrase.

1 The winner of the 2012 _____ ran two hours and eight minutes.
2 I want you to pretend that Jesse Owens is in _____.
3 That's the difference that track _____ has made.
4 Eddy Merckx set the _____ for the longest distance cycled in one hour at 30 miles, 3,774 feet.
5 While we haven't evolved into a new species in a century, the _____ within competitive sports certainly has changed.
6 The financial incentives and fame and glory afforded _____ skyrocketed and it tipped toward the tiny upper echelon of performance.
7 In some cases, the search for bodies that could push athletic performance forward ended up introducing into the _____ populations of people that weren't previously competing at all.
8 This is a vertical _____ of more than 8,000 feet, and Kílian went up and down in under three hours.

3 Match these sports with the statements. Two sports are used more than once.

| cycling | marathon | sprinting | swimming |

1 The 2012 Olympic winner finished in two hours and eight minutes. _____
2 This sport favors a body type similar to a canoe. _____
3 The Kalenjin tribe have been particularly successful in this event. _____
4 In this sport, the governing body decreed that competitors had to use the same technology as in 1972. _____
5 Starting blocks were an important innovation in this sport. _____
6 Scientists estimate that Jesse Owens would have finished less than one stride behind Usain Bolt in this sport, if he'd been using the same technology. _____

4 Choose the correct option to complete the sentences.

1 Every year, runners seem to get *faster / fastest*.
2 More sophisticated training methods mean that today's athletes are often *stronger / strongest* than the winners from one hundred years ago.
3 In cycling, the *longer / longest* distance traveled in one hour is only about 800 feet further than the record set by Eddy Merckx in 1972.
4 Michael Phelps is seven inches *taller / tallest* than Hicham El Guerrouj, even though their legs are the same length.
5 Today's gymnasts are significantly *shorter / shortest* than competitive gymnasts from several decades ago.
6 The *better / best* athletes in the world have more specialized body types today than they used to.
7 Humans are better suited to ultra-endurance sports than *more / most* primates.

VOCABULARY IN CONTEXT

5 Match the words and phrases (1–6) with the sentences where a synonym is used (a–f).

1 shrunk _____
2 fade away _____
3 the entire _____
4 essentially _____
5 change the face of _____
6 throughout _____

a Widespread use of specialized swimsuits has completely **changed the nature of** competitive swimming.
b Athletes at university are **basically** training at a professional level.
c The distance between certain records **has got smaller** over the years.
d **In all parts of** the world, technology gives people the opportunity to watch huge sporting events.
e Some people worry that certain sports will **disappear** from public notice if they are not included in the Olympics.
f I wonder whether **the whole** difference between Jesse Owens' and Usain Bolts' records can be explained by technology?

3E Surveys

SPEAKING

Useful language

Introducing main findings

The most surprising / interesting thing we found was that…

You won't be surprised to hear that… but one thing that was interesting was…

The main thing we discovered was…

(By far) the most popular… was…

Introducing other points

Another thing that was interesting was…

Apart from that, we found that…

Some other things worth mentioning are…

1 Put the words in parentheses in the correct order to complete the presentation. Then listen to check your answers. 🎧 25

Hello. We're here to present the findings of the class sports survey we conducted.
(1) (discovered / thing / was / the / we / main) _____

people do at least three hours of individual exercise a week.
(2) (most / the / thing / was / we / surprising / that / found) _____

everyone does at least two sports regularly. By far the most popular individual sport was swimming.
(3) (we / that, / that / found / from / apart) _____

one-third of the class go to the gym at least once a week.
(4) (was / another / was / that / interesting / thing) _____

the number of people who like mountain biking. A third of the class go mountain biking regularly, and over three-quarters do it from time to time.
Focusing on team sports, (5) (to / you / be / that / surprised / won't / hear) _____

most of the males play football, (6) (was / one / thing / was / but / that / interesting) _____

that over half of the females we surveyed play soccer regularly.

(7) (things / are / worth / some / mentioning / other) _____

that spinning classes were more popular with females than males, and that ten percent of the class play more than three team sports, including basketball.

2 Look at the data about Cybercrime. Prepare some notes for a presentation on this information. Remember to include the useful language. Then listen to the sample answer and compare your ideas. 🎧 26

Cybercrime by age (USA)

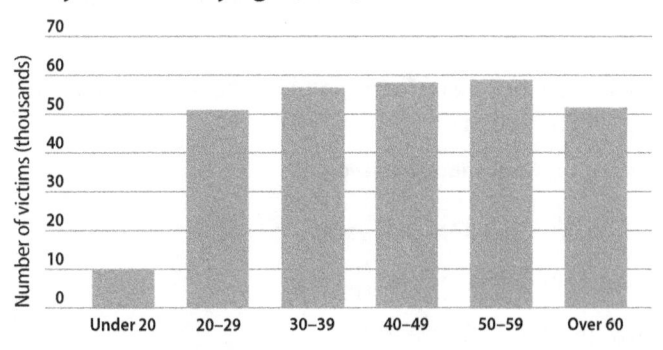

[Bar chart: Number of victims (thousands) by age group — Under 20: ~8; 20–29: ~50; 30–39: ~55; 40–49: ~57; 50–59: ~58; Over 60: ~50]

Source: U.S. Department of Justice / Federal Bureau of Investigation. Statistics shown are for 2015.

Cybercrime by age (USA)

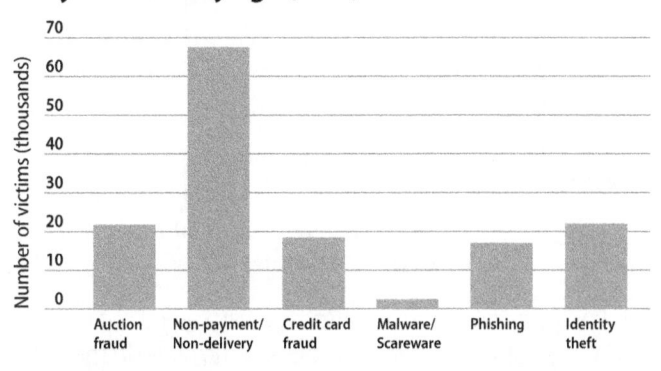

[Bar chart: Number of victims (thousands) by type — Auction fraud: ~20; Non-payment/Non-delivery: ~65; Credit card fraud: ~17; Malware/Scareware: ~2; Phishing: ~15; Identity theft: ~20]

3 You have been asked to talk about a sport that is typical in your country. Make notes about this topic. Use the useful language. Then listen to the sample answer. 🎧 27

Your comments should include:
- what the sport is
- how you play or do it
- when and how often people do it
- why you consider it a typical sport for your country

Faster, Higher, Stronger **35**

WRITING A survey

4 Choose the correct option to complete the sentences.

1 *More then half / More than half* of the participants were under 16.
2 *Under just two-thirds / Just under two-thirds* of the sports are free.
3 *Roughly a quarter / Roughly the quarter* of all scheduled events were canceled.
4 We can see that membership *double / doubled* in May.
5 *One on four / One in four* runners dropped out of the marathon.
6 The *vast majority of / vast majority in* students prefer doing team sports.
7 *Almost 40 percent of / 40 percent of almost* those surveyed live in cities.
8 Funding for sports *increased by / increased in* 15 percent over the period.

5 Look at the bar chart. Then complete the text with the missing phrases a–h.

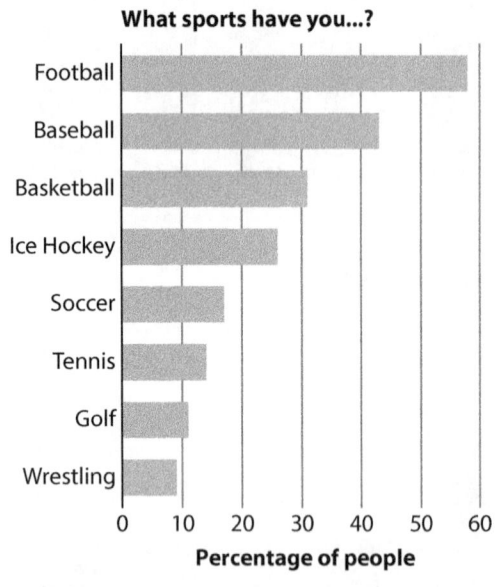

What sports have you…?

- Football ~58
- Baseball ~43
- Basketball ~32
- Ice Hockey ~27
- Soccer ~18
- Tennis ~15
- Golf ~11
- Wrestling ~8

Percentage of people

This bar chart shows the results of a survey carried out in a local city last year. A hundred adults participated in the survey, (1) _____.
All participants in the survey attended at least some spectator sports during the year. As can be seen from the chart, (2) _____. The lowest attendance was at wrestling, (3) _____. More than a quarter went to watch ice hockey, with almost one in three going to watch basketball games. The football statistics are not entirely surprising, given that the popularity of football is well documented. (4) _____ second most popular spectator sport in the survey.
(5) _____, as a highly successful baseball team is based in the region in which the surveyed city is located.
(6) _____, the numbers attending ice hockey were unexpected. The reason given by those interviewed was support for their children or other family members (7) _____. A lack of developed facilities in the local area has been suggested as the reason for the lower numbers (8) _____.

a Being higher than the national average
b with fewer than one in ten participants attending wrestling matches
c attending wrestling events
d which aimed to discover levels of annual attendance at sporting events
e Baseball was the
f well over half of those interviewed attended football matches
g participating in ice hockey
h This may be explained by geography

6 Read the text again. Then answer the questions.

1 What was the purpose of the survey?
  a to find out how many people are playing sports
  b to find out how many people are watching sports
2 How many people interviewed did not attend any sporting events?
  a none of them   b at least one
3 Which statistics are first mentioned in the text?
  a the national average for attendance at these sports
  b the sports with the best and worst attendance
4 Which sport did roughly one-third of all participants attend?
  a basketball   b golf
5 What reason is suggested for the high numbers attending football matches?
  a that the local team in this city is very successful
  b that football is known to have high levels of support
6 According to the text, why did so many people go to watch ice hockey?
  a because their relatives play ice hockey
  b because their city has extremely well-developed facilities for ice hockey

7 The chart below gives information about a group of people who were surveyed about their attitudes to gym class. Summarize the information by selecting and reporting the main features, and make comparisons where relevant.

	Elementary school students	High school students
Everyone should go to gym class	73.2	26.8
I enjoy gym class at school	82	18
I feel self-conscious in gym class	33.8	66.2
I enjoy school sports days	69.1	30.9
Sports are important for well-being	42	58
I'd prefer optional gym classes	24.6	75.4
I do sports outside school hours	48	52
I like watching sports	37	63

Review

1 Match the two parts of the sentences.

1 You scored a
2 He hasn't got a real
3 We competed
4 He's a skillful
5 She's a positive
6 I won
7 I want to set
8 You played a

a player.
b key role in the team.
c a new world record.
d passion for golf.
e in the championship.
f great goal.
g the race.
h role model.

2 Complete the sentences with the missing word.

1 I won a silver _____ at my school sports day.
2 He has a real _____ for gymnastics.
3 She smashed the world _____ by three minutes.
4 He didn't _____ any goals on Saturday.
5 Messi was the youngest player to _____ Argentina.
6 He played a key _____ in the team from the start.
7 They have a really great _____ towards their opponents.
8 Who _____ the championship?

3 Complete the sentences with these words. Write *x* if no word is necessary. Some words can be used more than once.

a	a few	a lot of
many	the	x

1 In the sport of extreme ironing, which started in England, people travel to _____ remote places to iron their clothes there.
2 At the Cooper's Hill Cheese-Rolling and Wake, "athletes" chase a wheel of cheese down a hill; the winner gets to keep _____ cheese.
3 Snow polo, _____ Swiss sport in which players play polo on a snowy field, is now played in other parts of the world.
4 Sweden gave us *kaninhop* (Bunny Jumping) in which _____ trained rabbits jump over small fences (similar to horses in show jumping).
5 "Octopush" is another name for underwater hockey in which _____ swimmers use a "pusher" to move a hockey puck into the goal.
6 Do you know _____ people who are interested in chessboxing? It combines a game of chess with a boxing match.

4 Choose the correct option to complete the sentences.

1 ____ of my friends are interested in trying out for the basketball team.
  a Far few   c Every
  b Hardly any
2 The Shanghai Tower isn't the world's ____ building any more.
  a as tall as   c tallest
  b quite a bit tallest
3 I couldn't go to the match because I had ____ homework.
  a many   c too
  b a lot of
4 Star soccer player Cristiano Ronaldo was born in ____.
  a a Madeira, Portugal   c Madeira, Portugal
  b the Madeira, Portugal
5 I didn't see ____ my friends at the match.
  a any of   c every of
  b any
6 Our team lost the match because we didn't score ____ the other team did.
  a as much points as   c slightly fewer points as
  b as many points as
7 I am two years ____ my sister.
  a as older then c the oldest
  b older than

5 Complete the comparative sentences with the information given.

1 Lima's population: almost ten million; Bogota's population: around nine million (slightly / big)
Lima is _____ Bogota.
2 the red shirt: $9.99; the blue shirt: $11.50 (not / quite / cheap)
The blue shirt _____ as the red shirt.
3 Always Dreaming time: 2:03.59; Smarty Jones time: 2:04.06 (fast)
The 2004 Kentucky Derby winner, a horse named Smarty Jones, _____ the 2017 winner Always Dreaming.
4 Brad: 5 feet 9 inches; Jackie: 4 feet 9 inches (quite / tall)
Brad is _____ than Jackie.
5 money China spent on Beijing Olympics: $40 billion; money Russia spent on Sochi Olympics: $50 billion (not / quite / expensive)
The Beijing Olympics _____ the Sochi Olympics.
6 River Volga length: 2,265 miles; River Congo-Chambeshi length: 2,920 miles (long)
The River Volga _____ as the River Congo.

4 Cultural Transformation

4A Putting the Town on the Map

VOCABULARY Cultural events

1 **Review** Choose the correct option to complete the sentences.

1 We saw a fantastic *broadcast / production* of *Hamlet* at the theater yesterday.
2 The photographs are on display in the *art gallery / concert hall*.
3 They are rehearsing in their new music *cultural center / studio*.
4 Can you write down the *sculpture / lyrics* of that song, please?
5 He painted a *mural / portrait* of the queen.
6 How many *listeners / viewers* watched the documentary on TV?

2 **Review** Are these words connected with art or music? Complete the table.

| concert hall | lyrics | mural |
| painting | portrait | verse |

Art	Music

Roskilde Festival Denmark

3 Complete the sentences with these verbs.

| attend | attracts | boost | brings | generates | holds |

1 Roskilde Festival is a music festival in Denmark that _____ music lovers from around the world every year.

2 Organizers expect thousands of people to _____ the week-long event next summer.
3 The arrival of tourists going to the festival will _____ the country's broader economy.
4 It's also a humanitarian event that _____ people together.
5 The festival _____ events that include a vote for which charities should receive support from the festival.
6 Attendees visit local restaurants and attractions during their stay, which _____ income for the local economy.

4 Choose the correct option to complete the sentences.

1 The event organizers are putting *on / in / by* a parade.
2 The large number of visitors has a big impact *to / at / on* the city.
3 There is wide support *with / for / to* public art.
4 Thousands of people take part *on / by / in* carnivals around the country.
5 Street artist Banksy helped to put his home town, Bristol, *on / at / in* the map.
6 The exhibit creates a sense of pride *to / for / in* their history.

5 Choose the correct option (a–d) to complete the sentences.

1 The new music venue has had a negative _____ on transportation.
   a support   c impact
   b opportunity   d sense

2 Cultural events are great for _____ people together.
   a putting   c offering
   b bringing   d attracting

3 Having public art creates a _____ of pride in the local area.
   a sense   c festival
   b parade   d venue

4 Local people had the opportunity to take _____ in the organization.
   a place   c role
   b together   d part

5 The film festival has put Cannes on the _____.
   a map   c road
   b party   d menu

6 The art gallery generates over one million _____ in income.
  a tourists   c opportunities
  b events   d dollars

7 The many cultural events _____ tourists from all over the world.
  a put on   c generate
  b boost   d attract

8 Many people _____ several events every day.
  a support   c generate
  b attend   d attract

6 Match the events or activities (1–8) with the benefits each one accomplishes (a–f). You can use the letters more than once.

1 Have a party for the planners of a music festival. _____
2 Advertise the different groups that will perform. _____
3 Sell tickets for the event. _____
4 Hire teens and young people to work at the festival. _____
5 Organize volunteers for the festival. _____
6 Sell merchandise at the festival. _____
7 Hold a party after the festival for everyone who worked and performed. _____
8 Film a documentary about the music festival. _____

a attracts tourists
b creates sense of pride
c brings people together
d boosts the economy
e generates income
f offers young people opportunities

7 **Extension** Read the clues and complete the crossword puzzle with these words.

Across
2 a performance of music
5 a person who directs the performance of an orchestra
6 a school where musicians are trained
8 a movie with singing and dancing in the story

Down
1 a style of popular music, originally from the United States
3 a person who writes music
4 a piece of music played in a particular way
7 a live performance by a musician or comedian

arrangement composer conductor conservatory
gig   jazz   musical   recital

8 **Extension** Choose the correct options to complete the text.

Every May, we organize a "fringe festival" that runs alongside the main festival in Brighton. There are hundreds of different events that are held over the five-day period. There is stand- (1) _____ comedy at the Bizarre Comedy Club, where there is also an (2) _____ mic for people who want to try stand-up comedy. There will be showing of the best of (3) _____ cinema, and poetry (4) _____ from new writers. There are also free events including dozens of outdoor (5) _____ performances and a (6) _____ launch on Saturday, where you can meet local authors and get signed copies of their books. Finally, come along to the City (7) _____ Hall to see a display of local children's artwork.

1 a off   **c** up
  b in   **d** down
2 a public   **c** private
  b closed   **d** open
3 a independent **c** fringe
  b main   **d** public
4 a writings **c** launches
  b readings **d** exhibits
5 a hall   **c** park
  b movie   **d** street
6 a comedy   **c** book
  b art   **d** photography
7 a Exhibit   **c** Exhibiting
  b Exhibition **d** Exhibited

Cultural Transformation

PRONUNCIATION

9 Listen to the sentences. Underline the word that you hear using contrastive stress. Then practice saying the sentences. 🎧 28

1 We were going to take the subway to the festival, but it was mobbed.
2 The forecast said it was going to be a chilly evening, but it was freezing.
3 I thought there would be about twenty guests, but loads of people showed up.
4 They thought the tickets would cost ten dollars, but they were way more expensive.
5 She was going to meet me there, but she never showed up.
6 He said he would sing a song for us, but he's got a terrible voice.
7 The parade was going to start at 9, but we waited for hours.
8 My friend promised the show would be great, but it was awful.

LISTENING

10 Listen to some people describing eight different cultural events. Choose the best answer. 🎧 29

1 Where is the man talking about going?
   a a music festival   c a magic show
   b a museum
2 Where does the woman want to take her friend?
   a a comedy club   c a music club
   b a night club
3 What is the man describing?
   a a music festival   c a parade
   b a symphony orchestra
4 Where did the woman go?
   a an art gallery   c an art festival
   b an art museum
5 Where was the woman going to meet the man?
   a the comedy club   c the theater
   b the art gallery
6 What is the woman describing?
   a a night club   c a parade
   b a food festival
7 What did the man go to see?
   a a movie   c a symphony orchestra
   b a play in a theater

Georgian architecture in Edinburgh, Scotland

11 Listen to a talk about Edinburgh, Scotland. Match the adjectives with nouns to form the collocations that you hear. 🎧 30

1 rolling   a streets
2 artistic   b museum
3 narrow   c appeal
4 elegant   d center
5 architectural   e proportions
6 residential   f design
7 aesthetic   g hills
8 pleasing   h area
9 cultural   i transformation

12 Listen again and answer the questions. 🎧 30

1 How many artistically interesting cities does the speaker mention?
   a one   c three
   b two
2 What does the speaker say Edinburgh is known for?
   a its rolling hills   c its romantic landscape
   b its cultural festivals
3 What was the motivation to construct New Town?
   a its foundation in the 12th century
   b an architectural competition
   c the unhealthy conditions in Old Town
4 What style of architecture is New Town?
   a Georgian   c British
   b Scottish
5 What residential area does the speaker mention?
   a Dundas Street   c Cumberland Street
   b Scotland Street

GRAMMAR Future forms 1

13 Correct the errors in the sentences. There is one error in each sentence.

In the future…

1 people will to read more digital books than print books.
2 we going to rely on our smartphones more than we expected.
3 people will subscribing to music streaming services rather than downloading songs.
4 people are going watch TV on the internet, not with cable.
5 you use your 3D printer to print things at home rather than buying them at a store.
6 electric cars is going to be "normal" cars.
7 drones are going deliver many of the products—and food!—that we order online.
8 self-driving cars will to take everyone to work.
9 we won't not use paper money anymore.

14 Choose the correct options to complete the sentences.

1 On Tuesday, my class *is attending / attends* a classical concert so we can learn more about the music.
2 Like most people, I *'ll be pretending / 'm pretending* to understand the modern art when we go to the gallery.
3 The school choir *performs / is performing* several songs at the assembly today.
4 She *is about to wear / will be wearing* her costume when she walks home from school.
5 On Sunday, I*'m going to meet / 'm about to meet* my friends at the food festival in the park.
6 I'll be really happy once we *will finish / finish* our exams.
7 My parents *are going to order / will order* a print of my favorite painting for my room.
8 Let's go! The teachers *are about to put / will put* the sculpture in the school lobby.

15 Put the words in the correct order to make sentences and questions.

1 on / evening / the lectures / Friday / start / .

2 be / the singer / the reporters / will / after / interviewing / the concert / ?

3 are / watch / we / about / the music video / on his laptop / to / .

4 when / on the art world / an impression / that young artist / make / starts / her show / will certainly / .

5 be / on / the musicians / working / tomorrow / will / their / song / new / ?

6 their drawings / going / the art class / to display / is / next week / in the hallway / .

7 think / he / be / time / don't / will / on / I / ready / .

8 my first book / have / ready / I / publish / enough / will / short stories / I / once / .

16 Complete the questions about the future with the correct form of the verbs in parentheses. Sometimes there is more than one correct answer.

1 _____ you _____ (know) when the documentary film about Salvador Dali will be shown?
2 When _____ the class _____ (film) the performance of the school musical?
3 _____ the band leader _____ (give) us a new song to learn for next week?
4 What time _____ your flight _____ (leave) on Saturday?
5 What _____ we _____ (do) this time next week?
6 _____ your friend _____ (dance) with the professional ballet dancers at the theater tonight?
7 It's late! _____ the show about _____ (finish)?

4B Painting the Town

VOCABULARY BUILDING Adjective and noun collocations 2

1 Choose the correct option to complete the sentences.

1 The students in my class are from *diverse / low / leading* backgrounds—everyone has a different perspective to share.
2 In this school we follow a *hard / strict / mixed* set of rules, and there are consequences if you break them.
3 With a lot of *driving / innovative / hard* work and effort, you can achieve all your goals.
4 My school is starting an *innovative / individual / mixed* program where students can volunteer to tutor other students who need extra help.
5 He won a scholarship that helps *mixed- / diverse- / low-* income students afford the fees at the private school.
6 She is a member of the *leading / straightforward / private* orchestra in the city, in which she plays the violin.
7 He never stops studying because of his *hard / leading / driving* ambition to get into the best college in the country.
8 Although the teacher worked hard to prepare the students, they received *straightforward / hard / mixed* results on the exam.

READING

2 Read the article. Sentences a–g below have been removed from the article. Decide which sentence belongs in each gap (1–6). There is one extra sentence that you do not need to use.

1 ____
2 ____
3 ____
4 ____
5 ____
6 ____

a They moved to the neighborhood, hired about twelve local residents and trained them to paint.
b They were built without any of the planning that makes cities functional and attractive.
c The Vila Cruzeiro project attracted attention from other cities trying to improve their struggling neighborhoods.
d Koolhaas and Urhahn hope to work in many more cities, all over the world.
e Koolhaas and Urhahn agree.
f However, they believe that bringing colorful art into disadvantaged neighborhoods does something else.
g While visiting these favelas, famous for their crime and drug problems, the artists saw something different—potential.

3 Choose the correct options according to the information in the article.

1 Why did Koolhaas and Urhahn want to paint the favelas?
 a They wanted to make them inspiring places to live.
 b They wanted to provide jobs for local workers.
 c They were making a documentary about local artists.
 d They enjoy street painting.
2 Who built most of the favelas in Brazil?
 a skilled carpenters
 b city planners
 c the people who live there
 d architects
3 Which of the following could replace the underlined word "accomplishment" in paragraph 4?
 a buildings
 b successful project
 c employment
 d stripes
4 Why do some people criticize Koolhaas and Urhahn's art projects?
 a They think the artists take advantage of local workers.
 b They do not believe that art can help local communities.
 c They believe the art does not help with the biggest problems in the communities.
 d They do not think that artists from another country can understand local communities.
5 What may be the best title for the article?
 a Art in the Favelas
 b Painting Buildings
 c How do you paint neighborhoods?
 d Can art save a neighborhood?

4 Do the statements match the information in the article? Write true (T), false (F), or information not given (NG).

1 Koolhaas and Urhahn grew up in neighborhoods like the ones they paint. ____
2 Koolhaas and Urhahn believe that painting can be done without much planning. ____
3 The majority of residents in Vila Cruzeiro were glad that the artists were painting their favela. ____
4 The project in Philadelphia took longer than the project in Vila Cruzeiro. ____
5 Urhahn believes that a painting project can help a neighborhood economically. ____

Painting the Town

A favela neighborhood in Rio de Janiero

1   Jeroen Koolhaas and Dre Urhahn, the pair of artists known as Haas and Hahn, grew up in Holland, far from the tough neighborhoods of Rio de Janeiro, Brazil, where they completed some of their most innovative street paintings. Koolhaas and Urhahn met as university students and began working together professionally when Koolhaas was making a documentary film about hip hop in Brazil's favelas—the informal, urban neighborhoods in which many of Brazil's very low-income families live. (1) What if they could paint the crumbling houses and dirty buildings and turn them into art? Could they help make these dangerous neighborhoods beautiful, inspiring places to live?

2   Most favelas in Brazil were built by the people who live in them as they moved to the cities in search of work. (2) Koolhaas and Urhahn wanted to do their paintings in the same way the favelas were built, using local people to paint and letting the paintings be created without too much planning.

3   First, they started spending a lot of time in Vila Cruzeiro, a favela neighborhood that they believed could become their first large painting project. The artists spent time in the neighborhood and got to know the people there. As local residents became excited about the project, Koolhaas and Urhahn began hiring local workers to plaster and paint the houses they selected. They worked together with the local artists for 18 months, and the result was colorful neighborhood paintings that cover dozens of buildings and bring art into one of Rio's poorest communities.

4   (3) After Vila Cruzeiro, Koolhaas and Urhahn were contacted by officials from North Philadelphia, one of the poorest neighborhoods in the United States. (4) The project took roughly two years to complete, but the new painters, along with Koolhaas and Urhahn, painted over 50 buildings to create a huge urban painting of colorful stripes. The City of Philadelphia recognized the efforts of the local painters by giving them an award for their <u>accomplishment</u>.

5   Critics of Koolhaas and Urhahn's art projects say that painting such troubled neighborhoods does not address the real problems they face, like poverty, unemployment, drugs, and crime. (5) They don't expect a painting to solve complex social and economic issues. (6) It inspires the local residents and gives them pride in their community. It changes attitudes.

6   So Koolhaas and Urhahn will continue to bring art to troubled communities. They have worked in Haiti and Curacao and receive emails from interested cities every week. They hope their work will encourage kids to pursue creative careers.

4C Things We Will Have Done and Learned

GRAMMAR Future forms 2

1 Match the two parts of the sentences.

1 She was going to play baseball,
2 It was starting to rain,
3 She promised
4 Yesterday my sister said
5 They were still playing baseball when it got dark,
6 She decided to go to the baseball game

a she was going to play baseball with her friends.
b because she hoped she would see her favorite player.
c but it started raining.
d so she knew she'd have to go inside soon.
e we would play baseball if it isn't too hot this afternoon.
f so we had to tell them to come inside.

2 Complete the sentences with these phrases.

I'll have cooked	I will have listened
she'll have visited	we'll have been swimming
will have been practicing	will have been studying

1 Once she gets to Greece next month, _____ nine different countries.
2 They _____ the songs for six weeks by the time they have their concert next month.
3 I _____ English for three years by the time I graduate.
4 After the birthday dinner I'm making for my mom next week, _____ all the recipes in Madhur Jaffrey's *Vegetarian India*.
5 _____ for an hour by the time you join us.
6 _____ to all of the band's music by the time I go to the concert next month.

3 Put the verbs in parentheses in the correct form of the future perfect simple or future perfect continuous.

1 By the time we go to the music festival in March, our band _____ (learn) several new songs.
2 I _____ (not have) time to finish all my homework by tomorrow.
3 Before the weekend, I _____ (pack) for the trip.
4 By the time our sister is able to meet us, we _____ (look around) the museum for about an hour.
5 They _____ (watch) the first movie in the series again before the second one comes out in June.
6 In ten minutes' time, we _____ (wait) for the train for two hours.
7 He _____ (take) acting lessons for six years by the time he graduates from high school.
8 I _____ (try out) for the school jazz band by the end of the month.

4 Put the words in the correct order to make sentences talking about the future in the past.

1 read / my / book / sister / to / but / couldn't / going / find / her / was
   _____
2 my / I / if / he / wondered / to / come / party / would
   _____
3 fell / I / to / going / call / was / you, / but / I / asleep
   _____
4 the / by the time / started / the / we / will / get / to / have / theater, / movie
   _____
5 have / sailing / two / by the time / arrive, / we'll / been / we / for / hours
   _____
6 saved / he'll / by the time / of / money / have / he / retires, / a lot
   _____

5 Which sentence, a or b, is closer in meaning to the original sentence?

1 They'll have set out all the food and put on some fun music by the time their friends arrive for the party.
   a When their friends arrive, there will be food out and music playing.
   b They'll turn on music and put out food after their friends arrive.
2 Niko told me he was going to camp in Yosemite National Park for a week with his family.
   a Niko told me he and his family camped for a week at Yosemite National Park.
   b When I talked to Niko, he hadn't gone camping with his family yet, but they were planning to go.
3 Once he goes to Yosemite, he'll have visited seven national parks.
   a He hasn't been to Yosemite yet, but he's planning to go. It will be the seventh national park he's visited.
   b He went to Yosemite once, and it was the seventh national park he'd visited.

44 Unit 4

4 By the time I put the bread in the oven, the beans will have been cooking for an hour.
   a Once I put the bread in the oven, the beans will cook for an hour.
   b The beans will cook for an hour. Then I'll put the bread in the oven.

5 He'll have been watching TV for 45 minutes by the time he has to go to bed.
   a He'll need to go to bed 45 minutes after he starts watching TV.
   b After 45 minutes of watching TV, he'll need to continue watching in bed.

6 Yen asked our teacher if we would visit the Louvre on our trip to Paris.
   a The trip to Paris occurred after Yen asked the question.
   b Yen asked the question while her teacher went to the Louvre.

7 By the time I go to my violin lesson on Tuesday, I'll have learned the song my instructor taught me last week.
   a I learned a new song from my instructor last week. I've been practicing it since then. I will know it well when I go to my lesson on Tuesday.
   b I will be practicing the song my instructor taught me last week when I go to my violin lesson on Tuesday.

6 Complete the sentences about the future in the past with the correct form of the verb in parentheses.

1 By the end of this week, I _____ (finish) writing my paper on architecture in medieval Europe.

2 I knew you _____ (plan to stay) in Hong Kong for a week, but I didn't know you were going to fly to Bangkok afterwards.

3 By the time we get to the south rim of the Grand Canyon, we _____ (hike) for three days.

4 I _____ (not read) JK Rowling's new book by the time I meet her at the book signing.

5 My pottery project _____ (finish drying) by the time I get to class on Thursday, so I can start painting it then.

6 He said he _____ (study) at the library after school today.

7 By the time we complete our volunteer hours at the park, we _____ (not spend) more than ten hours picking up litter.

7 Complete the text with the correct form of these verbs.

be	finish	hike	melt	plan	visit	welcome

Yosemite National Park is a beautiful site in northern California that has waterfalls, mountains, and amazing forests. In the year 2040, Yosemite (1) _____ a national park for 150 years. The park is always extremely popular; in fact, by the end of this season, the rangers (2) _____ more than three million visitors. I heard the other day that my friend Brian (3) _____ a trip to Yosemite. Actually, he (4) _____ last year but didn't have enough time. For this trip, though, Brian thought he (5) _____ to Mirror Lake to take photos of Half Dome, one of Yosemite's most famous landmarks. I reminded him that Highway 120, which runs through the park, will remain closed until June or July, when the snow (6) _____ from the road. He said he was planning to go in August and invited me. Perfect timing, actually, because I (7) _____ my classes by then!

The Half Dome in Yosemite National Park

8 Use the prompts to write sentences with the future in the past.

1 I / thought / we / enjoy / new exhibit
_____

2 By the time / you / take your Spanish exam / you / ready / go Costa Rica
_____

3 We / finish decorating / house / by July
_____

4 I / take drawing class / tomorrow / not enough time
_____

5 Students / read the book / by Monday
_____

6 I / hoped / the play / finish / earlier
_____

7 He / say / ride bike / meet us / museum
_____

8 We / had to leave early / because / he / arrive / 9:00
_____

4D Building a Park in the Sky

TEDTALKS

AUTHENTIC LISTENING SKILLS

1 Listen to the extracts from the TED Talk and complete the sentences with these words. 🎧 32

a lot of	even though	going to	or for worse
right after	sort of	to try to	you know

1 I'm going to fast-forward through _____ lawsuits and a lot of sort of community engagement.
2 So we commissioned an economic feasibility study _____ make the case.
3 We opened the first section in 2009. It's been _____ successful beyond our dreams.
4 And this has been designed by Renzo Piano. And they're _____ break ground in May.
5 And the city has planned—for better _____—twelve million square-feet of development that the High Line is going to ring around.
6 And honestly, _____ I love the designs that we were building, I was always frightened that I wouldn't really love it.
7 Just one quick example is I realized _____ we opened that there were all these people holding hands on the High Line.
8 I think that's, _____, the power that public space can have to transform how people experience their city and interact with each other.

WATCH ▶

2 Complete the sentences with one or two words.

1 But even with a cowboy, about one person a month was killed and _____.
2 But with the rise of interstate trucking, it was used less and _____.
3 It was a train loaded with frozen turkeys—they say, at Thanksgiving—from the meatpacking district. And then it was _____.
4 And what first attracted me, or interested me, was this . . . this view from the street—which is this, you know, steel structure, sort of rusty, this _____.
5 Mayor Bloomberg came in office, he was very supportive, but we still had to make the _____.
6 We opened the first section in 2009. It's been sort of successful beyond our _____.
7 The other thing, it's generated, obviously, a lot of economic value; it's also inspired, I think, a lot of great _____.

3 Choose the correct option to complete the sentences.

1 The railroad hoped that the "West Side Cowboy" *would / will* reduce the number of fatal accidents on the train tracks.
2 The city *would / was going to* demolish the High Line tracks before Hammond and his organization got involved.
3 Hammond thought it *would have been / would be* nice to incorporate wild flowers and plants into the park.
4 They commissioned a study and predicted that the project *will have / would* cost $100 million.
5 Hammond says that the Whitney *is moving / would move* downtown to build their new museum at the base of the High Line.
6 The final section of the High Line *would have gone / is going to go* around the rail yards.

VOCABULARY IN CONTEXT

4 Match the words and phrases (1–6) with the sentences where a synonym is used (a–f).

1 engagement ____
2 figure out ____
3 behind ____
4 run over ____
5 assumed ____
6 relic ____

a One of the major problems with the original rail line in the city was that people were frequently **hit by the trains** and killed.
b Many people simply **believed** that it would not make economic sense to turn the High Line into a park.
c Robert Hammond wanted to **try to understand** how to transform the High Line into a park that would improve the life of the city.
d One of the challenges Hammond faced was convincing people that the High Line could be part of the city's future, and wasn't simply an **object from the past**.
e Many citizens were interested in the fate of the High Line, and they held **several meetings** to debate what should be done with it.
f The community members who were **supportive** of the High Line Park were certain that it would provide great economic and social benefits.

4E What's the plan?

SPEAKING

Useful language

Making suggestions

Do you feel like going to…?

I was wondering if you'd like to go to…?

Rejecting suggestions

To be honest, it's not really my kind of thing.

Doesn't really sound like my kind of thing, I'm afraid.

Suggesting alternatives

OK. Well, in that case, how about going to…?

OK. Well, if you'd rather, we could always go to…

1 Read the two conversations. Decide which sentence (a–f) belongs in each gap (1–6). 🎧 33

a Doesn't really sound like my kind of thing, I'm afraid.
b OK. Well, in that case, how about going to the 90s party with a few of us on Friday?
c Do you feel like going to the zoo with me next Saturday?
d To be honest, it's not really my kind of thing. I'm more into pop music.
e I was wondering if you'd like to go to the Kamaal Williams gig that's on in town?
f Well, if you'd rather, we could always go to the sculpture park they've got there.

Conversation 1
A: Hey, what are you up to this weekend?
B: Well, I've got a project I was going to work on, but otherwise not too much, why?
A: (1) ____
B: Who's he? What kind of sound is it?
A: It's a kind of jazz funk music. He plays keyboard but he's got a band with him too.
B: (2) ____
A: (3) ____
B: You know, I'd like that. Thanks.
A: Great.
B: What time are you meeting?
A: I guess we'll head into town at about 8.

Conversation 2
A: (4) ____
B: What?
A: It's a big family trip. My cousins were coming but had to cancel, so my parents said I could bring a friend with me. What do you think?

B: (5) ____ There are all those animals and I really disagree with them being kept in captivity.
A: Oh, really? You know it's that sanctuary where they rescue them, so it's not that bad.
B: Hmm, sorry, I'm really not sure.
A: (6) ____ And there's also an animal art center. It's got some of those paintings done by horses and elephants and stuff.
B: Yeah, that sounds OK. Are you sure your parents won't mind us wandering off?
A: No, they'll be fine as long as I'm not on my own, and my little brother, Joe, won't let them take him anywhere near art.
B: Yeah, alright then.
A: Great!

2 Answer the questions about the conversations in Activity 1. You do not need to write complete sentences.

1 What style of music is the invitation for?

2 What instrument does the musician play?

3 Why does the invitation get rejected?

4 What do they arrange to do? ____
5 Are they going alone? ____
6 Why is Suzie invited to the zoo? ____
7 Does she want to go? Why? / Why not?

8 What's special about the zoo? ____
9 What part of the trip appeals to Suzie?

10 Why won't everyone be together on the trip?

3 Answer the following questions. Make notes and remember to include the useful language. Then, listen to the sample answers and compare your ideas. 🎧 34

- What do you enjoy doing in your free time?
- Do you listen to a lot of music in your free time?

Cultural Transformation 47

WRITING For and against essay

4 Complete the steps for writing a *for* and *against* essay.

against	brief	conclusion	four
in favor of	introduction	personal	relevant
support	three		

A *for* and *against* essay is usually
(1) _____ paragraphs long.
The opening paragraph is the (2) _____.
It states the topic and tells the reader why it is currently
(3) _____. It also gives a
(4) _____ overview of the topic.
The main body of the essay is made up of paragraphs
two and (5) _____. The
second paragraph should offer a few points
(6) _____, or for, the topic. The
third paragraph should supply two or three points
opposing, or (7) _____, the topic. It
is important to provide reasons and examples to
(8) _____ these points.
The closing paragraph is the (9) _____.
The writer sums up the essay and gives his or her
(10) _____ opinion on the topic.

5 Read the *for* and *against* essay. Then match the underlined items (1–8) with their function (a–h).

Local artists who improve our community should be given free housing. Do you support or oppose this idea?

(1) There has been a significant increase in community art projects in the past year. Local artists have been working with residents to create public murals, installations, and various sculptures around our city. (2) By and large, these creations are warmly received by the community. It also bears mentioning that many of these artists are struggling financially.

One very convincing argument in favor of giving free housing to local artists is the value they bring to our city. (3) The work they do helps to establish a stronger sense of community. It is sometimes said that cities are unfriendly, lonely places, but these shared collaborations bring people together and give them an opportunity to express themselves creatively. (4) In addition, such meaningful creations give people greater pride in their neighborhoods. Providing free housing to the artists would be a worthy gesture of thanks from the city.

(5) However, many people strongly disagree with this proposal. First of all, it has been reported that some residents dislike the murals and sculptures in their areas. (6) Secondly, it is worth remembering that artists who collaborate in community projects are paid for their work. It is also important to point out that a career in art is a personal choice. Why should one profession be rewarded more generously than another? Finally, as our city has a high number of homeless people, many feel it would be better to give free housing to the needy rather than to artists.

(7) To sum up, (8) it seems to me that free housing should be reserved for those who need it the most. While it is true to say that local artists are doing excellent work in the community, giving them free housing does not seem to be a popular prospect.

a sequencing points in a list _____
b introducing the conclusion _____
c introducing a general statement _____
d introducing an opposing view _____
e adding a further point _____
f introducing a personal opinion _____
g supporting a main point with a reason _____
h establishing the recent relevance of the topic _____

6 Read the *for* and *against* essay in Activity 5 again. Then answer the questions. Write *yes* or *no*.

1 Is the essay about a definite plan to give free housing to local artists? _____
2 Does the writer show that local artists bring value to the community? _____
3 Can we infer that only a few people are opposed to giving artists free housing? _____
4 Do artists collaborate in community projects for free? _____
5 Overall, is the writer against artists being given free housing? _____

7 The local government is planning to fund a major arts festival in your town next year. Do you support or oppose this plan? Write a 300-word essay to respond to this question.

Review

1 Complete the sentences with a word from this unit.

1. The food festival has a big _____ on the city.
2. The sculpture creates a _____ of pride in the community.
3. There is wide _____ for a new football stadium; everyone wants it.
4. The museum _____ together people from across the city.
5. The comedy club _____ a lot of students.
6. The title "European Capital of Culture" _____ the local economy.
7. We hope the event will _____ a lot of income for the museum.
8. Thousands of people _____ the film festival last year.

2 Circle the item that is NOT a correct definition.

1. to have an impact on: *to influence / to not influence / to cause changes*
2. to generate: *to hold back / to produce / to stimulate*
3. to hold an event: *to cancel an event / to schedule an event / to have an event*
4. to raise money: *to find money / to earn money / to collect money*
5. to fade: *to become less important / to grow in importance / to get lighter in color*
6. an innovative scheme: *an idea or plan that's been done before / a new method / an unusual method*
7. mixed results: *good results / different types of results / both good and bad results*
8. driving ambition: *weak ambition / strong ambition / long-lasting ambition*

3 Complete the sentences with these verbs.

was going to	was starting	would make
would start	would take	wouldn't go
wouldn't sell		

1. Hana didn't rush because she knew the concert _____ late.
2. The painter said he _____ a presentation of his work to the art class.
3. The gallery owner promised he _____ the painting to anyone else but me.
4. She already said that she _____ to the music festival.
5. They always thought their son _____ be a writer.
6. Ivan said he _____ a lot of pictures at the art exhibit.
7. The play _____ so we had to take seats quickly at the back of the theater.

4 Match the two parts of the sentences.

1. By dinner time, ____
2. I'm looking forward to going to dinner because ____
3. I'll be eating dinner after ____
4. I'll eat dinner when ____
5. I told him I was ____
6. I'm going to eat dinner and then ____
7. Before I went to dinner, I ____
8. I'm about to eat dinner and ____
9. Before I went to dinner, ____

a. going to eat dinner and then study.
b. was planning to study.
c. I thought I would study.
d. I study.
e. I'll have been studying for six hours.
f. then I'll study.
g. study.
h. I've finished studying.
i. I'll have finished studying by then.

5 Complete the sentences with the correct form of these verbs. Use one verb twice.

| give | go | have | live | play | wait |

1. I wondered if he _____ to hike all the way to the bottom of the Grand Canyon.
2. She _____ to come to the restaurant with us.
3. I thought I _____ until I got to the theater to buy my ticket.
4. He texted to say he _____ a presentation at our school next week.
5. I _____ in Buenos Aires for three months by the time you come to visit me.
6. I _____ three different art teachers by the time I go to college.
7. She _____ volleyball for eight years by the time she tries out for the national team.

5 It's Not Rocket Science

5A Steps in the Process

VOCABULARY Science in action

1 Review Choose the best options to complete the text.

Manuel Castillo is an experienced (1) ___, who has just been employed as a new member of the Help Team. Please contact him if you are having any problems with your computer (2) ___. Manuel can respond to your questions by email or he can come to your office and (3) ___ things face-to-face. He can also advise you on how to (4) ___ with other departments, (5) ___ for documents in the scientific library, and (6) ___ scientific research materials from other universities online.

1. a computing technician
   b computer technician
   c hacker
   d software developer
2. a equip
   b equipped
   c equips
   d equipment
3. a ask
   b search
   c explain
   d find
4. a join
   b connect
   c access
   d connection
5. a find
   b search
   c access
   d get
6. a access
   b invent
   c connect
   d ask

2 Review Complete the sentences with these words.

curious	data	discover	examine
proof	results	solution	technology

1. All the _____ the scientists collected is still being examined.
2. The _____ of the experiment were very disappointing. We did not learn anything new.
3. Many people still want to _____ if there is life on other planets.
4. The _____ to the problem still escapes us.
5. I won't believe you unless you give me _____ of your statement.
6. Children ask so many questions because they are naturally _____ about everything around them.
7. We will _____ all the ancient statues we found on our trip.
8. The _____ in computer science is changing every day.

3 Choose the correct option (a–d) to complete each sentence.

1. The first step is to ___ a hypothesis.
   a release   c track
   b record   d form
2. I ___ the substance under the microscope.
   a got rid   c recorded
   b placed   d formed
3. When did you carry ___ the experiment?
   a off   c over
   b in   d out
4. The substance ___ in the water.
   a released   c dissolved
   b got rid of   d added
5. The scientists ___ their eating habits over six months.
   a tracked   c rewarded
   b proved   d submitted
6. We ___ an experiment to test the effects of heat.
   a formed   c dissolved
   b designed   d placed
7. The action ___ a chemical reaction.
   a did   c proved
   b added   d created
8. He ___ the results of the experiment.
   a looked   c analyzed
   b carried out   d placed

4 Complete the sentences with these verbs.

| analyze | carry | dissolve | form |
| heat | prove | submit | track |

1 First, you need to _____ up the substance.
2 The team hopes to _____ the movement of the whales.
3 My goal is to _____ the hypothesis.
4 Doctors _____ the samples in a lab outside the hospital.
5 Make sure you _____ your report before the deadline.
6 I _____ out research as part of my job.
7 The salt didn't _____ in the cold water.
8 It's important to _____ an interesting hypothesis.

5 Number the steps of the research in order.

___ a Record the results of the experiment.
___ b Prove or discount your hypothesis.
___ c Carry out research.
___ d Design an experiment.
_1_ e Form a hypothesis.
___ f Analyze the data.

6 Cross out the mistake in each sentence and write the correct word.

1 The chemical reaction realized a gas.
_____
2 You should add referees at the end of your research report. _____
3 Scientists are carrying in research into cancer.
_____
4 We'll analysis the results at the end.
_____
5 He heated out the chemicals. _____
6 We designed the test to get rid with a chemical.
_____

7 Put the words in the correct order to make sentences.

1 researchers / demonstrate / their / experiment / to / designed / an / theory / .
_____
2 the / energy / chemical / released / reaction / .
_____
3 dissolved / the / heated up / substance / after / it / was / .
_____
4 data / form / a / before / collecting / hypothesis / .
_____
5 the / cell / placed / she / microscope / under / the / .
_____
6 the / gorillas' / tracked / eating / scientists / habits / .
_____

8 Extension Complete the table. Match these verbs with the noun they collocate with.

| conduct | disprove | formulate | perform | set up | test |

Hypothesis	Experiment

9 Extension Complete the sentences with these words.

| data | disprove | dissect | observation |
| performed | reacted | set | support |

1 After the experiment, we analyzed the _____ .
2 The chemicals _____ with each other.
3 She wanted to _____ her hypothesis and show it was false.
4 They _____ up the experiment in the laboratory.
5 We _____ the experiment over three days.
6 Students _____ animals as part of their biology course.
7 Biology is the study of the natural world through _____ and experimentation.
8 Does your data _____ your hypothesis?

PRONUNCIATION

10 Listen to the sentences. Underline the verb that is stressed in the passive construction. Then practice saying the sentences. 🎧 35

1 The heart was believed to be the center of intelligence until the Middle Ages.
2 It is claimed that computer training programs can limit the effects of aging on the brain.
3 Einstein's brain was said to be bigger than average, which explains his intelligence.
4 It's estimated that the human brain is about 75 percent water.
5 It's well known that most of the time we use only 10 percent of our brain capacity.
6 Doing exercise is thought to create chemicals that reduce your ability to think.
7 The part of the brain called the hippocampus is known to be connected to our sense of direction.
8 It has been generally accepted that creative people have a dominant right brain.

LISTENING

11 Listen to a short talk about accents and perception. What would you say is the main finding of the researchers? 🎧 36

a Looks and accent are the two traits that people perceive first.
b Good-looking people are generally perceived as more honest.
c The brain's response to different looks and accents is inconclusive.
d People with accents are sometimes perceived as outsiders.

12 Listen again. Then complete the text with the words that you hear. 🎧 36

When it comes to the way we speak, accents (1) _____ more than where we come from. (2) _____ at Germany's Friedrich Schiller University Jena found that speech wins out over looks when people (3) _____ someone based on those two (4) _____ alone. Accents may be key to social (5) _____ because they can affect whether listeners (6) _____ the speaker as being one of their own or part of a different group. Says Patricia Bestelmeyer, whose research at the University of Glasgow focuses on the brain's (7) _____ to different accents: "They can (8) _____ how much you prefer or trust someone."

A lion walks in the Okavango Delta.

13 Listen to a story about being overly curious. What do you think would be the best title for the story? 🎧 37

a The Curious Bayei
b Curiosity and a Cat
c A Curious Brother
d Curiosity Kills

14 Listen again and answer the questions. 🎧 37

1 How many lions are in the Okavango Delta?
  a 10,000   c nearly 80,000
  b more than 2,000 d around 20,000
2 What did the ancestors of the Bayei people hunt?
  a crocodiles   c lions
  b leopards   d hippopotamus
3 What raised the curiosity of the brothers?
  a lions calling   c elephants running
  b hippos swimming d Bayei learning
4 After wandering from camp, how did the brothers feel?
  a embarrassed   c curious
  b defenseless   d ashamed
5 What did the brothers not want the lions to think of them as?
  a naked   c inviting
  b curious   d threatening
6 How did the brothers get the lions to relax?
  a by staring at the lions
  b by reasoning with them
  c by focusing on some dung
  d by running towards them
7 What lesson did the brothers learn?
  a to be more cautious
  b to take more risks
  c to never be curious
  d to forget consequences

GRAMMAR Passives 1

15 Read about important inventions of the 21st century. Then choose the correct options to complete the text.

It might be said that some of the most important advances of the 21st century have been the iPhone, the iPod, YouTube, and Skype. Today, they are a part of everyday life, but our lives (1) *has been changed / have been changed / have changed* by all of them.

Music players existed before Apple's iPod, but the iPod changed people's relationship with music—especially how it (2) *was enjoyed / was to enjoy / enjoy*.

The iPod and Apple's music store, iTunes, (3) *was develop / were developing / were developed* in 2001. The iPod's modern design and its large storage capacity made it very popular. And because of iTunes, digital music has become normal.

YouTube (4) *founded / was being founded / was founded* in 2005 and is now the world's most popular video-sharing website. Videos (5) *can shared / can be shared / can share* by anyone from anywhere. Millions of hours (6) *spent / is spent / are spent* each month watching music videos, clips from TV programs and films, how-to tutorials, and even cat videos!

How people communicate (7) *also been changed / has also been changed / is also changing* because of Skype. Before this, telephone calls to friends abroad were expensive, but that changed with Skype's free, internet-based calls. Now anyone with an internet connection can (8) *been "called" / is "called" / be "called"* for free! What's more, they (9) *can be seen / can see / have seen* thanks to the video chat!

Apple's iPhone was the first user-friendly smartphone with a large touchscreen. It came out in 2007 and took over the cell phone market, and a new industry (10) *created / was creating / was created*—app development. To date, nearly 900 million iPhones (11) *has been sold / have been sold / are sold*.

The 21st century is still young. Who knows how our lives (12) *improved / will improved / will be improved* by other inventions in the next few years!

16 Complete the sentences with the passive forms of these verbs and the tenses in parentheses below.

cause	conduct	confirm	question	select
submit	track	transform	win	

1 We were told that more research _____ if there's enough funding. (modal + passive)

2 The other team's hypothesis _____ by the teacher. (past perfect passive)

3 The smoke _____ by escaping gas. (past continuous passive)

4 The results of the experiment _____ by the surprised researchers. (simple past passive)

5 The raw materials _____ into a unique substance. (present perfect passive)

6 Temperature changes _____ by the scientists. (future passive)

7 The winner of the competition _____ by the committee. (present perfect passive)

8 The innovation prizes _____ right now. (present continuous passive)

9 The teacher was happy that our homework _____ on time. (simple past passive)

17 Rewrite the passive sentences in active form and the active sentences in passive form.

1 An experiment was designed by the scientists to test the quality of the gold.
　_____

2 The fish had been released into the stream by the biologist.
　_____

3 The wire was attached to the battery, which started the experiment.
　_____

4 The powder is being dissolved in the liquid.
　_____

5 They used the smartphone to make a video of our experiment.
　_____

6 You can find the winners on our website or in our magazine.
　_____

7 The high cost has discouraged me from building a supercomputer.
　_____

8 Experts consider scientists from your country to be among the best in the world.
　_____

5B Playing to Learn

VOCABULARY BUILDING Adjective endings

1 Complete the table with the adjectives that go with these nouns.

| adaptation | beauty | curiosity | effect | help |
| hope | imagination | innovation | ~~treatment~~ | |

-able	-ful
treatable	

-ive	-ous

READING

2 Read the article and choose the best headings for paragraphs 1–6 from the list of headings below. You will not use all the headings.

Paragraph 1 ___
Paragraph 2 ___
Paragraph 3 ___
Paragraph 4 ___
Paragraph 5 ___
Paragraph 6 ___

a Guided play for learning
b Guided play for discovery
c How education is changing
d How children learn best
e Why rats play
f The problem with play
g Why animals play
h Playing for the future
i Play and the brain

3 Read the article again. Choose the answer that you think fits best according to the article.

1 In paragraph 2, what is the author's main point about animal play?
  a Play makes rats more social and less stressed.
  b Play is extremely important for animals to survive and succeed.
  c Playful animals live longer than animals who are not playful.
  d Rats, squirrels and bears are healthy animals because they play a lot.

2 The author gives examples of animals that play because
  a it is interesting information for the reader.
  b it is important information for teachers to understand.
  c it helps explain why play is important for human children.
  d scientists are focused on animal play.

3 In paragraph 4, what does the author suggest about guided play?
  a It is better for learning than many traditional teaching methods.
  b It should be used mainly to teach vocabulary.
  c It should be directed by teachers, not children.
  d It should be focused on fun more than on specific learning goals.

4 In paragraph 5, what is the author's purpose in describing the teacher's interaction with students about shapes?
  a to prove that this is a good teacher
  b to prove that guided play is important for children
  c to suggest that teachers should never talk more than children
  d to give an example of how guided play works

5 In the last paragraph, "this" refers to
  a research.   c guided play.
  b children.   d scientists.

4 Complete each sentence with the correct ending based on information from the article.

1 Rats that play regularly ___
2 Students in the past ___
3 The purpose of guided play is to ___
4 A teacher using guided play well will ___
5 Children learn best when they ___
6 Worksheets and flashcards ___

a have strong social skills.
b spend a lot of time listening.
c help students achieve learning goals.
d make connections to their own lives.
e do not always help students remember information.
f spent less time playing than they do now.

Playing to Learn

1. When most people think of school, we think of sitting in desks or at tables, listening to teachers, and taking exams. But today, especially in classrooms for young children, learning looks quite different. One of the biggest trends in early childhood education is for play-based learning. Instead of seeing children sitting at a desk, you might find them playing in a model kitchen or building towers of blocks. Rather than watching a teacher who stands at the front of the room, these students will be playing with their teacher in the park. What is play-based learning, and why do children need it?

2. To find some answers, we can look to the animal kingdom. Many species of animals have been observed playing, and scientists have begun to understand why. Animals play for a variety of reasons: to learn social skills, to master survival skills and to relieve stress. Rats are some of the most playful animals, and research shows that rats who play have better developed brains, are able to pay attention longer, and have better memories than rats who don't. Rats who play are also better in social situations with other rats; they get in fewer fights and have much lower stress levels. Squirrels are also playful animals. Scientists have found that squirrels who play have better coordination and even have more babies than those who don't. Brown bears who play as cubs are more likely to survive into adulthood than those who do not experience play. Play is crucial for animals to learn important social and survival skills, and might even create healthier brains.

3. It's not surprising, then, that human children also benefit from playing to learn. Educational researchers have found that children learn best when they are mentally active, interested, socially interactive, and able to make connections between what they are learning and their own lives. Teachers build on this research by practicing guided play in their classrooms.

4. Play is flexible, fun, and directed by children; guided play helps children focus their play to achieve a learning goal. For example, a teacher using guided play to teach farm animal vocabulary might read a book with the children and then let them play with toy horses, cows, and chickens. Studies show that this type of guided play helps children remember words better than regular school activities like worksheets or flashcards.

5. With guided play, teachers watch and listen more than they talk. If children are playing with toys of different shapes, a teacher might ask questions about the shape. This allows the child to learn about different shapes through discovery rather than instruction. They are able to form hypotheses of their own, test them, and become little scientists.

6. Research is showing that children learn better from playing, especially from guided play. Scientists are trying to learn more about what effects this has on the brain, but it is clear that play is an important part of development. Guided play helps prepare children to become curious, creative thinkers, and caring members of society. Many teacher training programs are now focusing on the importance of guided play so that the next generation gets the best education possible.

5C Mind-Blowing!

GRAMMAR Passives 2

1 Read the sentences. Are they active (A) or passive (P)?

1 My sister Roberta claims to be too busy to help me study. ___
2 It's well known that Beijing Capital International Airport is one of the busiest airports in the world. ___
3 I believe Barbara McClintock won the Nobel Prize in Physiology or Medicine in 1983 for her work in genetics. ___
4 The estimate the scientists made for how long it takes certain bacteria to multiply was accurate. ___
5 Louis Armstrong was said to be one of the most innovative jazz trumpeters. ___
6 Exercising every day is thought to lead to better sleep. ___
7 They said getting humans to the moon couldn't be done. ___
8 It's estimated that the world's population will be 9.7 billion by 2050. ___
9 Thoughts on the nature of the universe have changed throughout time. ___
10 Ella Fitzgerald was a well-known jazz singer. ___
11 Marie Curie was believed by many people to be one of the greatest scientists working in the early 20th century. ___

2 Choose the correct option to complete the sentences.

1 It ___ that human actions are increasing the negative effects of climate change.
   a is claimed
   b claimed
   c is known to be
   d is thought to
2 In the 1950s, it ___ by some people that women should not play sports.
   a believe
   b were believed
   c has been believed
   d was believed
3 The Space Launch System ___ a major step along the road to putting people in space to explore Mars as well as other aspects of deep space.
   a it's expected to be
   b is expecting to be
   c is expected to be
   d expecting
4 Rewriting your notes after class ___ help you learn the material better.
   a is thought to
   b known to be
   c thought to
   d knowing to
5 ___ that students who study every day get better grades.
   a Thought
   b It's considered
   c It's thinking
   d It's well known
6 British archaeologist Howard Carter ___ as the person who, in 1922, discovered Tutankhamun's tomb in Egypt.
   a seems
   b is said
   c considered
   d is known
7 In the 1400s, many people ___ India's spices were the best in the world.
   a were said
   b said
   c have generally accepted
   d have been said

3 Choose the correct option to complete the sentences about brain myths.

1 *It's said / It says* we use only 10 percent of our brain capacity.
2 Our brain *doesn't / is believed to be* work as well after we turn 50.
3 Brains *claim / are claimed* to be like computers.
4 It *generally accepts / is generally accepted* that we have only five senses.
5 *It's assumed / It assumes* that you have to speak one language well before you learn a new language.
6 Men's brains *were believed to / are* different in many ways from women's brains.
7 *It is thought / Thoughts* that adults can't grow new brain cells.

4 Which sentence, a or b, is closer in meaning to the original sentence?

1 Gabriel Garcia Marquez is said to be one of the greatest authors of the 20th century.
   a I think Gabriel Garcia Marquez is one of the greatest authors of the 20th century.
   b Many people think Gabriel Garcia Marquez is one of the greatest authors of the 20th century.
2 It's well known that tennis players who take extra lessons do better in competitions.
   a Tennis players know to take extra lessons and do well in competitions.
   b If tennis players take extra lessons, they generally do better in competitions.

56 Unit 5

3 Persuasive advertisements are thought to make customers buy more.
  a People generally think that customers buy more when they see persuasive advertisements.
  b Customers buy more items and like persuasive advertisements.

4 Lewis Hamilton is known to be one of the best Formula One drivers of all time.
  a Lewis Hamilton knows he is one of the best Formula One drivers of all time.
  b Many people think Lewis Hamilton is one of the best Formula One drivers of all time.

5 It's been generally accepted that science has made life better.
  a Though not everyone agrees, a lot of people think science has made our lives better.
  b Science making our lives better is accepted to be a general thought.

6 It's widely believed that teachers should encourage curiosity in their students.
  a Teachers generally want to encourage their students to be curious.
  b Most people think it's important for teachers to encourage their students to be curious.

5 Use *have* or *get* + *something* + past participle to write a new sentence in the passive that is related to the first sentence.

1 Someone took my photo for my new ID. (get)
I got my photo taken for my new ID.

2 They displayed my research project at the science fair. (have)
_____

3 They printed my aunt's favorite recipe in the newspaper. (get)
_____

4 They took my temperature at the clinic. (have)
_____

5 Some classmates finished Jamie's experiment for him. (get)
_____

6 Use the prompts to write present simple sentences with the impersonal *it*.

1 well / know / people / like / ice cream
It is well known (that) people like ice cream.

2 think / recording lectures / help / students / learn
_____.

3 assume / most students / need / study / regularly
_____.

4 think / exercise / good for / brain
_____.

5 claim / world / get / hotter / every decade
_____.

6 assume / scientific advances / help / people / live longer
_____.

7 well know / Mrs. Liu / be / best teacher / our school
_____.

7 Rewrite each passive sentence so that it does not use the impersonal *it*.

1 It is thought that studying abroad helps students become more curious about the world.
_____.

2 It's estimated that 37 percent of the people in our country have university degrees.
_____.

3 It was said that our experiment was doomed to failure since we didn't take into account the temperature.
_____.

4 It is claimed that brushing your teeth twice a day keeps your mouth healthy.
_____.

5 It's believed that fish such as salmon are good for the health of your brain.
_____.

6 It's thought that getting at least eight hours of sleep every night helps your brain work better.
_____.

5D Science is for everyone, kids included.

TEDTALKS

AUTHENTIC LISTENING SKILLS

1 Listen to the extract from Beau Lotto's TED Talk, and choose the filler words where he uses them. If he does not use a filler word, choose X. 🎧 39

Now, I want to tell you a story about seeing differently, and all new perceptions begin in the same way.
(1) *Right?* / *X* They begin with a question. The problem with questions is they create uncertainty. Now, uncertainty is a very bad thing. It's evolutionarily a bad thing. If you're not sure that's a predator, it's too late. (2) *OK?* / *X* Even seasickness is a consequence of uncertainty. (3) *Right?* / *X* If you go down below on a boat, your inner ears are telling you you're moving. Your eyes, because it's moving in register with the boat, say I'm standing still. (4) *OK?* / *X* Your brain cannot deal with the uncertainty of that information, and it gets ill. The question "why?" is one of the most dangerous things you can do, because it takes you into uncertainty. (5) *You know?* / *X* And yet, the irony is, the only way we can ever do anything new is to step into that space. So how can we ever do anything new? Well fortunately, evolution has given us an answer,
(6) *right?* / *X* And it enables us to address even the most difficult of questions. (7) *Yeah.* / *X* The best questions are the ones that create the most uncertainty. They're the ones that question the things we think to be true already. (8) *Right?* / *X* It's easy to ask questions about how did life begin, or what extends beyond the universe, but to question what you think to be true already is really stepping into that space.

WATCH ▶

2 Do Beau (B) or Amy (A) make each of these statements?

1 The brain takes meaningless information and makes meaning out of it, which means we never see what's there. ___
2 Science is not defined by the method section of a paper. It's actually a way of being, which is here, and this is true for anything that is creative. ___
3 We thought that it was easy to see the link between humans and apes in the way that we think, because we look alike. ___
4 Really, we wanted to know if bees can also adapt themselves to new situations using previously learned rules and conditions. ___
5 We asked the bees to learn not just to go to a certain color, but to a certain color flower only when it's in a certain pattern. ___
6 So the kids give me the words, right? I put it into a narrative, which means that this paper is written in kid speak. ___
7 It took four months to do the science, two years to get it published. ___
8 This project was really exciting for me, because it brought the process of discovery to life, and it showed me that anyone, and I mean anyone, has the potential to discover something new. ___

VOCABULARY IN CONTEXT

3 Match the words 1–6 with the sentences that show their meaning (a–f).

1 adapt ___
2 a voice ___
3 reward ___
4 surrounded ___
5 bother ___
6 link ___

a Joaquin's mother always told him that knowledge would be the **benefit he received** for his effort in school.
b Sometimes adults don't **make the effort** to take children's questions seriously, even though they can provide valuable insights.
c Amy and her classmates wanted to study the **connection** between the way humans solve problems and the way bees do.
d The students wondered whether the bees would **change** their behavior based on the experiments that they designed.
e When I go into the city, I have people and buildings **all around me**.
f Beau Lotto thinks that it is important for children to have **the opportunity to contribute** to scientific discussions.

5E Conducting Experiments

SPEAKING

Useful language

Staging

The first thing we'd need to do is…
  We'd also need to make sure that we (didn't)…
I suppose then we'd probably be best… -ing…

Preparing research questions

I wonder if / how / why…
It'd be good to know what / whether…
We'd need to try and work out…

Hypothesizing

I'd expect the results to show… I'd imagine that the data would probably reveal…
I would / wouldn't have thought it'd be possible to prove that…

1 Match each useful language phrase with its function: Talking about Staging (S), Preparing research questions (Q), or Hypothesizing (H).

1 I wonder if / how / why ___
2 We'd also need to make sure that we (didn't) ___
3 I would / wouldn't have thought it'd be possible to prove that ___
4 We'd need to try and work out ___
5 I guess then we'd probably be best…-ing ___
6 I'd expect the results to show ___
7 It'd be good to know what / whether ___
8 I'd imagine that the data would probably reveal ___
9 The first thing we'd need to do is ___

2 Listen to the conversation and decide what the experiment will be about. 🎧 40

a commerce   b science   c technology

3 Complete the conversation with phrases from the useful language box. Then listen again and check your answers. 🎧 40

A: So, how are we going to plan our science project together?
B: Well, I think (1) _____ design the experiment.
A: That's a good idea. So, if we're investigating the gas released in the chemical reaction with different metals, we need to use sound research methods.
C: (2) _____ we can measure the rate of gas produced.
B: (3) _____ measured and recorded the results accurately.
A: Yeah, and (4) _____ how the reaction occurs.
C: (5) _____ doing some research, forming a hypothesis about the reaction, and then proving it in our experiment.
B: Also, (6) _____ the quantity varies at different temperatures.
C: (7) _____ the speed of the reaction changes at different temperatures.
A: Yeah, (8) _____ an increase in volume at higher temperatures.
B: What about the different metals? Are they all going to be the same?
C: (9) _____ that one of the metals was the most reactive.
A: Right, let's decide how we're going to research this then.

4 Think about how you and some classmates would work together to plan one of the experiments from the list below (or an example of your own). Apply the research methods you learned in the unit to plan your task. Use the useful language to make notes. Then compare your ideas with the conversation in Activity 3.

- How do different building designs react in an earthquake?
- Frozen substances—expansion or contraction?
- How can we produce light without electricity (or fire)?
- The effectiveness of different materials to filter dirty water

5 Listen to part of a lecture from a biology course and answer the question below. 🎧 41

Using the information from the talk, describe the two main consequences of global warming and how the examples illustrate the concept.

Make notes and remember to use the useful language. Then listen to the sample answer. 🎧 42

WRITING A scientific method

6 Match the two parts of the sentences.

1 The experiment aimed to measure ___
2 The purpose of the experiment ___
3 Pavlov played the same sound ___
4 The reactions among the gases were studied in order to ___
5 During the experiment, the scientists ___
6 After the experiment, the properties ___

a determine their volumes.
b of radioactivity were described.
c was to demonstrate superconductivity.
d reproduced certain types of bacteria.
e so that the dogs knew they would be given food.
f the force of gravity in a laboratory.

7 Match each sentence with its function: Introducing the process (I), Linking the steps (L), or Explaining the steps (E).

1 The purpose of the experiment was to show the effects of gravity. ___
2 Next, the psychologist showed the child the choice of rewards. ___
3 A microscope was provided so that the cells could be seen. ___
4 The diagram illustrates the process used to complete the experiment. ___
5 The experiment aimed to prove that light travels faster than sound. ___

8 Complete the process for this scientific experiment using these words and phrases. Two items are not used.

after the experiment,	aim	before the experiment,
carried out	conform	discover
during the experiment,	finally	in order to
incorrect	once	then

The Asch conformity experiment

The (1) _____ of this 1950s experiment was to (2) _____ whether social pressure would make individual people conform. In other words, it tested whether individuals would (3) _____, that is, agree, with an answer given by a majority of others even though they knew this answer was (4) _____. The experiment was (5) _____ with 50 male students from a college in the United States.

(6) _____ seven participants were told what answer to give about a comparison between the length of lines on two different cards. One participant was not aware of this, and was not given any instruction.
(7) _____ this person was deliberately placed last in the line of participants, who were all required to answer the question aloud.
(8) _____ prove the theory, the first seven people were instructed to give the same incorrect answer.
(9) _____ these seven had answered, the final participant (10) _____ had to decide whether to conform and give the answer everyone else had given, or the one they personally knew to be correct.

9 Read the process in Activity 8 again. Then put the points (a–h) in the correct order (1–8).

a Before the experiment, seven of the eight people were told what answer to give. ___
b The plan was to ask the group to answer an obvious question. ___
c After hearing all seven answers, the eighth person had to decide whether to conform. ___
d Groups of eight people were formed to participate in this experiment. ___
e The eighth person didn't know the others had been told how to answer. ___
f The purpose was to find out whether people would conform to what others said. ___
g These seven people were all instructed to give the same incorrect answer. ___
h They had to answer aloud, so everyone in the group could hear their answer. ___

10 In your English class, you have been talking about robots. Now your English teacher has asked you to write an essay. Write 140–190 words in an appropriate style.

Today, scientists are developing more advanced robots that will carry out many functions for human beings in the future. Some people feel this is a bad idea. Do you agree?

Notes
Write about:
1 convenience
2 jobs
3 _____ (your own idea)

Review

1 Choose the correct option to complete the sentences.

1. She *recorded / formed* the results of the experiment on her tablet.
2. In a *reference / hypothesis* you try to explain an observation.
3. The scientists *carried out / tracked* the progress of the athletes.
4. The chemicals *dissolved / released* a gas.
5. Can you *add / place* it under the microscope, please?
6. The team *designed / formed* a hypothesis.

2 Complete the words to make the phrases.

1. s _ _ _ _ _ an assignment before the deadline
2. c _ _ _ _ _ a chemical reaction
3. a _ _ references at the end of a report
4. d _ _ _ _ _ an experiment
5. c _ _ _ _ o _ _ research
6. a _ _ _ _ _ _ the results of an experiment
7. p _ _ _ _ a hypothesis
8. g _ _ r _ _ o _ a chemical

3 Cross out the mistake in each sentence and write the correct word.

1. Music streaming being used by more and more people these days. _____
2. The electric car been developed to decrease our dependence on petroleum. _____
3. The driverless car has been dream of for many years, but now it is a reality. _____
4. Smartphones is now carried by the majority of adults. _____
5. Before I left school, tablet computers had introduced into most lessons. _____
6. The internet was using for research for the science project. _____
7. Wearables (small computer devices that you wear) being advertised as the latest tech gadget. _____
8. Her files stored in the cloud so she can access them from any computer with an internet connection. _____

4 Complete the sentences using the verbs in parentheses in the passive voice.

1. It _____ (generally agree) that travel sparks curiosity.
2. Certain senses and functions of the body _____ (control) by the brain.
3. In the 15th century, it _____ (say) that the world was flat.
4. The Copley Medal _____ (award) annually by the Royal Society, London, to persons in any field of science who show outstanding achievement.
5. The report _____ (write) after the students completed the experiment.
6. In the 16th century, the Earth _____ (believe) to be at the center of the universe.
7. In many circles, it _____ (claim) that scientific innovation depends on a solid secondary school education.

5 Read the questions. Choose the correct answer.

1. Who do you think the best soccer player is?
   a It's claimed that either Lionel Messi or Ronaldo is the best soccer player in the world.
   b I claims that either Ronaldo or Lionel Messi is the best soccer player.
2. Do I really have to study every day?
   a You'll got better grades if you study more.
   b Well, it's been generally accepted that the more you study, the better grades you'll get.
3. Name one of the happiest countries in the world.
   a Denmark says to be one of the happiest country in the world.
   b Denmark is said to be one of the happiest countries in the world.
4. How many people were in the world in the 1600s?
   a It's estimated that the population then was around 500 million.
   b The population in the 1600s it's estimated that it was around 500 million.
5. What can I do to stay healthy?
   a If you wash your hands frequently, I think you'll get sick less often.
   b It's well know washing your hands frequently leads to fewer illnesses.
6. Do you think I should join the drama club?
   a If you do join, I think you'll have got better grades and you had liked it.
   b Yes, I do! Participating in activities such as drama club is thought to help you get better grades. And I think you'll like it, too.
7. Didn't your hair use to be longer?
   a Yes, I have it cut last Monday.
   b Yes, I got it cut on Monday.

It's Not Rocket Science

6 Adapt to Survive

6A Evolution and Conservation

VOCABULARY Endangered species

1 Review Complete the sentences with these words.

drought	environmental	expedition	fishing
route	save	waste	wild

1 Many plant species die during a _____.
2 The world is facing an increasing number of _____ problems.
3 Many charities track illegal _____ boats using technology.
4 Everyone should change their daily routine to help _____ the environment.
5 Campaigners are encouraging restaurants not to _____ food.
6 Illegal hunters catch _____ animals in their habitats.
7 The scientific _____ to Antarctica lasted eight months.
8 The _____ the climbers chose was straight up the mountain.

2 Review Mark each sentence correct (C) or incorrect (I). Then cross out the incorrect words and write the correct ones.

1 The increase in people using cars has led to global cooling. ___ _____
2 A result of the bluehouse effect is the heating up of the Earth's surface. ___ _____
3 Governments need to take action against companies that damage nature. ___ _____
4 Building projects are destroying the nature environment. ___ _____
5 Schools are teaching children about how to protect the environment. ___ _____
6 Climate change is leading to less extreme weather. ___ _____

3 Choose the correct option (a–d) to complete the sentences.

1 The Javan rhino is at risk of _____.
  a endangered   c extinction
  b survival   d conservation

2 The zoo is running a _____ program for turtles.
  a hunting   c species
  b conservation   d habitat

3 Parents _____ on their genes to their children.
  a preserve   c breed
  b pass   d bring

4 Farming is _____ the natural habitat of plants and animals.
  a destroying   c losing
  b preserving   d improving

5 Scientists are concerned about the long-term _____ of the Western Lowland gorilla.
  a risk   c extinction
  b survival   d consequence

6 Increased water pollution will have lasting _____ on the area.
  a risks   c consequences
  b extinction   d species

4 Cross out the phrase that does NOT collocate with the noun.

1 *improve energy / bring a lasting / work in nature* + conservation
2 *discover a new / an endangered / work in nature* + species
3 *lose its natural / destroy the / pass on its* + habitat
4 *leave the / have serious / consider the* + consequences
5 *ensure its / preserve their / its long-term* + survival

5 Complete the phrasal verbs in the sentences with these prepositions.

for	from	on	out	to	to

1 Scientists benefit _____ new technology.
2 We had to adapt _____ the freezing temperatures during our stay.
3 We had to conform _____ the tribe's rules about exploring the area.
4 My parents passed _____ their love of bees to me.
5 Many species have died _____ in the last century.
6 We had to stop them hunting _____ the elephants.

A Namib Desert Darkling Beetle

6 Complete the text with these words.

| adapted | endangered | extinct | habitat |
| risk | species | store | survive |

Everyone knows that if your (1) _____ is the desert, there is one thing you lack: water. The Namib Desert Beetle may look ancient, but it is not (2) _____ or even (3) _____. How does this insect (4) _____? This (5) _____ of beetle has (6) _____ to its surroundings. Its back has bumps on it. The bumps contain something that attracts water. Once a day, these bumps collect moisture from the cool morning breeze and (7) _____ it on the beetle's back. When the bumps have collected enough, the water runs down into the beetle's mouth.

Now, using the same idea, a company is trying to make a self-filling water bottle for people and animals at (8) _____ of dehydration in the desert.

7 Listen to the descriptions. Match each description with the item it describes. 🎧 43

1 _____   a an animal that has adapted for survival in a difficult habitat
2 _____   b a species that was saved by conservation efforts
3 _____   c a species that is extinct
4 _____   d an insect that is beneficial to people
5 _____   e a species whose habitat is being destroyed
6 _____   f a species that is endangered by hunting

8 Extension Complete the table. Use a dictionary if necessary.

Noun	Adjective	Verb
conformity	conforming	
	modified	
	threatened	
habit		habituate
sustenance	sustaining, sustained	

9 Extension Complete the crossword.

Across
2 to obey a rule or law
3 the ability to do something unpleasant for a long time
6 a small change
7 a danger or risk
8 the chance or hope that something will happen

Down
1 protection from heat or cold, etc.
4 well known to you
5 a place that is safe from danger

Adapt to Survive

PRONUNCIATION

10 Listen to the sentences. Is the underlined *have* or *been* pronounced in its weak or strong form? Practice saying the sentences. 🎧 44

1 Those animals should <u>have</u> been protected.
   a weak   b strong
2 That article must <u>have</u> been fake.
   a weak   b strong
3 How have the gorillas <u>been</u> doing?
   a weak   b strong
4 He's <u>been</u> working with endangered species all his life.
   a weak   b strong
5 <u>Have</u> they benefited from the conservation efforts?
   a weak   b strong
6 Most of their habitat has <u>been</u> destroyed.
   a weak   b strong
7 What has <u>been</u> most rewarding about the work?
   a weak   b strong
8 I think we all might <u>have</u> done more.
   a weak   b strong

LISTENING

11 Listen to the conversation. Complete the collocations that you hear. 🎧 45

1 consider _____
2 an endangered _____
3 destroying _____
4 risk of _____
5 involved in a conservation _____
6 ensure the _____
7 pass on their _____
8 a potential _____

a crocodile bag

12 Listen again and answer the questions. 🎧 45

1 How did Janice react to what Laura showed her?
   a She was disappointed.
   b She wasn't interested.
   c She was a bit jealous.
   d She was very curious.
2 What did Janice criticize Laura for not considering?
   a how expensive the bag was
   b which country the bag came from
   c what the bag was made of
   d who actually made the bag
3 What did Janice tell Laura she was doing to crocodiles?
   a destroying their only habitat
   b ensuring their final extinction
   c not considering their rights
   d adding to the threat to them
4 How did the man describe Janice?
   a patronizing   c pessimistic
   b passionate   d perplexed
5 What was one of Janice's arguments in favor of conservation?
   a the possible benefits to humankind
   b stopping unnecessary cruelty to animals
   c reducing the amount of consumerism
   d ensuring the survival of the human race
6 In the end, how would you describe Laura's attitude?
   a She was even more offended.
   b She was a bit upset with the man.
   c She was rethinking her position.
   d She was finished with Janice.

13 Listen to the lecture. Match these scientific terms with their definitions. 🎧 46

1 species
2 habitat
3 troop
4 climate
5 adapt
6 behavior
7 primatologist
8 survival

a the usual weather conditions in an area
b a group of particular animals
c the ways in which a person or animal acts
d continuing to live despite difficult circumstances
e an animal's natural home or environment
f to change because of new or different conditions
g a group of similar individuals capable of breeding
h an expert in the study of primates

14 Listen again. Are the statements true (T) or false (F)? Practice saying the true sentences. 🎧 46

1 Male chacma baboons generally weigh more than 88 pounds. ____
2 Chacmas do not usually live in desert areas. ____
3 Long periods without water affects the baboons' behavior. ____
4 The baboons get water from the Kuiseb River all year round. ____
5 Chacmas in the Namib will sometimes sleep during the day. ____
6 Temperatures in the Namib are often higher than 113 degrees Fahrenheit. ____

64 Unit 6

GRAMMAR Modals and meaning

15 Choose the best option to complete the sentences.

1 The Korowai people in southeastern Papua, Indonesia, *can / may* disappear in the next generation because the young people are moving to nearby towns.
2 A drought in Kenya *shall / might* make life even more difficult for the Samburu people who travel across northern Kenya looking for water and food for their animals.
3 The Awa people in Brazil *can / should* be protected from the farmers and loggers who are coming into their homeland and destroying the habitat.
4 If the Tsaatan people in Mongolia *could / would* get help from the government, their culture and their reindeer, on which they depend, could survive.
5 Help from the Indian government *may / must* help the Ladakhis in the state of Jammu and Kashmir as their culture modernizes and changes very quickly.

16 Choose the best options to complete the text.

Even though we (1) *shall not / may not* realize it, language is always changing. It changes so slowly that we (usually) don't notice it. Some people (2) *may / must not* assume that language change is bad and the result of laziness or mistakes, but in truth, language change is neither good nor bad. It just *is*.

Language evolution (3) *shall / can* include changes in vocabulary, grammar, and pronunciation. Because it reflects the needs of its speakers, a language (4) *could / will* require new words if the needs of its speakers change, due to new technology, new products, or unique experiences.

Languages (5) *can / should* adapt by borrowing words (for example, *sushi*), by shortening words or phrases (*text messaging* has become *texting*), or by combining words to create a new word (*breakfast* + *lunch* = *brunch*).

Geography (6) *should / can* lead to language change, too. If a group of speakers is separated from other people who speak the same language, their language (7) *will / must* change differently or at a different speed than the other people. British and American English are an example of this.

If languages didn't change, we (8) *couldn't / wouldn't* have any words for the digital technologies that have appeared in the 21st century so far. Language (9) *must / could* change to keep up with the lives of its speakers.

17 Complete the sentences with these words. You may use the words more than once. There is more than one correct answer for some items.

can	could	may	might	must

1 In the plains and grasslands of North America, we _____ not interfere with the habitat of the bison or they, too, will become extinct.
2 The blue whale _____ die out if we don't stop polluting the Gulf of California.
3 Building roads in the jungle _____ destroy the habitat of the endangered bonobos in the Congo Basin.
4 We _____ protect the Galapagos Islands in order to save the giant tortoise.
5 You _____ borrow the binoculars, but please be careful with them.
6 In order for animals to survive, they _____ evolve along with their changing habitats.

18 Complete the sentences with these phrases.

can expect	couldn't connect	might even be
must call	must rely	should know

1 Reading a map is a disappearing skill. Now, we _____ on the sat nav on our smartphones.
2 Changing a car tire is a disappearing skill. Because no one can do it now, we _____ for help when we have a flat tire.
3 Knowing correct spelling and grammar is a disappearing skill. People these days _____ their computers, tablets, and smartphones to fix mistakes.
4 In the 21st century, people _____ how to use a smartphone.
5 It would be practically unthinkable if someone _____ to Wi-Fi these days.
6 It _____ dangerous if people didn't understand how online privacy settings work.

19 Choose the correct option to complete the sentences.

1 In the future, it's unlikely that people *will / would / must* wear watches to know what time it is.
2 People probably *should / shall / will* not have DVD players because they will stream movies from the internet.
3 People *shall / can / might* get by with just a cell phone these days so there's no need to have a landline.
4 Because their smartphones have built-in music players, people *might / can / must* not need stereo equipment in the future.
5 And because their phones have built-in cameras, fewer people *will / could / must* want digital cameras.
6 Email is such a popular way to communicate now, so I doubt anyone *might / would / must* need a fax machine.

Adapt to Survive

6B The Lynx Returns

VOCABULARY BUILDING Compound nouns

1 Match the words to form compound nouns.

1 social media   a creatures
2 sea   b products
3 science   c shop
4 animal   d age
5 rain   e campaign
6 ice   f teacher
7 book   g house
8 farm   h drop

READING

2 Read the article and choose the best summary (a–d).

a Without more European rabbits, the survival of the Iberian lynx is in question.
b Spanish pride in their native cat, the Iberian lynx, has never been higher.
c While still endangered, the Iberian lynx population is steadily recovering.
d Like many small cats, the Iberian lynx is able to blend in with its environment.

3 Choose the correct option according to the information in the article.

1 What can we infer from the first paragraph?
   a Iberian lynx like to live in and around olive trees.
   b It is usual for Iberian lynx to have two babies.
   c The cat is wearing some kind of electronic device.
   d Iberian lynx like to be around loud noises.

2 What has surprised Germán Garrote about the Iberian lynx?
   a their ability to survive without any rabbits to eat
   b their ability to adapt to strange environments
   c their devotion and caring for their newborns
   d their incredible strength for such a small size

3 What kind of fur does the Iberian lynx have?
   a striped
   b bushy
   c amber
   d spotted

4 How many Iberian lynx were there when the Iberlince project started?
   a less than 100
   b more than 2,000
   c approximately 176
   d around 60

5 Why have scientists been able to reintroduce so many lynx into the wild?
   a They know how to hide extremely well.
   b They can eat things other than rabbits.
   c They always have at least two babies.
   d They breed well, even when confined.

6 What is the current status of the lynx?
   a critically endangered
   b almost extinct
   c endangered
   d surviving in captivity

7 What are Simón and his team providing in order to save more lynx?
   a public information
   b underpasses
   c native cats
   d road crossings

4 Sentences a–g have been removed from the article. Decide which sentence belongs in each place (1–6). There is one extra sentence that you do not need to use.

1 _____   4 _____
2 _____   5 _____
3 _____   6 _____

a Four breeding centers and one zoo raised most of the cats, all of which were fitted with radio collars.
b Of the world's 38 wildcat species, 31 are considered small cats.
c Lynx are more adaptable than we thought, he explains.
d He says it's a beloved national figure.
e The team works closely with private landowners to earn their trust and persuade them to welcome lynx on their property.
f If it weren't for her radio collar, we'd never know that one of the world's rarest cats is hiding among the neat rows of trees.
g The lynx population was so small that it was suffering from dangerously low genetic diversity, making it vulnerable to disease and birth defects.

The Iberian Lynx

1. "She's very close," whispers Germán Garrote, pointing to a handheld receiver picking up Helena's signal. Somewhere in this olive grove* beside a busy highway in southern Spain, the Iberian lynx and her two cubs are probably watching us. (1) Helena has learned to blend into the human landscape, even hiding with her newborn cubs in a vacant house during a loud festival.

2. "Ten years ago we couldn't imagine that the lynx would be breeding in a habitat like this," says Garrote, a biologist with the Life+Iberlince project, a government-led group of more than 20 organizations working to help protect the Iberian lynx. The area where Helena lives is very hot for about five months of the year, and has heavy traffic on the roads. Garrote says that the spotted cat's future is to live in fragmented* areas. (2)

3. After many years of decline, the lynx population has started to increase. When Iberlince stepped in to rescue the lynx in 2002, fewer than a hundred of the cats were scattered throughout southern Spain. The numbers were drastically reduced by hunting and a virus that nearly killed all the region's European rabbits, the lynx's main food. (3)

4. Luckily for scientists, lynx breed well in captivity, and 176 have been reintroduced* into carefully selected habitats since 2010. (4) Sixty percent of the reintroduced cats have survived and some have done extremely well.

5. Two lynx traveled across the Iberian peninsula, each walking more than 1,500 miles to new territory, says biologist Miguel Simón, director of the reintroduction program. (5) In 2012, when the population hit 313—about half of which were old enough to breed—the International Union for Conservation of Nature upgraded the lynx's status from critically endangered to endangered.

6. Cars and trucks are the leading killers of lynx, so Simón and his team are working with the government to create wildlife underpasses* so the animals can cross beneath the roads. Simón says that everyone knows about the Iberian lynx and the Spanish are very proud of their native cat. (6) With Simón's and others' help, the remarkable feline should continue to inhabit the peninsula for which it is named.

grove *an area in which a certain kind of tree grows*
fragmented *broken up; not connected*
reintroduced *when an animal goes to live in the wild*
underpasses *walkways under roads*

Adapt to Survive

6C Mysterious Changes

GRAMMAR Modals and infinitive forms

Blue whale

1 Choose the correct option to complete the sentences.

1 Today there _____ only between 10,000 to 25,000 blue whales left.
  a be
  b have been
  c being
  d are

2 Blue whales can _____ from 82 to 105 feet and weigh up to 200 tonnes.
  a be ranging
  b ranged
  c range
  d have been ranged

3 Every day, the blue whale must _____ about 4.5 tons of food.
  a have eaten
  b be eating
  c eating
  d eat

4 Blue whales can _____ in every ocean.
  a being found
  b be found
  c find
  d found

5 Climate change could _____ the survival of blue whales.
  a being threat
  b threaten
  c have been threatened
  d threat

6 We should _____ into consideration the effects of pollution on blue whales' habitats.
  a be taking
  b have take
  c took
  d taking

7 More must _____ to help blue whales by preserving their environments.
  a be
  b have been
  c being done
  d be done

2 Listen and complete the sentences. 🎧 48

1 The pizza _____ cooked too long.
2 We _____ left earlier.
3 You _____ studying all night.
4 I don't know where they are. They _____ gone to the museum.
5 It _____ mattered if we had made more coffee.
6 They _____ set up the tent by now.
7 You _____ talking during class.

3 Choose the correct option to complete the sentences logically.

1 Paleontologists have discovered feather imprints in many dinosaur fossils. They now believe that most dinosaurs must *be / were / have been* covered in feathers.

2 The Carolina parakeet, the only parrot native to the United States, was extinct by 1904 as a result of hunting, deforestation, and disease. People *should / may / won't* have protected them.

3 NASA has found some interesting mineral deposits on Mars. Similar formations on Earth were formed by ancient bacteria. This means that life *can't / could / should* have existed on Mars.

4 Every year, people report seeing a yeti, Bigfoot, or Sasquatch—all large, hairy, human-like creatures from local legends. However, there is no scientific evidence that these creatures actually exist. They may *see / be seeing / be seen* an ape, a bear, or another animal.

5 The black-footed ferret was almost extinct, but biologists have been working hard to save the species. In fact, they are hoping that by 2020, the black-footed ferret *will have / will have been, / would have been* removed from the endangered species list.

6 The Amazon Rainforest is home to 10% of plant and animal species in the world. Unfortunately, humans are cutting down the forest at an alarming rate. We *wouldn't be / can't have been / shouldn't be* destroying this precious natural resource.

68 Unit 6

4 Complete the sentences with these phrases.

as you can see	could have been done
could have come	have to study
must have been	need I explain
should have seen	wouldn't have come

1 _____ how your new phone works?
2 We _____ for the final exam.
3 _____, the climate is getting warmer.
4 You _____ to the party.
5 I _____ to the party if I'd known Dominic would be here.
6 We _____ many more birds on our hike.
7 More _____ to clean up the river.
8 The book _____ really interesting. She was up until at least midnight reading.

5 Match the related sentences.

1 I didn't invite my friends on the camping trip last weekend.
2 The students all finished the test in less than 20 minutes.
3 The documentary wasn't great.
4 They went on a trip to Antarctica last year.
5 Friday is the last day for us to turn in our science projects.
6 Ten o'clock is definitely too late for us to arrive at the dinner party.
7 The students have a big test tomorrow.
8 Wait. Don't call the neighbors right now.

a It could have been better.
b It must have been exciting!
c It can't have been very difficult.
d They should be studying now.
e They will have finished eating by then.
f They might be eating dinner.
g They must be finished by then.
h They wouldn't have come.

6 Which option is closer in meaning to the original sentence?

1 You can't have cooked the rice long enough.
   a You didn't cook the rice long enough.
   b Next time you may want to cook the rice longer.
2 We must make more spaghetti next time.
   a We might want more spaghetti next time.
   b Next time we make spaghetti, we need to make more.
3 He can't drive his friend to the movies on Friday.
   a He won't be able to drive his friend to the movies on Friday.
   b On Friday, he may be able to drive his friend to the movies.
4 I can't believe how long it took to hike to the waterfall.
   a It took longer than I thought it would to hike to the waterfall.
   b The hike to the waterfall was really long.
5 We should set up our tents before we eat.
   a We might set up our tents before we eat.
   b It would be a good idea for us to set up our tents before we eat.
6 I shouldn't have taken five classes this semester.
   a I wish I had taken fewer classes this semester.
   b I shall take fewer classes next semester.

7 Put the words in the correct order to make sentences.

1 see / I / can / on / movie / Saturday / the / .
_____
2 studying / be / you / every / should / at / library / the / day / .
_____
3 Madagascar / summer / he / go / to / this / might / .
_____
4 she / new / need / bike / to / may / buy / a / .
_____
5 have / you / read / that / can't / book / entire / !
_____
6 he / the / might / more / have / beach / enjoyed / weather / better / in / .
_____
7 should / before / went / have / you / told / me / I / !
_____

8 Complete the sentences with the correct form of the verbs in parentheses.

1 An Amur tiger can also _____ (call) a Siberian tiger.
2 In the past, Amur tigers could _____ (find) in eastern Russia, northern China, and the Korean peninsula.
3 Experts say there might _____ (be) only 540 Amur tigers left in the world today.
4 In the 1940s, there may _____ (be) only 40 Amur tigers left because of hunting.
5 A reason these numbers could _____ (be) higher today is because the Russian government was the first to grant these tigers full protection.
6 There might not _____ (be) such an increase in numbers if the government hadn't stepped in to protect them.
7 We must _____ (encourage) industries such as logging, agriculture, and mining to consider the Amur tiger's habitat as they make business plans.

Adapt to Survive 69

6D You Have no Idea Where Camels Actually Come From

TEDTALKS

AUTHENTIC LISTENING SKILLS

1 Listen and complete each extract from the TED Talk with one, two, or three words. 🎧 49

1 She's a paleobiologist, which means she specializes in _____ really old dead stuff.
2 … maybe I'm looking _____ more closely and realizing it doesn't quite look like this has tree rings.
3 … and eventually collected 30 fragments of that exact same bone, _____ really tiny.
4 Having hit a wall, she showed one of the fragments to some colleagues of hers in Colorado, and they _____.
5 And usually, after so many _____, it breaks down.
6 And he processed it, and compared it to 37 known and modern-day mammal species. And _____ a match.
7 Well, scientists have known for _____, turns out, even before Natalia's discovery, that camels are actually originally American.
8 It went from being this ridiculously niche creature suited only to this one _____ environment…

WATCH ▶

2 Complete the sentences with a word or short phrase.

1 The Fyles Leaf Bed is located near the _____ Pole.
2 Over the years, Rybczynski collected 30 _____ of the same bone.
3 Eventually, Rybczynski used a 3D surface _____ to complete her work.
4 Collagen is what gives _____ to our bones.
5 The bone belonged to a camel that would have been _____ feet tall.
6 Camels are originally _____.
7 Camels' humps are filled with _____.
8 Llamas and alpacas are relatives of camels that live in _____.

3 Number these events from the talk in chronological order.

____ Eventually, the North American camels went extinct.
____ In 2006, Natalia Rybczynski discovered ancient camel bones in the Arctic.
____ Camels first evolved in North America, where there were around 20 species.
____ Now scientists are questioning whether camels may have evolved for cold climates, instead of the desert.
____ For a long time, people assumed camels originated in the desert.
____ Around 7 million years ago, camels migrated to South America and to Asia.

VOCABULARY IN CONTEXT

4 Match the words and phrases to the sentences that illustrate their meaning.

1 spot ____
2 willingness ____
3 hit a wall ____
4 surface ____
5 proof ____
6 camp ____

a The scientists knew they had to dig deeper than **the top layer of land** to find the oldest artifacts.
b They chose a quiet **place to set up their tents** and spend the night.
c Natalia went back to the same **place** to look for more bone fragments.
d She tried hundreds of different ideas, but eventually, she **reached a point where she couldn't make any more progress**.
e One of the key things we look for is **evidence** that our hypotheses are true.
f I was impressed by Natalia's **desire to keep trying** to find the answer even though it was a difficult challenge.

6E Finding a Solution

SPEAKING

1 Look at the photos. Match the anecdotes with the pictures. Write the correct letter in the space provided.

a   c

b   d

1 Last year, I had the opportunity to go scuba diving in the Red Sea. I felt a little frightened when I first got into the water, but I forgot all about my fear when I started seeing beautiful fish. ____
2 For their thirtieth wedding anniversary, my parents went whale watching. Seeing whales in their natural environment had always been their dream. ____
3 When I graduated from high school, my parents surprised me with plane tickets to South Africa. They'd made plans for us to visit an elephant sanctuary. ____
4 Over the summer, I went on a safari. It was an unforgettable experience. ____

2 Complete the conversation using these words and phrases. Some items may have more than one answer.

How amazing!   Really?
So, what did you do?   That must have been wonderful!
What happened?

A: Last year my family and I decided to visit a nature reserve.
B: (1) _____ I've always wanted to do that.
A: So had I! Anyway, we weren't quite sure where to go, but after considering several options, we decided to travel to Tanzania.
B: Wow. (2) _____
A: Yes, that's what I thought, but for the first few days we didn't see any animals.
B: Oh, no. How disappointing!
A: My parents were sure that eventually we would see something. After all, we were in the animals' natural habitat.
B: (3) _____
A: Well, on our last day, we were really lucky.
B: (4) _____
A: Well, very early in the morning we came across a herd of zebras. They were grazing by the side of the road and it was just beautiful.
B: (5) _____ Were you able to take any photos?

Now answer the following questions.

1 Which photo are the two friends speaking about?
_____
2 How would you feel if you were in Speaker A's situation?
_____
3 What other questions could Speaker B ask to find out more information?
_____

3 Choose one of the photos in Activity 1 and write your own anecdote. You can begin with one of these prompts or a sentence in Activity 1. Make notes below.

Last year, my family and I decided to…
Ever since I was a child, I had always wanted to…
Once, I had the opportunity to…
It had always been my dream to…
On my last vacation, my family and I…

4 Listen to an anecdote. Then write a list of questions you could ask to find out more. Use these expressions. 🎧 50

How did you feel when…?   What did you do when…?
What happened after…?   Who else…?
Why do you think…?

Now, write the ending to the story. Include some of the details you asked about in your questions.

5 Read the following questions. Make notes on how you would answer them. Listen and compare your ideas to the sample answers. 🎧 51

1 Would you like to go on a safari? Why? / Why not?
2 Does whale watching appeal to you? Why? / Why not?
3 Would you enjoy scuba diving? Why? / Why not?
4 What do you think is the best way to protect endangered species? Why?
5 What are the advantages of nature reserves compared to zoos?

Adapt to Survive   71

WRITING A problem-solution essay

6 Put the steps for writing a problem-solution essay into the correct order, 1–7.

a Also, try to start each new paragraph with a topic sentence. ___
b Begin the essay by outlining the problems and saying you will suggest solutions. ___
c First, read the essay topic carefully. ___
d Finally, if you have time, write a brief conclusion to sum up. ___
e Next, plan your essay. Make notes on your ideas and main points. ___
f Write about one problem and solution in each new paragraph. ___
g As you plan, do some research if possible. To give your main points greater authority, refer to other sources. ___

7 Complete the problem-solution essay with sentences a–h.

(1) ___

(2) ___ Apart from loss of habitat, these animals are also hunted for their meat. The worst issue of all, though, is frequent poaching, that is, they are illegally hunted for their horn. (3) ___

(4) ___ One of the greatest of these is deforestation (cutting down trees). (5) ___ Conservation groups such as Save the Rhino relocate, or move, the rhino to safer areas, and also run various projects to protect the animals.

People in developing countries often don't have enough to eat. This is not a new problem. (6) ___ I agree with the solution proposed by experts from Stirling and Oregon State universities to have local governments encourage their people to switch to alternative food sources.

(7) ___ In some countries, the horn is believed to provide medical benefits, although there is no scientific evidence for this. In recent years, some conservationists have been using chemicals to dye rhino horns pink, so that they become less valuable to poachers. (8) ___ It is not yet clear whether or not this solution is working, but it's certainly an interesting approach.

a Large animals, such as rhino, can provide meat for entire villages in some areas.
b Loss of habitat happens for a number of reasons.
c According to the Rhino Rescue Project, humans who consume these chemicals would become ill.
d How can we protect the world's rhino?
e In this essay, I will suggest solutions to these three problems.
f Being poached for their horn is the greatest threat the rhinos face.
g Today, most species of rhinoceros in the world are critically endangered.
h This forces the rhino to move to more open areas where they may not have enough food, and where they are more vulnerable to other threats.

8 Read the essay in Activity 7 again. Then match the questions (1–8) with the answers (a–k). Three answers are not used.

1 What are the three problems faced by the rhino? ___
2 Which of the problems is the worst? ___
3 What is one solution to the loss of habitat problem? ___
4 Why are rhino hunted for their meat in some areas? ___
5 Why are rhino poached for their horn? ___
6 What are some conservationists doing to the rhino horn? ___
7 What source claims that the dye could make people sick? ___
8 Is the dye and chemicals solution a success? ___

a moving the rhino to safer areas
b applying chemicals and pink dye to it
c it isn't yet known
d loss of habitat
e loss of habitat, being hunted for their meat, and being poached for their horn
f yes, it's very successful
g it's used as medicine in some countries
h poaching
i experts from Stirling and Oregon State universities
j the people in those villages are very hungry
k the Rhino Rescue Project

9 Read the text below and follow the instructions.

A number of zoos around the world are important centers for research and conservation of certain species. The animals in zoos may be well cared for, but they don't have freedom and aren't in their natural environment.

There are numerous benefits from having animals in zoos.

Do you agree or disagree? Write an essay giving your thoughts on this topic.

Review

1 Rewrite the sentences. Complete the sentences using the words in capital letters. Use between two and five words.

1 The Madagascan dwarf hippopotamus has become extinct.
  The Madagascan dwarf hippopotamus _____ _____. OUT
2 Sea turtles are endangered.
  Sea turtles _____. RISK
3 The animals haven't been able to live in the new environment.
  The animals _____ the new environment. ADAPTED
4 We are concerned that many birds won't survive for long.
  We are concerned about the _____ of many birds. TERM
5 The Amur tiger hasn't become extinct yet.
  The Amur tiger has _____. SAVE
6 I got my red hair from my mother.
  My mother _____ her red-hair gene to me. PASS

2 Complete the sentences with one word.

1 Tropical forests are the natural _____ of millions of species.
2 Conservation programs breed animals at _____ of extinction.
3 The Canarian oystercatcher was a _____ of bird.
4 We need to ensure the _____ of as many species as possible for future generations.
5 Your _____ can even determine the length of your life.
6 Millions of species have _____ to life in the rainforests.

3 Choose the correct option to complete the sentences. There may be more than one correct answer.

1 Scientists have plenty of ideas of how to rescue the elephants and they ____ need any more.
  a must not b may not c should not
2 If the government promises to protect our traditional way of life, it ____ survive for future generations.
  a must b will c can
3 The loggerhead turtles in the Mediterranean ____ be saved because several countries are working together.
  a could b shall c need
4 Stopping people from cutting down the trees in their habitat ____ help save the endangered bonobos.
  a should b would c must
5 The red panda ____ be protected because its forest habitat is being destroyed.
  a must b can c should
6 Habitat loss ____ be the most dangerous factor faced by snow leopards today.
  a should b might c must

4 Match the two parts of the sentences.

1 More money must ____
2 Now we should ____
3 I can't ____
4 As you can ____
5 You should ____
6 I don't think we could ____
7 Nicaragua must ____
8 If the Amur tiger hadn't been given protection, they would ____

a have been even more beautiful before so many of its trees were cut down.
b see, protecting the forest elephant's habitat is vital.
c have done more to protect Australia's Great Barrier reef.
d have died out.
e be spent on protecting the environment.
f be doing more to protect the environment.
g see why people hunt endangered species.
h have told us more about how Amur tigers protect their young.

5 Choose the correct option to complete the sentences.

1 **A:** Did Sasha have a lot of interesting things to say about the reading assignment?
  B: She didn't have much to say about the book in class. She *can't have / may have* read it very thoroughly.
2 **A:** Do you think we're lost?
  B: Yes, we *can have / must have* turned the wrong way.
3 **A:** I can't believe we're still going to be on the train at midnight.
  B: I know! Normally, I *shall be going / would be going* to bed by 10 o'clock.
4 **A:** Why didn't you take the early train?
  B: I *should've / wouldn't have* made it on time, even if I'd taken the early train.
5 **A:** We had such a great time on our trip to Puerto Rico.
  B: It *must have been / can have been* fun to explore the island and the old city.
6 **A:** Why didn't you study more for your exam?
  B: Studying more *would helped / wouldn't have helped* me do better on the exam.
7 **A:** But what can we do to help the environment?
  B: More animals *can't have lived / could live* here if we planted more trees and cleaned up the river.

7 Outside the Box

7A Rules of Creativity

VOCABULARY Breaking the mold

1 Review Rewrite the sentences. Complete the sentences using the word in capital letters. You may use between one and four other words in your answer.

1 Kate Robinson works as a photographer in New York.
  Kate Robinson _____ as a photographer. LIVING
2 I always do a lot with my time.
  I _____ of my time. MAKE
3 Many people don't understand abstract art.
  Abstract art _____ to a lot of people. SENSE
4 Please decide in the next few minutes.
  Please _____ in the next few minutes. MIND
5 The public loved Banksy's artwork in Calais.
  Banksy's artwork _____ in Calais. SPLASH
6 The movies *Planet Ocean* had a big effect on the viewers.
  The movies *Planet Ocean* _____ on the viewers. MADE

2 Review Cross out the mistake in each sentence. Write the correct words.

1 I'm sorry, but I really can make up my mind. I don't know what I want. _____
2 The mural will make a big different to the hospital. _____
3 Let's make the most for our gallery visit. _____
4 Supermarkets should make way to small, independent shops. _____
5 He makes a good live as an actor. _____
6 The documentary did quite a splash—people loved it. _____
7 Her novels don't make many sense to me. _____
8 Your photographs are going to make a big impressive. _____

3 Match the two parts of the sentences.

1 I'm going to create   a person.
2 He's made   b creatively.
3 She's a very creative   c to the problem.
4 He's an artist who breaks   d up some lyrics for the song.
5 We need a new approach   e something new to wear.
6 She thinks   f the rules.

4 Complete the sentences with these verbs.

adapt   create   follow   has   kill   make   score   work

1 Jazz musicians don't _____ traditional rules.
2 New Bollywood movies always _____ a lot of excitement.
3 Less money means we need to _____ existing ways of doing things.
4 Teaching more grammar in schools might _____ creativity.
5 Artists generally _____ high on intelligence tests.
6 I always _____ up new words in my poems.
7 He _____ an interesting approach to problem-solving.
8 The marketing team _____ very creatively together.

5 Choose the correct option to complete the sentences.

1 We couldn't come ___ with a solution.
  a up
  b down
  c in
  d out
2 I go to ___ writing classes twice a week.
  a create
  b creativity
  c creative
  d creatively

74 Unit 7

3 Street artists usually ___ the rules of traditional art.
  a obey
  b follow
  c solve
  d break

4 Let's ___ up a cool name for our band.
  a give
  b make
  c write
  d do

5 The team had a wide variety of ___ to the problem.
  a approaches
  b rules
  c creations
  d ways

6 He had to ___ his way of working when he moved to a new country.
  a follow
  b invent
  c break
  d adapt

6 Cross out the mistake in each sentence. Write the correct word.

1 We're going to creatively a storytelling group in our local library. _____
2 Boredom actually encourages creation in children. _____
3 The festival led to the create of a lot of opportunities for young people. _____
4 World leaders need to think more creative about solutions. _____
5 It's difficult to come up to a solution. _____
6 She made out a new way of singing. _____

7 **Extension** Circle the option that does not form a collocation.

1 create + *a scene / an email account / a bank account*
2 break + *the law / a deadline / someone's heart*
3 come up with + *an emotion / a plan / a theory*
4 follow + *your heart / your instinct / your resume*
5 *wealth / disease / job* + creation
6 *destroy / stifle / find out* + creativity

8 **Extension** Complete the sentences with these words.

| gift | imagination | ingenious |
| innovative | originality | vision |

1 Mozart had a creative _____ .
2 It was an _____ piece of work that showed skill and intelligence.
3 The play didn't have any new ideas and lacked _____ .
4 Creating storybooks is great for sparking children's _____ .
5 _____ artists experiment with forms and materials.
6 Any great project starts with its creator's _____ .

Outside the Box **75**

PRONUNCIATION

9 Listen to the sentences. Underline the words where the final consonant disappears. Then practice saying the sentences. 🎧 52

1 I'd rather you didn't take all the same classes as me.
2 My teacher says I should try to be more creative.
3 She still couldn't decide how to tell her parents.
4 Creativity doesn't mean the same thing to everybody.
5 I wish I could design my own house.
6 If only I hadn't stayed up all night.
7 He wishes he had a year off so he could travel.
8 I really can't believe how creative she is.

LISTENING

10 Listen to six different people talking. Match the speakers (1–6) with the statements (a–h). There are two extra statements. 🎧 53

Speaker 1
Speaker 2
Speaker 3
Speaker 4
Speaker 5
Speaker 6

a He wishes the classes weren't mandatory.
b If only she weren't so busy all the time.
c If only he had listened to his friend.
d He would rather have joined the other group.
e She wishes they could understand how she really feels.
f If only she'd been more serious about her studies.
g He wishes that he could have played basketball instead.
h She'd rather focus on less creative subjects.

11 Listen to part of an interview with Professor Richard Florida. What seems to be the main point of his theories? 🎧 54

a the loss of sense of community in our cities and the resulting damage
b the exploding populations of our cities and our inability to support this
c the increasing concentration of creativity and innovation in our cities
d decreasing innovation because of people and firms clustering together

12 Listen to some of Professor Florida's statements. Decide if they are fact (F) or opinion (O). 🎧 55

1 ___   2 ___   3 ___   4 ___
5 ___   6 ___   7 ___   8 ___

13 Listen to the interview again and answer the questions. 🎧 54

1 What does the professor say increasingly determines a person's prosperity?
  a location   b economic trends   c education
2 What word is in the title of both of Professor Florida's books?
  a economy   b city   c creative
3 How many world centers of innovation does the professor mention?
  a 3   b 4   c 5
4 What does the professor say is the downside to all of this innovation and development?
  a growing concentration
  b growing inequality
  c growing prosperity
5 What percentage of the population does the professor say now lives in cities?
  a less than 20 percent
  b more than 40 percent
  c more than 50 percent
6 How many of our new innovations does the professor say come from mega-regions?
  a less than 20 percent
  b 2/3
  c 90 percent
7 Why does the professor say that sense of community is so important?
  a because so many people have been dislocated
  b because so many people have anchors
  c because so many people want to live alone
8 What does the professor say he is attracted to?
  a a remade suburb
  b a place with a soul
  c a livable city

GRAMMAR First, second, third, and mixed conditionals

14 Choose the correct option to complete the sentences.

1. If teachers *had allowed / allow* creative students to daydream, they would be better prepared for their future.
2. Students *would have / will have* difficulty in the future if education doesn't include creativity because we are going to need workers who can think creatively.
3. How can we expect students to be creative if their assignments *have / would have had* very specific instructions?
4. If students *are / were* taught that there's only one solution to a problem, they won't be able to imagine creative solutions.
5. Students *are / would be* better prepared to be scientists or musicians if we didn't expect them to focus on memorizing facts and formulas.
6. If students *have been / were* able to decide what they want to learn about, they would be more interested in the subject.

15 Choose the correct option to complete the sentences.

1. If we *hadn't played / didn't play* the video game, we *aren't / wouldn't have been* in such a good mood, which often makes us more creative.
2. If you *would meditate / meditate*, you *will be able to think / could think* about a problem differently and perhaps come up with a new solution.
3. If you *had exercised / exercised* more often, your body—and mind—*are / would feel* more relaxed, which makes it easier to have creative ideas.
4. If you *look / would look* at something blue, you *had thought / might think* more clearly. (According to researchers, we associate blue with the sea, sky, and openness.)
5. If you *had taken / took* a walk outdoors, you *could think / thought* more creatively. (Being outdoors stimulates all five of your senses, which can stimulate creativity.)
6. We *hadn't been / might not have been* distracted by the background noise if we *had gone / went* to a cafe to do our work.
7. If I *hadn't taken / haven't taken* a nap, I *can think / wouldn't have been able to* tackle the problem in a creative way.

16 Correct the verb forms in bold. Sometimes there is more than one correct answer.

1. If creative people daydream, or let their minds wander, sometimes new ideas **came** into their minds while they are thinking about something else. _____
2. There would probably be fewer distractions if you **would work** late at night or early in the morning, like Benjamin Franklin or Ernest Hemmingway. _____
3. Creative people **were able to plan** their days more effectively if they know when they do their best work. _____
4. If they **hadn't taken** failure personally, creative people could learn from their mistakes and not be afraid of taking risks. _____
5. If J.K. Rowling hadn't been able to work anywhere, at any time, she **hadn't written** the *Harry Potter* books. _____
6. Beethoven and Tchaikovsky might not have been such brilliant composers if they **didn't walk** every day for exercise. _____
7. If creative people **are** motivated by money or awards, they might not find challenges so exciting. _____

17 Complete the sentences with the correct forms of the verbs in parentheses.

1. If she _____ (know) how other people solved similar problems, she _____ (find) a way to solve this problem.
2. You _____ (understand) the problem differently if you _____ (think) about it in a more creative way.
3. If I _____ (not start) listening to how other people solved their problems, I _____ (not learn) so many different ways of solving the problems I've been having.
4. She _____ (be) inspired to be more creative if she _____ (surround) herself with creative people when she starts university next month.
5. If he _____ (try) to solve his problem backwards, he _____ (understand) the problem differently, but he doesn't see that.
6. He _____ (not start) listening to what other people have to say if he _____ (not realize) how important it is.
7. If we _____ (not draw) a picture representing our problem, we _____ (not find) this amazing solution!
8. You _____ (realize) how similar these problems are if you _____ (research) different problems.

Outside the Box

7B Testing Times

VOCABULARY BUILDING Noun forms

1 Complete the chart by forming nouns from the verbs and adjectives.

Verb	Noun	Adjective	Noun
vary		useful	
publish		logical	
know		fluent	
conclude		flexible	
assess		intelligent	
analyze		concerned	

READING

2 Read the article. Match these words from the article with the definitions. Use the context to help you.

1 nurture ___
2 DNA ___
3 vulnerability ___
4 heredity ___
5 indistinguishable ___
6 IQ ___

a being unprotected from harm, either physically or emotionally
b a measure of intelligence, usually with a number score
c unable to identify as different
d the process of taking care of someone, for example, a baby
e the passing of mental or physical characteristics from parents to children
f the carrier of genetic information

3 The paragraphs in the article are numbered 1–6. Choose the most correct heading (a–g) for each paragraph. There is one extra heading.

Paragraph 1
Paragraph 2
Paragraph 3
Paragraph 4
Paragraph 5
Paragraph 6

a Separated at birth
b What is the role of DNA?
c Early research
d Human diversity
e Understanding identical twins
f Answering the questions
g Two areas of research

4 Complete the statements with one or two words from the article.

1 Twins that look the same are _____.
2 Twins that do not look the same are _____.
3 Comparing both kinds of twins help us understand the role of nature and _____.
4 Research on twins who had been separated _____ began in the 1980s.
5 People found the way the two Jims spoke to be _____.
6 Research at the University of Minnesota tried to answer some of the mysteries of _____.
7 Bouchard concluded that heredity was more important in determining _____ than education.
8 Everywhere scientists look, they find _____ shaping who we are.

A Thing or Two About Twins

1. To scientists, twins offer a special opportunity to understand the influence of genes and the environment—of nature and nurture. Identical twins share virtually the same genetic code. Any differences between them—one twin having younger-looking skin, for example—must be due to environmental factors such as less time spent in the sun.

2. Alternatively, by comparing the experiences of identical twins with those of fraternal twins, who share about half their DNA, researchers can measure the degree to which genes affect our lives. If identical twins are more likely to both have an illness than fraternal twins are, then vulnerability to the disease must come at least in part from heredity.

3. These two lines of research—studying the differences between identical twins to identify the influence of environment, and comparing identical twins with fraternal ones to measure the role of heredity—have been crucial to understanding the role of nature and nurture in determining our personalities, creativity, behavior, and vulnerability to disease.

4. The idea of using twins to measure heredity dates back to 1875, when the English scientist Francis Galton first suggested the approach (and came up with the phrase "nature and nurture"). But twin studies took a surprising turn in the 1980s, following the discovery of a number of identical twins who had been separated at birth.

5. The story began with the famous case of two brothers, both named Jim. Born in the US state of Ohio in 1939, Jim Springer and Jim Lewis were put up for adoption as babies and raised by different parents, who gave them the same first name by chance. When Jim Springer reconnected with his brother at age 39 in 1979, they uncovered many similarities. Both men were six feet tall and weighed 180 pounds. Growing up, they both had dogs named Toy and had taken family vacations in St. Pete Beach in Florida. As young men, they'd both married women named Linda, and then divorced them. Their second wives were both named Betty. They named their sons James Alan and James Allan. They'd both worked as part-time sheriffs, enjoyed home carpentry projects and suffered severe headaches. Although they wore their hair differently, their voices were indistinguishable.

6. Over the next two decades, the Jim twins and hundreds of other twins were studied by Thomas Bouchard Jr., a psychologist at the University of Minnesota. Bouchard and his colleagues tried to answer some of the mysteries of human nature: Why are some people happy and others sad? Why are some outgoing and others shy? Where does general intelligence come from? Bouchard's team reached a controversial conclusion: IQ depended more on heredity than on training or education. Until this time, most scientists thought that our brains were shaped more by experience. It was as if it didn't matter in which family the twins had been raised. They concluded that IQ scores were influenced more by genetics than parenting. Other studies found that heredity could predict criminal behavior and religious beliefs. Wherever scientists looked, they found genetic influence helping to shape our lives.

7C If only...

GRAMMAR Wish, if only, would rather

1 Choose the correct option to complete the sentences.

1 I wish I _____ play the guitar. I tried to learn when I was younger, but I wasn't very good.
 a would
 b had
 c could
 d was

2 I'm not a very creative person. If only I _____ been taught more about art at school.
 a have
 b could
 c would
 d had

3 I have never liked art galleries. I wish I _____ had to visit them when I was young, but my parents were really into art.
 a had
 b hadn't
 c wouldn't
 d could have

4 I am not a fan of modern art. I wish I _____ understand what the artist was trying to say.
 a could
 b would
 c were
 d can

5 I would _____ study a subject like media at college, but my parents really want me to do business.
 a prefer
 b like
 c rather
 d enjoy

6 If I _____ so shy, I would love to try acting.
 a was
 b would
 c wasn't
 d couldn't be

7 If only we _____ that movie, it was terrible. There are so many other movies we could have chosen.
 a had chosen
 b didn't choose
 c would choose
 d hadn't chosen

8 I wish he _____ talking about galleries and museums. I'm just not interested.
 a would stop
 b could stop
 c did stop
 d had stopped

2 Complete the conversation using *was*, *would*, or *could*. Then listen and check your answers. 🎧 57

A: Hi Julia, what are you doing?

B: Oh hi, Stephen. I'm just watching a short video about making videos to put online. I wish I (1) _____ creative like that.

A: Yeah, I know what you mean. If only we (2) _____ learn things like that at university. I wish they (3) _____ focus on things like that a little more.

B: Exactly, these kinds of skills are really important in the modern world. Ah, anyway. Are you going to come to the lecture tonight? It's on the future of creative marketing.

A: I wish I (4) _____ but I really have to do some work on my project.

B: That's a shame. I'm going with a few friends, but they will probably show up late. I wish they (5) _____ check their watches a little more often.

A: Ha ha. Yeah, we all have friends a bit like that. Well, I should get back to my project. I wish I (6) _____ coming tonight. Have fun.

B: I wish you (7) _____ come. Oh well. See you tomorrow.

A: Yeah, see you tomorrow.

3 Choose the correct option to complete the sentences.

1 I wish I *would / could* think like a child.
2 If only I *had / have* studied design at school.
3 I would *prefer / rather* listen to classical music.
4 I wish I *am / was* good at art.
5 I wish he *would / could* stop telling everyone how creative he is.
6 If only I *listened / had listened* to my parents. They told me to study media.
7 I wish advertisers *would stop / had stopped* making such abstract advertisements these days.
8 I would rather *go / gone* to the old town. There is a bit more culture in that part.

4 Read the sentences below and decide if they are correct or incorrect. Correct the incorrect sentences.

1 A lot of people say that creativity is about breaking the rules. Sometimes I wish I would be braver.
 _____

2 I wish I'd had more time to play at school. Scientists say play is really important for making us more creative.
 _____

3 I wish you could stop talking. You are really annoying me.
 _____

4 If only I haven't chosen this approach for my project. There's so much work to do and I think the presentation is going to be really detailed.
 _____

5 I wish we didn't have to go to the exhibition.
 _____

6 I would rather to go to the theater than to the movies.
_____

7 I wish they give additional marks in exams for original ideas. _____

8 If only I had more time for my hobbies. I'd love to spend more time painting. _____

5 Rewrite the second sentence so that it has the same meaning as the first using the word in parenthesis.

1 It would be amazing to be a fashion designer.
 (wish) _____

2 I would prefer to be at the beach right now.
 (rather) _____

3 My parents made me learn the violin. I hated it.
 (hadn't) _____

4 I have to practice for the concert but I don't want to.
 (wish) _____

5 He always tells me how to finish my writing. It's annoying.
 (would) _____

6 I did not finish my project on time. I really regret that now.
 (only) _____

7 I want to be like my brother.
 (was) _____

6 Complete the email with these phrases.

I wish I could go	I wish I'd chosen	I wish I'd signed
I wish you were	I'd rather make	I'd rather she had
If only I'd paid		

Hey Sara,

How are you? Well, I hope. You'll never believe what I did last weekend! Do you remember I signed up to that pottery course? Well, it started on Saturday and
(1) _____ up ages ago—it was amazing! (2) _____ in the class too though—you would have loved it!

At first, the teacher told us about how to treat the clay. To be honest, this part of the class was a bit boring.
(3) _____ let us start making things immediately, but I think it was an important thing to know.
(4) _____ more attention, the next part of the class might have been better! Next, she showed us how to turn the wheel and I was pretty good at that.

Finally, we got to use the clay. We could choose to make a bowl or a cup. I said (5) _____ a cup, but now (6) _____ a bowl. My cup wasn't very good, but the teacher said I was very creative ☺

(7) _____ every day—it is so much fun! You should come next time. The classes are on Saturday morning.

See you soon,

Yeon-soo

7 Put the words in the correct order to make sentences.

1 encouraged / me / my / had / play / to / wish / instrument / I / an / parents / .
_____

2 only / his / he / if / wasted / talent / hadn't / .
_____

3 neighbor / wish / practicing / drums / stop / all / day / I / my / would / .
_____

4 rather / I / in the book / the / was / more / likeable / would / main character / .
_____

5 open / I / the / was / really / wish / gallery / .
_____

6 didn't / I / have / to / invent / I / wish / solutions / all the time / .
_____

7 could / paint / only / like / Picasso / if / I / .
_____

8 teacher / freedom / would / the / more / gave / rather / us / I / .
_____

8 Complete the sentences so they are true for you.

1 I wish I could _____

2 I wish my parents would _____

3 I wish I had _____

4 If only I hadn't _____

5 I'd rather go to _____

6 I'd rather my family _____

7D Go Ahead, Make up New Words!

TEDTALKS

AUTHENTIC LISTENING SKILLS

1 Listen to these extracts from Erin McKean's TED Talk, and repeat the sentences. Listen especially to the speed of her speech, and try to match her pace and intonation.
🎧 58

1 Every language is just a group of people who agree to understand each other.
2 That rule lives in your brain. You never had to be taught this rule, you just understand it.
3 So we've been talking about this for a long time.
4 And I think that is, well, stupid.
5 "Motel" is a blend of "motor" and "hotel."

WATCH ▶

2 Choose the best options.

1 What is the main topic of this TED Talk?
   a Dictionaries are useful tools.
   b English grammar is so complicated it's easy to make mistakes.
   c It's OK to be creative with language.
   d A lot of English words come from Japanese.
2 According to McKean, what are the two types of rules language has?
   a old-fashioned rules and modern rules
   b formal rules and informal rules
   c rules based on Latin and rules based on German
   d unconscious rules and learned rules
3 What is McKean's attitude towards grammar rules?
   a They shouldn't stop people from inventing words.
   b They help you decide whether a word is acceptable.
   c They explain confusing patterns.
   d They are the only rules we should follow.
4 According to McKean, how are words like hats?
   a Both words and hats come in many forms.
   b Both words and hats are used by humans.
   c Both words and hats have "natural" and "learned" rules associated with them.
   d You can find the word "hat" in the dictionary.
5 How does McKean organize her recommendations about creating new words?
   a She begins by telling a story.
   b She describes six ways to form new words and gives examples.
   c She compares and contrasts word formation in English with other languages.
   d She starts with simple words and ends with complex words.
6 Why does McKean say, "OMG"?
   a to give a humorous example of a word formed with the first letters of a phrase.
   b to show shock that the audience likes NASA.
   c to emphasize her point that anyone can create new words.
   d to demonstrate that she disagrees with formal grammar rules.

3 Choose the correct option to complete the sentences.

1 If you look at the word NASA, *you'll / you would* notice that the letters come from "National Aeronautics and Space Administration".
2 If we didn't borrow words from other languages, we *don't have / wouldn't have* the word "kumquat" in English.
3 If the word "brunch" did not exist, what *do we call / would we call* a late breakfast?
4 If you want a job making dictionaries, you *should / should have* become a lexicographer.
5 If you hadn't been taught what a "wug" was, you *would still know / will still know* how to form the plural, "wugs".
6 If you learn a language as a child, you *understand / would understand* some grammar rules unconsciously.
7 If you use unusual words when you speak, people *will pay / paid* more attention to what you say.
8 If we didn't create new words in English, how *do we name / would we name* new technologies?

VOCABULARY IN CONTEXT

4 Match the words (1–6) with the sentences that show their meaning (a–f).

1 get your meaning across ___
2 manners ___
3 grab ___
4 heartbroken ___
5 edit ___
6 electrocute ___

a It's always a good idea to use **polite behavior.**
b Miguel was **very sad** when his team didn't win the basketball tournament.
c During the storm, the electricity company warned people that fallen power lines could **seriously injure** them.
d Lily works for her school newspaper; she **decides what information should be included** in each issue.
e When you know more words, you have more ways to **explain your ideas**.
f When you say something surprising or unexpected, you can **attract** people's attention.

7E Creative Solutions

SPEAKING

1 Read the sentences. Match each one with its function: Raising concerns (C), Making suggestions (S), or Giving reasons (R).

1 That way we will be sure to finish on time. ___
2 If we do that, we can save time and money. ___
3 Wouldn't that approach lead to other problems? ___
4 I can't see how that would work. ___
5 If you ask me, we should do it a different way. ___
6 This approach will enable us to be more efficient. ___
7 I propose doing it differently. ___
8 What do you think about this idea? ___
9 I can see several issues with that. ___
10 Wouldn't it be better to consider an alternative? ___
11 That will allow us to complete the project faster. ___

2 Choose the correct response to each question or statement.

1 How do you feel about the plan?
  a Personally, I can't see how it would work.
  b It allowed us to make progress more quickly.
2 Do you agree with the approach we're taking?
  a On the other hand, I can't think of any alternatives.
  b If you ask me, we should consider an alternative.
3 What is the main advantage?
  a Doing it this way will allow us to save money.
  b Wouldn't it be better to do it a different way?
4 Can you see any problems with this strategy?
  a I can think of three main issues.
  b If we do that, it will definitely work.
5 I think we should work on it as a group.
  a If you ask me, we should do it that way.
  b If we do that, won't it take longer?
6 Why do you think that?
  a Well, it will enable us to get better results.
  b The thing is, I can't see how that would work.

3 Complete the conversation with these words and phrases.

if we do that, won't it	my only issue is
it would allow us	that way we could
maybe we should	what do you think about

A: I'm worried we're not going to be able to finish the project on time. You know, we only have two days left.
B: I agree. (1) _____ asking for an extension?
A: Hmm... (2) _____ affect our final grade?
B: Yes, maybe. But on the other hand, (3) _____ to put in some extra time this weekend.
A: Yes, and (4) _____ go to the library this afternoon to do more research.
B: Exactly.
A: (5) _____, I asked for an extension a couple of months ago.
B: Oh, I see. I didn't realize that.
A: (6) _____ see how much we get done this evening, and think about it again tomorrow.
B: That's a good idea.

4 Choose one of the situations below and suggest a better approach. Make notes about your ideas in the space provided. Use these expressions to help you.

I'd suggest…
If you ask me, I think you should…
My recommendation would be to…
Perhaps it would be better to…
That way, you would/could…
That would enable/allow you to…
Wouldn't it be better to…?

a Your friend is considering running a half marathon, but he hasn't done very much training.
b Two of your classmates have had an argument, but they need to work together on a school assignment.
c Your sister doesn't like her part-time job and she is considering leaving it.

5 Read the following text and listen to the conversation that follows it. 🎧 59

Public Bikes in Stoney Bridge

Town leaders in Stoney Bridge are thinking about implementing a public bicycle system. They want to install thirty stations around the town, each of which will have ten bikes. For a monthly fee, anyone will be able to borrow a bike and use it to get from place to place. Several neighboring towns recently put similar systems in place and research has shown that they are an effective way to reduce congestion and improve air quality. In addition, cycling is a good way to promote a healthy lifestyle and encourage exercise.

Make notes on what you would say to answer the question below. Then listen to the sample answer and compare your ideas. 🎧 60

Question: Why does the mayor want to install the bike system now? What is the council member's concern?

Outside the Box 83

WRITING A report

6 Read the sentences from various reports. Underline those that make recommendations.

1 We might consider adding an extra five minutes to the school lunch break.
2 In order to represent everyone, we interviewed both students and teachers.
3 This report will also explain what the background issues are.
4 I would strongly recommend revising the rules for cell phone use at school.
5 We explored a range of possible solutions before completing our report.
6 It is clear that many students are unhappy with the "no jewelry" policy at school.
7 We would suggest making more space available for students' bicycles.
8 I propose giving senior students the opportunity to design part of the curriculum.

7 Complete the report with these words and phrases.

Background	Findings
Methods of investigation	Purpose
Recommendations	This report will
We might consider	We then surveyed

Creating a gardening section on school grounds

Introduction

(1) _____

The aim of this report is to establish how we could create a new gardening area at school. (2) _____ make recommendations on the best location for the garden, as well as on how to get students involved in the project.

(3) _____

Our principal, Mr. Barboza, introduced a suggestion box for students to share their ideas about what improvements could be made at school. A number of students expressed an interest in having a dedicated area at school for growing vegetables, herbs, fruit, and flowers.

(4) _____

In order to approach this from an informed perspective, a team of us carried out some research on other schools that have gardening areas. This gave us a realistic sense of how much space would be required for the project. (5) _____ the school grounds carefully and considered a number of possible locations before agreeing on the best spot for our purposes.

(6) _____

Although there is a good-sized green area outside the assembly hall, it is frequently in the shade, and therefore not ideal for planting and growing. The best space appears to be outside the library, but there is one issue to be overcome: the entire area is paved in concrete.

(7) _____

To solve this problem, we would recommend keeping the paved area, and creating a garden using plant pots of various sizes. (8) _____ recycling containers brought in from home by students. This would enable us to use our ideal location, while also getting students to contribute materials to the new garden.

8 Read the report in Activity 7 again. Then choose the correct option to complete the statements.

1 The main aim of the report was to establish the *right spot / best schedule / overall costs* for the new school garden.
2 The idea for a school garden was suggested by *the principal / students / teachers*.
3 *One student / Two students / A group of students* worked on the report.
4 One method of investigation was *improving / researching / recommending* other school gardens.
5 The first decision was about the amount of *space / soil / vegetables* the garden would need.
6 Several possible *plants / perspectives / places* were considered before a decision was reached.
7 A possible green area was not selected because of not getting enough *rain / sunlight / interest*.
8 The problem with the area selected is that it's covered in *soil / concrete / shade*.
9 The proposed solution is to plant everything *indoors / in the library / in containers*.
10 An added advantage is that it provides a way to get other students *involved / surveyed / informed*.

9 Your head teacher has asked you to write a report on the school cafeteria. You should include an overview of what the cafeteria currently offers, comment on any recent dissatisfaction, and make some recommendations.

Write your report in 140–190 words in an appropriate style.

Review

1 Complete each sentence with a word based on the root word *create*. You can use the same word more than once.

1 The exercises encourage _____ thinking.
2 We don't have time to _____ anything new today.
3 The government is discussing job _____ .
4 Children should have more time for _____ play.
5 He cooks _____ with the ingredients.
6 The writing course encouraged his _____ .

2 Read the phrases. Underline those that describe something creative.

1 adapt existing ways of doing things
2 break the rules
3 come up with new ways of doing things
4 follow sets of rules
5 invent things
6 make up words
7 obey the rules
8 write definitions

3 Are the words in bold correct or incorrect? Correct those that are incorrect.

1 If we **would want** technology to help students, we need to see computers as creative tools, not as televisions to entertain us or machines for finding information. _____
2 If we believe that all children are born with creativity, we **should use** technology to keep that creativity alive. _____
3 If teachers **encouraged** students to create comics to explain concepts or describe historical figures, they will be more engaged with the topics. _____
4 Students **feel** more responsible for their own learning if they were encouraged to write blog posts for their friends and family to read. _____
5 If students **won't use** mind maps or brainstorming in class, they probably wouldn't try thinking outside the box. _____
6 If the school hadn't encouraged us to make videos, we **wouldn't develop** our creative skills. _____
7 Students **wouldn't be able** to try any of these techniques if they didn't have access to computers.

4 Choose the correct option to complete the sentences.

1 If you like broccoli, I imagine _____ like cauliflower as well.
  a you'll   **c** she will
  b you want to   **d** she'd
2 I _____ forgotten all about Sibran's birthday if you hadn't reminded me.
  a will have   **c** would have
  b had   **d** might
3 My mother _____ I wanted to study abroad.
  a wish   **c** wishes
  b is wishing   **d** had been wish
4 He might take his classes more seriously _____ he understood how important good grades are.
  a if   **c** through
  b when   **d** how
5 She'd _____ text than call someone.
  a wish   **c** would
  b only   **d** rather
6 _____ I didn't have so much homework, I could go for a walk.
  a Rather   **c** Wish
  b If   **d** So
7 _____ I were more interested in the theatre.
  a Rather   **c** If wish
  b If   **d** If only

5 Match each trait shared by many creative people to the statement someone with that trait might say.

1 They take time to be alone sometimes.
2 They daydream.
3 They take advantage of new experiences.
4 They sometimes take risks.
5 They look for beauty in their everyday lives.
6 They look for the good in bad situations.

a I'd rather try something new, even if I'm not sure it will work.
b If only I hadn't failed that test. Now I know I need to study a lot more for the next one.
c I'd rather spend time by myself this afternoon.
d I wish I had seen the sunset with you. It must have been gorgeous!
e I'd rather travel to new places and meet the people who live there.
f I wish I had more time to just sit back and let my mind wander.

Outside the Box

8 Common Ground

8A Cultural Crossings

VOCABULARY Identity and communication

1 Review Complete the sentences with these words.

connect	get	have	join
make	pay	respond	share

1 Drivers _____ distracted by their cell phones.
2 The project is encouraging older people to _____ on social media.
3 Why don't you ever _____ to texts?
4 Users need to sign in to _____ photos from the album.
5 What point was he trying to _____ ?
6 You need to _____ attention during the debate.
7 Teachers regularly _____ in on professional online forums.
8 People complain when doctors don't _____ very good interpersonal skills.

2 Review Circle the option that does not form a collocation.

1 get — my message out / distracted / a chat
2 connect — online / a message / on social media
3 make — photos / connections / a point
4 post — on social media / photos / texts
5 face-to-face — conversation / on the phone / skills
6 share — my message out / photos / posts

3 Match the sentence halves.

1 We need to sort ___
2 The best ___
3 They've had a ___
4 I feel really ___
5 He's made a negative ___
6 She didn't mean ___

a awkward about it.
b to offend you.
c misunderstanding.
d it out.
e comment.
f response is to walk away.

4 Are the phrases associated with positive or negative ways of communicating? Complete the table.

avoid discrimination   be offended
create an awkward silence   discriminate against
have a misunderstanding   pay a compliment
sort something out   stereotype people

Positive association	Negative association

5 Choose the correct option to complete the sentences.

1 The rules _____ against foreign workers.
  a discourage   c discriminate
  b offend   d stereotype
2 The teacher _____ me a compliment about my work.
  a said   c felt
  b had   d paid
3 He _____ we should go home.
  a avoided   c discouraged
  b hinted   d reacted
4 People are more _____ of racism nowadays.
  a reaction   c conscious
  b awkward   d offended
5 She hasn't spoken to me since we had our _____ .
  a misunderstanding   c compliment
  b reaction   d response
6 The teacher's negative comments are _____ him.
  a responding   c sorting
  b discouraging   d hinting

7 The best _____ is to ignore him.
   a comment
   b hint
   c response
   d compliment
8 I didn't know what to say and there was _____ silence.
   a a negative
   b a positive
   c a conscious
   d an awkward

6 Cross out the mistake in each sentence and write the correct word.
   1 We tried to discourage him for going.
   _____
   2 He always takes offend at what I say.
   _____
   3 My initial react was to laugh.
   _____
   4 I'm consciously of the situation.
   _____
   5 She was very compliment about my artwork.
   _____
   6 He's a stereotype actor.
   _____

8 Extension Complete the sentences with these words.

| enthusiasm | flatter | insult | pay |
| praise | put | reaction | swallowed |

1 They always _____ tribute to well-respected actors at the Oscars.
2 Sportspeople shouldn't _____ their opponents during a game.
3 I tried to _____ him off leaving the country.
4 Fans of *Star Wars* have so much _____ for the movies.
5 She wanted to _____ him for his hard work.
6 People will often _____ you with false praise when they want something.
7 I _____ the insult and kept silent.
8 I had a delayed _____ to his insult. I got angry the next day.

7 Extension Are the statements true (T) or false (F)?
1 If you praise somebody, you are paying that person a compliment. ___
2 A flattering comment will cause offense. ___
3 We pay tribute to people we admire. ___
4 An insult is a positive comment. ___
5 If you put someone off doing something, you're encouraging them. ___
6 If someone compliments you and then you return the compliment, you say the same thing. ___
7 A back-handed compliment is offensive. ___

Common Ground **87**

PRONUNCIATION

9 Listen to the conversations. Underline the word or phrase that is stressed for clarification. Then practise saying that sentence. 🎧 61

1. **A:** There must be hundreds of different languages in the world.
   B: Actually, there are thousands of different languages.
2. **A:** We should get going. The movie starts at seven.
   B: What? I thought you said that it started at eight.
3. **A:** I'm driving up to see my sister this weekend.
   B: By yourself? Didn't you tell me that you're not allowed to drive alone?
4. **A:** She has to move to Europe with her parents.
   B: And leave college? I thought she didn't have to go with them.
5. **A:** My mother just turned 58.
   B: Oh, that makes sense. At first I thought you said 98.
6. **A:** I've decided to start studying Mandarin.
   B: That's a surprise. I'm sure you told me that you weren't interested in Chinese.

LISTENING

10 Listen to the lecture on cultural globalization. Match the words and phrases you hear. 🎧 62

1 developing	a marketplace
2 experiencing	b change
3 global	c societies
4 human	d communication
5 barriers	e entertainment
6 cross-border	f global culture
7 worldwide	g and connections

11 Listen again to the lecture and complete the sentences. There are no more than three words for each answer. 🎧 62

1. There's no doubt that we are experiencing change at an ever _____.
2. The term *globalization* is most often used to describe the _____.
3. Cultures leave behind _____ that can be studied and tracked over time.
4. The thousands of _____ are coming together on just a handful of global languages.
5. What is lost and what is gained in each case _____ us personally and globally.

Languages depend on older generations passing them on to younger generations.

12 Listen to the lecture on languages. What is the main idea of the talk? 🎧 63

a language provides insight into cultures
b the variety of languages under threat
c linguists don't all agree on what language is
d some countries don't have a variety of languages

13 Now listen to the lecture again and answer the questions. 🎧 63

1. How do linguists classify languages?
   a by narrow classifications
   b by age of the language
   c by location and features
2. What determines higher-level family groupings of languages?
   a particular spoken features
   b ancient linguistic origins
   c geographical locations
3. How does the speaker describe language use today?
   a there are many people who speak many languages
   b there are few people who speak few languages
   c there are many people who speak few languages
4. What does the speaker say should happen next?
   a rare languages should be brought back
   b new film and audio technologies should be developed
   c less common languages should be recorded
5. What does the speaker say helped create some multi-cultural countries?
   a a wide variety of languages
   b trade and cultural exchange
   c people of the same culture
6. How many countries does the speaker mention as having multiple surviving ethnic groups?
   a 3   b 4   c 5
7. What determines when a language dies?
   a every 14 days
   b no recording for posterity
   c its last speaker
8. How is language usually passed on?
   a within family groups
   b by cultural identity
   c recordings for posterity

GRAMMAR Reported speech

14 Read the statements. Choose the correct option to complete the sentences.

1 Caitlin: "Americans are very, very friendly; sometimes it seems that they're *too* friendly."
She answered that Americans *were / are / will be* very friendly and that sometimes they're *too* friendly.

2 Yui: "There is public transportation in most American cities but not in smaller towns."
She advised that most American cities *have / have had / would had* public transportation but not smaller towns.

3 Natalia: "Americans eat dinner kind of early: 6 o'clock."
She complained that Americans *eat / have eaten / would eat* dinner too early.

4 Ye-jun: "There's a special relationship between Americans and their cars."
He confirmed that Americans *are having / has / have* a special relationship with their cars.

5 Nora: "Soft drinks and water are served with ice, so you need to tell the server if you don't want ice."
She reminded us that soft drinks and water are always *served / serve / serving* with ice in the US.

6 James: "Americans are usually on time and appreciate it if you are, too."
He repeated that Americans *like / would liked / have liked* it when you are on time.

15 Complete the sentences with the correct forms of the verbs in parentheses.

Read these travelers' comments on visiting Peru.
- museumlover commented that while in Lima he (1) _____ (visit) a lot of great museums.
- foodie67 added that the Inca ruins (2) _____ (be) the most interesting he'd ever seen.
- iloveperu explained that ceviche (3) _____ (be) the most popular dish in Peru.
- inkaking02 told us that the Norte Chico people (4) _____ (build) a civilization in Peru more than 5,000 years ago, long before the Inca.
- travelismylife confirmed that it (5) _____ (take) her a while to get used to the high altitude in the Sacred Valley, and she (6) _____ (warn) that the sun is very strong there.
- limaismyhome announced that he (7) _____ (think) the dry season (May to October) was the best time to visit Peru.
- pacificsurfer said she (8) _____ (be) able to see Machu Picchu because she didn't buy tickets in advance.

16 Put the words in the correct order to create reported speech questions.

1 **Jens asked if** / was / funny / for making / there / a championship / faces / .
_____
_____

2 **Monika asked whether** / Turkey / camel wrestling / in / there / was / .
_____
_____

3 **Chen asked what** / to celebrate / weddings / Germans / did / .
_____
_____

4 **Wilma asked how** / China and Japan / business cards / exchanged / people / in / .
_____
_____

5 **Hasan asked if** / a monkey festival / was / Thailand / there / in / .
_____
_____

6 **Petra asked whether** / unusual / to close / was / is / it / while another / person / speaking / for people / their eyes / .
_____
_____

7 **Ana asked where** / in the world / took / tomato fight / place / the biggest / .
_____
_____

8B The Third Wave

VOCABULARY BUILDING Compound adjectives

1 Match the adjectives with the nouns to form compound adjectives. Note that one of the compound adjectives is not hyphenated (-).

1 well-
2 long-
3 heart
4 two-
5 like-
6 deep-
7 world-
8 open-
9 highly-
10 cost-

a faced
b effective
c minded
d respected
e broken
f wide
g mannered
h rooted
i minded
j lasting

READING

2 Read the article and choose the best summary.

a The "cultural assault" of Western influences will severely weaken other cultures.
b Globalization continues a long tradition of cultural connections, but at a faster pace.
c Countries like Brazil that have a mix of civilizations will dominate world culture.
d Many cultures will be unrecognizable as a new "global culture" gets more powerful.

3 Complete the statements with one or two words from the article.

1 Changes in politics, business, health and entertainment all fall under the umbrella of _____.
2 Teenagers all over the world are one of the _____ driving the new global culture.
3 Commercial and _____ are nothing new. Humans have been making them for centuries.
4 A _____ is that goods, people and ideas move. At the same time, cultures change.
5 Alvin Toffler's first book, _____, was a best-seller and very influential around the world.
6 Toffler says that in our current world, _____ economies will dominate the others.
7 Toffler is optimistic that countries can still have a _____ based on their core culture.

4 Read the article again and answer the questions.

1 In paragraph 1, the word "merging" is closest in meaning to
   a coming together
   b moving forward
   c going backward
   d changing into
2 Which of the following can be inferred from the statement in paragraph 2 that globalization is a reality, not a choice?
   a Globalization has already happened and now we have to find a better way.
   b There was actually more globalization in the past than what we're seeing now.
   c Even with globalization, the reality is that we still have a great deal of choice.
   d People opposed to globalization need to accept its reality and deal with it.
3 According to paragraph 2, what is one example given of change in the 1800s?
   a radio   c newspapers
   b television   d air transport
4 In paragraph 4, what do some social scientists fear could result from globalization?
   a more Western companies
   b English replacing other languages
   c the weakening of all cultures
   d a kind of cultural cloning
5 In paragraph 4, the word "wave" is closest in meaning to
   a movement   c signal
   b flood   d crashing
6 What word does Toffler use in paragraph 4 to describe industrial economies?
   a knowledge-based c agrarian
   b smokestack   d trisection
7 Which of the following can be inferred from Toffler's comment that "You can have a unique culture made of your core culture. But you'll be the Chinese of the future, not of the past."?
   a the global culture of the future will include all cultures
   b the cultures of the past will be replaced by new modern ones
   c unique cultures will survive based on their central values
   d Chinese culture will take over the new global culture

90 Unit 8

The Third Wave

1 Today we are in the middle of a worldwide reorganization of cultures, a change in habits and dreams that social scientists call *globalization*. It's a broad term for sweeping changes in politics, business, health and entertainment. The huge number of teenagers—800 million in the world—with time and money to spend is one of the powerful engines of merging global cultures. Kids travel, they hang out, and above all, they buy stuff.

2 How people feel about all this depends a great deal on where they live and how much money they have. Yet globalization, as one report stated, "is a reality, not a choice". Humans have been creating commercial and cultural connections for centuries. In the 19th century the postal service, newspapers, transcontinental railroads and great steam-powered ships brought huge changes. Telegraph, telephone, radio and television made further connections between individuals and the wider world. Now computers, the internet, smartphones, social media, cable TV and cheaper air transportation have made these connections both easier and more complicated.

3 Still one basic truth remains the same: Goods move. People move. Ideas move. And cultures change. The difference now is the speed of these changes. It took television 13 years to get 50 million users; the internet took only five.

4 Alvin Toffler is an author whose book *Future Shock* was published in 1970. He also wrote *The Third Wave* with his wife, Heidi. Waves, he explains, are major changes in civilization. The first wave came with the development of agriculture, the second with industry. Today we are in the middle of the third wave, which he says is based on information. "What's happening now is the trisection of world power," he says. "Agrarian nations on the bottom, smokestack countries in between, and knowledge-based economies on top." There are a number of countries—Brazil, for example—where all three civilizations are present.

5 "Culturally we'll see big changes," Toffler says. "You're going to turn on your TV and get Nigerian TV and Fijian TV in your own language. People ask, "Can we become third wave and still remain Chinese?" "Yes," Toffler says. "You can have a unique culture made of your core culture. But you'll be the Chinese of the future, not of the past."

8C That's What They Told Me

GRAMMAR Patterns after reporting verbs

1 Choose the correct option to complete the sentences.

1 My parents *suggested / convinced* me to go on the exchange trip when I was at school.
2 My pen pal *reminded / claimed* me to take warm clothes when I visited her.
3 My school *assured / arranged* for me to go abroad for my work experience.
4 My sister *admitted / promised* to take photographs of her travels.
5 I *suggested / persuaded* that we should try new restaurants to experience different foods.
6 Doctors have *claimed / confessed* that new experiences make us happier.
7 I *persuaded / pretend* my friends to watch more international movies.
8 I was lucky because my school *recommended / encouraged* us to learn about different cultures.

2 Complete the sentences with these prepositions. Some sentences do **not** need a preposition.

for (x2)	of	on	to

1 She accused her friend _____ copying her style.
2 My host family insisted _____ collecting me from the airport.
3 My parents forced _____ me to read about different cultures as a child.
4 I have always blamed my brother _____ writing in my favorite books.
5 We were talking about fashion and I admitted _____ being a goth when I was young.
6 I used to imagine _____ traveling all around the world.
7 I decided _____ study languages so I could have a year abroad.
8 It is important to forgive people _____ their mistakes.

3 Read the interview with Yasmin about her trip to London and choose the correct option to complete each sentence. Sometimes both words may be correct.

A: So Yasmin, you are just back from your trip. How was it?
B: Oh, it was all so amazing. At first I was worried as my friends and family had (1) *explained / warned* me that London was going to be very cold. They all (2) *suggested / advised* me to take lots of warm clothes, but it wasn't so bad. I will (3) *confess / consider* that I wore a lot of sweaters for the first few days though.
A: What do you think you learned most from the experience?
B: Well, that is hard to say, I feel as if I learned so much. When I went I had (4) *claimed / intended* to try to visit as many places as I could. I would definitely (5) *suggest / recommend* going to the museums and what is amazing is that most of them are free! Also, my host family (6) *persuaded / decided* me to go and visit some other places like the Lake District, which was so beautiful.
A: Yes, people always say that. Do you have any advice for people going on a similar trip?
B: Hmmm, well, I would (7) *tell / recommend* that people try to plan what they really want to see. Oh, and don't be afraid to (8) *ask / offer* people to help you. The people were helpful. One last thing, I would (9) *consider / invite* trying to stay a bit longer next time.

4 Read the sentences below and decide if they are correct or incorrect. Correct the incorrect sentences.

1 A lot of people claim to me that modern technology makes the world smaller. _____
2 Katarina warned us for avoiding the city center on Saturday as it was busy. _____
3 Michael urged us to visit him in the summer for their local festival. _____
4 When I was younger, I used to pretend being an explorer. _____
5 The government declared that companies should pay men and women equally. _____
6 Schools should avoid to make some subjects like woodwork only for boys. _____
7 Clement thanked Makie to the advice she gave him. _____
8 Denise asked to help her choose traditional local gifts for her family. _____

5 A word is missing in each sentence. Choose the <u>two</u> correct options to complete each sentence.

1 The presentation _____ me to do more to fight discrimination.
   a suggested **c** recommended
   b persuaded **d** convinced
2 My parents always _____ me not to believe stereotypes.
   a warned **b** suggested **c** advised **d** insisted
3 My colleague _____ to forgetting to update the company's website.
   a confessed **b** declared **c** promised **d** admitted

92 Unit 8

4 She _____ him for using offensive language and upsetting the guests.
 a blamed   b criticized   c refused   d told

5 Max advised my brother to _____ working abroad as it was good for his resume.
 a offer   c carry on
 b consider   d claim

6 A family friend _____ that I learn to ignore people who make negative comments.
 a thanked   c recommended
 b suggested   d avoided

7 The news report _____ that Iceland was the best place to live if you were female.
 a claimed   c assured
 b told   d announced

8 My sister _____ to help me with my project on international co-operation.
 a encouraged c insisted
 b offered   d promised

6 Rewrite the second sentence so that it has the same meaning as the first using the word in capital letters. Use between two and five words.

1 "You should be careful of believing stereotypes," he said.
He _____ stereotypes. WARNED

2 The speaker put forward the idea that we could learn from other cultures.
In the talk it _____ we could learn from other cultures. ARGUED

3 My parents didn't let me dye my hair when I was younger.
My parents _____ my hair when I was younger. REFUSED

4 Most modern companies want to employ people with good intercultural communication skills.
Most modern companies _____ people with good intercultural communication skills. INSIST

5 "You should go to a place if you want to understand the people," she said.
She _____ a place to understand the people. SUGGESTED

6 Society should make companies react strongly to any discrimination in the workplace.
Companies should _____ strongly to any discrimination in the workplace. FORCED

7 Challenging social norms is a normal part of teenage years, scientists have said.
Scientists have _____ social norms is a normal part of teenage years. STATED

7 Put the words in order to make sentences.

1 threatened to / more cost-effective / dismiss workers / The company / to be / .
_____

2 I / to make / urge everyone / like-minded / would / friends / .
_____

3 notified us that / by email / the tickets / The company / had been sent / .
_____

4 discriminated against / He denied that / anyone / he had / .
_____

5 being called / She / a goth / resented / .
_____

6 for being / He thanked / well-mannered / the audience / so / .
_____

7 always asked / My / my clothes / to borrow / sister / .
_____

8 people / I / staying away from / would recommend / two-faced / .
_____

8 Complete the paragraph with these words.

| announced | claimed | confess |
| deny | insist | persuade |

Writers have recently (1) _____ that there is a new subculture among the country's youth: meet Seapunk, which is (2) _____ to be a mix of punk and pirates, and features the use of lots of marine colors. The followers of this new trend (3) _____ that it is completely original and (4) _____ being influenced by anyone. Instead they try to (5) _____ us that this new subculture grew from online sites. There is no denying that the movement is humorous and doesn't take itself too seriously. But, I must (6) _____ that it will be a while before I am brave enough to experiment with this new fashion.

9 Complete the sentences so they are true for you.

1 My parents warned me not to

2 When people ask me about where to go in my hometown, I always advise them

3 I was lucky my parents encouraged me

4 When I was younger, I always tried to avoid

5 Last week I asked

6 I think it is wrong to criticize someone for

Common Ground

8D Why I Keep Speaking up, Even When People Mock My Accent

TEDTALKS

AUTHENTIC LISTENING SKILLS

1 Listen to the extracts from Safwat Saleem's TED Talk and select which meaning of *just* he uses in each statement.
🎧 65

1 I just had to grunt a lot for that one.
   a soon   b simply   c exactly
2 I just sat there on the computer, hitting "refresh."
   a simply   b recently   c soon
3 This was just the first of a two-part video.
   a exactly   b only   c recently
4 I just could not do it.
   a exactly   b soon   c simply
5 if I stutter along the way, I just go back in and fix it.
   a simply   b soon   c only
6 And just the year before, that number was about eight percent.
   a soon   b exactly   c only
7 Just like the colour blue for Ancient Greeks, minorities are not a part of what we consider normal.
   a recently   b exactly   c only

WATCH ▶

2 Are the following statements true (T) or false (F)?

1 Saleem was self-conscious about his accent when he was a boy. ___
2 Saleem uses very different accents for each of his animated characters. ___
3 Saleem realized that people were reacting to his accent because they didn't think it was normal for an editor to have an accent. ___
4 At first, Saleem took the comments about his accent very personally. ___
5 Historical texts include more reference to colours than do modern texts. ___
6 Studies show that people are treated differently because of the expectations that we have. ___
7 Saleem says that it isn't enough to tell children they can do anything; we have to show them examples of people like them who have been successful. ___
8 Saleem says it is easy for him to be on stage. ___

3 Read the sentence and paragraph. Look at the places in the text marked by a, b, c, and d. In which place could the sentence be added to the paragraph? Choose a, b, c, or d.

And the most popular theory for why that might be the case is that cultures begin to recognize a colour only once they have the ability to make that colour.

Let me give you an example. I came across this story about the Ancient Greek writer, Homer. Now, Homer mentions very few colours in his writing. **(a)** And even when he does, he seems to get them quite a bit wrong. For example, the sea is described as wine red, people's faces are sometimes green and sheep are purple. But it's just not Homer. If you look at all of the ancient literature—Ancient Chinese, Icelandic, Greek, Indian, and even the original Hebrew Bible—they all mention very few colours. **(b)** So basically, if you can make a colour, only then can you see it. A colour like red, which was fairly easy for many cultures to make—they began to see that colour fairly early on. **(c)** But a colour like blue, which was much harder to make—many cultures didn't begin to learn how to make that colour until much later. They didn't begin to see it until much later as well. So, until then, even though a colour might be all around them, they simply did not have the ability to see it. **(d)** It was invisible. It was not a part of their normal.

VOCABULARY IN CONTEXT

4 Match each word with the sentence that shows its meaning.

1 somewhat constructive ___
2 breakdown ___
3 around ___
4 humorous ___
5 huge step ___
6 self-conscious ___

a Sometimes misunderstandings can lead to **funny** situations.
b Saleem has always felt a little **embarrassed** about the way he speaks.
c The comments people made about Saleem's accent were **a little helpful**, but also a little offensive.
d When I arrived at school, I was surprised not to see anyone **in the building or nearby**.
e Getting positive feedback from people who didn't know him was **a very important event** for Saleem to increase his self-confidence.
f Sometimes people have so many problems all at the same time that they get **anxious and upset and can't do anything**.

8E Agreeing, Disagreeing, and Challenging

SPEAKING

1 Match the expressions (1–8) with the explanations (a–h).

1 I'm in favour of the idea.
2 That's crazy.
3 I'm against the idea.
4 I'm totally for it.
5 I don't get what you mean.
6 From my point of view…
7 I mean…
8 Are we supposed to…

a I completely support that.
b What I think is…
c I don't agree.
d What I want to say is…
e I strongly disagree.
f Do we have to…
g I agree with that.
h I don't understand.

2 Complete the sentences with these words. Two options will not be used.

as a	for	from
I mean	I think	I'm in
it doesn't mean	it's crazy	just because
point of view	speaking as	totally supports

1 _____ that's how it was done in the past, _____ we have to do it that way now.
2 If you look at it _____ your parents' _____, you might see the matter differently.
3 _____ someone who has done it before, I don't think it's a good idea.
4 Everyone else _____ the proposal, but personally, I think _____.
5 _____ young person, _____ doing it this way has a lot of advantages.
6 There are a lot of reasons I'm for the idea. _____, first of all, it will help us save time.

3 Read the statements. Do you agree or disagree? Write your response and use these expressions.

I don't get that.	I totally support that.
I'm against the idea.	I'm in favour.
I'm totally for the idea.	That's crazy.

1 More people should adopt a vegetarian diet.
2 Driving should be taught in schools.
3 All universities should be free.
4 Standardized tests should be eliminated.
5 All schools should be bilingual.
6 Art and music should be required subjects.

4 Complete the conversation. Use one word in each space. Then listen and check your answers. 🎧 66

Kim: I was thinking of going to the cinema tonight.
Carlos: I'd be in (1) _____ of that.
Kim: Yeah…
Carlos: You sound a little uncertain. (2) _____ wrong?
Kim: Well, I suggested the idea to Adam, and he told me he doesn't want to come.
Carlos: Oh, I see. But (3) _____ because he's not into the idea, that (4) _____ mean we can't go, does it?
Kim: No, I suppose you're right.
Carlos: If you look at it (5) _____ his point of (6) _____, it makes sense. He's had quite a long week.
Kim: Yes, he has.
Carlos: I (7) _____, he must be pretty tired.
Kim: Well, even if he doesn't want to join us, (8) _____ you still want to go?
Carlos: Sure. I'm all (9) _____ it. What do you want to see?
Kim: How about watching a thriller?
Carlos: I (10) _____ support that idea. I love movies with a lot of suspense.

5 Choose one of the topics below. Think about how you would answer and make notes. Practice saying your response out loud. You should speak for one to two minutes and record yourself. Then listen to the sample responses. 🎧 67

1 Your best friend wants to go on a road trip this summer. You should say:
  • Whether you like this idea
  • Why you are in favour or against it
  • Where you would like to go
2 Your parents want you to get a part-time job. You should say:
  • Whether you like this idea
  • Why you are for or against it
  • What type of job you would like to get
  • What you will do if you don't get a job

Common Ground

WRITING A complaint

6 Match the sentence halves.

1 I am writing to complain about an offensive term ___
2 This is a matter that ___
3 Your article implied that most women are ___
4 While I value freedom of expression, ___
5 I realize it was meant as a joke, ___
6 As a student myself, I was very upset ___
7 I feel it is highly inappropriate ___
8 I would like you to ___

a should be taken very seriously.
b however, I feel it was irresponsible.
c publish a formal apology as soon as possible.
d I believe it is important to remain respectful.
e used in last night's broadcast.
f by your implication that all students are lazy.
g mean to each other, which is simply untrue.
h to make a claim such as this on a popular website.

7 Complete the complaint with these words and phrases.

as it suggests	however
I am writing to complain	I suggest
I would like you to	problems
stereotype	the attitude
There is a risk	While

Dear Sir/Madam,

1 _____ about an article on the issue of homelessness, which was published in your magazine last week. This article is extremely insulting to homeless people, _____ they are deliberately trying to ruin our towns and cities. It also implies that their _____ are entirely their fault and, furthermore, that they could easily improve their situation if they wanted to.

2 I was very distressed by _____ expressed in this article. With some students from my school, I was recently involved in a fundraising event for the homeless, and I learned how difficult their lives really are. _____ it might make us uncomfortable to see homeless people sleeping on our streets, it is important to remember that they are human beings, and many of their stories are heartbreaking.

3 I understand that this was an opinion piece, _____ , I feel it is irresponsible and dangerous to _____ homeless people in this way. _____ that it could make other readers lose sympathy for these disadvantaged people who need our help. In fact, it could even make residents angry towards the homeless.

4 _____ publish a revised version of the article, this time offering a more balanced view. In addition, _____ you make a donation to a homeless shelter to show your support for those in our society who are vulnerable.

Yours faithfully,
Kasia Baran

8 Read the complaint in Activity 7 again, paying attention to the paragraph numbers. Then read the list of points mentioned, and highlight the paragraph or paragraphs they appear in.

a where the article appeared   1 2 3 4
b the reason for complaining   1 2 3 4
c helping the homeless   1 2 3 4
d the effects the article could have 1 2 3 4
e specific problems with the article 1 2 3 4
f how the article made the writer feel 1 2 3 4
g what action the writer expects 1 2 3 4
h how the article represents the homeless 1 2 3 4

9 The chart below gives information about a survey carried out in one high school in Mexico, in Germany, and in Korea over a 30-year period. The survey shows how many students identified themselves with a sub-culture.

Summarize the information by selecting and reporting the main features, and make comparisons where relevant.

You should spend about 20 minutes on this task. Write at least 150 words.

Percentage of students who identified themselves with a sub-culture

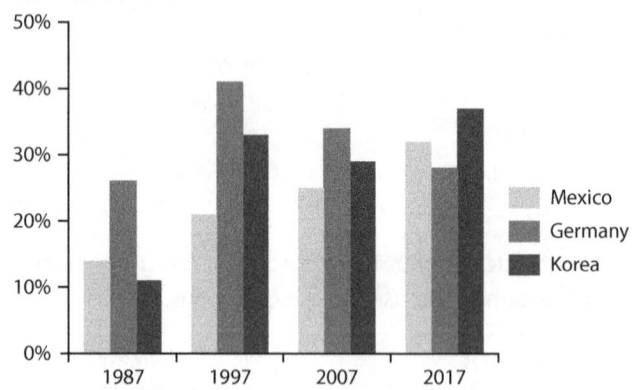

Year	Mexico	Germany	Korea
1987	14%	26%	11%
1997	21%	41%	33%
2007	25%	34%	29%
2017	32%	28%	37%

96   Unit 8

Review

1 Rewrite the sentences. Complete the sentences using the words in capital letters. Use between two and five words.

1. They need to resolve their differences.
   They need to _____ . SORT
2. Your words upset me very much.
   I _____ by your words. OFFENDED
3. She made a nice comment about my hair.
   She _____ my hair. PAID
4. It's better to say that you're busy that day.
   The _____ to say that you're busy that day. RESPONSE
5. They don't want me to go abroad.
   They're trying to _____ abroad. DISCOURAGE
6. I didn't feel comfortable talking to the manager.
   I _____ talking to the manager. AWKWARD

2 Complete the crossword.

Across

4. The children were quiet and polite. They were well-_____.
6. It is _____ to hire only people under age 50.
7. When she broke up with him, he was _____.
8. There is no _____ medicine against the common cold.

Down

1. We agree about everything. We are like-_____.
2. She told me one thing and my friend the opposite. She is very two-_____.
3. She said she liked my new dress and my shoes. She was very _____.
5. Not so long ago, women were _____ as housewives on TV.

3 Complete the reported statements with the verbs in parentheses. Some sentences have more than one correct answer.

1. Chul asked if I _____ (take) offence when he asked how old I was.
2. Chailai answered that it _____ (seem) unusual for no one to be at home.
3. Apo announced that he _____ (make) plans to visit his grandparents.
4. Anurak asked how the tourists _____ (react) when they saw the whale.
5. Ja-kyung observed that some people _____ (clap) to get his attention.
6. Wayna explained that she _____ (expect) everyone to help plan the trip.

4 Rewrite the sentences with the words in parentheses.

1. I avoid studying at the weekends.
   _____
   (tell / you)
2. I convinced her that seeing a doctor was a good idea.
   _____
   (tell)
3. He insists that studying in Cairo was a great experience.
   _____
   (assure / his parents)
4. We invited our friends to join us at the poetry reading.
   _____
   (insist on)
5. Did you tell him to study at the library after school?
   _____
   (ask)

5 Which sentence is closest in meaning to the original sentence?

1. He admitted telling her my secret.
   a. He admitted that he had been telling her my secret.
   b. He admitted that he told her my secret.
2. She denied that she had eaten all the cake.
   a. She denied eating all the cake.
   b. After eating all the cake, she wanted to deny it.
3. He reported that he had passed the test.
   a. He told he passed the test.
   b. He reported passing the test.
4. I propose that we take the train to Mumbai.
   a. Perhaps we may take the train to Mumbai.
   b. I propose taking the train to Mumbai.

Common Ground **97**

9 Lend a Helping Hand

9A In Times of Crisis

VOCABULARY Dealing with disaster

1 Review Read the email. Complete the sentences with these words.

| disastrous | flooded | impact | level |
| rescued | saved | shelter | |

Hi Nicole,

I just wanted to let you know that we're safe, but we've had a (1) _____ few days here. On Saturday, the sea (2) _____ just kept getting higher and higher. Eventually it (3) _____ the railway line. By noon the water had reached our house and we had to be (4) _____ in boats. We went to a (5) _____ and we spent the night there. However, the water has completely ruined the furniture in our house downstairs. The flood has had a terrible (6) _____ on the community. There are a dozen families whose homes couldn't be (7) _____ .
—Mark

2 Review Cross out the mistake in each sentence and write the correct word(s). One sentence has two mistakes.

1 Being an aid worker is a very challenge job.
   _____

2 The work hours are sometimes longer.
   _____

3 The job can be stress and demanding.
   _____

4 You have to be flexibility and creative.
   _____

5 If you feel a responsible to help people in need, this job might be reward for you. _____

3 Put the words in the correct order to make sentences.

1 The / destroyed / infrastructure / completely / was / city's / .
   _____
   _____

2 roads / The / blocked / main / were / .
   _____

3 The / struck / earthquake / center / the / city / .
   _____

4 a / gas / shortage / of / There / was / .
   _____

5 had / Volunteers / the / of / rebuilding / task / .
   _____

6 They / flee / tried / the / area / to / .
   _____
   _____

4 Choose the correct option to complete the sentences.

1 The earthquake led to widespread _____.
   a infrastructure
   b crisis
   c devastation
   d impact

2 The government evacuated _____.
   a the people
   b the debris
   c the food
   d the water

3 It is a serious _____.
   a aid
   b debris
   c strike
   d crisis

4 The charity _____ to the public for money.
   a asked
   b responded
   c reacted
   d appealed

5 The drought led to food _____.
   a limits
   b shortages
   c blocks
   d supplies

6 The government agreed to send ___ to the area.
  a charity
  b debris
  c aid
  d relief effort

7 People started to flee the ___ zones.
  a humanitarian
  b disaster
  c blocked
  d rescue

8 There was a ___ in the number of homeless people after the second earthquake.
  a shortage
  b strike
  c rise
  d drop

5 Match the sentence halves.

1 Helicopters dropped food
2 There were food
3 They had to first clear the
4 The charity launched a
5 It damaged the
6 They asked for help from the

  a international community.
  b debris.
  c relief effort.
  d supplies.
  e infrastructure.
  f shortages.

6 Circle the option that does not form a collocation.

1 The earthquake *fled / struck / devastated* the region.
2 The war led to a humanitarian *crisis / infrastructure / disaster*.
3 There were shortages of *roads / water / food*.
4 Helicopters dropped *debris / food / aid*.
5 The government launched *an appeal / a relief effort / an aid*.
6 There was widespread *infrastructure / destruction / devastation*.

7 Extension Complete the table.

Noun	Verb
devastation	
	destroy
	appeal
supplies	
	provide
	evacuate

8 Extension How many types of extreme weather and natural disaster do you know? Complete the crossword.

Across
4 A very large and destructive wave in the ocean
5 A sudden violent movement of the Earth's surface
6 A period of time when the weather is much hotter than is normal
7 When a large amount of water covers an area that should be dry

Down
1 A long period of very dry weather
2 A time when the electricity supply to an area is cut off
3 A storm with strong winds and heavy rain
6 Frozen rain

Lend a Helping Hand

PRONUNCIATION

9 Listen to the sentences. Write the *-ing* word that you hear. Then practice saying the sentences. 🎧 68

1 _____
2 _____
3 _____
4 _____
5 _____
6 _____
7 _____

LISTENING

10 Listen to part of an interview at a disaster scene and answer the questions. 🎧 69

1 What does the captain say about the storm?
 a The strongest part of the storm is approaching.
 b The strongest part of the storm is happening now.
 c The strongest part of the storm is over.
2 What seems to be the biggest continuing problem?
 a flooding b high winds c casualties
3 What is the captain's advice for residents?
 a Get to a rescue centre quickly.
 b Stay in place if you're safe.
 c Go to the hospital for food and water.
4 Are there any rescue centres operating?
 a Yes, there are three.
 b None have opened yet.
 c So far, only the hospital.
5 What is the situation with casualties?
 a there are many life-threatening injuries
 b no injuries that she has heard of
 c no deaths have been reported

6 How is the hospital doing?
 a Luckily, it never lost power.
 b It's operating with a generator.
 c It's overwhelmed with injuries.
7 What does the captain say about the community?
 a It's pulling together.
 b It's restoring power.
 c It's clearing roads.

11 Listen to the talk about a tornado. Match the phrases you hear. 🎧 70

1 cost of the   a frame by frame
2 the loss   b and path
3 more questions   c was personal
4 destroyed everything   d in its path
5 turn his grief   e damage
6 a storm's strength   f day and age
7 revealed   g into action
8 in this   h than answers

12 Listen to the talk again. From what you've heard, how would you best describe Anton Seimon? 🎧 70

a fatalistic and discouraged
b overwhelmed and overworked
c resilient and determined
d defeatist and dispirited

13 Listen again. Are the statements true (T) or false (F)? 🎧 70

1 It was the widest tornado ever recorded. ___
2 Seimon's vehicle was carried nearly a mile. ___
3 Seimon left the area because of his grief. ___
4 He decided to create a visual representation of the storm. ___
5 Seimon put the videos in order by time. ___
6 Seimon focused on the storm's strength and path. ___
7 Seimon hoped to inspire engineers with his work. ___
8 Seimon believes that deaths caused by tornados are inevitable. ___

GRAMMAR Relative clauses

14 Choose the correct relative pronoun to complete the sentences. Choose *x* if no pronoun is needed.

1 The students, *who / whose / who's / whom* were happy about missing a day of school, celebrated the news that a blizzard was expected last night.
2 The wind inside a tornado, *who / which / x* normally moves from southwest to northeast, blows in the opposite direction in the Northern Hemisphere.
3 The waves of a tsunami, *which / who / x* are caused by an underwater earthquake, can be as tall as 98 feet.
4 The blizzard *who / whom / x* they predicted dropped about three feet of snow and stranded people in their homes.
5 Hurricanes, like the one *that / who / x* hit New Orleans, can be more than 590 miles across.
6 Most of the survivors, *who / whose / who's / whom* homes were destroyed by the tornado, are now homeless.
7 More than 216,000 people in fourteen different countries died in the 2004 tsunami *that / who / x* occurred in the Indian Ocean.
8 We went to the parade for the rescuers, *who / whose / who's / whom* the president called heroes.

15 Choose the correct relative pronoun to complete the sentences.

1 The oil *whom / that* leaks into the environment is poisonous to both animals and plants.
2 The oil covers birds' feathers, *who / which* makes it difficult for them to maintain their body heat.
3 Animals *that / whom* accidentally swallow the oil soon die from poisoning.
4 The animals *whom / that* are most affected by oil spills live on or near the shoreline.
5 Seabirds, *whom / which* are the most common victims of oil spills, can be washed and often survive oil spills.
6 Volunteers *which / who / whom* haven't been properly trained should not try to wash birds.

16 Combine the sentences into one sentence using a relative pronoun.

1 There is new technology. It was designed for use in disaster zones.
___
2 Dr. Paul Gardner-Stephen is a computer researcher at a university in Australia. He developed a way for people to communicate after a natural disaster.
___
3 He designed a new technology that lets people communicate by cell phone where there is no wireless network or the wireless network has been destroyed. It is called "mesh networking."
___
4 In mesh networking, each phone sends and receives data for the whole network. The data could be text messages, phone calls, or files.
___
5 Google started a drone program. The drones could deliver aid to hard-to-reach places.
___
6 Google also developed project Loon. It is a way to provide internet connections to remote places with a network of high-altitude balloons.
___

17 Put the words in the correct order to create sentences with relative clauses.

1 which / created / solar generator / Michael and Kenny Ham / is / the All Terrain Solar Trailer, / a / .
___
2 that / in disaster areas / cameras and software / OpenRelief / a drone / will use / to identify and locate / people / is developing / .
___
3 which / allows / The PLOTS spectrometer, / costs / people / about $10 / their drinking water, / to test / .
___
4 which / can / terrain / carry / was invented / The Aid Necessities Transporter (ANT), / by Brian Lee, / supplies / over rough / .
___
5 which / disaster aid / Anna Stork and Andrea Sreshta / makes / it / a solar-powered light, / easier / to distribute / created / .
___

18 Cross out the mistake in each sentence and write the correct word. Each sentence contains one mistake.

1 Every eight minutes, the Red Cross, who responds to more than 60,000 disasters each year, responds to an emergency somewhere in the world.
___
2 In 2013, the Red Cross, that has 97 million volunteers worldwide, helped 100 million people.
___
3 When a disaster strikes, the Red Cross, which it opens shelters in disaster areas, ensures that people have somewhere to stay. ___
4 Red Cross health volunteers go to disaster areas to help people which need first aid, shelter and medical care.
___
5 People whose volunteer with the Red Cross provide hot meals, snacks and water as part of emergency response.
___
6 The Red Cross reunites families whom have been separated by natural disasters. ___

Lend a Helping Hand **101**

9B Bridges to Prosperity

VOCABULARY BUILDING the + adjective

1 Complete each sentence with *the* + one of these adjectives.

best	brave	old	poor
rich	traumatized	young	worst

1 Mental health experts were on the scene to help _____.
2 Many would argue that _____ have a moral responsibility to help _____.
3 Only _____ would dare enter such a disaster scene to rescue others.
4 The old saying goes, "Youth is wasted on _____."
5 In a real crisis you will encounter _____ and _____.
6 It was especially difficult for _____, who had lived there all their lives.

READING

2 Read the article and choose the best headings for paragraphs 1–4 from the list of headings below. You will not use all the headings.

Paragraph 1 ___
Paragraph 2 ___
Paragraph 3 ___
Paragraph 4 ___

a Destroying a Bridge
b An Organization Is Born
c Bridges Around the World
d It All Started with a Photo
e Donkeys Can Do It
f Innovate, Educate, Inspire

3 Answer the questions below. Use one word and/or one number from the article for each answer.

1 What word describes the way Ken thinks of himself? _____
2 What were the Ethiopians using to cross the river before Ken arrived? _____
3 What does Ken hope to create for people with his organization? _____
4 What kind of steel design was chosen for the bridge? _____
5 How were the bridge supplies transported to the site? _____
6 How many thousands of dollars did the first bridge cost? _____
7 What word describes the third part of the organization's strategy? _____
8 What kind of bridge did the organization construct in Indonesia? _____

4 Sentences a–g below have been removed from the article. Decide which sentence belongs in each gap. One sentence is extra.

1 ___
2 ___
3 ___
4 ___
5 ___
6 ___

a Being appropriate to the community is key—one size does not fit all.
b Ten men would stand on either side of the broken span and pull themselves across.
c In addition to local governments, it also works with other charitable organizations.
d Rural, isolated areas almost always have higher levels of poverty and disease.
e Happily, this "boy" owns a construction company.
f Additionally, both farming productivity and labour rates increase by more than 30%.
g "Now they can trade, get to hospitals and schools on the other side, and see family members they haven't seen for years."

Bridges to Prosperity

A suspension bridge in Nepal

1 Ken Frantz decided to fix an Ethiopian bridge because, he says, "I'm a boy, and boys love bridges." (1) Ken, 52 at the time, was waiting for mechanics to service a truck in his hometown of Gloucester, Virginia in the US, when he picked up an issue of *National Geographic* magazine. He saw a photo of Ethiopians being hauled on a rope across the Blue Nile river. (2) The 360-year-old bridge located there had been destroyed during the Italian occupation of 1935–1941. "I looked at the photo once, twice, three times," Ken recalls, "and it came to me: What I want to do is repair that bridge."

2 Having made his decision, Ken helped launch Bridges to Prosperity, an organization dedicated to building bridges to help create wealth in developing nations. The group surveyed the site, won backing from tribal elders, and chose a lightweight steel design. Donkeys carried in 25,000 pounds of supplies, and Ken, his crew, and Ethiopian volunteers rebuilt the bridge in ten days at a cost of $108,000, largely donated by the organization's founders. "Half a million people live near the bridge," he says. (3)

3 Bridges to Prosperity has three main strategies that determine where and how they build. First, build to innovate: Using local knowledge and materials, the bridges must be cost-effective and appropriate for the community. (4) Second, build to educate: Each project has to involve the community and local labourers to increase their knowledge of bridge building. Finally, build to inspire: Community members must take responsibility for the project, including providing volunteers for construction, and maintenance of the bridge after completion.

4 Bridges to Prosperity is a non-profit organization that works at the local level. (5) Since its founding, Bridges to Prosperity has built more than 200 footbridges in countries across Africa, Southeast Asia, and Central and South America—cableways in Nepal, a suspension bridge in Indonesia, and a second Ethiopian bridge. A study conducted by the University of Notre Dame found that bridge connectivity has a huge effect on rural communities and the people that live there. For example, the study concluded that each family's income increases by an average of 32%.
(6) The organization's central goal is the same today as when it started: to reduce poverty by eliminating rural isolation.

9C Ready to Help

GRAMMAR Participle clauses

1 Choose the correct option to complete the sentences.

1 Countries *affecting / affected* by disasters often need international aid.
2 Students *wanting / wanted* to help raise money for the appeal should meet in the library at 2pm.
3 I find it hard to watch news of disasters *including / included* images of children.
4 Donations *making / made* by the public will be sent to the victims of the earthquake.
5 Many countries give development aid to countries *damaging / damaged* by war.
6 The headquarters of the U.N., *basing / based* in New York, was set up in 1945.
7 There has been an increase in companies *investing / invested* in green technologies.
8 There has been a series of natural disasters *leading / led* to a food shortage.

2 Rewrite the sentences from Activity 1 using a full relative clause.

1 _____
2 _____
3 _____
4 _____
5 _____
6 _____
7 _____
8 _____

3 Read the article and then change the relative clauses in bold into reduced relative clauses.

Torrey Canyon

The *Torrey Canyon* was one of the largest oil tankers of its day when it was first built in 1959. It had a capacity of 66,000 tons, (1) **which was enlarged** to 132,000 tons in Japan. The ship, (2) **which was traveling** to Milford Haven, was full of oil, when it hit rocks off the coast of Britain. As soon as the ship started to break up, there was an attempt to prevent the oil escaping, (3) **which included** the use of detergent. When this was unsuccessful the government decided to try to set fire to the oil. Jets from the air force dropped bombs (4) **that were filled** with fuel to start the blaze. These all failed because of the weather. Eventually the ship sank, but the oil damaged a lot of the coastal areas of the UK and northern France. The chemicals (5) **that were used** often did more harm than good and the government was criticized. However, the disaster did lead to changes in the law and the mistakes (6) **that were made** did mean countries were better prepared for future disasters.

1 _____
2 _____
3 _____
4 _____
5 _____
6 _____

4 Read the sentences below and decide if they are correct or incorrect. Correct the sentences that are wrong.

1 Attending the UNICEF conference, the other students asked me all about it. _____
2 Wanted to remain neutral, the UN works with many countries and charities. _____
3 Providing role models to children globally, the youth assembly is an important project. _____
4 Having fleeing the disaster zone, many people find themselves homeless. _____
5 Watching the terrible news reports, people began sending donations. _____
6 Making money, the rich have a responsibility to give assistance when appeals are launched. _____
7 Facing with an earthquake, I would leave my home. _____
8 Working in a disaster zone, the rescuers were in danger. _____

5 Rewrite the second sentence so that it has the same meaning as the first using the word in capital letters. The answer will be between two and five words.

Example: He attended the conference, then returned to his university.
Having attended the conference, he returned to his university. HAVING

1 If I was forced to flee my home, I would take my diary with me.
_____
I would take my diary with me. FORCED

2 They were totally exhausted so they had to abandon the search for survivors.
_____,
they had to abandon the search for survivors. EXHAUSTED

3 Because she was in an unfamiliar place, she felt nervous.
_____,
she felt nervous. BEING

4 He realized he had forgotten his conference notes after he left the room.
_____,
he realized he had forgotten his conference notes. LEFT

5 He took notes while he listened to the other delegates.
He took notes _____.
LISTENING

6 Because he lacked money, he decided to get a part-time job.
_____,
he decided to get a part-time job. LACKING

6 Read about a group of school friends who decided to become involved in charity. Complete the text with these phrases. Capitalize words as necessary.

after appointing	asking them to make donations
having decided	having done so
having met	raising half of the required funds
recently destroyed by fire	

(1) _____ in their first year at school, a group of students decided to do something to restore their local community center. The center, which had been (2) _____, was the home of many local groups. It was especially important to the older members of the community who used it as a place to meet. (3) _____
to try to raise money to rebuild the center, they began by holding a sponsored silence.
(4) _____, the event was a success. However, they then decided to become more serious. (5) _____ a committee, they tried to involve local businesses,
(6) _____. This proved successful and they soon reached their target, but
(7) _____, they decided to continue their work. So far the group has raised money for many projects based in the local area and abroad and it is a reminder to us all that we can all make a difference.

7 Complete these sentences with the correct form of the word in parentheses.

1 International response to disasters, _____ (cause) by extreme weather, is fast.

2 _____ (travel) to the disaster zone, he met other aid workers.

3 _____ (have) headquarters all over the world, it is a global company.

4 The Red Cross, _____ (set up) in 1881, provides emergency assistance to people in need.

5 _____ (join) the NGO, she was sent abroad where she helped to build infrastructure projects.

8 Complete these sentences so they are true for you.

1 Having finished school, I
_____

2 I love watching TV shows based on
_____

3 Studying a new language, I discovered that
_____

4 Using wireless technology, it is easier to
_____

Lend a Helping Hand

9D (Re)Touching Lives Through Photos

TEDTALKS

AUTHENTIC LISTENING SKILLS

1 Listen to an extract from Becci Manson's TED Talk. Decide whether the intonation on the bold words is rising or falling. Choose the correct answer. 🎧 72

Once a **week** (1) (rising / falling), we would set up our scanning equipment in the temporary photo libraries that had been set up, where people were reclaiming their **photos** (2) (rising / falling). The older **ladies** (3) (rising / falling) sometimes hadn't seen a scanner **before** (4) (rising / falling), but within 10 minutes of them finding their lost **photo** (5) (rising / falling), they could give it to us, have it **scanned** (6) (rising / falling), uploaded to a cloud **server** (7) (rising / falling), it would be downloaded by a **gaijin** (8) (rising / falling), a stranger, somewhere on the other side of the **globe** (9) (rising / falling), and it'd start being **fixed** (10) (rising / falling).

WATCH ▶

2 Listen to the extracts from the TED Talk. Choose the correct answers. 🎧 73

1 What was Mason's profession?
   a a fashion model
   b a photo retoucher
   c a rescue worker
2 What had happened in Ofunato?
   a It had been devastated by the wave.
   b It had a large fish market.
   c 50,000 people had died.
3 What happened at the onsen?
   a People started taking baths at the onsen again.
   b The volunteers prepared a community dinner.
   c The volunteers collected the photos they had found.
4 What is a *gaijin*?
   a a stranger
   b a photo retoucher
   c a computer technician
5 Why does she compare cleaning photos to doing a tattoo?
   a because both are artistic
   b because both are permanent
   c because both use many colours
6 Which is NOT a reason Mason gives to explain the importance of photographs?
   a They are important legal documents.
   b They preserve people's memories.
   c They help people feel connected.
7 What does Manson say she learned from the project?
   a how difficult it is to recover from natural disaster
   b how similar people are in all parts of the world
   c how beautiful Japanese kimonos are

3 Put the statements about the photo retouching process in order.

___ a The photo retouchers worked very carefully on the photos—sometimes for weeks or months—to make sure that the photographs were restored to their original state.
___ b The volunteers realized that these photos must contain important memories for their owners, so they brought the photos to the onsen, where Manson was collecting them.
___ c Once the restoration was complete, the photos were returned to the families.
___ d People from the town came to the photo libraries to identify and reclaim their photos.
___ e As the volunteers cleaned up the debris from the giant wave, they found photo albums that people had lost when they fled their homes.
___ f Once the townspeople had reclaimed their photos, they scanned the photos and sent them to photo retouchers around the world.
___ g Very carefully, the team cleaned the photos.

VOCABULARY IN CONTEXT

4 Match the words with the sentences that show their meaning.

1 sirens ____
2 give it a go ____
3 struck a chord ____
4 globe ____
5 on the ground ____
6 unfolded ____

a I'll never forget the events that **developed** that day.
b The police were **at the location of the problems** within 20 minutes.
c Sharon was afraid the problem would be too complex, but she decided to **try**.
d The **loud warning noise** from the ambulance woke the baby.
e People from all over the **world** went to Japan to help out after the tsunami.
f When she looked at the photographs of other people's families, she **felt an emotional connection** to those people.

9E Give It a Try

SPEAKING

1 Circle the option that correctly completes each expression.
1. Now, I know *which / what / about* you might be thinking…
2. I realize *there's / that's / have* a perception that…
3. I'm obviously not *to deny / denial / denying* that…
4. To begin *with / of / about*, consider the fact that…
5. On *above / top / plus* of that…
6. Let's *do not / not / cannot* forget that…
7. And finally, it's important *note / noting / to note* that…

2 Match the sentence halves.
1. Let's not forget that anyone ___
2. Among many people, there's ___
3. I'm obviously not denying the ___
4. To begin with, consider the fact ___

a. fact that evacuations are difficult to carry out.
b. that there are widespread food shortages.
c. can be affected by a natural disaster.
d. a perception that aid is mismanaged.

3 Put the story in order. Write the numbers 1–7 in the spaces provided. Use the underlined expressions to help you.

___ **a** Now, I know you're probably thinking, isn't that a difficult line of work?

___ **b** On top of that, I really feel like I'm making a difference. Very often, the people that I meet have lost everything.

___ **c** Two years ago, I decided to look for a job in disaster relief. Even though I didn't have very much experience, I was very motivated.

___ **d** To begin with, I organize food, clothing, transportation, and health services. Later, my team and I help people try to rebuild their lives.

___ **e** It's important to remember that anyone can be affected by a disaster. One day, we might need someone to help us, too.

___ **f** I'm obviously not denying that it's hard. It's very stressful at times. On the other hand, it's also very fulfilling.

___ **g** Now I work as an Emergency Response coordinator. When there is a crisis, my job is to get people the help they need as quickly as possible.

4 Complete the radio program with these expressions. Then listen and check your answers. 🎧 74

Let's not forget that	It's also important to
final points you want to note	I'm obviously not going to deny that
On top of	To begin with
what do you recommend	Now, I know what you might be thinking
Today I want to speak to you	it's too late

A: On today's show, we have the opportunity to speak to Angela Park. She is an expert in crisis management. Ms. Park, it's a pleasure to have you with us.

B: Thank you. (1) _____ about an important issue.

A: What's that?

B: The need to be prepared in the event of an emergency. (2) _____. Everyone already knows how important it is to be prepared!

A: Well, (3) _____.

B: The thing is, many people think they know what to do in a crisis, but when the time comes, they realize that they didn't take the necessary steps.

A: I see. And by then, perhaps (4) _____.

B: Exactly.

A: So, (5) _____?

B: (6) _____, all people should have a disaster supplies kit ready in their homes. (7) _____ essentials like food and water, people should stock batteries, flashlights and mobile phone chargers. (8) _____ a first aid kit is also extremely important.

A: I see.

B: (9) _____ keep a list of emergency telephone numbers written down somewhere. Often, people forget to do this, and then they have no way of getting in touch when they need help.

A: That makes a lot of sense. OK, and are there any (10) _____?

5 Read the questions below and make notes for how you would answer them. Then listen to sample answers and compare your ideas with them. 🎧 75

1. Lending a helping hand
   - Describe a time when you helped a friend or family member.
   - What did you learn from the experience?
   - How did the experience make you feel?
2. Community Service and Volunteer Work
   - Have you ever done this type of work?
   - Why did you decide to volunteer?
   - What did you learn from the experience?
3. Responding to Crises
   - What skills do you have that might be useful in a crisis?
   - What is the best way to help when a crisis happens?
   - How can we raise awareness when emergencies happen?

WRITING A letter of application

6 Read the sentences from a letter of application. Then choose the correct option. Write (I) for Introducing a subject that you want to discuss or (E) for Explaining your suitability.

1 I believe I can make a difference because I'm very enthusiastic and I'm a fast learner. ___
2 With regard to qualifications, I took a first aid course at school last year. ___
3 I feel I would be suitable because I am hardworking and dependable. ___
4 As far as language skills go, my English is quite good, and I am also learning Japanese. ___
5 I'm also prepared to take on extra responsibilities because I believe it is very important to be flexible. ___
6 With regard to my availability, I finish my exams in late June. ___

7 Match the topics with the sentences from a young man's letter of application for a voluntary position.

1 basic information about himself ___
2 his personal traits ___
3 his plans for the future ___
4 his skills and experience ___
5 how he found out about the post ___
6 main reason for writing ___
7 requesting information ___
8 what he is doing now ___

a I'm writing in relation to the opportunity for volunteers to work at this year's film festival in Edinburgh.
b I came across the advertisement on your website today.
c I was wondering if you could send more details about the post, and instructions on how to apply.
d My name is Antonio Conti. I'm 18, and I'm from Naples in the south of Italy.
e I'm currently in my final year of high school.
f I have a positive attitude and I'm very organized. In addition, I have always been passionate about movies.
g In September I'll be starting at college.
h My level of English is very good, and I also worked at our local movie theater last summer.

8 Write the missing words to complete the letter of application for a voluntary post. The first letters have been provided for you.

Hello,
I'm writing in (1) r_____ (8-letter word) to the ad for (2) v_____ (10-letter word) to visit the elderly in our local hospital. I came across your ad on the community website. Please let me know what I need to do to
(3) a_____ (5-letter word).

My name is Lisa Liu. I'm 16, and I'm a student at the international high school in Beijing. As biology is my best subject, I would like to become a doctor in the (4) f_____ (6-letter word). I'm keen to volunteer for two reasons. (5) F_____ (5-letter word), I think this is a very worthwhile program, and I would like to do something nice for the elderly in our community. Second, I would value spending time in a (6) h_____ (8-letter word) environment and observing how patients are cared for. With (7) r_____ (6-letter word) to what I would (8) b_____ (5-letter word) to the program, everyone says I'm a very friendly person, and I believe that would make me a (9) s_____ (8-letter word) volunteer for hospital visits. In addition, I have quite a lot of confidence, so I find it easy to chat to others, and I enjoy hearing their stories. I'm also very reliable. Although I don't have any formal (10) e_____ (10-letter word), when my aunt broke her leg last year, I visited her at home every day for a month and she said I was really good company.
I hope this convinces you of my suitability for the program, and I look (11) f_____ (7-letter word) to hearing from you soon.
Best wishes,
Lisa

9 Read Lisa Liu's letter of application in Activity 8 again. Is the information true (T), false (F), or not given (NG)?

1 This voluntary program is specifically for visiting old people in the hospital. ___
2 Lisa saw the ad on a community website. ___
3 She requests some information about applying. ___
4 Lisa is in her final year at high school. ___
5 She wants to be a doctor. ___
6 She would like to volunteer for the program because she has lots of free time. ___
7 Lisa spends some time describing her personality. ___
8 She also gives details of her past experiences as a hospital volunteer. ___

10 Write 140–190 words in an appropriate style.

In your English class you have been talking about community action against crime. Now your English teacher has asked you to write an essay.

There is a growing trend in community action against crime, where local residents volunteer to help tackle crime in their community. What are the advantages and disadvantages of community action against crime?

Notes

Write about **(1)** lower crime rates, **(2)** risk to participating residents, and **(3)** _____ (your own idea).

Review

1 Complete the sentences with the correct forms of these verbs.

| block | evacuate | flee | flood |
| launch | rescue | rise | survive |

1 Humanitarian aid workers _____ dozens of people in the community.
2 Women and children were _____ first.
3 The organization _____ an appeal for more funds.
4 The risk of disease has started to _____.
5 All of the residents _____ the earthquake.
6 Rising sea levels _____ the coastal area every year.
7 We tried to _____ the danger.
8 The army _____ the roads.

2 Complete the words in the sentences.

1 The earthquake had an i_____ on the whole city.
2 The worst-a _____ areas were by the coast.
3 Bridges and roads are part of a country's i_____.
4 The disaster z_____ was heavily damaged by the floods.
5 Everyone in the building died—there weren't any s_____.
6 There was a s _____ of drinking water.
7 The richer countries sent medical s_____.
8 Falling d_____ from the building made it dangerous.

3 Choose the correct word to complete the text.

For more than 40 years, Save the Whales has worked to educate people about how they can protect the ocean and the animals (1) *who / that* live in it. It was founded in 1977, by a mother and daughter (2) *who / whom* volunteered their time by handing out information about saving whales.

Save the Whales worked with other groups to stop the US Navy from exploding bombs in the Pacific Ocean. This has saved more than 10,000 marine animals, (3) *who / which* include whales, dolphins, and seals. It also supports a rescue boat, (4) *which / who* saves whales, dolphins, seals, and birds (5) *who/ that* are trapped in fishing nets.

Save the Whales is best known for its educational programs. Scientists (6) *which / who* have studied the habitat and lives of marine animals teach these programs.

They teach students how they can take action to save whales and sea life. Save the Whales programs, (7) *which / who* more than 300,000 students have already participated in, are taught at many schools in California.

In 2015, Save the Whales was awarded the "Best of Seaside Awards for Environmental, Conservation, and Ecological Organizations" for the fourth year in a row, (8) *who / which* means it is now part of the Seaside Business Hall of Fame. In 2017, it was named a "top rated" nonprofit organization.

4 Are the words in bold correct or incorrect? Correct those that are incorrect. Use reduced relative clauses when possible.

1 People **lived** in Australia are called Australians. _____
2 A type of pastry **is calling** a doughnut is often served with coffee. _____
3 Tokyo is a city **who is famous** for its excellent subway and train lines. _____
4 We are grateful for people, **who are willing to help,** after a disaster. _____
5 Cyclones are storms **that** usually occur from late spring to early autumn. _____
6 I love **coffee which** many people in my country drink at breakfast. _____
7 My new shirt, **which I bought online,** fits perfectly! _____

5 Rewrite the sentence with a reduced relative clause.

1 When I was younger, I had a good friend. Her name was Megan.
   _____
   _____

2 There is a man reading by the pool. He is my father.
   _____
   _____

3 Many people went to the concert. It was held at the park.
   _____
   _____

4 Did you see the email? It was sent by Kailash.
   _____
   _____

5 I love the dress the girl who is walking ahead of us is wearing.
   _____
   _____

6 The boy who is riding the blue bike isn't looking where he's going.
   _____
   _____

Lend a Helping Hand 109

10 Life-changing

10A Road to Recovery

VOCABULARY Illness and injury

1 Review Complete the sentences with these verbs.

| absorb | beats | breathe | infect |
| pass | support | tastes | use |

1 Veins do not allow substances to _____ through their walls.
2 Our lungs do not _____ all of the oxygen that we breathe in.
3 Over 200 bones _____ the body.
4 Mosquitoes _____ humans with malaria.
5 It is a myth that we only _____ 10% of our brain.
6 We _____ at different rates when we are asleep.
7 A newborn baby's heart _____ very fast.
8 Your tongue _____ food.

2 Review Choose the correct option to complete the sentences.

1 Nutrients are *absorbs / absorbed* from the food we eat.
2 Many types of *bacteria / bacterias* are good for the body.
3 She's got a lung *infection / infected*.
4 Taste, touch, and smell are examples of *sensories / senses*.
5 He had an irregular *heartbeat / heartbeats*.
6 There are three types of *muscular / muscles*.
7 The *digestion / digestive* system absorbs food.
8 The sense of *touch / touching* is extremely important when you can't see.

3 Match the two parts of the phrases.

1 control the   a normal life
2 a head   b intensive care
3 be in   c injury
4 speech   d therapy
5 be left   e stomach
6 keep down   f paralyzed
7 lead a   g food
8 an upset   h symptoms

4 Write these words in the correct column in the table.

| antibiotics | bleeding | cancer |
| operation | physical therapy | stroke |

Illness	Treatment

5 Choose the correct option to complete the sentences.

1 She's in a wheelchair because she's paralyzed from the *wrist / wheel / waist* down.
2 I've been out of *active / action / the act* since the accident.
3 It's dangerous to play with doors, you may *crash / slam / injury* your finger.
4 The infection cleared *up / out / off* after three weeks.
5 It's vital to detect cancer early before it *cures / prescribes / spreads* to other parts of the body.
6 She's *made / done / had* a full recovery.
7 After a week in the hospital, his chest *damage / infection / bleeding* was much better.
8 He had severe brain *damaged / damaging / damage* after the stroke.

6 Complete the crossword.

Across
2 Don't _____ about the bad things, only the good things.
3 I've broken my leg so I'm out of _____ for six weeks.
5 My grandfather can't walk anymore so he uses a _____.
8 The infection _____ to different parts of his body.

Down
1 They were able to _____ the illness early.
4 After the surgery, she was in _____ care for one week.
6 There is no _____ for the common cold.
7 She complained of _____ pains so she went to the hospital.

7 **Extension** Choose the correct words to complete the paragraph.

A stroke is a life-threatening medical (1) _____. There is increased risk of a stroke if you suffer from diabetes or high (2) _____ pressure. You should seek urgent treatment if you think someone is having a stroke. What are the main symptoms of stroke? The face, mouth, or eye may be (3) _____ on one side. A person may not be able to (4) _____ both arms. Your fingers, hands, or jaw may feel (5) _____. You might not be able to speak or your speech may be (6) _____. Any delay in seeking treatment will increase the risk of brain injury or a permanent (7) _____. In order to recover from a stroke, people often undergo a long period of (8) _____.

1 a symptom
  b sign
  c condition
  d injury
2 a blood
  b bleed
  c bleeding
  d bloody
3 a droops
  b drooped
  c drooping
  d a droop
4 a lift
  b carry
  c hold
  d hang
5 a normal
  b numb
  c dizzy
  d hurt
6 a slipped
  b stopped
  c slurred
  d paralyzed
7 a disabled
  b disabling
  c disable
  d disability
8 a habitat
  b rehabitat
  c habilitation
  d rehabilitation

8 **Extension** Put the words in order to make sentences.

1 attacks / disability / can / heart / cause / .
_____
2 the / his / felt / in / legs / numbness / patient / .
_____
3 conditions / from / he / suffers / medical / a range of / .
_____
4 hospital / people / the / rehabilitation / start / in / .
_____
5 became / her / slurred / speech / .
_____

Life-changing 111

PRONUNCIATION

9 Listen to these exchanges. Underline the auxiliary verb that is stressed for contrast. Then practice saying that sentence. 🎧 76

1 **A:** Are you saying that just so I don't worry?
  B: No, really, I **am** feeling better.
2 **A:** I'm sorry, but I really think he needs to see a doctor.
  B: But he **has** seen a doctor.
3 **A:** I think you need to take it slower. You were doing too much.
  B: You're wrong. I **was** taking it easy.
4 **A:** That's not good. You've been skipping your physical therapy.
  B: No, I **haven't**. I go every week.
5 **A:** They were insensitive to the situation. Rude, actually.
  B: No, they **weren't**. They were just upset.
6 **A:** It doesn't look to me like the injury is healing very quickly.
  B: But it **is**. It's much better than it was.
7 **A:** That store still hasn't installed a ramp for wheelchairs.
  B: No, they **have** installed it. I saw it yesterday.
8 **A:** Sometimes I think he doesn't even try.
  B: But he **has** tried. It's just very difficult.

LISTENING

10 Listen and complete the sentences with the missing word or phrase that you hear. Then practice saying the sentences. 🎧 77

1 The doctors believe she is capable of making a full _____.
2 The man was complaining of debilitating _____.
3 He was initially a little _____ to trying art therapy.
4 Rather than _____ more medications, can we try something else?
5 There is a growing _____ of brain injuries.
6 Some traditional doctors can be resistant to new _____.

11 Listen to the talk on brain injuries. What do you think would be the best title for this talk? 🎧 78
  a The Art of Recovery
  b An Impossible Diagnosis
  c Broken Dreams, Lost Lives
  d The Brain of an Artist

12 Listen again and choose the correct options. 🎧 78

1 What do these two soldiers have in common?
  a They both suffered arm and leg injuries.
  b They were together when a bomb went off.
  c They are both in the US Air Force.
  d Neither of them suffered visible injuries.
2 How does Major Hall describe himself?
  a injured, but he is still the same man
  b as not the same person he once was
  c not even feeling like a human being
  d able to forget the worst experiences
3 How many wars are mentioned?
  a two
  b three
  c four
  d five
4 What medical condition is not mentioned?
  a sleep disorders
  b headaches
  c seizures
  d stomach aches
5 What kind of treatment is being described here?
  a reading therapy
  b art therapy
  c writing therapy
  d physiotherapy
6 What does Major Hall compare his mask to?
  a painting
  b speaking
  c thinking
  d writing

13 Match the comments with the speakers. You can use the speakers more than once. Listen again if necessary. 🎧 78

1 "Most of my injuries are invisible, and the rest are hidden." _____
2 "I am just not the same human being as I used to be." _____
3 "I was wrong," _____
4 "I don't know why, but that's what needed to come out of me." _____
5 "… The artwork is like a printed page—it is there if you want to read it." _____
  a Staff Sergeant Robert "Bo" Wester
  b Army Staff Sergeant Perry Hopman
  c Army Major Jeff Hall

112 Unit 10

GRAMMAR Expressing past ability

14 Choose the best option to complete the sentences.

1 Jae-Hwa *could / managed to* lose some weight by eating less and exercising more every day—he looks great now!
2 Lena knew she *could / managed to* eat healthy snacks on her diet.
3 Jae-Hwa *could / managed to* read the nutrition facts labels on food.
4 Lena *could / was able to* choose foods with less sugar.
5 If Jae-Hwa *could / managed to* ride his bike to school instead of taking the bus, he could get more exercise.
6 Lena *was able to / succeeded in* get enough exercise by walking to and from school.
7 Jae-Hwa *could / managed to* get all of his homework done—and still sleep eight hours every night.
8 Lena *was able to / managed* lose 10 pounds thanks to diet and exercise.

15 Choose the correct options to complete the questions.

1 **A** *Could / Was* your friend *able to / manage* go back to school last week?
   B No. She still had a temperature, so her mother made her stay home.
2 **A** *Did / Was* he *able / managed* to play in the football game yesterday?
   B No. He had sprained his ankle, so he just watched the game.
3 **A** *Was / Did* she *able go / manage to go* to the party last night?
   B No, she was still feeling bad, so she decided to stay at home.
4 **A** *Did / Was* he *able / succeed* in talking to his doctor about the prescription?
   B Yes. He left several messages, and the doctor finally called him back.
5 **A** *Were / Did* the doctors *succeeded in / able to* cure his condition?
   B No, not yet. They're still researching new drugs that might be effective.
6 **A** *Could / Was* she *manage to walk / walk* around the school after her surgery?
   B Well, at first she needed to use a wheelchair, but after a while she was fine.
7 **A** *Did / Were* you *managed / able* to visit your grandmother in hospital this morning?
   B No. The nurses asked us to wait until tomorrow because she was very tired this morning.
8 **A** *Did / Was* your cousin *manage / able to* to find a physiotherapist near his house?
   B Yes, eventually. His new physiotherapist isn't that far away.

16 Choose the correct option to make the sentences negative. In some cases, both options are correct.

1 Guilherme _____ raise his arm after his bicycle accident.
   a couldn't   **b** didn't manage
2 Guilherme _____ or write with his left hand after the accident.
   a couldn't draw   **b** wasn't able to draw
3 Luiza _____ take the test on Friday because she was ill.
   a wasn't able to   **b** didn't manage
4 Luiza _____ work as a lifeguard at the pool because she didn't do the first aid course.
   a couldn't   **b** wasn't able to
5 Henrique couldn't focus during the game and _____ in scoring a goal.
   a didn't manage   **b** didn't succeed
6 Henrique _____ to exercise last week because of his sore muscles.
   a didn't manage   **b** couldn't
7 After she fell, Ester _____ to walk to the school nurse's office.
   a wasn't able   **b** didn't manage
8 Ester _____ go on the school trip.
   a didn't manage to   **b** couldn't

17 Complete the questions with the correct form of the verbs in parentheses.

1 **A:** What was the first medicine people _____? (could, buy)
   B: Aspirin was the first medicine you could buy. Felix Hoffman created it from a chemical in willow bark in 1899.
2 **A:** When _____ companies _____ aspirin as tablets? (be able to, manufacture)
   B: The first aspirin was a powder, but they were able to make it into a tablet in 1900.
3 **A:** How many chemical compounds _____ scientists _____ in coffee? (manage to, identify)
   B: Scientists have managed to identify more than 1,000 chemical compounds in a cup of coffee. Together they make up the special flavor of coffee.
4 **A:** How _____ doctors _____ a cure for smallpox in the last century? (succeed in, find)
   B: They didn't cure the disease, but it was eradicated due to the success of vaccinations.
5 **A:** When _____ doctors _____ blood transfusions? (be able to, give)
   B: The first transfusion of human blood was in 1818.

10B Medical Possibilities

VOCABULARY BUILDING Dependent prepositions

1 Complete the sentences with these words. Pay attention to the preposition that follows each of them.

aimed	awareness	capable	chance
devoted	resistant		

1 You're in great shape. I think you have a good _____ of finishing the marathon.
2 She's done a great job of raising _____ of that illness.
3 With all the new technology, who knows what we're _____ of doing.
4 I'm usually _____ to change at first. It takes me a while to get used to things.
5 His life has been _____ to helping those less fortunate.
6 The campaign against smoking is especially _____ at young people.

READING

2 Read the article and choose the correct options.

1 The word "devoted" in paragraph 1 could best be replaced by
  a enthusiastic   c dedicated
  b caring   d affectionate
2 The word "justify" in paragraph 2 is closest in meaning to
  a support   c produce
  b explain   d question
3 The word "sightless" in paragraph 2 could best be replaced by
  a eyeless   c sighted
  b deaf   d blind
4 The word "function" in paragraph 3 could best be replaced by
  a behavior   c work
  b performance   d service
5 In stating "… the immune system restrains itself…," the author means that the immune system
  a holds back   c calls out
  b moves forward   d stays on
6 The word "privileged" in paragraph 4 is closest in meaning to
  a unfortunate   c private
  b explained   d advantaged

7 In stating "Gene therapy offers the promise…," the author means that gene therapy
  a gives hope   c provides confirmation
  b guarantees   d suggests

3 According to the article, are the following statements true (T), false (F), or not stated (NS)?

1 More than 200 million people on Earth are blind. ____
2 Medical advances in ending blindness are promising. ____
3 The eye acts as a kind of laboratory for the body. ____
4 A "control" gives you valuable perspective on what you're doing. ____
5 If something is "immune privileged" it makes things more complicated. ____
6 Unlike the eye, the brain is not "immune privileged". ____

4 Read the article again. For the following questions, choose the answer that you think fits best according to the text.

1 In the first paragraph, what is the author's main point?
  a the worsening global blindness problem
  b the severe limitations of people who are blind
  c the heavy cost of global vision loss
  d the unfair burden on the relatives of the blind
2 How many new medical treatments does the author mention?
  a two   c four
  b three   d five
3 What is another way to say "bionic"?
  a implanted   c electronic
  b advanced   d biomedical
4 What does the author suggest about new treatments for the eye?
  a They are specific to the eye because of its uniqueness.
  b They may lead to treatments for the entire body.
  c Some treatments are promising, but a lot more time is needed.
  d They are limited because it's hard to find a control.
5 We can infer from what the author says that the immune system
  a usually attacks invaders in organs of the body.
  b has a much stronger response in the eyes.
  c attacks inflammation in the organs of the body.
  d makes gene therapy problematic in the eyes.
6 We can infer from the text that neuroscientists' main focus of work is
  a the eyes.   c the brain.
  b the organs of the body.   d the immune system.
7 What is the promise of biomedical implants?
  a replacing eyes   c replacing genes
  b replacing bodies d replacing organs

A Cure in Sight

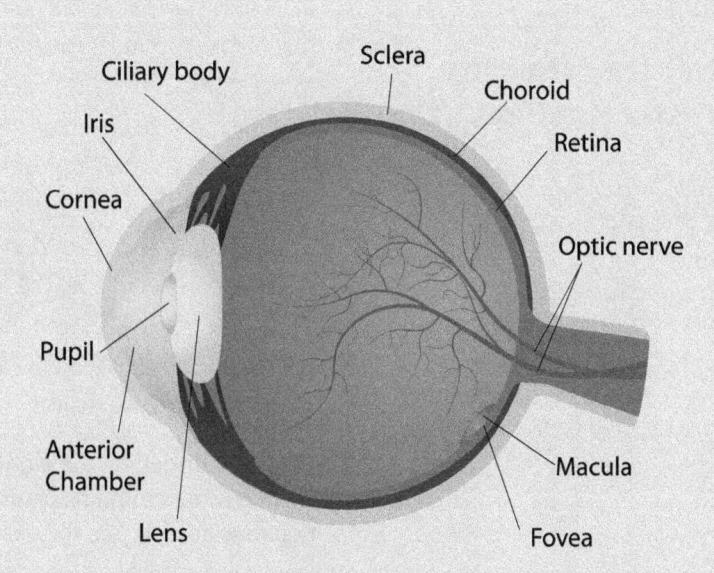

1 Roughly one in every 200 people on Earth—39 million of us—can't see. Another 246 million have poor vision, which is serious enough that it complicates their lives. Vision loss also affects hundreds of millions more people, often relatives, devoted to helping their family members who can't see.

2 These problems alone justify the search for new treatments. Within roughly the past decade, efforts in gene-replacement, stem cells, and biomedical, or "bionic," implants have given at least some sight to people previously sightless. These advances encourage talk of something unthinkable just 10 or 20 years ago: ending human blindness, and soon.

3 Yet the eye is also getting increased attention because it provides a safe, available place to test treatments that might also be used elsewhere in the body. To start with, researchers can look directly into the eye to see what's wrong and whether a treatment is working. Likewise, the patient can see out of the eye (or not), providing a quick, important measure of function. The eye also offers feedback such as pupil dilation* or electrical activity in the optic nerve. In addition, a researcher running an experimental treatment on one eye can usually use the other as a control. In an experiment, a control is something that doesn't change so you can compare the effects of the treatment against it.

4 The eye is also tough. Within the eye's round shelter, the immune system restrains itself in a way that makes the eye "immune privileged." This means that the eye doesn't react with inflammation like other organs. Therefore, it is safer to try a treatment in the eye, such as gene therapy, which might cause major problems elsewhere in the body.

5 Neuroscientists like the eye because "it's the only place you see the brain without drilling a hole," as one put it. The retina, visible through the pupil, is basically a bowl of nerve cells tied to the brain by the optic nerve; the eye as a whole is an "outpouching of the brain," formed as a baby develops, by stretching away from it. Like the eye, the brain enjoys immune privilege, so treatments that work in the eye may readily transfer to the brain or spinal cord.

6 These advantages take on extra importance because experimental strategies now focused on the eye may advance future treatments for the whole human body. Gene therapy offers the promise of fixing faulty genes that cause illnesses of all kinds. Stem cells offer the promise of replacing entire body parts; bionic implants may replace failing organs. The eye is becoming a window to the possibilities—and limits—of healing methods on which medicine's future may depend.

pupil dilation *when the pupil in the eye becomes larger*

10C Medical Advances

GRAMMAR Emphatic structures

1 Put the words in the correct order to make sentences.

1 increased / The invention of antibiotics / did / life expectancy / lead to /.
_____
2 the invention of antibiotics / Only after / surgery / did / become more common /.
_____
3 new treatments / have people / the need for / Not until recently / realized /.
_____
4 the negative effect / would have / Little would people / fast food / have guessed /.
_____
5 your / exercise / improve / Regular / health / does /.
_____
6 all the improvements / little did / in medicine / As a child, / I imagine /.
_____
7 most diseases / are invented / will we / be able / Not until / to cure / new drugs /.
_____
8 has there been / of penicillin / a luckier accident / Rarely / than the discovery /.
_____

2 Choose the correct option to complete the sentences.

1 Little *did* / *do* she realize how much exercise would change her life.
2 In no way *was* / *am* I ready for the news the doctors gave me.
3 Rarely *have* / *do* I seen such a fast recovery.
4 Only after my leg *had* / *have* healed could I walk without pain.
5 At no time when I was a child *did* / *could* I want to be a doctor.
6 Not until I graduated from medical school *was* / *am* I allowed to diagnose patients.
7 Nowhere in the world *is* / *are* healthcare so cheap.
8 Only when I found out I was cured *can* / *could* I relax.

3 Complete the paragraph with these words and phrases.

did	in no way	little
not only	only after (2x)	

I've always been quite a sporty person, but I have also often had accidents while playing sport. (1) _____ have I had bumps and bruises, but I have also had a few breaks. Most of these were fairly minor, for example, when I broke my fingers. While it (2) _____ hurt, (3) _____ did it really have an impact on my everyday life. I was lucky that I broke the fingers on my left hand. In fact, despite all my injuries, (4) _____ breaking my toe did I really understand how painful broken bones could be. Even worse, I didn't break my toe playing sport, I broke it trying to stop a vase from smashing on the floor. (5) _____ did I expect as I stuck out my foot how painful it would be. The vase broke anyway and (6) _____ a couple of months did the pain go completely. My advice: if you are going to try and catch a falling vase, use your hands, not your feet!

4 Read and underline the eight structures that make the writing more emphatic by using either the verb *do* or a negative adverb. See the example.

Cystic Fibrosis

Cystic Fibrosis was first discovered in 1938. It is a disease that affects all sufferers differently, but it has some common symptoms. For example, <u>not only</u> are people with *CF* more likely to get chest infections, <u>but many also</u> cannot digest food without medication.

For many years, being diagnosed with *CF* did mean a shorter life. These days, it is different. Little can they have imagined when it was first discovered the changes that would happen in the next century. Even when I was growing up things were different. Not until I was ten was I allowed to eat chocolate after new drugs were developed. To be honest, when I was younger, I didn't really think much about my illness. Rarely did it make much of a difference to my life. Only after I was sick when I was 16 did I begin to think about it more.

These days, although I have to take a lot of medication, I also know that without CF, I would not be me. So, rarely do I let it get me down. Also, in recent years the treatment has got so much better, and despite there being no cure, the medication does let me lead a pretty normal life.

1 *not only… but also*
2 _____
3 _____
4 _____
5 _____
6 _____
7 _____
8 _____

5 Rewrite the second sentence so that it has the same meaning as the first using the word in capital letters. Use between two and five words including the word given.

1. As he checked the results he didn't expect what he found.
   Little _____ found when he checked the results. **DID**
2. They only found a cure after testing many plants.
   Only _____ they find a cure. **AFTER**
3. It is unusual for patients to recover completely.
   _____ completely. **RARELY**
4. He was not at all to blame for the accident.
   In _____ blame for the accident. **WAY**
5. I didn't understand anything they were discussing in the program.
   At no _____ what they were discussing in the program. **DID**
6. People live longer in Japan than anywhere else.
   Nowhere _____ in Japan. **DO**

6 Read the paragraph and think about how the numbered sentences could be made more emphatic. Rewrite the emphatic phrases using the words and phrases below.

Clean Hands Stop Disease

(1) Most people don't know what a huge difference washing your hands could make to your health. However, dirty hands have been found to be one of the biggest spreaders of infections. A World Health Organization survey has shown that (2) most people don't wash their hands very often and they also don't use soap. (3) This area of the country seems to be the worst for hygiene. So we are here to tell you to wash, soap, dry. (4) Then we will have improved health.

1. Little _____
2. Not only _____
3. Nowhere in _____
4. Only _____

7 Complete these sentences so they are true for you.

1. Not only do I _____, but I also _____.
2. Only after I finished _____, did I _____.
3. Not until I was _____, did my parents let me _____.
4. In no way am I a fan of _____.
5. Rarely do I have time to _____.
6. Only when I have _____, am I able to _____.

10D A Broken Body Isn't a Broken Person

TEDTALKS

AUTHENTIC LISTENING SKILLS

1 Listen to the extract from Janine Shepherd's TED Talk. Write down three key adjectives she uses and three key nouns. 🎧 80

Adjectives:
1 _____
2 _____
3 _____

Nouns:
1 _____
2 _____
3 _____

WATCH ▶

2 Choose the option that best completes the sentences.

1 Before her accident, Shepherd was a competitive
  a cyclist.
  b cross-country skier.
  c pilot.
2 Before her accident, Shepherd had dreamed of
  a becoming a pilot.
  b moving to New York City.
  c competing in the Olympics.
3 The doctors told her that her back
  a had been crushed.
  b would recover completely.
  c was only slightly damaged.
4 In the acute spinal ward, Shepherd
  a became depressed because she had no one to talk to.
  b learned about the possibility of flying school.
  c formed close friendships even though she couldn't see the people she was talking to.
5 When Shepherd went home from hospital, the nurse warned her
  a that she would become depressed.
  b that she would miss her friends in the hospital.
  c that she should be very careful in her wheelchair.
6 Maria was Shepherd's friend in the hospital who
  a had also been a skier.
  b always had a positive attitude.
  c encouraged her to try flying.
7 During her first flying lesson, Shepherd
  a was not allowed to touch the controls.
  b regretted signing up for the lesson.
  c flew over the spot where she'd had her accident.
8 Shepherd's parents
  a also got their pilot's licences.
  b have never been up in the plane with her.
  c told her she should just accept her circumstances.

3 Choose the correct option to complete the sentences and add emphasis to their meaning.

1 When Shepherd started her training ride that day, *little / small* did she know that her life would change.
2 Even though Maria could hardly move, *in no time / at no time* did she lose her positive attitude.
3 While the doctors *did / do* try everything they could, they did not believe Shepherd would walk again.
4 It was *only after / in no way* Shepherd's accident that she decided to learn to fly.
5 *In no way / Not until* Shepherd had received her aerobatics licence was she satisfied with her progress.
6 *Nowhere else / Rarely* had Shepherd been in a situation where she formed deep friendships without ever seeing the people she was talking to.
7 While Shepherd had worked hard in her Olympic training, *never before / little* did she have to overcome emotional obstacles as she did after the accident.
8 The flying school *does / did* accept Shepherd as a student, even though many instructors doubted that she would be able to fly.

VOCABULARY IN CONTEXT

4 Match the words (1–6) with the sentences that show their meaning.

1 superficial _____
2 nickname _____
3 set _____
4 extensive _____
5 out of my comfort zone _____
6 grasp _____

a Shepherd's friends were deeply concerned when they learned about **the large number and different types** of injuries that she had resulting from the accident.
b It took a long time for Shepherd to truly **understand** how much her life had changed.
c Suddenly, the things that used to worry her seemed **silly and unimportant**.
d Shepherd's friends often called her by **a special name** that reflected her strength and perseverance.
e Before the accident, Shepherd's focus and her training were **fixed** on competing in the Olympics.
f Shepherd realized that one of the most important things she could do to help her recovery was to spend time **doing things that were difficult for her in unfamiliar situations**.

10E Developing the Conversation

SPEAKING

1 Choose the correct response to each statement

1 Last week I had a cold, but now I'm much better.
   a I'm thinking of you.   c You must be fed up.
   b I'm glad to hear that.

2 Sara hasn't been feeling well recently.
   a Tell her I'm thinking of her.
   b That's really good news.
   c Apparently she's not well.

3 The doctor told me that I need physical therapy.
   a That's awesome.   c You're kidding!
   b Say "hi" from me.

4 The antibiotics are quite expensive.
   a Oh no!   b Wow, that's cool!   c Amazing!

5 Luckily, the infection hasn't spread.
   a Poor you.   c That's good news.
   b Are you OK?

6 Julian has been ill for weeks.
   a I know. I'm not kidding.
   b I heard he was in the hospital.
   c Yes, apparently he's been ill.

2 Listen to the conversations. Decide if the second speaker is surprised, sympathetic or if he or she wants to pass on a message. Circle the correct answer. 🎧 81

1 surprised   sympathetic   passing on a message
2 surprised   sympathetic   passing on a message
3 surprised   sympathetic   passing on a message
4 surprised   sympathetic   passing on a message

3 Read the sentences. Write a response in the space provided. Use these expressions to help you.

You're kidding!	Oh no!	Wow, that's great!
Awesome!	Poor guy/girl!	Say "hi" from me.
No, what happened?	Is he/she OK?	

1 Did you hear about Veronica?
_____

2 My wallet was stolen this afternoon.
_____

3 Apparently Yumi has a new job.
_____

4 Did you hear the news? Peter has broken his leg.
_____

5 You'll never guess what happened. I got a raise!
_____

6 I'm seeing Jordan this afternoon.
_____

4 Complete the conversation. Use one word in each space. Then listen and check your answers. 🎧 82

Jack: Have you (1) _____ the news?
Linda: No, I haven't. What (2) _____?
Jack: (3) _____ the class is cancelled.
Linda: You're (4) _____! How come?
Jack: Nobody seems to know.
Linda: I (5) _____ Ms. Davis's dog has been ill. (6) _____ she had to go take care of him.
Jack: (7) _____ Ms. Davis!
Linda: She lives near me. Maybe I'll knock on her door and see if she's (8) _____.
Jack: That's a good idea. If you go, will you (9) _____ her I'm (10) _____ of her?
Linda: Of course.

5 The following photos show people who are ill. Make notes about how you think the people are feeling. Then, speak about the photos, and make comparisons, for one minute. Record yourself.

1

2

Listen to a student compare the photos. 🎧 83

Is this response similar to what you would say? Add to the ideas in your notes if you need to.

Now make notes about the following questions.

- Which person do you think feels worse? Why?
- When you are ill, what do you do to try to make yourself feel better?

Now listen to the sample answers. Add to your answers as necessary. 🎧 84

Life-changing   **119**

WRITING A success story

6 Read the sentences. Is this how you felt before succeeding (B) or after succeeding (A)?

1 I'd tried absolutely everything. ____
2 It was a day that changed my life. ____
3 It was a moment I'll never forget. ____
4 It was a truly memorable experience. ____
5 It was the best day of my life! ____
6 I was absolutely terrified. ____
7 I was ready to just give up. ____
8 I was sure I was going to fail. ____

7 Choose the most descriptive verb to complete each sentence.

1 I _____ as quietly as possible from the living room to the front door.
   a crept   **b** walked   **c** ran

2 "Somebody, HELP! I can't swim!" I _____.
   a said   **b** asked   **c** screamed

3 Wasting no time, the firefighters immediately _____ inside the building!
   a went   **b** rushed   **c** walked

4 I _____ the door as hard as I could, and then called the police.
   a shut   **b** closed   **c** slammed

5 Suddenly, a large dog _____ over a garden fence and began to chase me!
   a stepped   **b** leapt   **c** moved

6 I was too frightened to stay there so I _____ my backpack and ran back to town.
   a took   **b** picked up   **c** grabbed

8 Put the missing sentences in the correct places to complete the success story.

> (1) ___ When my friends all went swimming, I'd pretend I didn't feel like it. No one knew I couldn't swim because I was too embarrassed to tell them.
>
> Then, my best friend got an extraordinary graduation present: a boat trip for a full week! Everyone in our group of friends was invited and we were thrilled. (2) ___
>
> I didn't want to miss out, so I secretly started taking swimming lessons. (3) ___ Once, when my feet couldn't touch the bottom, I panicked! (4) ___
>
> My instructor was patient, but after several lessons I was ready to give up, and then a strange thing happened. I got into the pool one day and I actually liked how the water felt. (5) ___ It was a moment I'll never forget. It felt amazing! Soon after that, I was able to swim, very slowly at first, but then with more confidence. (6) ___ Our boat trip is next month, and I can't wait!

a The next thing I knew, I was floating.
b The first few times I went to the pool I was terrified.
c Now I love it.
d I've always been scared of water.
e But there was a rule… you had to know how to swim.
f I was screaming, believing I was going to drown.

9 Listen to a lecture. Then read the text. Write an essay summarizing the points made in the lecture you just heard, explaining how they cast doubt on points made in the reading. 🎧 85

If you think we're at our peak in terms of medical science, think again. Thanks to science and technology, we now have driverless cars, space travel, and the internet… but medical developments seem to be moving at a very slow pace indeed.

True, we have better machines than we used to have, but how many people can afford the best medical treatments and procedures, which are usually the most expensive. The true picture in many countries is that health services are struggling to cope due to lack of resources. Hospitals are overcrowded and staff can barely cope with demands. In this day and age, we should have much better systems in place.

And while vaccines have revolutionized modern medicine, how long ago was the last one discovered? And it is well-known that antibiotics are losing their efficiency as we are seeing more and more superbugs that can resist them. So why aren't scientists developing medicines and cures at a faster rate?

With all of today's technology and awareness, we should be the picture of health, but are we? According to the World Health Organization (WHO), heart disease is the number one cause of death worldwide, and that is particularly shocking given that many of those conditions are lifestyle-related. Levels of stress are also rising globally, especially stress in the workplace. And, today, one in four people suffers with a mental health issue.

So, while it may be true that we can now treat many diseases, we are certainly not preventing or curing enough of them.

Review

1 Rewrite the sentences. Complete the sentences using the words in capital letters. Write between two and five words.

1 I'm fit again now.
  I'm _____. BACK
2 I've fully recovered.
  I've _____. MADE
3 There isn't any permanent damage after the accident.
  The accident _____
  any permanent damage. LEFT
4 He couldn't do anything for a few weeks.
  He _____ for a few
  weeks. ACTION
5 He's like he was before.
  He's _____ now. BACK

2 Complete the sentences with these words.

care	cure	infection	injury
physical therapy	prescribe	stroke	wheelchair

1 Many athletes have _____ following an injury.
2 Scientists are still searching for a _____ for cancer.
3 A _____ is when the blood supply to the brain is damaged.
4 Doctors _____ antibiotics and drugs to patients.
5 She had a chest _____ and couldn't go swimming.
6 Football players with a serious _____ usually come off the field.
7 He was in intensive _____ after the car accident.
8 He lost the use of his legs and needs to use a _____.

3 Find and correct the mistakes in the sentences.

1 My mother is very strong; she managed walk a short distance the day after her surgery. _____
2 The patient made a miraculous recovery and was able leave the hospital after a few days. _____
3 The doctor couldn't found the cause of the infection, so she prescribed antibiotics. _____
4 The doctor succeeded curing the patient with an experimental treatment. _____
5 We couldn't to meet with the doctors because one of them was with another patient. _____
6 The athletes managed to can avoid injuries by stretching and warming up before each race. _____
7 From the x-ray, the doctor could be able to see that her arm was broken. _____
8 I didn't managed to get to the prescription from the pharmacy before it closed. _____

4 Complete the sentences with these words and phrases.

are	can	is
little did we know	must	may be

1 _____ that antibiotics could usher in a new age of superbugs.
2 Patients who _____ infected by a superbug are separated from other patients.
3 People _____ pick up superbugs when they go to hospital for another issue such as a broken leg.
4 Superbugs _____ sometimes found in public areas such as gyms and schools.
5 Superbugs _____ be considered to be a major threat to public health.
6 One strategy that _____ impacting the war on superbugs is educating people about not asking for antibiotics every time they feel ill.

5 Write the words in the correct order to make sentences with negative adverbs and phrases.

1 have / I / last night / a concert / as / much / enjoyed / as / rarely / I / did /.
   _____
2 did / he / know / we / little / were / a / surprise party / for / his / sixteenth birthday / planning /.
   _____
3 realize / bought / only / couldn't / after / I / the tickets / did / I / I / go / to the movie /.
   _____
4 end up / at / no / did / think / I / time / I'd / in / the / hospital / of / a bite from a spider / because /.
   _____
5 better / else / in / our / sells / ice cream / nowhere / than / my uncle's shop / town /.
   _____
6 underestimate / in / should / way / you / the / of / a good education / importance / no /.
   _____

Life-changing

VOCABULARY LIST

UNIT 1

Review

a bike ride (n)	/ə baɪk raɪd/
backpacking (n)	/ˈbækˌpækɪŋ/
commute (v)	/kəmˈjut/
cruise (n)	/kruz/
destination (n)	/ˌdɛstəˈneɪʃən/
flight (n)	/flaɪt/
ride (v)	/raɪd/
route (n)	/rut/
taxi (n)	/ˈtæksi/
train (n)	/treɪn/

Unit Vocabulary

accessible (adj)	/ækˈsɛsəbəl/
B&B (n)	/ˈbi ən ˈbi/
ban (v)	/bæn/
basically (adv)	/ˈbeɪsɪkli/
be up for (phr v)	/bi ˈʌp ˌfɔr/
budget (n)	/ˈbʌdʒɪt/
cause (v)	/kɔz/
come across (phr v)	/ˈkʌm əˈkrɔs/
community (n)	/kəˈmjunɪti/
culture shock (n)	/ˈkʌltʃər ˌʃɒk/
date back (phr v)	/ˈdeɪt ˈbæk/
deal (n)	/dil/
decline (v)	/dɪˈklaɪn/
established (adj)	/ɪˈstæblɪʃt/
evaluate (v)	/ɪˈvæljuˌeɪt/
extensive (adj)	/ɪkˈstɛnsɪv/
fluent (adj)	/ˈfluənt/
food poisoning (n)	/ˈfud ˌpɔɪzənɪŋ/
genuinely (adv)	/ˈdʒɛnjuɪnli/
get a real feel for (phr v)	/ˌgɛt ə ˈrɪəl ˈfil fɔr/
get used to (the food) (phr v)	/ˌgɛt ˈjuzd tu/
grand (adj)	/grænd/
hiking (n)	/ˈhaɪkɪŋ/
honesty (n)	/ˈɒnɪsti/
host family (n)	/ˈhoʊst ˈfæməli/
ideal (adj)	/aɪˈdɪəl/
incredibly (adv)	/ɪnˈkrɛdəbli/
independence (n)	/ˌɪndɪˈpɛndəns/
individual (n)	/ˌɪndɪˈvɪdʒuəl/
influence (v)	/ˈɪnfluəns/
investment (n)	/ɪnˈvɛstmənt/
left to (your) own devices (idiom)	/ˈlɛft tu (yər) ˈoʊn dɪˈvaɪsɪz/
legal (adj)	/ˈligəl/
lie around (phr v)	/ˈlaɪ əˈraʊnd/
look back (phr v)	/ˈlʊk ˈbæk/
major (adj)	/ˈmeɪdʒər/
media (n)	/ˈmidiə/
move on (phr v)	/ˈmuv ˈɒn/
necessarily (adv)	/ˌnɛsəˈsɛrəli/
negotiate (v)	/nɪˈgoʊʃiˌeɪt/
opt (v)	/ɒpt/
overseas (adv)	/ˈoʊvərˌsiz/
participant (n)	/pɑrˈtɪsəpənt/
perspective (n)	/pərˈspɛktɪv/
reinforce (v)	/ˌriɪnˈfɔrs/
reliability (n)	/rɪˌlaɪəˈbɪləti/
reputation (n)	/ˌrɛpjəˈteɪʃən/
resource (n)	/ˈrisɔrs/
restriction (n)	/rɪˈstrɪkʃən/
revolution (n)	/ˌrɛvəˈluʃən/
ridiculous (adj)	/rɪˈdɪkjələs/
robbery (n)	/ˈrɒbəri/
roots (n)	/ruts/
servant (n)	/ˈsɜrvənt/
sights (n)	/saɪts/
simply (adv)	/ˈsɪmpli/
spread (v)	/sprɛd/
standard (n)	/ˈstændərd/
stare (v)	/stɛər/
step out (phr v)	/ˈstɛp ˈaʊt/
strongly (adv)	/ˈstrɒŋli/
turn out (phr v)	/ˈtɜrn ˈaʊt/
tutor (n)	/ˈtutər/
upgrade (n)(v)	/ˈʌpˌgreɪd/
vice versa (adv)	/ˈvaɪsə ˈvɜrsə/
voyage (n)	/ˈvɔɪədʒ/
wealth (n)	/wɛlθ/
welcoming (adj)	/ˈwɛlkəmɪŋ/
worry (v)	/ˈwɜri/

Extension

amenities (n)	/əˈmɛnətiz/
availability (n)	/əˌveɪləˈbɪləti/
downtime (n)	/ˈdaʊnˌtaɪm/
excursion (n)	/ɪkˈskɜrʒən/
overbooked (adj)	/ˈoʊvərˌbʊkt/
secluded (adj)	/sɪˈkludɪd/
tourist trap (n)	/ˈtʊrəst træp/
wander (v)	/ˈwɑndər/

Vocabulary Building

break down (phr v)	/ˈbreɪk ˈdaʊn/
come down to (phr v)	/ˌkʌm ˈdaʊn tu/
hang out (phr v)	/ˈhæŋ ˈaʊt/
line up (v)	/laɪn ʌp/
look after (phr v)	/ˈlʊk ˈæftər/
pick up (phr v)	/ˈpɪk ˈʌp/
pull over (v)	/pʊl ˈoʊvər/

Vocabulary in Context

anxiety (n)	/æŋˈzaɪəti/
broke (n)	/broʊk/
keep in touch (idiom)	/ˈkip ɪn ˈtʌtʃ/
rush (v)	/rʌʃ/
trip up (phr v)	/ˈtrɪp ˈʌp/
up for it (idiom)	/ʌp fɔr ɪt/

UNIT 2

Review

career prospects (phr)	/kəˈrɪr ˈprɑspɛkts/
flexible (adj)	/ˈflɛksəbəl/
full-time (adj)	/fʊl-taɪm/
in charge of (phr v)	/ɪn tʃɑrdʒ ʌv/
industry (n)	/ˈɪndəstri/
job market (n)	/dʒɑb ˈmɑrkət/
long hours (phr)	/lɔŋ ˈaʊərz/
part-time (adj)	/ˈpɑrt ˌtaɪm/
physically demanding (phr)	/ˈfɪzɪkəli dɪˈmændɪŋ/
poorly paid (phr)	/ˈpʊrli peɪd/
responsible (adj)	/rɪˈspɑnsəbəl/
stressful (adj)	/ˈstrɛsfəl/
well-paid (adj)	/wɛl-peɪd/
work on (phr v)	/wɜrk ɑn/

Unit Vocabulary

(a) matter (of) (idiom)	/əˈmætər ʌv/
adapt (v)	/əˈdæpt/
aspect (n)	/ˈæspɛkt/
assume (v)	/əˈsum/
attach (v)	/əˈtætʃ/
automatically (adv)	/ˌɔtəˈmætɪkli/
backup (n)	/ˈbækˌʌp/
banking (n)	/ˈbæŋkɪŋ/
bargain (n)	/ˈbɑrgɪn/
barrier (n)	/ˈbæriər/
be based (phr v)	/bi ˈbeɪst/
beg (v)	/bɛg/
businessperson (n)	/ˈbɪznɪsˌpɜrsən/
campaign (n)	/kæmˈpeɪn/
capable (adj)	/ˈkeɪpəbəl/
climate change (n)	/ˈklaɪmɪt ˌtʃeɪndʒ/
code (n)	/koʊd/
confirm (v)	/kənˈfɜrm/
corporate (adj)	/ˈkɔrpərɪt/
cut down (phr v)	/ˈkʌt ˈdaʊn/
data (n)	/ˈdeɪtə/
demonstrate (v)	/ˈdɛmənˌstreɪt/
detect (v)	/dɪˈtɛkt/
discourage (v)	/dɪsˈkɜrɪdʒ/
distant (adj)	/ˈdɪstənt/
distribute (v)	/dɪˈstrɪbjut/
distribution (n)	/ˌdɪstrəˈbjuʃən/
diverse (adj)	/dɪˈvɜrs/
edit (v)	/ˈɛdɪt/
email (n)	/ˈiˌmeɪl/
entrepreneur (n)	/ˌɒntrəprəˈnʊər/
executive (n)	/ɪgˈzɛkjətɪv/
expand (v)	/ɪkˈspænd/
export (v)	/ˈɛkspɔrt/
failure (n)	/ˈfeɪljər/
filter (n)	/ˈfɪltər/
fund (n)	/fʌnd/
fund (v)	/fʌnd/
gender (n)	/ˈdʒɛndər/
guarantee (n)	/ˌgærənˈti/
handle (v)	/ˈhændl/
harvest (v)	/ˈhɑrvɪst/
illegal (adj)	/ɪˈligəl/
impressive (adj)	/ɪmˈprɛsɪv/
inbox (n)	/ˈɪnˌbɒks/
infect (v)	/ɪnˈfɛkt/
invent (v)	/ɪnˈvɛnt/
investor (n)	/ɪnˈvɛstər/
leadership (n)	/ˈlidərˌʃɪp/
market (n)	/ˈmɑrkɪt/
network (v)	/ˈnɛtˌwɜrk/
origin (n)	/ˈɔrɪdʒɪn/
post (v)	/poʊst/
potential (n)	/pəˈtɛnʃəl/
pressure (n)	/ˈprɛʃər/
profile (n)	/ˈproʊfaɪl/
profit (n)	/ˈprɒfɪt/
publisher (n)	/ˈpʌblɪʃər/
put together (phr v)	/ˈpʊt təˈgɛðər/
raise money (phr v)	/ˈreɪz ˈmʌni/
reality (n)	/riˈæləti/
recover (v)	/rɪˈkʌvər/
risk (n)	/rɪsk/
scam (n)	/skæm/
social media (n)	/ˈsoʊʃəl ˈmidiə/
solar (adj)	/ˈsoʊlər/
source (n)	/sɔrs/
spam (n)	/spæm/
statement (n)	/ˈsteɪtmənt/
store (v)	/stɔr/
strategy (n)	/ˈstrætɪdʒi/
summarize (v)	/ˈsʌməˌraɪz/
supplier (n)	/səˈplaɪər/
tribe (n)	/traɪb/
victim (n)	/ˈvɪktɪm/
wealthy (adj)	/ˈwɛlθi/

Extension

chair (n)	/tʃɛr/
delicate (adj)	/ˈdɛləkət/
founder (n)	/ˈfaʊndər/
outsource (v)	/ˌaʊtˈsɔrs/
proactive (adj)	/proʊˈæktɪv/
self-starter (n)	/sɛlf-ˈstɑrtər/
systematic (adj)	/ˌsɪstəˈmætɪk/
team player (n)	/tim ˈpleɪər/

Vocabulary Building

distant relatives (col)	/ˈdɪstənt ˈrɛlətɪvz/
luxury hotel (col)	/ˈlʌgʒəri hoʊˈtɛl/
normal price (col)	/ˈnɔrməl praɪs/
personal details (col)	/ˈpɜrsɪnl dɪˈteɪlz/
well-paid job (col)	/wɛl-peɪd dʒɑb/

Vocabulary in Context

go too far (idiom)	/ˈgoʊ ˌtu ˈfɑr/
intrigue (v)	/ɪnˈtrig/
knock on the head (idiom)	/ˈnɒk ɒn ðə ˈhɛd/
matter (v)	/ˈmætər/
out of hand (idiom)	/ˈaʊt əv ˈhænd/
turn up (phr v)	/ˈtɜrn ˈʌp/

UNIT 3

Review

achieve (v)	/əˈtʃiv/
bounce (v)	/baʊns/

coach (n)	/koutʃ/
do yoga (phrase)	/du ˈjougə/
encourage (v)	/ɛnˈkɜrɪdʒ/
go cycling (phrase)	/gou ˈsaɪkəlɪŋ/
kick (v)	/kɪk/
net (n)	/nɛt/
play a role (phrase)	/pleɪ ə rou/
referee (n)	/ˌrɛfəˈri/
represent (v)	/ˌrɛprəˈzɛnt/
rink (n)	/rɪŋk/
spectator (n)	/ˈspɛkteɪtər/
swing (v)	/swɪŋ/
throw (v)	/θrou/
track (n)	/træk/
train (v)	/treɪn/

Unit Vocabulary

accelerate (v)	/ækˈsɛləˌreɪt/
advance (n)	/ædˈvæns/
agree with (phr v)	/əˈgri ˌwɪð/
amount (n)	/əˈmaunt/
anticipate (v)	/ænˈtɪsəˌpeɪt/
athletic (adj)	/æθˈlɛtɪk/
attitude (n)	/ˈætɪˌtud/
awareness (n)	/əˈwɛərnɪs/
billion (n)	/ˈbɪljən/
brand (n)	/brænd/
bronze (adj)	/brɒnz/
captain (v)	/ˈkæptən/
championship (n)	/ˈtʃæmpiənˌʃɪp/
change the face of (idiom)	/ˈtʃeɪndʒ ðə ˈfeɪs əv/
closely (adv)	/ˈklouslɪ/
compete (v)	/kəmˈpit/
conquer (v)	/ˈkɒŋkər/
debt (n)	/dɛt/
determine (v)	/dɪˈtɜrmɪn/
elite (adj)	/ɪˈlit/
energetic (adj)	/ˌɛnərˈdʒɛtɪk/
entire (adj)	/ɛnˈtaɪər/
essentially (adv)	/ɪˈsɛnʃəli/
establish (v)	/ɪˈstæblɪʃ/
evolution (n)	/ˌɛvəˈluʃən/
evolve (v)	/ɪˈvɒlv/
expense (n)	/ɪkˈspɛns/
fade away (v)	/ˈfeɪd əˌweɪ/
fame (n)	/feɪm/
formal (adj)	/ˈfɔrməl/
forward (n)	/ˈfɔrwərd/
funding (n)	/ˈfʌndɪŋ/
gardening (adj)	/ˈgɑrdnɪŋ/
glory (n)	/ˈglɔri/
goal (n)	/goul/
greatly (adv)	/ˈgreɪtli/
hold (a record) (v)	/hould/
host (v)	/houst/
injury (n)	/ˈɪndʒəri/
instantly (adv)	/ˈɪnstəntli/
intensively (adv)	/ɪnˈtɛnsɪvli/
junk food (n)	/ˈdʒʌŋk ˌfud/
largely (adv)	/ˈlɑrdʒli/
long-term (adj)	/ˈlɔŋ ˌtɜrm/
marathon (n)	/ˈmærəˌθɒn/
medal (n)	/ˈmɛdl/
muscle (n)	/ˈmʌsəl/
nation (n)	/ˈneɪʃən/
participate (v)	/pɑrˈtɪsəˌpeɪt/
pay off (phr v)	/ˈpeɪ ˌɔf/
percentage (n)	/pərˈsɛntɪdʒ/
personality (n)	/ˌpɜrsəˈnælɪti/
popularity (n)	/ˌpɒpjəˈlærɪti/
positive role model (phrase)	/ˈpɒzɪtɪv ˈroulˌmɒdl/
preferably (adv)	/ˈprɛfərəbli/
principle (n)	/ˈprɪnsəpəl/
psychological (adj)	/ˌsaɪkəˈlɒdʒɪkəl/
quote (n)	/kwout/
ranking (n)	/ˈræŋkɪŋ/
real passion (phrase)	/ˈriəl ˈpæʃən/
recreation (n)	/ˌrɛkriˈeɪʃən/
represent (v)	/ˌrɛprɪˈzɛnt/
role model (n)	/ˈroul ˌmɒdl/
roughly (adv)	/ˈrʌfli/
schedule (n)	/ˈskɛdʒul/
season (n)	/ˈsizən/
select (v)	/sɪˈlɛkt/
set (a new record) (v)	/sɛt/
set up (phr v)	/ˈsɛt ˌʌp/
shrink (v)	/ʃrɪŋk/
slightly (adv)	/ˈslaɪtli/
slow down (phr v)	/ˈslou ˌdaun/
smash (v)	/smæʃ/
specialize (v)	/ˈspɛʃəˌlaɪz/
specific (adj)	/spəˈsɪfɪk/
spirit (n)	/ˈspɪrɪt/
stamina (n)	/ˈstæmɪnə/
status (n)	/ˈsteɪtəs/
subsequently (adv)	/ˈsʌbsɪkwəntli/
subway (n)	/ˈsʌbˌweɪ/
suit (v)	/sut/
sum (n)	/sʌm/
surface (n)	/ˈsɜrfɪs/
tackle (v)	/ˈtækəl/
target (n)	/ˈtɑrgɪt/
technique (n)	/tɛkˈnik/
technological (adj)	/ˌtɛknəˈlɒdʒɪkəl/
tend to (phr v)	/ˈtɛnd tu/
terminal (n)	/ˈtɜrmɪnl/
throughout (prep)	/θruˈaut/
top (adj)	/tɒp/
vast (adj)	/væst/

Extension

aware (adj)	/əˈwɛr/
awareness (n)	/awareness/
competition (n)	/ˌkɒmpəˈtɪʃən/
competitive (adj)	/kəmˈpɛtətɪv/
energy (n)	/ˈɛnərdʒi/
energetic (adj)	/ˌɛnərˈdʒɛtɪk/
passion (n)	/ˈpæʃən/
passionate (adj)	/ˈpæʃənət/
positive (adj)	/ˈpɒzətɪv/
skill (n)	/skɪl/
skillful (adj)	/ˈskɪlfəl/

Vocabulary Building

amount (n)	/əˈmaunt/
elite (adj)	/ɪˈlit/
establish (v)	/ɪˈstæblɪʃ/
money (n)	/ˈmʌni/
selected (adj)	/səˈlɛktəd/
talent (n)	/ˈtælənt/

Vocabulary in Context

but (conj)	/bʌt/
conversely (adv)	/ˈkɒnvərsli/
rather than (phr)	/ˈræðər ðæn/

UNIT 4

Review

art gallery (n)	/ˈɑrt ˈgæləri/
broadcast (n)	/ˈbrɔdˌkæst/
concert hall (n)	/ˈkɑnsərt hɔl/
listener (n)	/ˈlɪsənər/
lyrics (n)	/ˈlɪrɪks/
mural (n)	/ˈmjurəl/
painting (n)	/ˈpeɪntɪŋ/
portrait (n)	/ˈpɔrtrət/
production (n)	/prəˈdʌkʃən/
sculpture (n)	/ˈskʌlptʃər/
verse (n)	/vɜrs/

Unit Vocabulary

actual (adj)	/ˈæktʃuəl/
authority (n)	/əˈθɔrɪti/
behind (prep)	/bɪˈhaɪnd/
boost (v)	/bust/
carnival (n)	/ˈkɑrnɪvəl/
choir (n)	/kwaɪər/
claim (v)	/kleɪm/
comedy club (n)	/ˈkɒmɪdi ˌklʌb/
commitment (n)	/kəˈmɪtmənt/
confidence (n)	/ˈkɒnfɪdəns/
construction (n)	/kənˈstrʌkʃən/
costume (n)	/ˈkɒstum/
creation (n)	/kriˈeɪʃən/
creativity (n)	/ˌkriɛˈtɪvɪti/
demolish (v)	/dɪˈmɒlɪʃ/
desperate (adj)	/ˈdɛspərɪt/
discipline (n)	/ˈdɪsəplɪn/
dramatic (adj)	/drəˈmætɪk/
duration (n)	/duˈreɪʃən/
economist (n)	/ɪˈkɒnəmɪst/
economy (n)	/ɪˈkɒnəmi/
emphasize (v)	/ˈɛmfəˌsaɪz/
engagement (n)	/ɛnˈgeɪdʒmənt/
expression (n)	/ɪkˈsprɛʃən/
factor (n)	/ˈfæktər/
fatal (adj)	/ˈfeɪtəl/
festival (n)	/ˈfɛstɪvəl/
figure out (phr v)	/ˈfɪgjər ˌaut/
found (v)	/faund/
foundation (n)	/faunˈdeɪʃən/
fulfill (v)	/fulˈfɪl/
gallery (n)	/ˈgæləri/
gang (n)	/gæŋ/
generate (v)	/ˈdʒɛnəˌreɪt/
impact (n)	/ˈɪmpækt/
income (n)	/ˈɪnkʌm/
industrial (adj)	/ɪnˈdʌstriəl/
initially (adv)	/ɪˈnɪʃəli/
inspiration (n)	/ˌɪnspəˈreɪʃən/
lead to (phr v)	/ˈlid tu/
literally (adv)	/ˈlɪtərəli/
mayor (n)	/ˈmeɪər/
minister (n)	/ˈmɪnɪstər/
minority (n)	/mɪˈnɔrɪti/
museum (n)	/mjuˈziəm/
official (adj)	/əˈfɪʃəl/
organizer (n)	/ˈɔrgəˌnaɪzər/
parade (n)	/pəˈreɪd/
physical (adj)	/ˈfɪzɪkəl/
poverty (n)	/ˈpɒvərti/
pride (n)	/praɪd/
private company (n)	/ˈpraɪvɪt ˈkʌmpəni/
process (n)	/ˈprɒsɛs/
professional (n)	/prəˈfɛʃnl/
public art (n)	/ˈpʌblɪk ˈɑrt/
redevelopment (n)	/ˌridɪˈvɛləpmənt/
rehearse (v)	/rɪˈhɜrs/
reject (v)	/rɪˈdʒɛkt/
relic (n)	/ˈrɛlɪk/
remarkable (adj)	/rɪˈmɑrkəbəl/
rhythm (n)	/ˈrɪðəm/
run over (phr v)	/ˈrʌn ˌouvər/
sell out (phr v)	/ˈsɛl ˌaut/
signal (v)	/ˈsɪgnl/
skilled (adj)	/skɪld/
stand for (phr v)	/ˈstænd fɔr/
straightforward process (phrase)	/ˌstreɪtˈfɔrwərd ˈprɒsɛs/
struggling (adj)	/ˈstrʌgəlɪŋ/
supposedly (adv)	/səˈpouzɪdli/
take charge (phr v)	/ˈteɪk ˈtʃɑrdʒ/
theater (n)	/ˈθiətər/
venue (n)	/ˈvɛnju/
violence (n)	/ˈvaɪələns/
vital (adj)	/ˈvaɪtl/
viewer (n)	/ˈvjuər/
volunteer (n)	/ˌvɒlənˈtɪər/
widely (adv)	/ˈwaɪdli/

Extension

arrangement (n)	/əˈreɪndʒmənt/
book launch (n)	/ˈbuk lɔntʃ/
composer (n)	/kəmˈpouzər/
conductor (n)	/kənˈdʌktər/
conservatory (n)	/kənˈsɜrvətɔri/
exhibition hall (n)	/ˌɛksəˈbɪʃən hɔl/
gig (n)	/gɪg/
independent cinema (n)	/ˌɪndɪˈpɛndənt ˈsɪnəmə/
jazz (n)	/dʒæz/
musical (n)	/ˈmjuzɪkəl/
open mic (n)	/ˈoupən maɪk/
poetry reading (n)	/ˈpouɪtri ˈrɛdɪŋ/
recital (n)	/rəˈsaɪtəl/
stand-up comedy (n)	/ˈstænd ʌp ˈkɒmədi/
street performance (n)	/ˈstrit pərˈfɔrməns/

Vocabulary Building

diverse social background (col)	/dɪˈvɜrs ˈsouʃəl ˈbækˌgraund/
driving ambition (col)	/ˈdraɪvɪŋ æmˈbɪʃən/
hard work (col)	/ˈhɑrd ˈwɜrk/
innovative program (col)	/ˌɪnəˌveɪtɪv ˈprouˌgræm/
leading orchestra (col)	/ˈlidɪŋ ˈɔrkɪstrə/
low income (col)	/ˈlou ˈɪnkʌm/
mixed results (col)	/ˈmɪkst rɪˈzʌlts/
strict set (col)	/ˈstrɪkt ˈsɛt/

Vocabulary in Context

assume (v)	/əˈsum/
behind (prep)	/bɪˈhaɪnd/
engagement (n)	/ɛnˈgeɪdʒmənt/

figure out (phr v) /ˈfɪgjər aʊt/
relic (n) /ˈrɛlɪk/
run over (v) /rʌn ˈoʊvər/

UNIT 5

Review

access (v) /ˈæk,sɛs/
connect (v) /kəˈnɛkt/
curious (adj) /ˈkjʊriəs/
data (n) /ˈdeɪtə/
discover (v) /dɪˈskʌvər/
equip (v) /ɪˈkwɪp/
equipment (n) /ɪˈkwɪpmənt/
examine (v) /ɪgˈzæmɪn/
explain (v) /ɪkˈspleɪn/
hacker (n) /ˈhækər/
proof (n) /pruf/
results (n) /rɪˈzʌlts/
search (v) /sɜrtʃ/
software developer (n) /ˈsɔf,twɛr dɪˈvɛləpər/
solution (n) /səˈluʃən/
technology (n) /tɛkˈnɑlədʒi/

Unit Vocabulary

alter (v) /ˈɔltər/
arm (v) /ɑrm/
assignment (n) /əˈsaɪnmənt/
beautiful (adj) /ˈbjutəfəl/
belief (n) /bɪˈlif/
bother (v) /ˈbɒðər/
browser (n) /ˈbraʊzər/
bubble (n) /ˈbʌbəl/
bulb (n) /bʌlb/
capacity (n) /kəˈpæsɪti/
chemical (n) /ˈkɛmɪkəl/
circumstance (n) /ˈsɜrkəm,stæns/
conduct (v) /kənˈdʌkt/
consume (v) /kənˈsum/
cooperation (n) /koʊˌɒpəˈreɪʃən/
cooperative (adj) /koʊˈɒpərətɪv/
curiosity (n) /ˌkjʊəriˈɒsɪti/
deadline (n) /ˈdɛd,laɪn/
determining (adv) /dɪˈtɜrmɪnɪŋ/
discovery (n) /dɪˈskʌvəri/
dissolve (v) /dɪˈzɒlv/
dominant (adj) /ˈdɒmɪnənt/
downwards (adv) /ˈdaʊnwərdz/
effective (adj) /ɪˈfɛktɪv/
electrical (adj) /iˈlɛktrɪkəl/
embrace (v) /ɛmˈbreɪs/
engage (v) /ɛnˈgeɪdʒ/
evidence (n) /ˈɛvɪdəns/
function (n) /ˈfʌŋkʃən/
genius (n) /ˈdʒiniəs/
grasp (n) /græsp/
helpful (adj) /ˈhɛlpfəl/
hopeful (adj) /ˈhoʊpfəl/
identify (v) /aɪˈdɛntəˌfaɪ/
imaginative (adj) /ɪˈmædʒənətɪv/
increasingly (adv) /ɪnˈkrisɪŋli/
innovation (n) /ˌɪnəˈveɪʃən/
innovative (adj) /ˈɪnəˌveɪtɪv/
intelligence (n) /ɪnˈtɛlɪdʒəns/
journal (n) /ˈdʒɜrnl/
labor (n) /ˈleɪbər/
lid (n) /lɪd/
link (n) /lɪŋk/
listener (n) /ˈlɪsənər/
make matters worse (phrase) /ˈmeɪk ˈmætərz ˈwɜrs/
mark (v) /mɑrk/
mature (v) /məˈtʃʊər/
mechanical (adj) /mɪˈkænɪkəl/
medical (adj) /ˈmɛdɪkəl/
mode (n) /moʊd/
movement (n) /ˈmuvmənt/
myth (n) /mɪθ/
network (n) /ˈnɛt,wɜrk/
place (v) /pleɪs/
pleasurable (adj) /ˈplɛʒərəbəl/
pleasure (n) /ˈplɛʒər/
practical (adj) /ˈpræktɪkəl/
previously (adv) /ˈpriviəsli/
ray (n) /reɪ/
reaction (n) /riˈækʃən/
reference (n) /ˈrɛfərəns/
release (v) /rɪˈlis/
researcher (n) /rɪˈsɜrtʃər/
return (v) /rɪˈtɜrn/
reward (n) /rɪˈwɔrd/
sample (n) /ˈsæmpəl/
scan (n) /skæn/
social (adj) /ˈsoʊʃəl/
society (n) /səˈsaɪəti/
sophisticated (adj) /səˈfɪstɪˌkeɪtɪd/
submit (v) /səbˈmɪt/
substance (n) /ˈsʌbstəns/
surgeon (n) /ˈsɜrdʒən/
surgery (n) /ˈsɜrdʒəri/
surround (v) /səˈraʊnd/
survey (n) /ˈsɜrveɪ/
theory (n) /ˈθɪəri/
threat (n) /θrɛt/
transform (v) /trænsˈfɔrm/
transparent (adj) /trænsˈpærənt/
tremendous (adj) /trəˈmɛndəs/
ultimate (adj) /ˈʌltəmɪt/
uncertainty (n) /ʌnˈsɜrtənti/
use (n) /jus/
useful (adj) /ˈjusfəl/
voice (n) /vɔɪs/

Extension

conduct (v) /ˈkɑndʌkt/
disprove (v) /dɪˈspruv/
experiment (n) /ɪkˈspɛrəmənt/
formulate (v) /ˈfɔrmjəˌleɪt/
hypothesis (n) /haɪˈpɑθəsəs/
perform (v) /pərˈfɔrm/
set up (v) /sɛt ʌp/
test (v) /tɛst/

Vocabulary Building

adaptive (adj) /əˈdæptɪv/
beautiful (adj) /ˈbjutəfəl/
curious (adj) /ˈkjʊriəs/
effective (adj) /ɪˈfɛktɪv/
helpful (adj) /ˈhɛlpfəl/
hopeful (adj) /ˈhoʊpfəl/
imaginative (adj) /ɪˈmædʒənətɪv/
innovative (adj) /ˈɪnəˌveɪtɪv/
treatable (adj) /ˈtritəbəl/

Vocabulary in Context

a voice (n) /ə vɔɪs/
adapt (v) /əˈdæpt/
bother (v) /ˈbɑðər/
link (n) /lɪŋk/
reward (n) /rɪˈwɔrd/
surrounded (v) /səˈraʊndəd/

UNIT 6

Review

climate change (n) /ˈklaɪmət tʃeɪndʒ/
drought (n) /draʊt/
environmental (adj) /ɪnˌvaɪrənˈmɛntəl/
expedition (n) /ˌɛkspəˈdɪʃən/
fishing (n) /ˈfɪʃɪŋ/
global warming (n) /ˈgloʊbəl ˈwɔrmɪŋ/
greenhouse effect (n) /ˈgrinˌhaʊs ɪˈfɛkt/
protect (v) /prəˈtɛkt/
route (n) /rut/
save (v) /seɪv/
waste (v) /weɪst/
wild (adj) /waɪld/

Unit Vocabulary

administration (n) /ədˌmɪnəˈstreɪʃən/
agriculture (n) /ˈægrɪˌkʌltʃər/
alarming (adj) /əˈlɑrmɪŋ/
anger (n) /ˈæŋgər/
arise (v) /əˈraɪz/
assess (v) /əˈsɛs/
breed (v) /brid/
capture (v) /ˈkæptʃər/
catch on (phr v) /ˈkætʃ ˈɒn/
characteristic (n) /ˌkærɪktəˈrɪstɪk/
chase (v) /tʃeɪs/
clue (n) /klu/
compensate (v) /ˈkɒmpənˌseɪt/
concern (n) /kənˈsɜrn/
consequence (n) /ˈkɒnsɪˌkwɛns/
conservation (n) /ˌkɒnsərˈveɪʃən/
constantly (adv) /ˈkɒnstəntli/
cure (n) /kjʊər/
die out (v) /ˈdaɪ ˈaʊt/
diversity (n) /dɪˈvɜrsɪti/
domestic (adj) /dəˈmɛstɪk/
emotion (n) /ɪˈmoʊʃən/
endanger (adj) /ɛnˈdeɪndʒər/
ensure (v) /ɛnˈʃʊər/
equivalent (adj) /ɪˈkwɪvələnt/
extinct (adj) /ɪkˈstɪŋkt/
fake (adj) /feɪk/
feature (n) /ˈfitʃər/
fox (n) /fɒks/
gene (n) /dʒin/
genetic (adj) /dʒəˈnɛtɪk/
growth (n) /groʊθ/
habitat (n) /ˈhæbɪˌtæt/
historian (n) /hɪˈstɔriən/
hunt (v) /hʌnt/
indicate (v) /ˈɪndɪˌkeɪt/
influential (adj) /ˌɪnfluˈɛnʃəl/
inspire (v) /ɪnˈspaɪər/
interfere (v) /ˌɪntərˈfɪər/
mammal (n) /ˈmæməl/
mass (adj) /mæs/
misunderstanding (n) /ˌmɪsʌndərˈstændɪŋ/
mysterious (adj) /mɪˈstɪəriəs/
overcome (v) /ˌoʊvərˈkʌm/
polar bear (n) /ˈpoʊlər ˌbɛər/
psychologist (n) /saɪˈkɒlədʒɪst/
purely (adv) /ˈpjʊərli/
put forward (phr v) /ˌpʊt ˈfɔrwərd/
rainfall (n) /ˈreɪnˌfɔl/
rate (n) /reɪt/
rethink (v) /riˈθɪŋk/
reveal (v) /rɪˈvil/
revenge (n) /rɪˈvɛndʒ/
save (v) /seɪv/
short-term (adj) /ˈʃɔrt ˈtɜrm/
shorten (v) /ˈʃɔrtn/
significantly (adv) /sɪgˈnɪfɪkəntli/
species (n) /ˈspiʃiz/
sponsor (v) /ˈspɒnsər/
strengthen (v) /ˈstrɛŋkθən/
sudden (adj) /ˈsʌdn/
surroundings (n) /səˈraʊndɪŋz/
survival (n) /sərˈvaɪvəl/
survive (v) /sərˈvaɪv/
suspect (v) /səˈspɛkt/
suspicious (adj) /səˈspɪʃəs/
take to (phr v) /ˈteɪk tu/
unique (adj) /juˈnik/
unwilling (adj) /ʌnˈwɪlɪŋ/
wipe out (phr v) /ˈwaɪp ˈaʊt/

Extension

conform (v) /kənˈfɔrm/
conforming (adj) /kənˈfɔrmɪŋ/
conformity (n) /kənˈfɔrməti/
endurance (n) /ˈɛndərəns/
familiar (adj) /fəˈmɪljər/
habit (n) /ˈhæbət/
habitual (adj) /həˈbɪtʃuəl/
habituate (v) /həˈbɪtʃueɪt/
hazard (n) /ˈhæzərd/
insulation (n) /ˌɪnsəˈleɪʃən/
modify (n)(v) /ˈmɑdəˌfaɪ/
modification (n) /ˌmɑdəfəˈkeɪʃən/
modified (adj) /ˈmɑdəˌfaɪd/
prospect (n) /ˈprɑspɛkt/
sanctuary (n) /ˈsæŋktʃuˌɛri/
sustain (v) /səˈsteɪn/
sustained (adj) /səˈsteɪnd/
sustaining (adj) /səˈsteɪnɪŋ/
sustenance (n) /ˈsʌstənəns/

Vocabulary Building

animal product (n) /ˈænəməl ˌprɒdəkt/
book shop (n) /ˈbʊk ʃɑp/
farm house (n) /fɑrm haʊs/
ice age (n) /aɪs eɪdʒ/
rain drop (n) /ˈreɪn drɑp/
science teacher (n) /ˈsaɪəns ˌtitʃər/
sea creature (n) /ˈsi ˌkritʃər/
social media campaign (n) /ˈsoʊʃəl ˈmidiə kæmˌpeɪn/

Vocabulary in Context

camp (n)	/kæmp/
hit a wall (idiom)	/ˈhɪt ə ˈwɔl/
proof (n)	/pruf/
spot (n)	/spɒt/
surface (n)	/ˈsɜrfəs/
willingness (n)	/ˈwɪlɪŋnɪs/

UNIT 7

Review

make a living (phrase)	/meɪk ə ˈlɪvɪŋ/
make a splash (phrase)	/meɪk ə splæʃ/
make an impression (phrase)	/meɪk ən ɪmˈprɛʃən/
make sense (phrase)	/meɪk sɛns/
make the most of (phrase)	/meɪk ðə moʊst ʌv/
make up your mind (phrase)	/meɪk ʌp jʊər maɪnd/
make way (phrase)	/meɪk weɪ/

Unit Vocabulary

additional (adj)	/əˈdɪʃənl/
alternative (adj)	/ɔlˈtɜrnətɪv/
approach (n)	/əˈproʊtʃ/
assessment (n)	/əˈsɛsmənt/
bacteria (n)	/bækˈtɪəriə/
break (v)	/breɪk/
brick (n)	/brɪk/
combination (n)	/ˌkɒmbɪˈneɪʃən/
commonly (adv)	/ˈkɒmənli/
contribute (v)	/kənˈtrɪbjut/
create (v)	/kriˈeɪt/
creative (adj)	/kriˈeɪtɪv/
creatively (adv)	/kriˈeɪtɪvli/
demonstration (n)	/ˌdɛmənˈstreɪʃən/
desire (n)	/dɪˈzaɪər/
detailed (adj)	/ˈditeɪld/
displace (v)	/dɪsˈpleɪs/
external (adj)	/ɪkˈstɜrnəl/
extreme (adj)	/ɪkˈstrim/
follow (v)	/ˈfɒloʊ/
format (n)	/ˈfɔrmæt/
freedom (n)	/ˈfridəm/
functional (adj)	/ˈfʌŋkʃənl/
genuine (adj)	/ˈdʒɛnjuɪn/
imaginary (adj)	/ɪˈmædʒəˌnɛri/
implication (n)	/ˌɪmplɪˈkeɪʃən/
integrate (v)	/ˈɪntɪˌgreɪt/
learner (n)	/ˈlɜrnər/
lifestyle (n)	/ˈlaɪfˌstaɪl/
make up (phr v)	/meɪk ˈʌp/
measure (v)	/ˈmɛʒər/
needle (n)	/ˈnidl/
obey (v)	/oʊˈbeɪ/
original (n)	/əˈrɪdʒənl/
outcome (n)	/ˈaʊtˌkʌm/
preference (n)	/ˈprɛfərəns/
realistically (adv)	/ˌriəˈlɪstɪkli/
recommendation (n)	/ˌrɛkəmənˈdeɪʃən/
rely on (phr v)	/rɪˈlaɪ ɒn/
resolve (v)	/rɪˈzɒlv/
safety (n)	/ˈseɪfti/
score (v)	/skɔr/
sketch (n)	/skɛtʃ/
solution (n)	/səˈluʃən/
stimulate (v)	/ˈstɪmjʊˌleɪt/
supervise (v)	/ˈsupərˌvaɪz/
task (n)	/tæsk/
treatment (n)	/ˈtritmənt/
truly (adv)	/ˈtruli/
usage (n)	/ˈjusɪdʒ/
variety (n)	/vəˈraɪəti/

Extension

break someone's heart (phrase)	/breɪk ˈsʌmˌwʌnz hɑrt/
break the law (phrase)	/breɪk ðə lɔ/
create a scene (phrase)	/kriˈeɪt ə sin/
create an email address (phrase)	/kriˈeɪt ən iˈmeɪl ˈæˌdrɛs/
creative gift (phrase)	/kriˈeɪtɪv gɪft/
come up with (phr v)	/kʌm ˈʌp ˌwɪð/
destroy creativity (phrase)	/dɪˈstrɔɪ ˌkriˈeɪtɪvəti/
follow your heart (phrase)	/ˈfɒloʊ jʊər hɑrt/
follow your instinct (phrase)	/ˈfɒloʊ jʊər ˈɪnstɪŋkt/
imagination (n)	/ɪˌmædʒəˈneɪʃən/
innovative (adj)	/ˈɪnəˌveɪtɪv/
job creation (phrase)	/dʒɒb kriˈeɪʃən/
originality (n)	/əˌrɪdʒəˈnæləti/
stifle creativity (phrase)	/ˈstaɪfəl ˌkriˈeɪtɪvəti/
vision (n)	/ˈvɪʒən/
wealth creation (phrase)	/wɛlθ kriˈeɪʃən/

Vocabulary Building

analysis (n)	/əˈnæləsɪs/
analyze (v)	/ˈænəˌlaɪz/
assess (v)	/əˈsɛs/
concern (n)	/kənˈsɜrn/
concerned (adj)	/kənˈsɜrnd/
conclude (v)	/kənˈklud/
conclusion (n)	/kənˈkluʒən/
fluent (adj)	/ˈfluənt/
flexibility (n)	/ˌflɛksəˈbɪlɪti/
flexible (adj)	/ˈflɛksəbəl/
fluency (n)	/ˈfluənsi/
intelligence (n)	/ɪnˈtɛləʤəns/
intelligent (adj)	/ɪnˈtɛlɪdʒənt/
knowledge (n)	/ˈnɒlədʒ/
know (v)	/noʊ/
knowledge (n)	/ˈnɒlɪdʒ/
logic (n)	/ˈlɒdʒɪk/
logical (adj)	/ˈlɒdʒɪkəl/
publication (n)	/ˌpʌblɪˈkeɪʃən/
publish (v)	/ˈpʌblɪʃ/
useful (adj)	/ˈjusfəl/
usefulness (n)	/ˈjusfəlnɪs/
variation (n)	/ˌvɛriˈeɪʃən/

Vocabulary in Context

edit (v)	/ˈɛdət/
electrocute (v)	/ɪˈlɛktrəˌkjut/
get (your) meaning across (phrase)	/ˈgɛt (jər) ˈminɪŋ əˌkrɔs/
grab (v)	/græb/
heartbroken (adj)	/ˈhɑrtˌbroʊkən/
manners (n)	/ˈmænərz/

UNIT 8

Review

connect (v)	/kəˈnɛkt/
face-to-face conversation (phrase)	/feɪs-tu-feɪs ˌkɑnvərˈseɪʃən/
get distracted (v)	/gɛt dɪˈstræktəd/
get a message out (phrase)	/gɛt ə ˈmɛsəʤ aʊt/
interpersonal skills (phrase)	/ˌɪntərˈpɜrsənəl skɪlz/
join in (v)	/dʒɔɪn ɪn/
make a point (phrase)	/meɪk ə pɔɪnt/
make connections (phrase)	/meɪk kəˈnɛkʃənz/
pay attention (phrase)	/peɪ əˈtɛnʃən/
post photos (phrase)	/poʊst ˈfoʊˌtoʊz/
respond (v)	/rɪˈspɒnd/
share (v)	/ʃɛr/

Unit Vocabulary

abuse (n)	/əˈbjus/
accuse (v)	/əˈkjuz/
acknowledge (v)	/ækˈnɒlɪdʒ/
apparently (adv)	/əˈpærəntli/
appropriate (adj)	/əˈproʊpriɪt/
associate with (phr v)	/əˈsoʊʃiˌeɪt ˌwɪð/
assumption (n)	/əˈsʌmpʃən/
assure (v)	/əˈʃʊər/
awkward (adj)	/ˈɔkwərd/
awkwardness (n)	/ˈɔkwərdnɪs/
belong (v)	/bɪˈlɒŋ/
bully (v)	/ˈbʊli/
campaign (v)	/kæmˈpeɪn/
cardboard (n)	/ˈkɑrdˌbɔrd/
citizen (n)	/ˈsɪtəzən/
classic (n)	/ˈklæsɪk/
combine (v)	/kəmˈbaɪn/
compliment (v)	/ˈkɒmpləˌmɛnt/
conscious (adj)	/ˈkɒnʃəs/
conservative (adj)	/kənˈsɜrvətɪv/
criticize (v)	/ˈkrɪtɪˌsaɪz/
decoration (n)	/ˌdɛkəˈreɪʃən/
define (v)	/dɪˈfaɪn/
deliberately (adv)	/dɪˈlɪbərɪtli/
deny (v)	/dɪˈnaɪ/
diplomat (n)	/ˈdɪpləˌmæt/
discriminate (v)	/dɪˈskrɪməˌneɪt/
dishonest (adj)	/dɪsˈɒnɪst/
elect (v)	/ɪˈlɛkt/
element (n)	/ˈɛləmənt/
elsewhere (adv)	/ɛlsˈwɛər/
encounter (v)	/ɛnˈkaʊntər/
enthusiasm (n)	/ɪnˈθuziˌæzəm/
equality (n)	/ɪˈkwɒlɪti/
experiment (v)	/ɛkˈspɛrəˌmɛnt/
fed up (phr v)	/ˈfɛd ˈʌp/
fingernail (n)	/ˈfɪŋgərˌneɪl/
firmly (adv)	/ˈfɜrmli/
forget (v)	/fərˈgɛt/
generalization (n)	/ˌdʒɛnərələˈzeɪʃən/
global (adj)	/ˈgloʊbəl/
identity (n)	/aɪˈdɛntɪti/
ignore (v)	/ɪgˈnɔr/
immigrant (n)	/ˈɪmɪgrənt/
incident (n)	/ˈɪnsɪdənt/
insist on (v)	/ɪnˈsɪst ˌɒn/
intense (adj)	/ɪnˈtɛns/
interpret (v)	/ɪnˈtɜrprɪt/
invisible (n)	/ɪnˈvɪzəbəl/
make fun (phr v)	/ˈmeɪk ˈfʌn/
massive (adj)	/ˈmæsɪv/
misbehave (v)	/ˌmɪsbɪˈheɪv/
misunderstand (v)	/ˌmɪsʌndərˈstænd/
modify (v)	/ˈmɒdɪˌfaɪ/
norm (n)	/nɔrm/
notion (n)	/ˈnoʊʃən/
obsession (n)	/əbˈsɛʃən/
offended (adj)	/əˈfɛndɪd/
phenomenon (n)	/fəˈnɒmɪˌnɒn/
policy (n)	/ˈpɒləsi/
praise (n)	/preɪz/
presence (n)	/ˈprɛzəns/
pretend (v)	/prɪˈtɛnd/
proportion (n)	/prəˈpɔrʃən/
protest (v)	/ˈproʊtɛst/
racism (n)	/ˈreɪsɪzəm/
react (v)	/riˈækt/
refresh (v)	/rɪˈfrɛʃ/
regional (adj)	/ˈridʒənl/
response (n)	/rɪˈspɒns/
shopkeeper (n)	/ˈʃɒpˌkipər/
sort (it) out (phr v)	/ˈsɔrt (ɪt) ˈaʊt/
statistic (n)	/stəˈtɪstɪk/
stereotype (n)	/ˈstɛriəˌtaɪp/
stock (n)	/stɒk/

Extension

back-handed compliment (phrase)	/bæk-ˈhændəd ˈkɑmpləmənt/
flatter (v)	/ˈflætər/
insult (v)	/ˈɪnˌsʌlt/
pay a compliment (phrase)	/peɪ ə ˈkɑmpləmənt/
pay tribute (col)	/peɪ ˈtrɪbjut/
put someone off (phr v)	/pʊt ˈsʌmˌwʌn ɔf/
reaction (n)	/riˈækʃən/
return a compliment (phrase)	/rɪˈtɜrn əˈkɑmpləmənt/

Vocabulary Building

cost-effective (adj)	/ˈkɔst ɪˌfɛktɪv/
deep-rooted (adj)	/ˈdipˈrutɪd/
heartbroken (adj)	/ˈhɑrtˌbroʊkən/
highly-respected (adj)	/ˈhaɪli rɪsˈpɛktɪd/
like-minded (adj)	/ˈlaɪkˈmaɪndɪd/
long-lasting (adj)	/ˈlɔŋ ˈlæstɪŋ/
open-minded (adj)	/ˈoʊpənˈmaɪndɪd/
two-faced (adj)	/ˈtuˌfeɪst/
well-mannered (adj)	/ˈwɛl ˈmænərd/
worldwide (adj)	/ˈwɜrlˈdwaɪd/

Vocabulary in Context

around (prep)	/əˈraʊnd/
breakdown (n)	/ˈbreɪkˌdaʊn/
huge step (phrase)	/hjudʒ stɛp/
humorous (adj)	/ˈhjumərəs/
self-conscious (adj)	/ˈsɛlfˈkɒnʃəs/
somewhat constructive (phrase)	/ˈsʌmˌwʌt kənˈstrʌktɪv/

UNIT 9

Review

aid worker (n)	/eɪd ˈwɜrkər/
demanding (adj)	/dɪˈmændɪŋ/
disastrous (adj)	/dɪˈzæstrəs/

VOCABULARY LIST 125

flood (n) /flʌd/
impact (n) /'ɪmpækt/
rescue (v) /'rɛskju/
save (v) /seɪv/
shelter (n) /'ʃɛltər/
sea level (n) /si 'lɛvəl/
stressful (adj) /'strɛsfəl/

Unit Vocabulary

absence (n) /'æbsəns/
affect (v) /ə'fɛkt/
aid (n) /eɪd/
ally (n) /'ælaɪ/
appeal (v) /ə'pil/
assistance (n) /ə'sɪstəns/
block (v) /blɒk/
care for (phr v) /'kɛər ˌfɔr/
coastal (adj) /'koʊstl/
convention (n) /kən'vɛnʃən/
cope (v) /koʊp/
corrupt (adj) /kə'rʌpt/
crisis (n) /'kraɪsɪs/
debris (n) /də'bri/
delegate (n) /'dɛlɪgɪt/
devastation (n) /ˌdɛvə'steɪʃən/
disaster (n) /dɪ'zæstər/
donation (n) /doʊ'neɪʃən/
earthquake (n) /'ɜrθˌkweɪk/
edit (n) /'ɛdɪt/
evacuate (v) /ɪ'vækjuˌeɪt/
flee (v) /fli/
frustrate (v) /'frʌstreɪt/
global warming (n) /'gloʊbəl 'wɔrmɪŋ/
graduate (n) /'grædʒuɪt/
greed (n) /grid/
headquarters (n) /'hɛdˌkwɔrtərz/
homeless (adj) /'hoʊmlɪs/
housing (n) /'haʊzɪŋ/
humanity (n) /hju'mænɪti/
imprison (v) /ɪm'prɪzən/
inclusive (adj) /ɪn'klusɪv/
infrastructure (n) /'ɪnfrəˌstrʌktʃər/
initiative (n) /ɪ'nɪʃətɪv/
interactive (adj) /ˌɪntər'æktɪv/
joy (n) /dʒɔɪ/
launch (v) /lɔntʃ/
limited (adj) /'lɪmɪtɪd/
neutral (adj) /'nutrəl/
on behalf of (phr v) /ˌɒn bɪ'hæf əv/
overlook (v) /ˌoʊvər'lʊk/
panel (n) /'pænl/
portrait (n) /'pɔrtrɪt/
precious (adj) /'prɛʃəs/
programmer (n) /'proʊgræmər/
psychological (adj) /ˌsaɪkə'lɒdʒɪkəl/
realization (n) /ˌriələ'zeɪʃən/
reconstruction (n) /ˌrikən'strʌkʃən/
recovery (n) /rɪ'kʌvəri/
relief (n) /rɪ'lif/
reminder (n) /rɪ'maɪndər/
remote (adj) /rɪ'moʊt/
representative (n) /ˌrɛprɪ'zɛntətɪv/
restore (v) /rɪ'stɔr/
right (n) /raɪt/
rise (v) /raɪz/
satellite (n) /'sætlˌaɪt/
scale (n) /skeɪl/
senior (adj) /'sinjər/
shelter (n) /'ʃɛltər/
shortage (n) /'ʃɔrtɪdʒ/
skip (v) /skɪp/
staggering (adj) /'stægərɪŋ/
supply (n) /sə'plaɪ/
survivor (n) /sər'vaɪvər/
sustainable (n) /sə'steɪnəbəl/
the loud (n) /ðə 'laʊd/
the outgoing (n) /ðɪ 'aʊtˌgoʊɪŋ/
the stupid (n) /ðə 'stupɪd/
trap (v) /træp/
unfamiliar (adj) /ˌʌnfə'mɪljər/

Extension

blackout (n) /'blæˌkaʊt/
destroy (v) /dɪ'strɔɪ/
devastate (v) /'dɛvəˌsteɪt/

drought (n) /draʊt/
hail (n) /heɪl/
heatwave (n) /'hit weɪv/
hurricane (n) /'hɜrəˌkeɪn/
provide (v) /prə'vaɪd/
tsunami (n) /tsu'nɑmi/

Vocabulary Building

the best (n) /ðə 'bɛst/
the brave (n) /ðə 'breɪv/
the old (n) /ðɪ 'oʊld/
the poor (n) /ðə 'pʊər/
the rich (n) /ðə 'rɪtʃ/
the traumatized (n) /ðə 'trɔməˌtaɪzd/
the young (n) /ðə jʌŋ/
the worst (n) /ðə wɜrst/

Vocabulary in Context

give (something) a go (phr v) /'gɪv ə 'goʊ/
globe (n) /gloʊb/
on the ground (phrase) /'ɒn ðə 'graʊnd/
siren (n) /'saɪrən/
strike a chord (phr v) /'straɪk ə 'kɔrd/
unfold (v) /ʌn'foʊld/

UNIT 10

Review

absorb (v) /əb'zɔrb/
bacteria (n) /bæk'tɪriə/
digestion (n) /daɪ'dʒɛstʃən/
heartbeat (n) /'hɑrtˌbit/
infect (v) /ɪn'fɛkt/
muscle (n) /'mʌsəl/
sense (n) /sɛns/
touch (n) /tʌtʃ/

Unit Vocabulary

actively (adj) /'æktɪvli/
address (v) /ə'drɛs/
aim (v) /eɪm/
allergic (adj) /ə'lɜrdʒɪk/
amazement (n) /ə'meɪzmənt/
antibiotics (n) /ˌæntibaɪ'ɒtɪks/
apocalypse (n) /ə'pɒkəˌlɪps/
award (v) /ə'wɔrd/
bench (n) /bɛntʃ/
bestseller (n) /'bɛst'sɛlər/
blindness (n) /'blaɪndnɪs/
blink (v) /blɪŋk/
cast (n) /kæst/
category (n) /'kætɪˌgɔri/
cell (n) /sɛl/
chance (n) /tʃæns/
cheer (v) /tʃɪər/
chest (n) /tʃɛst/
clarify (v) /'klærəˌfaɪ/
clear up (phr v) /'klɪər 'ʌp/
close down (phr v) /'kloʊz 'daʊn/
combine (v) /kəm'baɪn/
concentration (n) /ˌkɒnsən'treɪʃən/
consciousness (n) /'kɒnʃəsnɪs/
considerable (adj) /kən'sɪdərəbəl/
contribute (v) /kən'trɪbjut/
convert (v) /kən'vɜrt/
darkness (n) /'dɑrknɪs/
deadly (adj) /'dɛdli/
dependent (adj) /dɪ'pɛndənt/
design (v) /dɪ'zaɪn/
determined (adj) /dɪ'tɜrmɪnd/
device (n) /dɪ'vaɪs/
devote (v) /dɪ'voʊt/
diagnose (v) /'daɪəgˌnoʊs/
dictate (v) /'dɪkteɪt/
disgust (n) /dɪs'gʌst/
disturbing (adj) /dɪ'stɜrbɪŋ/
dose (n) /doʊs/
drug (n) /drʌg/
editor (n) /'ɛdɪtər/
efficiently (adv) /ɪ'fɪʃəntli/
expose (v) /ɪk'spoʊz/
express (v) /ɪk'sprɛs/

extract (n) /ɪk'strækt/
fascinated (adj) /'fæsəˌneɪtɪd/
flash (v) /flæʃ/
force (v) /fɔrs/
get out (phr v) /'gɛt 'aʊt/
gripping (adj) /'grɪpɪŋ/
heath care (n) /'hɛlθˌkɛər/
helmet (n) /'hɛlmɪt/
honor (n) /'ɒnər/
house (v) /haʊz/
inability (n) /ˌɪnə'bɪlɪti/
inevitable (adj) /ɪn'ɛvɪtəbəl/
infection (n) /ɪn'fɛkʃən/
insufficient (adj) /ˌɪnsə'fɪʃənt/
intensive (adj) /ɪn'tɛnsɪv/
keep down (phr v) /'kip 'daʊn/
lead (v) /lid/
lung (n) /lʌŋ/
make the most of (phrase) /'meɪk ðə 'moʊst əv/
misery (n) /'mɪzəri/
optimistic (adj) /ˌɒptə'mɪstɪk/
partial (adj) /'pɑrʃəl/
peer (v) /pɪər/
portion (n) /'pɔrʃən/
precisely (adv) /prɪ'saɪsli/
prescribe (v) /prɪ'skraɪb/
prescription (n) /prɪ'skrɪpʃən/
procedure (n) /prə'sidʒər/
punishment (n) /'pʌnɪʃmənt/
rapid (adj) /'ræpɪd/
resistant (adj) /rɪ'zɪstənt/
respond (v) /rɪ'spɒnd/
risk (n) /rɪsk/
run away (v) /'rʌn ə'weɪ/
slam (v) /slæm/
slide (v) /slaɪd/
slow (v) /sloʊ/
stroke (n) /stroʊk/
sweat (n) /swɛt/
symptom (n) /'sɪmptəm/
thankfully (adv) /'θæŋkfəli/
therapist (n) /'θɛrəpɪst/
therapy (n) /'θɛrəpi/
think through (phr v) /'θɪŋk 'θru/
threatening (adj) /'θrɛtnɪŋ/
treat (v) /trit/
turn to (phr v) /'tɜrn tu/
vision (n) /'vɪʒən/
visual (adj) /'vɪʒuəl/
waist (n) /weɪst/
ward (n) /wɔrd/
watch out (phr v) /'wɒtʃ 'aʊt/

Extension

blood pressure (n) /blʌd 'prɛʃər/
disability (n) /ˌdɪsə'bɪlɪti/
heart attack (n) /hɑrt ə'tæk/
medical condition (n) /'mɛdəkəl kən'dɪʃən/
numb (adj) /nʌm/
rehabilitation (n) /ˌrihəˌbɪlə'teɪʃən/
slur (v) /slɜr/

Vocabulary Building

aim at (phr v) /eɪm æt/
chance of (phr v) /tʃæns ʌv/
devoted to (phr v) /dɪ'voʊtəd tu/
raise awareness of (phrase) /reɪz ə'wɛrnəs ʌv/
resistant to (phr v) /rɪ'zɪstənt tu/

Vocabulary in Context

comfort zone (n) /'kʌmfərt ˌzoʊn/
extensive (adj) /ɪk'stɛnsɪv/
grasp (v) /græsp/
nickname (n) /'nɪkˌneɪm/
set (n) /sɛt/
superficial (adj) /ˌsupər'fɪʃəl/